ENGLAND
MILES
0
50
100
200
300
Leasowes
Birmingham
Worcester
Stratford on Avon
Banbury
Blenheim
Buckingham
Oxford
Reading
Windsor
LONDON
Esher
Portsmouth
Canterbury
Dover
Cowes
Calais
The Hague
Rotterdam
Nijmegen
Kleve
Antwerp
Duisburg
Düsseldorf
St. Omer
Brussels
Mons
Cologne
Bonn
Abbeville
Valenciennes
Cambrai
Andernach
Coblenz
Havre
Nassau
Wiesbaden
Seine
Rouen
Roy
Frankfurt
Mainz
Hanau
Chantilly
Mannheim
Versailles
PARIS
Château Thierry
Speyer
Heidelberg
Fontainebleau
River
Epernay
Sens
Châlons sur M.
Karlsruhe
Orléans
Vermanton
Nancy
Strassburg
Angers
Tours
Blois
Loire
R.
Dijon
FRANCE
Châlons sur Saône
Mâcon
Lyon
R.
Vienne
ITALY
Rhone
MILAN
Turin
Certosa
Po R.
Pavia
R.
Agen
Orange
Pont du Gard
Genoa
Nîmes
Vaucluse
Coni
Noli
Sestri
Montpellier
Arles
Avignon
Tenda
Toulouse
Carcassonne
Cette
Aix
Nice
Vintimiglia
Marseille
Frejus
Toulon
Hyères
D1130740

JEFFERSON

THE SCENE OF EUROPE

1784–1789

Books by Marie Kimball

THE THOMAS JEFFERSON COOK BOOK

THE MARTHA WASHINGTON COOK BOOK

JEFFERSON: THE ROAD TO GLORY

JEFFERSON: WAR AND PEACE

JEFFERSON: THE SCENE OF EUROPE

JEFFERSON IN PARIS. By John Trumbull. Angelica Church's miniature. (*Courtesy of the Metropolitan Museum of Art*)

JEFFERSON THE SCENE OF EUROPE

1784 to 1789

by

Marie Kimball

Coward-McCann, Inc., New York

Published simultaneously in the Dominion of Canada by Longmans, Green & Company, Toronto

MANUFACTURED IN THE UNITED STATES OF AMERICA

VAN REES PRESS • NEW YORK

Author's Note

Once again the author wishes to express her indebtedness to the Alderman Library of the University of Virginia, to the Library Company of Philadelphia, the American Philosophical Society, the Bibliothèque Nationale and the Archives Nationales of Paris. Above all she wishes to acknowledge her debt to André Carlhian, who generously permitted her free use of his superb library on old Paris.

Her very particular thanks are due to Thomas R. Coward of New York, who has consistently believed in her, as well as to Fiske Kimball, who has taught her to know and revere Jefferson's Paris.

Contents

I.	The Vaunted Scene	3
II.	The Law of Nations	17
III.	Minister to France	35
IV.	The World of Art	55
V.	The Circle of Literati	78
VI.	The Elysian Fields	108
VII.	England and Its Gardens	127
VIII.	A Last Romance	159
IX.	The Remains of Roman Grandeur	184
X.	America's War Debts	202
XI.	Jefferson's Rhine Journey	218
XII.	Americans in Europe	242
XIII.	The French Revolution through Jefferson's Eyes	264
XIV.	Farewell to France	301
	Notes	311
	Index	343

Illustrations

Jefferson in Paris, by John Trumbull		*Frontispiece*
The Château de la Roche-Guyon	Facing page	86
The Model of the Virginia Capitol		87
The Hôtel de Langeac		118
Pont de Neuilly with Mont Valérien		119
The Temple and Obelisk at Chiswick		150
The Temple of Concord and Victory at Stowe		151
Maria Cosway		162
Ruggieri's Vauxhall		163
The Column at the Désert de Retz		170
The Salon of 1785		171
The Pont du Gard		182
A Gallery at Düsseldorf		183
The Opening of the States-General		294
Martha Jefferson		295

JEFFERSON

THE SCENE OF EUROPE

1784–1789

I. The Vaunted Scene

When Thomas Jefferson sailed out of Boston harbor at dawn on July 5, 1784, he was at last realizing a dream he had cherished for many years—that of visiting Europe. The idea had haunted him since early manhood. Although farther away in time than now, Europe was spiritually near to the eighteenth-century American. Many, in their hearts, still considered it home, even though their families might have been settled in the New World for several generations. The more conservative of the Virginia planters continued to send their sons to England for education until the latter half of the century, and after that a European tour continued to be very much *de rigueur*.

In his dream, to be sure, Jefferson had not pictured himself as going to Europe in the exalted station of minister plenipotentiary to France. He had, however, been appointed to that post just two months before and was now proceeding on the *Ceres*, a vessel belonging to Captain Nathaniel Tracy of Newburyport, to take up his post. With Jefferson was his little daughter Martha, whom he called Patsy, now nearing her twelfth birthday. He was likewise accompanied by a servant named James, one of his slaves, whom he subsequently had trained in Paris to become the cook at Monticello,[1] and later freed. If Patsy had a maid, as she probably did for every Virginia girl of that period was given a colored girl to act as such when she was eleven or twelve years old, no mention is made of her.

"We had a lovely passage in a beautiful new ship that had made only one voyage before," Martha writes her old friend, Elizabeth Trist of Philadelphia. "There were only six passengers all of whom Papa knew, and a fine sunshine all the way, with a sea which was as calm as a river."[2] Jefferson observes that it was "remarkably short, being only 19 days from land to land,"[3] that is from Cape Cod "from which the departure was taken at 3 P.M." to the lighthouse at Scilly, reached at 10 P.M. on July 24. The distance covered was 2,728 geographical miles, and "the wind was so favorable through the whole passage that we never deviated from the direct course more than was necessary to avoid shoals, etc."[4]

Every day at noon Jefferson entered in his private log the latitude and longitude, the number of miles covered in the preceding twenty-four hours, and the temperature. A column headed "miscellaneous circumstances" records the minor events that combined to relieve the monotony of life at sea. He lists the shearwaters, the long-winged hagdons and petrels, skimming close above the foaming of the white-caps, along with the sharks and the whales. For three days the ship was becalmed off the Grand Banks and the party spent the time fishing. Jefferson notes on the eleventh that he "caught cod." His daughter informs us that "the epicures of the cabin feasted on fish tongues and sounds, leaving the rest of the fish for the sailors, of which much was thrown overboard for want of salt to preserve it."[5] There was no further excitement until the nineteenth when a Portuguese man-of-war was sighted. The following day the passengers saw "2 sail," and for the next few days this was a common event.

In contrast to his usual energetic activity, Jefferson seems to have used the journey to rest and to enjoy the company of his fellow passengers, very likely over the four dozen bottles of wine he had taken the precaution to have put on board. If we may believe John Quincy Adams' statement, made after dining with Jefferson in 1804, the latter is said to have claimed that he learned Spanish "with the help of a Don Quixote lent him by Mr. Cabot, and a grammar" during this voyage.[6] Not the least of his pleasures was the association with the owner of the vessel, a man of wide knowledge and cultivation, whose intimate acquaintance with the commerce and economic condition of his native Massachusetts Jefferson did not hesitate to tap. Having received "assurance from every quarter that I might derive from Mr. Tracy the fullest information as to the commerce of this state," he had written Elbridge Gerry on the eve of his departure, "I have referred much of the enquiries I wished to make to the vacant hours of our voyage." [7]

Like most travelers, as the voyage drew to a close, Jefferson sent an account of it to old friends. We find him writing John Adams, Benjamin Harrison, and his fellow congressman Samuel Hardy and recommending Mr. Tracy to the Count van Hogendorp, who had returned to Europe. As usual, the trip had had practical results. A letter to Colonel Archibald Cary of Ampthill informs him that Captain St. Barbe will deliver some European hares, warren rabbits, and partridges. Jefferson begs him to raise these creatures and turn out breeders. He is likewise adjured to give some to Nicholas Lewis, in charge of Monticello, and ask him to do the same. It was with no small disappointment that he later wrote his old friend James Currie, "I was unlucky as to the pheasants, hares and rabbits which I had ordered for Virginia. The vessel in which I came over was to have returned to Virginia and to Warwick. I knew I could rely on the captain's care . . . but the destination of the vessel was changed and the poor colonists all died while my friend was looking out for another conveyance." [8]

The twenty-fifth of July found Jefferson noting in his account book that he "gave servants on board the *Ceres* 12 dollars" and on the twenty-sixth that he landed at West Cowes. On reaching the English Channel he had hoped, as he says, to fall in with a vessel "which could take me and put me on the French coast," but, "having very thick weather as we approached the coast of Europe," [9] he was obliged to give up this plan and disembark on the Isle of Wight. After breakfasting here, he crossed the broad waters of Spithead, so reminiscent of his native Hampton Roads, to Portsmouth, where he put up at the Crown Inn.

Several days before landing, Martha had been taken with a fever, and she was a very sick child when they reached England. Her father called in Dr. Meeks, who attended her twice, and he likewise engaged nurses to care for her. At the end of three days, reassured by the doctor and confident that his child was in good hands, Jefferson set out to see the sights. He hired a chaise and made a circuit of the harbor, driving first through Portchester with its ancient Roman walls and bastions, to Fareham, and thence to Titchfield. Here he had the unusual pleasure of calling on an old friend of his Williamsburg days, Elizabeth Blair, daughter of the President of the Council. In 1769 she had married Samuel Thompson, who was later to become an admiral in the British Navy. At the time of Jefferson's call she was "confined upstairs by a little one (I had just lost)." Her stupid servant she says, should have told this to Jefferson "instead of saying I was not at home.... Had I known you was in the house, I should certainly have introduced you into my Bed Chamber.... Captain T. set out the next day in hopes of meeting you, but had the mortification of hearing you was gone."[10] Jefferson was thus obliged to console himself by viewing the main objects of interest in the town, the remains of an ancient abbey founded in 1222 and later converted into a residence by the Earl of Southampton, and the famed bridge erected in 1445 at the time of the marriage of Margaret of Anjou and Henry VI. Satiated with his first glimpse of antiquity, charmed, no doubt, by the fresh green countryside, he continued on to Gosport, the ancient God'sport, where he took the ferry back for Portsmouth.

On the thirtieth Jefferson started upon the last stage of his journey. The apothecary, the nurses, and the innkeeper were paid, and after settling with "Capt. Grey passage to Havre, £ 8-8," he embarked at six o'clock in the evening. His little daughter has given a vivid picture of that grim voyage across the channel. "I cannot say that this voyage was as agreeable as the first, tho it was much shorter," she writes. "It rained violently and the sea was exceedingly rough all the time, and I was almost as sick as I was the first time when I was sick two days. The cabin was not more than three feet wide and about four feet long. There was no other furniture than an old bench which was fast to the wall. The door by which we came in at was so little that one was obliged to enter on all fours. There were two little doors on the side of the cabin, the way to our beds, which were composed of two boxes and a couple of blankets without either bed or mattress, so that I was obliged to sleep in my clothes. There being no window in the cabin we were obliged to stay in the dark for fear of the rains coming in if we opened the door."[11]

Despite the rough weather, Jefferson reached Havre at seven o'clock the next morning. "I fear we should have fared as badly at the arrival," Martha continues, "for Papa spoke very little French and I not a word, if an Irish gentleman, an entire stranger to us, who, seeing our embarrassment, had not been so good as to conduct us to a house and was of great service to us." [12] The hotel was L'Aigle d'Or, and Jefferson remained there until the third of August. That morning James was given seventy-two francs "to bear expenses etc, to Rouen," and after early coffee the journey was resumed. How James made out with an unknown language, a foreign currency, and the quaint customs of the French remains unrecorded. That he was equal to the situation seems obvious, however, for he returned half the money to his master on arrival at Rouen that evening.

The next day was spent in the ancient city of Rouen, the capital of Normandy. At that time it was still a cluster of old houses, half toppling into narrow, crooked streets, still surrounded by the old walls that had successfully defied the onslaught of Henry V of England and, later, of Henry IV of France. Whether Jefferson observed the unexcelled richness of its medieval architecture, whether he enjoyed the glory of its cathedral or of St. Maclou, to say nothing of the Palais de Justice, we do not know. He has left no written account and there is no recorded payment for "seeing things." We only know that his expenses on that day were most practical in character, such as a knife, a lock, some nuts, and, as usual when opportunity offered, books.

On the fifth, after paying 32 fr., 12 for entertainment at the Pomme de Pin, Jefferson was on his way again. His road lay along the gentle valley of the Seine, through the country later to be portrayed with such loving sympathy by Monet and Pissarro and endeared to half the world. The calm flow of the river, the white chalk hills, the old towns that slumber today much as they did in Jefferson's time, unfolded to his view. Through Gaillon with its famous château, one of the first monuments of the Renaissance in France, on to the old fortified town of Vernon with its frowning tower built in 1123 by Henry I of England, thence to Mantes, and finally to Meulon and Triel. Here, almost within sight of Paris, Jefferson halted for the night. He had driven seventy miles in his phaeton this day. The scene that passed before him he had, as always, viewed with an eye to the practical. He writes Monroe that he had been "thro' a country than which nothing can be more fertile, better cultivated and more elegantly improved. It was at the time when harvest was beginning, and it is principally a farming country—" [13] a scene that always delighted him.

Martha Jefferson, however, regarded their experiences with the fresh eye of youth. Her lively letter to Mrs. Trist continues her impressions of the trip. "It is amazing to see how they cheat the strangers," she remarks on an old French custom. "It cost Papa as much to have the baggage brought from the shore to the house, which was about half a square, as the bringing it from Philadelphia to Boston. From there [Havre] we should have had a very agreeable voyage to Paris, for Havre de Grace is built at the mouth of the Seine and we follow the river all the way thro' the most beautiful country I ever saw in my life—it is a perfect garden—if the singularity of our carriage[14] had not attracted the attention of all we met and whenever we stopped we were surrounded by beggars. One day I counted no less than nine where we stopped to change horses.

"We saw a great number of chalk hills near Rouen, where we saw also a church built by William the Conqueror," she continues, indicating that some sight-seeing was done, "and another at Ment [Mantes], which had as many steps to go to the top as there are days in the year. There are many pretty statues in it, the architecture is beautiful, all the windows are check glass of the most beautiful colours that form all kinds of figures." [15]

The sixth found Jefferson and his daughter once more making an early start. Driving through St. Germain with, seemingly, hardly a glance at its superb prospect of Paris and the valley of the Seine and, so far as we know, not even a look at the ancient château, they proceeded the few leagues to Marly, where Jefferson could not resist stopping. It was not to see the château, which was ultimately to have its influence on the design of the University of Virginia, that he halted, but to view the famous Machine de Marly. This was the hydraulic machine constructed under Louis XIV a hundred years before when mechanical science was in its infancy. It was designed to carry the water of the Seine to the cascades that adorned the gardens of Versailles and Marly. Still regarded as one of the wonders of the world, it was something Jefferson could not lightly pass by.

On arriving in Paris, Jefferson went at once to the Hôtel d'Orléans, a well-known *hôtel des voyageurs* on the rue de Richelieu near the Bibliothèque du Roi. He was no more than settled when he started out to follow the advice of John Adams, who had written on his arrival two years before, "The first thing to be done in Paris is always to send for a tailor, a perukemaker and shoemaker, for this nation has established such a domination over the fashion that neither clothes, wigs nor shoes made in any other place will do in Paris." [16] And Mrs. Adams had observed that "to be out of fashion is more criminal than to be seen in a state of nature, to which the Parisians are not averse." [17]

Within a week Jefferson had acquired a new outfit. We find him buying a hat, a sword, a belt, knee buckles, shoe buckles, shirts, and paying the tailor "Dubuquoy for clothes etc. in full 681 f 5." These garments had scarcely been delivered before he had to hurry back, as we learn from Mrs. Adams. "There is now court mourning," she writes, "and every foreign minister with his family must go into mourning for a prince of eight years old, whose father is an ally of the King of France. This mourning is ordered by the court and is for eleven days only. Poor Mr. Jefferson had to hie away for a tailor to get a whole new black silk suit made up in two days; and at the end of eleven days should another death happen, he will be obliged to have a new suit of mourning of cloth, because that is the season when silk must be left off." [18]

At the same time Jefferson had to turn his attention to the wardrobe of his daughter, still a little country girl despite a winter in Philadelphia. Once more Patsy gaily describes the happenings of this day.

"I wish you could have been with us when we arrived. I am sure you would have laughed for we were obliged to send immediately for the stay maker, the mantua maker, the milliner and even a shoemaker before I could go out. I have never had the *friseur* but once, but I soon got rid of him and turned down my hair in spite of all they could say, and I defer it now as much as possible for I think it always too soon to suffer." [19]

Jefferson remained in the rue de Richelieu only six days when he moved to another Hôtel d'Orléans in the rue des Petits-Augustins, on the Left Bank. It was the same one in which John Jay had lived before his departure for America. Like the first one, this was an *hôtel des voyageurs,* and it was run by a Madame Mayan. The rue des Petits-Augustins, named for a religious sect that had its quarters there, was the present rue Bonaparte, running at right angles to the quay as far as the rue Jacob. On the left, walking in from the quay, was the splendid *hôtel* of the Rochefoucauld family, with its beautiful gardens. Although numerous old houses still exist in this street, it has been impossible to identify the one in which Jefferson lived as neither the name of Mayan nor of the *hôtel* appear on any map or in any guide book which the writer has been able to find.[20]

Jefferson paid twenty louis a month for his rooms at the Hôtel d'Orléans. Meals were not served in the *hôtel* but sent in by a *traiteur* or eating-house keeper. Jefferson immediately engaged the services of one Gaspard to act as major-domo and likewise took into his employ as "*valet de chambre* a man named Marc at 40 louis a year, and he feeds himself."[21] What Jefferson called "table furniture" seems to have been lacking, for he made quite extensive purchases of china, glass, table linen, silver, and plated ware during these days. The Virginia phaeton no longer seemed adequate, and a coach was hired at sixteen louis a month, along with a coachman at two francs a day.

The Hôtel d'Orléans was, after all, for transients and not a suitable place of residence for a man of Jefferson's station—and he was eager to do what was proper in regard to his establishment as well as his clothes. He began looking about for a proper house and by mid-October had found what he describes as a "small hôtel," which he rented for 1,500 francs a quarter. It was at No. 5 cul-de-sac Taitbout and belonged to one Guireau.[22] This little street, not far from the rue de la Chausée d'Antin and the present rue Lafayette, is now known as the rue Helder. It is lost in a morass of office buildings adjacent to the Galeries Lafayette. Every trace of the old houses that once graced it has been swept away.

Jefferson moved into his new house on the seventeenth of October and became a real householder, as his account book reminds us with its renewed and frequent entries for lamps, china, silver, and household utensils of every sort. He was likewise forced to expand his staff. "It is the policy of this country to oblige you to a certain number of servants," Mrs. Adams writes, "and one will not touch what belongs to the business of another. . . . In the first place there is a coachman who does not an individual thing but attend to the carriages and horses; then the gardener, who has business enough; then comes the cook; then the maître d'hôtel; his business is to purchase articles in the family and oversee that nobody cheats but himself; a *valet de chambre* . . . There is another indispensable servant who is called a *frotteur;* his business is to rub the floors." [23] Jefferson was shortly to find himself with all these functionaries in his employ.

He was, of course, not living alone. His family, as he called it, consisted at this time of David Humphreys, "a dark complexioned, stout, well-made, warlike looking gentleman about thirty years old," [24] formerly aide-de-camp to General Washington and recently appointed secretary to the commission of which Jefferson was a member. He tells us that Jefferson's "politeness and generosity extended so far as to insist that I should live with him during our residence in Europe." [25] Then there was the mysterious Mr. Williamos, who had been with Jefferson in Boston and now seems to have lived with him until Williamos' sudden death late in 1785 or early in 1786. Mrs. Adams describes him as "a Swiss by birth, a very sensible, obliging man, who is a very great intimate of Mr. Jefferson's, which alone would be enough to recommend him." [26] She observes that "he always dined with Mr. Jefferson." William Short, Jefferson's protégé and private secretary, "modest and soft in his manners," [27] completed the family.

The problem of his outfit was one that caused Jefferson great concern as it had Adams and Jay before him—indeed Mrs. Adams states that "Mr. Jay went home because he could not support his family here with the whole salary." [28] She adds that it "would take two years of an American minister's salary to furnish the equipage of plate which you will find upon the tables of all the foreign ministers here." [29] In a letter to Monroe, written not long after his arrival, Jefferson unburdens himself to his old friend and asks his intervention in Congress. "I must say a word on my own affairs," he writes, "because they are likely to be distressed. All the ministers who came to Europe before me, came at a time when all expenses were paid and a sum allowed in addition for their time. Of course they all had their outfit. Afterwards they were put on fixed salaries, but still these were liberal. Congress in the moment of my appointment struck off 500 guineas of the salary, and made no other provision for the outfit but allowing me to call for two quarters' salary in advance. The outfit has cost me near a thousand guineas, for which I am in debt, and which, were I to stay here seven years, I could never make good by savings out of my salary, for be assured we are the lowest and most obscure of the whole diplomatic tribe. . . .

"I live here about as well as we did in Annapolis. I keep a hired carriage and two horses. A riding horse I cannot afford to keep. This is still far below the level. Yet it absorbs the whole allowance, and return when I will to America, I shall be the outfit in debt to Congress. I think I am the first instance in the world where it has not been given. . . . I ask nothing for my time, but I think my expenses should be paid in a style equal to that of those with whom I am classed." [30]

Nearly a year after his arrival, the matter had still not been settled. In refusing a loan at this time to Colonel David Franks, who had acted as his amanuensis in Annapolis, he observes, "The uneasiness which this has given me for some time past has preyed upon my spirits night and day." [31] And once more he unburdens himself to Monroe. "For the articles of household furniture, clothes and a carriage, I have already paid 28,000 livres and have still more to pay. For the greatest part of this I have been obliged to anticipate my salary. . . . I find that by rigid economy, bordering on meanness, I can save perhaps $500 a month, at least in the summer. The residue goes for expenses so much of course and of necessity that I cannot avoid them without abandoning all respect to my public character. Yet I will pray you to touch this string, which I know to be a tender one with Congress, with the utmost delicacy. I'd rather be ruined in my fortune, than in their esteem." [32]

Quite as much of a problem, meanwhile, had been the task of finding a suitable school for his daughter. Through the offices of the Marquise de Lafayette, she was placed in the ancient Abbaye de Panthemont, situated at No. 10 rue de Grenelle. The building which housed it at that time is still standing. Jean-Armand Tronchin, the minister of the Republic of Geneva in Paris and a correspondent of Jefferson, writes of it, "I did not choose the convent of Panthemont without reason. The abbess in charge is a woman of the world who understands the direction of young Protestant girls. There are often English girls. The daughter of Mr. Jefferson is a pupil there, and I know it is understood that one does not talk to them about religion, or rather controversial topics are not discussed. They certainly emerge quite as good Protestants as when they entered." [33]

Patsy wrote her impressions of her new circumstances to Mrs. Trist. "I was placed in a convent on my arrival and I leave you to judge of my situation," she says. "I did not speak a word of French and no one here knew English but a little girl of two years old that could hardly speak French. There are about fifty or sixty pensioners in the house so that, speaking as much as I could with them, I learned the language very soon. At present I am charmed with my situation ... There come in some new pensioners every day. The class is four rooms, exceedingly large, for the pensioners to sleep in, and there is a fifth and sixth one for them to stay in in the day, and the other in which they take their lessons. We wear the uniform which is crimson, made like a frock laced behind, with the tail like a *robe de cour*, hooked on, muslin cuffs and tuckers. The masters are always very good, except that for the drawing ..." [34]

Scarcely was one child happily settled than Jefferson was struck down by news of the death of another. He had left his two younger daughters, Maria, a little girl of six, and Lucy Elizabeth, just two years old, with their maternal aunt, Elizabeth Eppes, in Virginia. He had done this before, after the death of his wife, when he attended Congress. A letter from Dr. James Currie, a friend and associate of many years, apprised him of the event. "I am sincerely sorry, my dear friend," Currie writes, "to acquaint you of the demise of poor Miss L. Jefferson, who fell a martyr to the complicated evils of teething, worms and hooping cough.... I was called too late to do anything. ... Mr. Eppes lost his own youngest child from the same cause." [35]

How heartsick this news made Jefferson, we can merely surmise. Of his six children only two survived. His wife had died two years before, and even his young stepson had early succumbed. His grief and bitterness may well have contributed to the sad state of health in which he found himself at this time. In November he wrote his Dutch friend Van Hogendorp that he had "relapsed into that state of ill health in which you saw me in Annapolis, but more severe. I have had few hours wherein I could do anything." [36] On December 9 Mrs. Adams notes that "Mr. Jefferson has been sick and confined to his house for six weeks. He is upon the recovery, though very weak and feeble." [37] In writing to Monroe, the following March, he was more explicit. "I have had a very bad winter," he says, "having been confined the greatest part of it. A seasoning, as they call it, is the lot of most strangers, and none, I believe, have experienced a more severe one than myself. The air is extremely damp, and the water very unwholesome. We have had for three weeks past a warm visit from the sun (my almighty physician) and I find myself reestablished. I begin now to be able to walk four or five miles a day and find myself much better for it." [38] By April he reports being able "to walk six or eight miles a day, which I do very regularly." [39]

There is no doubt that his grief added to the sense of loneliness and frustration that filled him at this time. "I am here burning the candle of life without present or future object," he wrote Mrs. Trist not long after his arrival. "A dozen or twenty years ago this scene would have amused me, but I am past the age for changing habits." [40] To Dr. Currie he sent a most touching letter. "I thank you again and again for the details it contains," he writes his friend, "these being precisely of the nature I would wish. Of political correspondents I can find enough, but I can persuade nobody to believe that the small facts which they see daily passing under their eyes are precious to me at this distance, made more interesting to the heart than events of higher rank." It was the cry of the expatriate in every land.

"Fancy to yourself a being," he continues, "who is withdrawn from his connections of blood, of marriage, of friendship, of acquaintance in all their gradations, who for years should hear nothing of what has passed among them, who returns again to see them and finds the one half dead. This strikes him like a pestilence sweeping off the half of mankind. Events, which, had they come to him one by one and in detail, he would have weathered as other people do, when presented to his mind all at once are overwhelming. Continue, then, to give me facts, little facts, such as you think every one imagines beneath notice, and your letters will be the most precious to me. They will place me in imagination in my own country, and they will place me where I am happiest." [41]

In the months following his arrival in Paris, Jefferson took occasion, in letters to various friends, to picture his reaction to his new environment. The contrast in the two civilizations was, of course, staggering. He was to find, as many have since, that however much he might expect to feel familiar with European life and thought as a result of reading, reality was very different. Seldom has it made a man a more ardent advocate of his native country. The famous letter to Carlo Bellini, that rarely sensitive Italian who had emigrated to Virginia in 1774 and become a member of Jefferson's household until he was made professor of modern languages at the College of William and Mary, sums up Jefferson's impressions at the end of a year of observation. "Behold me at length on the vaunted scene of Europe!" he writes. "You are, perhaps, curious to know how this new scene has struck a savage of the mountains of America. Not advantageously, I assure you. I find the general fate of humanity deplorable.... It is a true picture of that country to which they say we shall pass hereafter, and where we are to see God and his angels in splendor, and crowds of the damned trampled under their feet. While the great mass of people are thus suffering under physical and moral oppression, I have endeavored to examine more nearly the condition of the great, to appreciate the true value of the circumstances in their situation which dazzle the bulk of spectators, and, especially, to compare it with that degree of happiness which is enjoyed in America by every class of people."

His conclusions were not flattering. "Intrigues of love occupy the younger, and those of ambition the elder part of the great," he observes. "Conjugal love having no existence among them, domestic happiness, of which that is the basis, is utterly unknown.... Much, very much inferior is this to the tranquil, permanent felicity with which domestic society in America blesses most of its inhabitants, leaving them to follow steadily those pursuits which health and reason approve, and rendering truly delicious the intervals of those pursuits.

"In science," he continues, "the mass of the people are two centuries behind ours; their literati half a dozen years before us. Books, really good, acquire just reputation in that time, and so become known to us and communicate all their advances in knowledge. Is not this delay compensated by our being placed out of the reach of that swarm of nonsensical publications which issues daily from a thousand presses, and perishes almost in issuing?" [42]

European manners, in contrast to American, seem to have made a deep impression upon him. "The roughnesses of the human mind are so thoroughly rubbed off with them," he wrote Mrs. Trist, "that it seems as if one might glide through a whole life among them without a jostle." [43] And to Bellini he made a similar observation. "In the pleasures of the table," he continues, "they are far before us because with good taste they unite temperance. They do not terminate the most sociable meals by transforming themselves into brutes. I have never yet seen a man drunk in France, even among the lowest of the people."

The letter concludes on a high note—his glory in the ineffable treasures of European art. "Were I to proceed to tell you how much I enjoy their architecture, sculpture, painting, music," he exults, "I should want words. It is in these arts they shine. The last of them, particularly, is an enjoyment, the deprivation of which, with us, cannot be calculated. I am almost ready to say, it is the only thing which from my heart I envy them, and which, in spite of all the authority of the Decalogue, I do covet." [44]

II. The Law of Nations

THE FIRST MEETING of the American Ministers Plenipotentiary took place on August 30, 1784. In deference to the aged Dr. Franklin, it was held at his house in Passy, a village about three miles from Paris. There he lived in what he describes as "a fine house . . . with a large garden to walk in." [1] Adams, with his tendency to look at the dark side of the picture, says it "was called the *basse cour* de Monsieur LeRay de Chaumont, which was, to be sure, not a title of great dignity for the mansion of ambassadors, though they were no more than American ambassadors. Nevertheless it had been nothing less than the famous Hôtel de Valentinois, with a motto on the door, '*Se sta bene, non si muove,*' which I thought a good rule for my conduct." [2] On the seventeenth, Adams had arrived from London, where he had gone to meet his wife. He was now established at nearby Auteuil. Inevitably, this meeting, after so many eventful years, must have recalled to the minds of the three men their last famous collaboration—the Declaration of Independence.

Jefferson brought with him "the necessary papers with the twenty commissions" [3] for the treaties, further directions from Congress, as well as his own famous and revolutionary "Instructions to the Ministers Plenipotentiary appointed to negotiate Treaties of Commerce with European Nations," which had been passed by Congress the preceding seventh of May. This "sensible, judicious man," as a fellow congressman described him,[4] likewise carried with him the high hopes of that body for securing a respected place for the new United States among the nations of the world. His colleagues were jubilant and confident that this would take place. Monroe summed up their feeling when he wrote the Governor of Virginia this same May, "At length our foreign affairs are put upon as excellent an establishment as we could desire.

As respectable talents as these states possess, with characters eminent for integrity and attachment to the public interest, collected also in such manner from the different parts of the Union as to possess a knowledge of the local interests of the whole, are concenter'd in the three gentlemen, Mr. Adams, Mr. Franklin, and Mr. Jefferson." [5]

It is evident that, until he had received his baptism of fire in international diplomacy and intrigue, Jefferson shared the optimistic spirit of Congress. Even then, although he might write, "We do not find it easy to make commercial arrangements in Europe," [6] he maintained a freshness of outlook and a directness of approach that at once sustained him and baffled his adversaries. Thus at the end of his life he was able to write of the Comte de Vergennes, the French foreign minister with whom he had his first dealings, that he "had the reputation, with the diplomatic corps, of being wary and slippery in his diplomatic intercourse; and so he might be with those whom he knew to be slippery and double-faced themselves. As he saw that I had no indirect views, practised no subtleties, meddled in no intrigues, pursued no concealed objects, I found him as frank, as honorable, as easy of access to reason, as any man with whom I had ever done business; and I must say the same for his successor, Montmorin, one of the most honest and worthy of human beings." [7]

When "our instructions were made out," Jefferson tells us, "they were conceived on a general scale and supposed that all the European nations would be disposed to form commercial connections with us." [8] That this idea was somewhat naïve, that the European powers were not animated by the same enthusiasm as the Americans, that, as Jefferson observed, "they seemed, in fact, to know little about us, but as rebels, who had been successful in throwing off the yoke of the mother country," did not take long for the commissioners, as they were called, to realize. "They were ignorant of our commerce," Jefferson continues, "which had always been monopolized by England, and of the exchange of articles it might offer advantageously to both parties. They were inclined, therefore, to stand aloof, until they could see better what relations might be usefully instituted with us." [9] Indeed, nearly a year later, Jefferson was writing that until lately he had not "been able to discover the smallest token of respect towards the

United States in any part of Europe. There was an enthusiasm towards us all over Europe at the moment of peace," he adds, but "the torrent of lies published unremittingly in every day's London paper first made an impression and produced a coolness. The republication of these lies in most of the papers of Europe (done probably by authority of the governments to discourage emigrations), carried them home to the belief of every mind. They supposed everything in America was anarchy, tumult and civil war." [10]

Jefferson, however, saw more than the rosy lining, he saw positive good stemming from these maneuvers. "They have produced effects the most desirable of all others for us," he observes to Hogendorp. "They have destroyed our credit and thus checked our disposition to luxury; and, forcing our merchants to buy no more than they have ready money to pay for, they force them to go to those markets where that ready money will buy most. . . . They are doing us another good turn. They attempt without disguise to possess themselves of the carriage of our produce and to prohibit our own vessels from participating of it. This has raised a general indignation in America. The states see, however, that their constitutions have provided no means of counteracting it. They are therefore beginning to invest Congress with the absolute power of regulating their commerce. . . . This will consolidate our federal building very much, and for this we shall be indebted to the British." [11]

The anomalous situation of a central government, loosely organized and essentially powerless, and thirteen individual states each nursing its own ego and intent upon preserving it, thus making concerted action difficult if not impossible, must indeed have been a spectacle that amazed the Europeans. It likewise gave Jefferson much food for thought. In a letter to Monroe written after he had been in Europe some months struggling with the difficulties of treaty making, he sets down at considerable length his "thoughts on the policy of entering into treaties with the European nations, and the nature of them. I am not wedded to these ideas," he writes, "and therefore shall relinquish them cheerfully when Congress shall adopt others, and zealously endeavor to carry theirs into effect. First as to the policy of making treaties, Congress, by the Confederation, have no original and inherent power over the commerce of the states. But by the 9th article they are authorized to enter into treaties of commerce. The moment these treaties are concluded, the jurisdiction of Congress over the commerce of the states springs into existence.... There are two restrictions only on the exercise of the power of treaty by Congress," which he details. "Leaving these two points free, Congress may by treaty establish any system of commerce they please.... You see that my primary object in the formation of treaties is to take the commerce of the states out of the hands of the states, and to place it under the superintendence of Congress, so far as the imperfect provisions of our constitution will admit until the states shall by new compact make them more perfect. I would say, then, to every nation on earth, *by treaty*, your people shall trade freely with ours and ours with you, paying no more than the most favored nation, in order to put an end to the right of individual states acting by fits and starts to interrupt our commerce or to embroil us with any nation." [12]

Nevertheless, a spirit of optimism prevailed at this first meeting of the commissioners, and no time was lost. After reading the instructions "paragraph by paragraph," they "agreed to meet every day at this place until the objects of the commissions should be properly arranged, and put as far as may be into the best train of execution." [13] The following day they determined to "announce officially to the Court of Versailles the object of their mission as early as possible," and they informed the British Minister, David Hartley, "that they had received a commission for negotiating a treaty of amity and commerce with the Court of London, and desired that he would announce to his Court that they were ready to proceed on the negotiation." [14]

The commissioners who had negotiated the treaty of peace in 1783 had been given the power to include a commercial convention with Great Britain, but they did not succeed in this. Although England had acknowledged the independence of the United States, she still regarded them, essentially, as rebels and seemed uncertain how to treat them. A lingering hope that the weak confederation might disintegrate, as, indeed, at times seemed not unlikely, may have been behind her policy of procrastination. In any case, the temper had not changed by the time of Jefferson's arrival. For a good five or six years after that England paid as little attention as possible to America and had as little to do with her.

On the sixteenth of September Mr. Hartley, "having previously requested a meeting with the American Ministers," was suddenly recalled to London. He was replaced by the Duke of Dorset, whom Humphreys describes as "the plainest and best bred Englishman I have seen at Paris," [15] and whom Jefferson distinguishes as "an honest man." [16] Nevertheless when Humphreys waited upon the Duke to deliver him two letters from the American Ministers, he replied "that being entirely unacquainted with the negotiations proposed through Mr. Hartley to the Court of London, he could say nothing on that subject, except that he would write concerning it to his court." [17]

Ten days later Jefferson wrote Monroe in disgust. "With England nothing will produce a treaty but an enforcement of the resolutions of Congress proposing that there should be no trade where there is no treaty," he observes. "The infatuation of that nation seems really preternatural.... Deaf to every principle of common sense, insensible to the feelings of man, they firmly believe they shall be permitted by us to keep all the carrying trade and that we shall attempt no act of retaliation because they are pleased to think it our interest not to do so." [18] That Jefferson was not too harsh in his estimate of the British, as some of his critics have claimed, is evident to anyone who has read the correspondence of this period between the Duke of Dorset and the Marquis of Carmarthen, the British foreign minister.[19]

On the twenty-fourth of November the Duke informed the commissioners on behalf of His Majesty's Ministers "of their readiness to take into consideration any proposals coming from the United States that can tend to the establishing of a system of neutral and permanent advantage to the two countries, and reminds them of a previous stipulation proposed by my court that the United States should send a person properly authorized ... to London, as more suitable to the dignity of either power than would be the carrying on, at a third place, negotiation of so great importance." [20]

Jefferson found this proposal extraordinary, as he wrote Monroe, and was confident that "they only want to gain time to see how their schemes will work without a treaty." [21] Nevertheless, on December 9, the commissioners wrote the British envoy that "although we have no apprehension that it is inconsistent with the dignity of the United States to treat in any third place . . . we are so desirous of showing a respect for the sentiments of your Court, that we would readily repair to London." Nothing came of the proposal, however. Matters dragged along until the following February when John Adams was appointed minister to the Court of St. James. Even then the British continued evasive. It was not until 1794, long after Jefferson had returned to the United States, that a treaty with that country was finally concluded.

The commissioners had been empowered to negotiate and conclude treaties of amity and commerce with sixteen nations, supplementary ones with three others where treaties already existed, as well as with Morocco, Algiers, Tunis, and Tripoli. It was a bold if unrealistic stroke for the young, unorganized country—an early first instance of American naïveté in its approach to European politics. Trade with Europe in the colonial days, only just ended, had been highly restricted. Exports were permitted solely to England, Africa, the West Indies, and Europe south of Cape Finisterre. The whole of northern Europe was closed to them. The liberal terms of commerce that the United States, with no colonies to protect and no understanding of that problem, was now prepared to offer to the various powers, wily, seasoned, and bred in a policy of restriction and exclusion, were impossible for them to accept. Their response was varied—from amazement and incredulity to complete disregard. "Without urging," Jefferson was later to write, "we sounded the ministers of several European nations, at the Court of Versailles, on their dispositions towards neutral commerce, and the expediency of encouraging it by the protection of a treaty. Old Frederick of Prussia met us cordially and without hesitation. . . . Denmark and Tuscany entered also into negotiations with us. Other powers appearing indifferent, we did not think it proper to press them."[22]

Although, as he says, the various reluctant powers were not pressed, countless communications passed between them and the American commissioners. "I have not eat the bread of idleness," David Humphreys, secretary to the commissioners wrote Washington in the spring of

1785. "I have been pretty constantly employed in writing of one kind or another. Besides the correspondence which have been opened with Russia, the Emperor, Denmark, Sweden, Saxony, Sicily," and he names all the rest, "I have kept an accurate record of the proceedings of the Ministers, the minutes of which have already filled two large folio volumes. Tho' treaties have been proposed to be entered into with all the before mentioned powers . . . yet none of them appear to be near a completion." [23]

After six months of negotiating, Jefferson had few illusions left and had concluded what were the important aspects of his mission. He wrote Monroe in February, 1785, "Our business goes on very slowly. No answers from Spain or Britain. The backwardness of the latter is nothing new. . . . The effecting treaties with the powers holding positions in the West Indies I consider the important part of our business. It is not of great consequence whether the others treat or not. Perhaps trade may go on with them well enough without. But Britain, Spain, Portugal and France are consequent, and Holland, Denmark, Sweden may be of service, too." [24]

A treaty with Spain was, of course, considered of the utmost importance. Not only was she one of the most powerful nations of Europe, but she was mistress of a vast empire in America and had a most extensive and profitable commerce. As early as 1779 John Jay had been appointed minister to Madrid to negotiate a treaty. He was empowered to guarantee the two Floridas to Spain in return for free navigation of the Mississippi on the part of this country. The Spanish government, however, declined to entertain the proposal. It was now the turn of Jefferson and his fellow commissioners to see what could be done. The Count de Aranda, Spanish ambassador to Versailles, followed much the same tactics of procrastination as had the Duke of Dorset. He likewise sought to induce the commissioners to repair to Madrid, bolstering his suggestion with the statement that "the customs of my Court (the most regular and systematic of all others) in matters between its Crown and any other Power, is to negotiate between themselves without availing themselves of a third place." [25]

This suggestion presented another problem to the American Ministers. They considered it for a month. On October 28, 1784, after giving up "hope that in the meantime he would get an answer from his court which would save us the difficulty of answering him," [26] they took a firm position. They wrote the Count that Congress "had been willing their Ministers should attend on this side of the Atlantic," that they had already "communicated to many courts through their Ministers at their own residence," and that "however desirous we may be of showing our respect to the Court of Madrid by repairing thither, it will be difficult for us to leave this place until we shall have finished the business already begun, which may take up much time." [27]

No further word was forthcoming from the Count or his court. The situation remained static for some years, until Jefferson became secretary of state. Late in 1792 William Carmichael, chargé d'affaires at Madrid, and William Short, minister to the Hague, were appointed commissioners to negotiate a treaty. This again fell through and it was not until 1795, when Thomas Pinckney of South Carolina was sent as envoy extraordinary of the United States, that the treaty was finally concluded.

"Old Frederick of Prussia," as intimated, proved to be of quite different temper. This wily monarch had been keeping an eye on the rise of the United States. Knowing, according to Adams, that "as his subjects had occasion for our tobacco and some other things, and as . . . we had occasion for Silesia linens and some other productions of his dominions . . . he thought an arrangement might be made between his Crown and the United States which would be beneficial to both." [28] Early in 1784 he instructed his ambassador to the Netherlands, the Baron de Thulemeier, to communicate with John Adams, then minister plenipotentiary to that court. "I wrote him in answer," says Adams, "that I would have the honor of receiving him at twelve o'clock the next day. . . . At the hour I had mentioned his Excellency appeared at my house in the habiliments and with the equipage of his ministerial character. He said that the King, his master, had ordered him to visit me and ask my opinion of a connection and treaty between Prussia and the United States of America." [29] Adams' answer was, "Be pleased, Sir, to present my most profound respects to his Majesty and inform him that, though I have no commission or instructions to enter into official conferences upon the subject, I am very sensible of the high honor done me by this communication, and have no hesitation in expressing my private opinion, that such a connection between the United States and his Majesty's dominions would be highly honorable and advantageous, and I have no doubt Congress would be unanimous in the same sentiments."

This conversation occurred on the eighteenth of February. Adams promptly wrote Benjamin Franklin and John Jay in Paris. They replied on the twenty-eighth that "the respect with which the reputation of that great Prince has impressed the United States early induced them to consider his friendship as a desirable object," [30] and proposed they draft a treaty. The King ultimately agreed to Adams' suggestion that the recently negotiated commercial treaty with Sweden be used as a model. After an interchange of numerous letters between Thulemeier, on behalf of the King, and Adams, the latter on April 10 sent a copy of the projected treaty to the President of Congress. "I should hope," he writes, "it might be examined by Congress, or by a committee, and that instructions may be sent concerning any changes to be made in the articles, together with a commission to treat and conclude, to such person or persons as Congress shall be pleased to appoint." [31] Congress' answer was to send Thomas Jefferson to replace John Jay, who was returning to the United States, and to entrust him with the instructions and commissions.

On the ninth of September the three American Ministers informed Thulemeier that they were in a position "to enter on the negotiation and to reconsider and complete the plan of a treaty which has already been transmitted by your Excellency to your Court." [32] Jefferson's pen can be seen in the word reconsider. The revolutionary "instructions" he had brought with him, which he had drafted during his last days in Congress, were to be embodied in this first treaty he was to assist in negotiating. As first submitted to Congress, with revisions by Adams and Frederick, it was what might be called a standard commercial treaty of twenty-seven articles, largely designed to advance as well as to protect the interests of both parties to the covenant.

On the eighth of October Thulemeier acknowledged the letter of the commissioners and sent a copy of his power to conclude the treaty, asking at the same time that they would "have the goodness to communicate your ideas to me on the manner in which you desire to proceed." [33] The reply to this was an entirely new draft of the project, embodying the humane and enlightened principles of warfare to which Jefferson was the first to give voice. These were, as the commissioners stated in the enclosing letter, to be included in all treaties with European powers, "by instructions from the Congress, our Sovereign." [34] The documents were accompanied by a paper entitled, "Reasons in Support of the New Proposed Articles in the Treaties of Commerce." Its high moral tone was doubtless concurred in by Jefferson's associates; the phrasing, however, marks it as the work of the idealist that was Jefferson. "By the original law of nations," it reads, "war and extirpation were the punishment of injury; humanizing by degrees, it admitted slavery instead of death; a farther step was the exchange of prisoners instead of slavery.... Why," he asks, "should not this law of nations go on improving? ... Why should it not be agreed to as the future law of nations, that in any war hereafter the following descriptions of men should be undisturbed, have the protection of both sides, and be permitted to follow their employments in surety, viz:

"1st. Cultivators of the earth, because they labor for the subsistence of mankind.

"2nd. Fishermen, for the same reason.

"3rd. Merchants and traders in unarmed ships, who accommodate different nations by communicating and exchanging the necessaries and conveniences of life.

"4th. Artists and mechanics inhabiting and working in open towns. It is hardly necessary to add that the hospitals of enemies should be unmolested; they ought to be assisted.

"It is for the interest of humanity in general, that the occasions of war, and the inducements to it, should be diminished.

"If rapine is abolished, one of the encouragements to war is taken away, and peace therefore more likely to continue and be lasting." [35]

What Frederick, that most crafty and sophisticated of monarchs, thought of these lofty phrases penned "by a savage of the mountains of America," as Jefferson once referred to himself, we do not know. He may well have raised a cynical eyebrow. That he "made a thousand questions on American affairs" we learn from Lafayette, who visited him in 1786. Lord Cornwallis was one of the company, and the waggish King "took care to invite him at table to a seat by me, having the British King's son [Duke of York] on the other side." [36]

There is no reference to Jefferson's idealistic phrases in the counter proposals of the King submitted on January 24, 1785.[37] His Minister, however, permitted himself to observe that "the twenty-third article is dictated by the purest zeal in favor of humanity. Nothing can be more just than your reflections on the noble disinterestedness of the United States of America. It is to be desired that these sublime sentiments may be adopted by all the maritime powers without any exception. The calamities of war will be much softened and hostilities, often provoked by the cupidity and inordinate love of gain, of more rare occurrence." [38] To this the forthright Adams replied, "I am charmed to find the King do us the honor to agree to the platonic philosophy of some of our articles, which are at least a good lesson to mankind, and will derive more influence from a treaty ratified by the King of Prussia, than from the writings of Plato or Sir Thomas More." [39]

After further formalities, the treaty was ultimately signed in the late summer of 1785. The following October it was sent to Congress in the care of young Mr. Fitzhugh, of the well-known Virginia family, who had been traveling in Europe. It was Jefferson's first important achievement in his new sphere of activity. What had started out to be John Adams' revision of Benjamin Franklin's treaty with Sweden, had become essentially Jefferson's.[40] John Adams observed at the time that "it is not every ambassador, however high his rank or numerous his titles or magnificent his appointments, who arrives at the honor of concluding a treaty. It is this distinction which is made an object of ambition, and is much desired." [41] Jefferson had done more than that. To have had his humanitarian views adopted without protest by an important power of an already world-weary Europe was no small accomplishment. If he felt a certain sense of satisfaction, it was not undeserved.

The final section of the general instructions that had been issued to the three Ministers dealt with one of the most complicated and vexing problems that faced the new nation. This was to find a modus vivendi with the so-called Barbary States—Morocco, Algiers, Tunis, and Tripoli. For centuries the commerce of the Mediterranean had been menaced by attacks committed by the pirates of the North African coast—a practice that was not finally suppressed until well into the nineteenth century. Before the revolutionary war the very considerable trade of the American colonies in the Mediterranean, which, according to Jefferson, amounted to one sixth of the wheat and flour exported, one fourth in dried and pickled fish, and some rice,[42] was carried on under the protection of the British. With independence, the Americans found themselves fair prey. Their ships were seized, the crews taken captive and held for high ransom, particularly by the Algerines.

With the sending of ministers plenipotentiary to negotiate treaties of amity and commerce, it seemed to an inexperienced and trusting Congress that a way out of the difficulties was at hand. The Ministers were instructed to enter into such treaties with the countries mentioned "for the term of ten years, or for a term as much longer as can be procured." [43]

The Emperor of Morocco was singled out for special treatment. According to Franklin, as early as 1768, he had "published an edict declaring himself at peace with all the world" [44] and forbidding the corsairs who had operated from the important port of Salee to cruise any more. Early in the revolution he had recognized the independence of the colonies and in May, 1779, we find Franklin writing the Committee of Foreign Affairs of the Continental Congress that "his Imperial Majesty wondered we had never sent to thank him for being the first power on this side of the Atlantic that had acknowledged our independence and opened his ports to us." [45] Now Congress directed its representatives to "make known to the Emperor of Morocco the great satisfaction Congress feel from the amicable disposition he has shown towards these states, and his readiness to enter into alliance with them." [46]

The first report of the commissioners to Congress, dated November 11, 1784, reveals a certain surprised dismay. No communications had as yet been made with the Barbary States. They write that "treaties with these powers are formed under very peculiar circumstances. Not only the expenses of the negotiations on their part are to be borne by the other negotiating power, but great presents and an annual tribute are requisite with some of them. The contributions under which they thus lay the powers of Europe are as heavy as they are degrading.... We wish it were in our power to conjecture the sums which might be necessary; and have endeavored to learn what is given by the European powers, as we might thence form some estimate what would be required from us. As yet we have been unable to obtain this information.... Presents or war is their usual alternative."[47]

Meanwhile Humphreys wrote Washington in the same strain. "It is scandalous and humiliating beyond expression to see the powerful maritime kingdoms of Europe tributary to such a contemptible banditti," he observes. "This sinister policy will force us in some degree to the same measure."[48] Jefferson was no less outraged at the idea of these people asking "such a tribute for the forbearance of their piracies. When this idea comes across my mind," he writes, "my faculties are absolutely suspended between indignation and impotence."[49] He must, however, have been unable to suppress a smile when Humphreys told him what he had learned from a man from Morocco with whom he fell in. "He informs me," Humphreys writes, that "in negotiation at that court the novelty of a present is frequently of more consequence than the intrinsic value of it. He mentioned, as an instance in proof, that the Emperor appeared more pleased with a hand organ than with any other present which he gave him."[50]

This, however, was followed by a letter of William Carmichael written from Cadiz, informing Jefferson that the Emperor must have an envoy and presents from the United States soon "or he will not be our friend." Mr. Carmichael also enclosed as a guide "a list of presents made by the States General to the Emperor of Morocco in 1784." This included large numbers of supplies for ships, such as 69 masts from 50 to 91 feet in length, cables, cordage anchors, wood for oars, sea charts, compasses, etc., and "extraordinary presents" ranging from 2 pieces of scarlet cloth, a barrel containing 1,072 pounds of sugar, 2 sets of India porcelain to "1 very large watch."[51]

In a private letter to Monroe, written the same day as the report to Congress, Jefferson makes a proposal extraordinary for a man who abhorred war as he did. "I do expect that they [the Barbary powers] would tax us at one, two, or perhaps three hundred thousand dollars a year," he says. "Surely our people will not give this. Would it not be better to offer them an equal treaty? If they refuse, why not go to war with them? Spain, Portugal, Naples, France, and Venice are now at war with them. Every part of the Mediterranean therefore would offer us friendly ports." To underline his argument he urges that America "ought to begin a naval power, if we mean to carry on our own commerce. Can we begin on a more honorable occasion, or with a weaker foe? I am of opinion that Paul Jones with half a dozen frigates would totally destroy their commerce."[52] That John Jay, then secretary of foreign affairs, agreed with Jefferson, we gather from a letter of January 19, 1786. Even though he realizes that "our country in general desires peace with them," for his part, he writes, he prefers "war to tribute, and that sentiment was strongly expressed in my report on that subject."[53]

The drastic step of war was not taken. Although continued residence in Europe inevitably imparted to Jefferson a greater understanding of international problems and relations, thus making him rather less of a firebrand than his letters indicate he was on first arrival, he nursed the idea of war well into 1786. In the summer of that year he and Adams entered into a detailed discussion of the question of tribute versus war, against the almost hopeless background of the financial situation of the United States. Jefferson made one last defense of his position. He was stung, no doubt, by Adams' exasperated statement that unless a lethargic Congress roused itself "you and I, as well as every other servant of the United States in Europe ought to go home, give up all points, and let all our exports and imports be done in European bottoms. My indignation is roused beyond all patience to see the people in all the United States in a torpor, and them a prey to every robber, pirate and cheat in Europe."[54] In a long letter to Adams written on July 11, Jefferson lists six reasons why he is in favor of war. They range from the idealistic point of view that justice and honor favor it, to more practical reasons, concluding, "If it be admitted, however, that war, on the fairest prospects is still exposed to uncertainties, I weigh against this the greater uncertainty of the duration of a peace bought with money, from such a people, from a Dey 80 years old, and by a nation who, on the hypothesis of buying peace, is to have no power on the sea to enforce an observance of it." [55]

By November of this same year, Jefferson had evolved another scheme for keeping the Barbary powers in order. This was a union of the "several powers at war with the piratical states of Barbary." The "object of the convention" he optimistically states, "shall be to compel the piratical states to perpetual peace, without price, and to guarantee that peace to each other." [56] To obtain this he proposed that a naval force not "so considerable as to be inconvenient to any party . . . but half a dozen frigates with as many tenders or xebecs," supplied by the various participants in the covenant, "be kept cruising along the coast of the Barbary powers." [57] It was his firm if optimistic conviction, which he communicated to Congress, that "by all exclusion of them from the sea" it would be possible "to change their habits and characters from a predatory to an agricultural people." [58] This proposal was communicated to the representatives of the various powers in Paris. Portugal, Naples, the two Sicilies, Venice, Denmark, and Sweden concurred. Vergennes assured Jefferson that France was favorably disposed and that England "dare not" interfere "in behalf of those piratical governments."

As usual Jefferson had talked the matter over with Lafayette, and as usual that fiery young man was prepared to spring into action. He wrote Jefferson, "Our last evening's consultation, together with the Neopolitan ideas, have raised into my head a plan of which I will speak to you tomorrow. It is to propose myself as a chief of the antipiratical confederacy. I will ask a sum of money from Naples, Portugal, Rome, Venise and some German towns, naval stores and seamen from America, a treaty with Malta, a harbor in Sicily, and keep up two or three fifties, six large brigs, and a number of the privateers. . . . The devil of it will be to make it agreeable to this ministry that I should meddle." [59] Nothing came of this chimerical proposal, however.

All that was needed for Jefferson's hopes and plans was the concurrence of Congress—along with a frigate and the funds for its maintenance. "The recommendatory powers for obtaining contributions were so openly neglected by the several states," he writes with the delicacy characteristic of him, "that they declined an engagement which they were conscious they could not fulfill with punctuality; and so it fell through." [60]

Meanwhile, early in 1785, Congress decided to send Thomas Barclay as agent to Morocco and John Lamb to Algiers, each bearing a draft of a treaty approved by Congress. Eighty thousand dollars were appropriated. The resulting negotiations, as reflected in the letters exchanged between these men, Jefferson and the Secretary of Foreign Affairs, are a dismal story of a dying and ineffective Congress, of powerless ministers, of no money and of incredible hardship and suffering for the unfortunate seamen who were victims of the pirates and who were reduced to slavery in all its degradation, as understood by the eighteenth century.[61] In vain the Ministers might write Congress: "We are as yet uninstructed from what sources to call for the moneys necessary for conducting and concluding treaties with them [the Barbary States], and no steps can be taken without cash in hand." [62] In a long conference with Vergennes, whose advice he sought, Jefferson "told him we had calculated, from the demands and information of the Tripoline Ambassador at London, that to make peace with the four Barbary States would cost us between two and three hundred thousand guineas if bought with money. The sum," he adds, "did not seem to exceed his expectations." [63]

In May, 1786, Lamb reported that the Dey of Algiers refused to treat for peace under any circumstances and that to redeem the twenty-one men recently seized on two ships by the Algerines would cost the United States $6,000 a head for a captain, $4,000 for a mate, and the same for passengers. Sailors were a bargain at $1,400. With the tax, so to speak, or "eleven percent to be added according to custom," the total amount requisite was $59,496. Congress had authorized the payment of $200 a man. Eventually, Jefferson recommended accepting the offer of the general of the religious order of Mathurins, who made it their business to ransom Christians held in slavery by the Barbary powers. They "redeem, I believe, on better terms than any other body, public or private," Jefferson wrote Jay. Their "last considerable redemption was of about three hundred prisoners, who cost them upward of fifteen hundred livres a piece; but [I am informed] that they should not be able to redeem ours as cheap as they do their own." [64] Congress ultimately availed itself of this opportunity, but with the revolution in France this body, like so many others, went out of existence. It is small wonder that Jefferson was led to write Jay, "I enclose the dispatches relative to the Barbary negotiations received since my last. It is painful to me to overwhelm Congress and yourself continually with these voluminous papers, but I have no right to suppress any part of them; and it is one of those cases where, from a want of well-digested information, we must be contented to examine a good deal of rubbish in order to find a little good matter." [65]

Meanwhile, the treaty with Morocco progressed more favorably. Although a Moroccan cruiser had seized a United States ship before Barclay's appointment, through the intervention of the court of Spain the captives were released and the owners indemnified for the cargo and vessel. The Emperor, furthermore, was prepared to be friendly. On July 31, 1786, Barclay announced the consummation of the treaty, and on November 2 it was laid before Congress. Adams and Jefferson signed it in January, 1787, and it was subsequently ratified by Congress.

With this the treaty-making activities of the American commissioners sent to Europe for that purpose came to an end. Although appointed for a term of three years, as a body they had long since ceased to exist. Adams had been the first to go when he was appointed minister to Great Britain in 1785. Franklin had returned home in the summer of the same year and Jefferson had been appointed to succeed him as minister to France. If it cannot be said that they had distinguished themselves, there are several things that must be taken into consideration. Compared to the European diplomats, who for centuries had been born and bred in intrigue, the Americans were the merest amateurs. They were likewise hampered by Congress in various ways, some of which we have discussed. Furthermore, as we have observed, the commercial principles advocated by that body were so liberal as to be entirely unacceptable to those European powers who still had colonies in America. In addition, even at this early time, our national specter of an uncertain foreign policy had already raised its head. Small wonder Jefferson was led to complain of the difficulties of "the business of treaty, and I own it does not hold out the most flattering prospects." [66]

Meanwhile people at home were beginning to wonder about these treaties with their rosy promises of increased trade and more stable conditions for their vessels and sailors on the seas. Indeed, they were beginning to wonder about many things. The general discouragement is nowhere better expressed than in the words of William Grayson, a member from Virginia of the dying Continental Congress, when he wrote Short, in 1787, "I am sorry to inform you that American affairs in general wear the worst aspect one can possibly conceive. The public treasury without money, the people discontented and the states either refusing or not complying with the requisitions of Congress... Our negotiations with Spain go but slowly, indeed we have got ourselves into a dilemma which it will be hard to extricate ourselves from.... The treaty with Morocco is arrived. With respect to Tripoli, Tunis and Algiers, the people begin to think the same not worth the candle, and I believe there will be no farther attempts made in that business. If we make a treaty today, they may break it tomorrow, and we have no fleet to punish or intimidate them.... Congress are, I think, beginning to recover from their *treaty madness.* Indeed it is high time... they begin to understand (though at this late hour) the doctrine of the right of the most favored nation; they will eer long begin also to see the folly of a weak disjointed nation contracting with a strong one, who can explain the contract as he pleases." [67]

III. Minister to France

IN FEBRUARY, 1785, the question of Franklin's return to his native country, "where he wishes to lay his bones," [1] became imminent. The old statesman's pleas could no longer be ignored, and Congress took it "in contemplation to permit him to return." [2] Jefferson, our correspondent continues, "who is peculiarly acceptable to the Court of Versailles, will probably be appointed his successor at the Court." [3] This took place the following month, and on the twenty-second of March John Jay, secretary of foreign affairs, dispatched Jefferson's commission and letter of credence in the care of Paul R. Randall, who was setting out for Europe to join Thomas Barclay as agent to Algiers, as we have seen.

The commission, addressed "to our trusty and well-beloved Thomas Jefferson," with the seal still affixed, reposes to this day among the Jefferson papers, a proud document in fulfillment of the hopes and dreams of many years. It reads, "We reposing special trust and confidence in your integrity, prudence and ability, have nominated, constituted, and appointed . . . you . . . our Minister Plenipotentiary to reside at the Court of his most Christian Majesty, and do give you full power and authority there to represent and do and perform all such matters and things as to the said place or office doth appertain, or as may by our instructions be given unto you in charge. This commission to continue in force for the space of three years from this day, unless sooner revoked." [4]

Jefferson received his commission on the second of May, as he wrote Jay. "I beg permission through you, Sir," he says, "to testify to Congress my gratitude for this new mark of their favor, and my assurances of endeavoring to merit it by a faithful discharge of the duties annexed to it. Fervent zeal is all which I can be sure of carrying into their service, and where I fail through a want of those powers which nature and circumstances deny me, I shall rely on their indulgence, and much also on the candor with which your goodness will present my proceedings to their eye. The kind terms in which you are pleased to notify this honor to me," he concludes, "require my sincere thanks." [5]

Although Jefferson states that a fervent zeal is all he can bring to his new station, his claim was obviously much too modest. In February, 1783, John Adams had taken occasion to write Robert R. Livingston, then secretary of foreign affairs, his idea of the qualifications necessary for an American foreign minister. Reading it in retrospect, it would almost seem as though his friend Thomas Jefferson had served as a model. "In the first place," Adams writes, "he should have had an education in classical learning, and in the knowledge of general history, ancient and modern, and particularly the history of France, England, Holland and America. He should be well versed in the principles of ethics, of the law of nature and nations, of legislation and government, of the civil Roman law, of the laws of England and the United States, of the public law of Europe, and in the letters, memoirs and histories of those great men, who have heretofore shone in the diplomatic order, and conducted the affairs of nations, and the world. He should be of an age to possess a maturity of judgement, arising from experience in business. He should be active, attentive, and industrious, and, above all, he should possess an upright heart and an independent spirit, and should be one who decidedly makes the interest of his country, not the policy of any other nation, nor his own private ambitions or interest, or those of his family, friends, and connections, the rule of his conduct." [6]

On the fourteenth of May Jefferson, as he reported to Jay, "communicated to the Count de Vergennes my appointment as Minister Plenipotentiary to this court, and on the 17th delivered my letter of credence to the King at a private audience." [7] He adds, in the offhand manner characteristic of him, that he "went through the other ceremonies usual on such occasions." There is no description of the scene, no record of his remarks. David Humphreys, who was presented at the same time, wrote Washington, "I have passed through the ceremony of going to court and being presented to the King and Royal family. The King, who is rather fat and of a placid, good tempered appearance, is thought to possess an excellent heart and to aspire only to the distinction of being considered as the father of his people." [8]

The Comte de Cheverny, whose duty it was to make the presentations, has left a rather more graphic picture of such a scene. Whether Jefferson was accorded the full honors of such a ceremony, we do not know, but it was the usual one. At ten in the morning, says the Count, the carriages of the gentlemen who were to be received arrived before the two *écuries* that flank the entrance to the palace. The French and Swiss guards were drawn up in the great court. "After having made the tour of the court," he continues, "in passing beneath the windows of the King, we entered the hall of the ambassadors, where the entire diplomatic corps was assembled. I went to the King's apartments to await the hour of the audience, and I also passed through the apartment of the whole royal family. At the hour fixed, I went to get the ambassador. The carriages had reassembled. My footmen were lined up, an equal distance apart, from the door to the foot of the great staircase, the *valets de pied* of the ambassador, stood in a similar manner at the foot. Preceded by the pages of the ambassador, followed by the gentlemen of the embassy, we climbed the stairway, the secretary of legation following. The ambassador found the great staircase lined with a hundred Swiss guards in full dress, the officers at their head, within the hall the bodyguard, with its officers, the sentinels saluting. The two Swiss guards before the King's apartment stood at their posts in the *Oeuil-de-boeuf*. The captain of the bodyguard stood at the left with the *introducteur*, as he could never leave the left of the ambassador having to instruct him what to do.

"On arrival in the King's bedroom, we found him seated surrounded by his leading officers, the grand chamberlain, all the dukes and people of title—in short the courtiers. When the King observed the ambassador, he removed his hat and rose. The ambassador, escorted by a prince and the *introducteur*, advanced, followed by his secretary of legation and his staff. He made three deep bows at equal distances. Then the King seated himself and replaced his hat. The ambassador did likewise. The princes, the dukes and the others also put on their hats. The ambassador then began his discourse. Each time he mentioned the name of their Majesties, he uncovered his head. The King did the same, and the courtiers followed faithfully. At the conclusion of the ambassador's remarks, the King responded. The ambassador then presented the secretary of legation and all the personnel, whereupon they retired as they had come in, again making three deep bows. Then we went to the Queen's apartments, and to those of all the royal family, going through much the same ceremony each time.

"At two o'clock we returned to the hall of the ambassadors. A table with fifty covers was set in the Council Chamber. All the people who had been presented were there. One of the King's *maîtres d'hôtel* was present to do the honors. Everyone was served by the gentlemen of the bedchamber, and one stood behind each chair. Swiss in uniform passed the platters about." [9]

In Jefferson's case, according to Humphreys, the whole of the diplomatic corps dined with the Comte de Vergennes. "It is curious to see forty or fifty ambassadors, ministers or other strangers of the first fashion from all the nations of Europe," he writes, "assembling in the most amicable manner and conversing in the same language. What heightens the pleasure is their being universally men of unaffected manners and good dispositions." [10] Following this, in the course of the next week, the ministers of all powers, great or small, ecclesiastical and temporal, called upon Jefferson, signed his register, and left a card of which that of the Baron Grimm is typical: *"Frederick Melchior Baron de Grimm, Ministre Plénipotentiaire de Saxe-Gotha a été pour l'avoir l'honneur de faire son compliment à Monsieur Jefferson de ce qu'il a eu ses premières audiences du Roi, de la Reine, et de la Famille Royale en qualité de Ministre Plénipotentiaire des Etats-Unis d'Amerique près sa Majesté très Chrétienne."* [11]

With these preliminaries over, Jefferson settled down to the routine of his work as minister. In his autobiography he remarks that "my duties at Paris were confined to a few objects. The receipt of our whale-oils, salted fish, and salted meats on favorable terms; the admission of our rice on equal terms with that of Piedmont, Egypt and the Levant; a mitigation of the monopolies of our tobacco by the Farmer-General, and a free admission of our productions into their islands, were the principal commercial objects which required attention."[12]

However casually Jefferson may have referred to his activities in retrospect, he did not take them lightly in reality. Before leaving America, he had prepared himself for his duties, as we have seen, by a tour of the northern states. A memorandum preserved among his papers indicates that he had informed himself by questioning the governors of the various states, or other knowledgeable persons, on the state of trade, the laws governing it, articles of trade and the annual value, fisheries, the building of ships, as well as the number of consuls employed, the immigration laws, and the rate of settlement.[13] Numerous other lengthy memoranda testify to the thoroughness with which the indefatigable Jefferson pursued his quarry. Ralph Izard, whom Jefferson had known in Congress, in reply to a letter asking information "relative to the products, exports, imports and other commercial matters" of his native South Carolina, enclosed a detailed report compiled by the Chamber of Commerce of that state. The exportation of rice, for which there was sharp competition from Italy and the Levant, was given particular attention in comprehensive reports from various sources. The all important tobacco trade was likewise scrutinized in such documents as "Observation on the actual state of commerce in tobacco between the United States and France, from 1782 [on]," or the "State of the tobacco trade with the United States at 11 French ports and summary of same from January 1, 1786 to September 3, 1787." There is likewise a detailed account, in the form of a table, of the amount of commerce with France and England, as well as a list of all ships sailing for the United States from January, 1782, with the names of the captains, the port of departure, and the cargo,[14] to give only a sample. These formed the basis of his reports to Jay and to the French Foreign Minister.

In his rôle as minister from the United States, Jefferson was kindly received. "I found the government entirely disposed to befriend us on all occasions," he writes, "and to yield us every indulgence, not absolutely injurious to themselves."[15] This was, of course, neither accidental nor due to Jefferson's personal charms but rather to the fact that that stout hater of England, Vergennes, had been largely responsible for supporting the revolution in America and for forming an alliance with the new state.

For his part, Jefferson never for a moment let out of sight the importance of cultivating the French, of keeping "up the affection of this country for us, which is considerable. A court has no affections," he writes, "but those of the people whom they govern influence their decisions, even in the most arbitrary governments."[16] And again he admonished Madison, his alter ego, whom he relied on for helping influence public opinion at home, "nothing should be spared, on our part, to attach this country to us. It is the only one on which we can rely for support, under any event. Its inhabitants love us more, I think, than they do any other nation on earth."[17]

On the fifteenth of September, 1784, Jefferson paid his first visit to Versailles. What impression was made upon him as he drove the length of the tree-bordered Avenue de Paris and miraculously came upon the dazzling ensemble of a palace more regal than any the Western world had known, with gardens that complemented it in beauty and sumptuousness, we do not know. We cannot doubt that it must have left a man of his artistic sensibilities awed and breathless. However, with the reticence which his biographers find baffling and stubborn, he merely records that he "paid for chair here at Versailles, 3 f."[18]

On this occasion Jefferson first paid his respects to the Comte de Vergennes. The latter was a man approaching seventy. He had seen distinguished service as minister, subsequently ambassador, to Turkey and later to Sweden. On the accession of Louis XVI, he was made minister of foreign affairs. Jefferson had the highest opinion of him but, at the same time, was not blind as to his motives. As he wrote Madison, "he is a great minister in European affairs, but has very imperfect ideas of our institutions, and no confidence in them"—which was, of course, to be expected. "His devotion to the principles of pure despotism," Jefferson continues, "renders him unaffectionate to our governments. But his fear of England makes him value us as a makeweight. He is cool, reserved in political conversations but free and familiar on other subjects, and a very attentive, agreeable person to do business with. It is impossible to have a clearer, better organized head; but age has chilled his heart," he concludes.[19]

Vergennes had, according to Jefferson, "two eyes," Rayneval and Hennin. "The former is the more important character," Jefferson observes, "because of possessing most of the confidence of the Count. He is cunning, rather than wise, his views of things being neither great nor liberal. He governs himself by principles which he has learned by rote, and is fit only for the details of execution. His heart is susceptible of little passions, but not of good ones. He is brother-in-law to M. Gérard," Jefferson adds, mentioning the first French Minister to the United States, "from whom he received disadvantageous impressions of us which cannot be effaced. He has much duplicity." Hennin, however, in whose department the affairs of the United States unfortunately did not fall, Jefferson considered "a philosopher, sincere, friendly, liberal, learned, beloved by everybody; the other by nobody." [20]

Another official of the first importance with whom Jefferson came much in contact was the brilliant if unscrupulous Calonne. In November, 1783, as the affairs of the kingdom approached ever closer to disaster, he had been summoned to the post of controller-general, which was, to all intents and purposes, minister of finance, in the hope that with his extraordinary business capacity, he might retrieve the situation. That he succeeded in convincing the government of his ability to do so, until his fall in April, 1787, and that many of his bold ideas were subsequently adopted by Necker on his recall to the government in 1788, is well known. There is no doubt that Jefferson had a high idea of his singular qualities. There is likewise no doubt that when the ailing Vergennes confided the negotiations with Jefferson to Calonne in the latter half of 1786, the dealings between the two countries proceeded at a more rapid pace. In sending a copy of a *Mémoire de M. Calonne,* a defense of his conduct, to a friend in October, 1787, Jefferson writes, "You will read it with pleasure. It has carried comfort to my heart, because it must do the same to the King and the nation. Though it does not prove M. de Calonne to be more innocent than his predecessors, it shows him not to have been that exaggerated scoundrel, which the calculations and the clamors of the public have supposed. It shows that the public treasuries have not been so inconceivably squandered as the parliaments of Grenoble, Toulouse, etc. had affirmed. In fine, it shows him less wicked, and France less badly governed, than I had feared." [21]

Jefferson's negotiations with Vergennes on the conditions and terms of commerce between his country and France began shortly after his appointment as minister in 1785. They form a long and complicated chapter in his life as envoy to that country. There were certain difficulties inherent in the situation that added to the complexity. First, since he was the newest and least important member of the *corps diplomatique,* was the almost insuperable difficulty of seeing Vergennes at all. As Jefferson wrote Jay concerning a proposed conference on the next levee day at Versailles, "the number of audiences of ambassadors and other ministers, which take place of course before mine . . . seldom, indeed, leave me an opportunity of audience at all." [22] Furthermore, the Count was a diplomat of the old school, brought up and trained in the ancient traditions of an ancient court. Jefferson, twenty-five years younger, was an emissary from a new country, which was making traditions instead of following them. Indeed, rather than conform to old customs that were, of necessity, those of England, there was a definite tendency to assert independence in this regard, too, and make all dealings as simple and direct as possible. Jefferson himself relates an instance of this. In discussing the tobacco monopoly with Vergennes he tells of his unprecedented suggestion to the Count how without reducing the King's revenue this "monopoly should be put down . . . in the simplest manner, by obliging the importer to pay, on entrance, a duty equal to what the King now received, or to deposit his tobacco in the King's warehouses, till it was paid, and then permitting him a free sale of it. '*Ma fois,*' gasped the astonished Count, '*c'est une bonne idée; il faut y penser.*' " [23]

In a letter to Jay, dated January 2, 1786, Jefferson encloses two long reports on conversations he had with Vergennes. They indicate that when Jefferson did have an opportunity to confer with the Count he made the most of it. Each man brought to the meeting a firm belief in his own preconceptions. Each was convinced that his theories were vital to the life of his country. "Our conversation began with the usual topic," Jefferson writes of their important discussion on December 9, 1785, "that the trade of the United States had not yet learned the way to France, but continued to centre in England, though no longer obliged by law to go there. I observed that the real cause of this was to be found in the difference of the commercial arrangements of the two countries, that merchants would not and could not trade but where there was to be some gain, that the commerce between two countries could not be kept up but by an exchange of commodities; that if an American merchant was forced to carry his produce to London, it could not be expected that he would make a voyage from thence to France with the money, to lay it out here . . . that if he could bring his commodities with advantage to this country, he would not make another voyage to England with the money to lay it out there, but would take, in exchange, the merchandise of this country. The Count de Vergennes agreed to this." [24]

Jefferson, for his part, after reviewing the productions of the United States that "could be brought here to advantage, such as rice, indigo, flour, fish, peltry, whale oil," and certain others, came back to the vital subject of the tobacco trade. Again he urged a mitigation of the monopoly of the purchase of tobacco by the Farmers-General and a simplification in the manner of collecting the duty. He observed, he writes, "that France at present paid us ten millions of livres for this article, that for such portion of it as were bought in London, they sent the money directly there, and for what they bought in the United States was still remitted to London in bills of exchange. Whereas, if they would permit our merchants to sell this article freely, they would bring it here and take the returns on the spot in merchandise, not money." [25]

The tired Count, who was nearing the end of his days, observed that Jefferson's "proposition contained what was doubtless useful, but . . . that the collection of this revenue, by way of farm, was of very ancient date, and that it was always hazardous to alter arrangements of long standing, and of such infinite combinations with the fiscal system." M. de Rayneval, who was present at the meeting, explained to the Count more in detail the advantages and the simplicity of it; then, philosopher that he was, he "concluded by observing to me that it sometimes happened that useful propositions, though not practicable at one time, might become so at another."[26]

The negotiations, says Jefferson, "were interrupted at times with collateral matters. One of these was important"—as, indeed, it was, for it struck root at the essential weakness of the tenuous American government as it then existed. "The Count de Vergennes," Jefferson continues, "complained, and with a good deal of stress, that they did not find a sufficient dependence on arrangements taken with us. This was the third time, too, he had done it." Jefferson discusses these occasions in detail adding that, in the present conversation, the Count had charged that the state of Georgia had violated the eleventh article of the treaty between the United States and France. "He observed, too," Jefferson adds, "that the administration of justice with us was tardy, inasmuch as their merchants, when they had money due them within our states, considered it as desperate; and that our commercial regulations in general were disgusting to them. These ideas were new, serious, and delicate.

"I decided therefore, not to enter into them at that moment," Jefferson continues, "and the rather as we were speaking in French, in which language I did not choose to hazard myself." However, he did say a few words in defense of his country by withdrawing, as he says, "from the objections of the tardiness of justice with us, and the disagreeableness of our commercial relations, by a general observation that I was not sensible they were well founded."[27] He then went home and prepared a learned treatise on the laws and regulations of the United States as applied to the charges made by Vergennes, concluding that they are administered "with a purity and integrity of which few countries afford an example." This he handed Rayneval to give the Count, under the heading "Explanations on some of the subjects of the conversation which I had the honor of having with his Excellency, the Count de Vergennes, when I was last at Versailles."[28]

Jefferson used this occasion to discuss once more with Rayneval "the subject of the farms, which were now understood to be approaching a conclusion. He told me that he himself was decidedly of opinion that the interest of the state required the farm of tobacco to be discontinued; that he had, accordingly, given every aid to my proposition which laid within his sphere; that Count de Vergennes was very clearly of the same opinion, and had supported it strongly with reasons of his own when he submitted it to the Comptroller General," who was, unfortunately, of the opinion that "the contract with the Farmers General was now so far advanced that the article of tobacco could not be withdrawn from it without unravelling the whole transaction." Jefferson, "having understood that in this contract there was always reserved to the Crown a right to discontinue it at any moment, making just reimbursements to the Farmers," got Rayneval to agree that "it might still be practicable to have it discontinued, as to the article of tobacco, at some future moment." With this triumph, minor in character, yet pregnant for the future, Jefferson concluded that "upon the whole, the true obstacle to this proposition has penetrated in various ways through the veil which covers it." [29]

Meanwhile, American merchants were pressing to conclude contracts for furnishing tobacco to the Farmers-General. Early in 1785 Robert Morris had, indeed, secured one, but it was scarcely to the advantage of his country.[30] For the time being it was impossible for any other American to make similar arrangements. "I have been fully sensible of the baneful influence on the commerce of France and America which this double monopoly will have," Jefferson wrote the Governor of Virginia.[31] He figured that Virginia and Maryland stood to lose 400,000 pounds by the reduction in the price of their tobacco. Morris, he declared, "had thrown the commerce of that article in agonies. He had been able to reduce the price in America from 40 to 22 livres lawful the hundred weight, and all other merchants being deprived of that medium of remittance, the commerce between America and that country, so far as it depended on that article, which was very capitally too, was absolutely ceasing." [32]

Jefferson now directed his energies toward a mitigation of this state of affairs. At this point the Marquis de Lafayette returned from a tour of Germany and Austria, where, in addition to improving himself "by the inspection of famous fields of battle, the conversation of the greatest generals, and the sight of excellent troops," he had acted as America's first ambassador at large. "The kind reception I met with in every part of my journey," he writes Jefferson, "has given me the means to hear and to speak much on the affairs of America. I find the misrepresentations of Great Britain have not been fruitless. The strength of the union, the powers of Congress, the dispositions of the people, and the principles of trade, are points upon which I have had many opportunities to give the lie to false assertions of newspapers, and to set to rights the false ideas of misinformed people." [33]

Now, on his return to Paris, his help was once more invoked. He responded with "the zeal which commands them [his services] on every occasion respecting America," Jefferson writes. "He suggested to me the meeting of two or three gentlemen well acquainted with this business." [34] As a result, a committee was proposed "for considering the means of promoting the general commerce of America." Lafayette, who, as early as December, 1783, had already addressed a memorial to Vergennes on the subject,[35] was named a member of it. "His influence in obtaining that establishment was valuable," Jefferson comments, "but his labors and his perseverance as a member of it became infinitely more so." [36]

Matters came to a head on the twenty-third of May with the arrival of a letter from some merchants at Lorient "complaining of their having six thousand hogsheads of tobacco on hand, and of the distress they were under from the loss of this medium of remittance." [37] Vergennes called a meeting of the committee for the following day at Berni, the seat of the Comptroller General. Again Jefferson asked "if I was to consider the expunging that article from the farm as desperate." Again, Vergennes replied that "the difficulty of changing so ancient an institution was immense." [38] In the end, "the only question agitated," Jefferson tells us, "was how best to relieve the trade under its double monopoly. The committee found themselves supported by the presence and sentiments of the Count de Vergennes." [39] The results of the discussion were announced in a letter from the Count to Jefferson, dated Versailles, May 30, 1786, enclosing a copy of the resolves of the committee.

"I take the earliest opportunity to inform you," Vergennes writes, "that notwithstanding the treaty which the Farmers General have made with Mr. Robert Morris, for the delivery of a certain quantity of tobacco [60,000 hogsheads] they have just concluded to take in the way of trade as much as fifteen thousand hogsheads per annum. To let you understand better the extent of the decision in question, I send it to you in the extract enclosed. I beg that you will make it known both in America, as also to the American owners of vessels who may be found in our ports, so that they may direct their commercial speculations accordingly." [40] It was Jefferson's first important victory in diplomacy. Robert Morris never forgave him.[41]

Lafayette's helpfulness on this committee marked what might be called the second alliance between the Marquis and Jefferson. The latter could not be too appreciative of his efforts. In a letter to the American Secretary of Foreign Affairs he observes that "the assistance of M. de Lafayette in the whole of this business has been so earnest and so efficacious, that I am in duty bound to place it under the eye of Congress, as worthy of their notice. On this occasion their thanks, or such other notice as they should think proper, would be grateful to him without doubt. He has richly deserved, and will continue to deserve it, whenever occasion shall arise of rendering service to the United States." [42]

Time did not dim the happiness of the relationship between the two men. When they had worked together even longer, with the inevitable opportunities for clash of temperaments, Jefferson was able to write Madison, "The Marquis de Lafayette is a most valuable auxiliary to me. His zeal is unbounded, and his weight with those in power, great. His education having been merely military, commerce was an unknown field to him. But his good sense enabling him to comprehend perfectly whatever is explained to him, his agency has been very efficacious. He has a great deal of sound genius, is well remarked by the King, and rising in popularity. He has nothing against him but the suspicion of republican principles.... His foible is a canine appetite for popularity and fame; but he will get above this." [43]

On the fourteenth of August, 1786, the eve of the *Assomption*, which even today finds Paris deserted, Jefferson wrote David Humphreys, who had meanwhile returned to the United States, "I am laboring hard with the assistance of M. de Lafayette to get the general commerce of the United States with this country put on a favorable footing, and I am not without hopes. The Marquis is gone into Auvergne for the summer. The rest of the *beau monde* are also vanished for the season. We give and receive them, you know, in exchange for the swallows." [44] Before Lafayette left, and at his instigation, Jefferson sent him a long letter, enclosing a detailed report of several pages on the estimated exports of the United States to Europe and the West Indies together with an estimate of the imports from those countries, a subject with which his committee was totally unfamiliar. "Calculations of this kind," Jefferson writes, "cannot pretend to accuracy, where inattention and fraud combine to suppress their objects. Approximation is all that can be arrived at. Neither care nor candor have been wanting on my part to bring them as near the truth as my skill and materials would enable me to do. I have availed myself of the best documents from the custom-houses, and have been able to rectify these in many instances by information collected by myself on the spot in many of the states. Still, remember, however, that I call them but approximations, and that they must present some errors as considerable as they were unavoidable." [45] The report gave the Marquis something to think about during the long summer days in Auvergne. In October, negotiations were resumed.

Meanwhile, Lafayette had not been idle. He had circulated Jefferson's reports among the members of the committee, whom he found "well disposed." They agreed, furthermore, Jefferson writes, "to report not only the general measures which they thought expedient to be adopted, but the form of the letter to be written by the Minister of Finance to me for the communication of these measures. I received the letter this morning." [46] The letter, a document some nine pages in length, dated Fontainebleau, October 22, 1786, can only be described as bristling with amiability and favors. Calonne announces, among other things, that the King has decided to grant the United States four free ports, instead of two, to suppress the duty on the exportation of brandy and various wines, to suppress or reduce certain other duties on a large number of articles imported from the United States, such as pelts, all kinds of wood fit for shipbuilding, books and papers of all sorts, potash and pearlash, and to permit the exportation of arms, guns, and gunpowder on French or American vessels. In regard to whale oil, one of the most important American products, there was granted for a period of ten years, "the same favors, the same diminution of duties which the Hanse-Towns enjoy." Only "the consolidation of ship duties and the encouragements for the importation of rice" remained for future negotiation.[47]

Jefferson was overjoyed. It was his second victory—a greater one than he had dared hope for. He wrote Jay the same day. The diplomatic pouch bulged with copies of all the correspondence involved in the negotiations, with translations of the *arrêts* of the King's Council of State reducing or suspending the various duties and superseding previous *arrêts* dating back to the year 1687. With these went Jefferson's own report in which he exulted happily that Calonne's letter was "a proof of the disposition of the King and Ministers to produce a more intimate intercourse between the two nations." With his eye always on the people, of whom he was so stout a champion, he continued, "Indeed, I must say that, as far as I am able to see, the friendship of the people of this country towards us is cordial and general, and that it is a kind of security for the friendship of the Ministers, who cannot in any country be uninfluenced by the voice of the people. To this we may add that it is to their interest as well as ours to multiply the bands of friendship between us. As the regulations stated in the Minister's letter are immediately interesting to those concerned in our commerce," he concludes, "I send printed copies of it to the seaport towns of France." [48]

On receiving what he believed to be "the final decision" on the questions just discussed, Jefferson proposed to avail himself "of the pause which that would produce in order to visit the seaport towns with which we trade chiefly, and to collect that kind of knowledge of our commerce, and of what may be further useful to it, which can only be gathered on the spot and suggested by one's own inspection." [49] This he proceeded to do during the spring of 1787, as we shall see. Meanwhile he had not reckoned with two eventualities, the death of the Comte de Vergennes on February 13, 1787, and the fall of his protégé Calonne the following April.

The Comte de Montmorin, jovial, stoutish, a man of Jefferson's age, whom he considered "one of the most honest and worthy of human beings," [50] "though indolent and inattentive, too, in the extreme,"[51] was appointed to succeed Vergennes. Montmorin had been ambassador to Madrid and was governor of Brittany at the time he was called as foreign minister. He was a great admirer of Necker, whose political fortunes he followed, and a loyal adviser to the King, even after the latter's flight. With his appointment, it became necessary for Jefferson to rehearse the whole negotiations. This he did in a long and persuasive letter of July 23, 1787,[52] and in a succinct résumé contained in a memorandum headed, "Observations on the letter of Monsieur Calonne to Monsieur Jefferson, dated Fontainebleau, October 22, 1786."[53] Although Jefferson had been "extremely pleased with his modesty, the simplicity of his manners, and his disposition towards us," and had promised himself "a great deal of satisfaction in doing business with him,"[54] subsequent correspondence reveals the gradual misunderstandings, conscious and unconscious, and the countless minor irritations that ensued. These were caused by such things as the failure of the farms to purchase the amount of tobacco agreed upon and the consequent glut of the market, the failure to obey the new regulations and not collect the ancient duties abolished by the King, and the discovery of various *droits locaux*, which the wily French customs officials were so adept at recalling or discovering.

A major problem that confronted Jefferson and Montmorin was the revision of the consular convention between France and the United States. In 1784, before Franklin's departure, he and Vergennes had entered into such an agreement. "It contained many things absolutely inadmissable by the laws of the several states," Jefferson writes. "Dr. Franklin, not being a lawyer, and the project offered by the Count de Vergennes being a copy of the conventions which were established between France and the despotic states on the continent (for with England they never had one) he seems to have supposed it a formula established by universal experience, and not to have suspected that it contains matters inconsistent with the principles of a free people.... The most objectionable matters were the privileges and exemptions given to the consuls, and their powers over persons of the nation, establishing a jurisdiction independent of that of the nation in which it was exercised, and uncontrollable by it. The French government valued these because they then apprehended a very extensive emigration from France to the United States, which this convention enabled them to control." [55]

Jefferson appears to have had a philosophical aversion to the office of consul. "As to ourselves," he writes, "we do not find the institution of consuls very necessary.... He is generally a foreigner, unpossessed of the little details of knowledge of greatest use to them. He makes national questions of all the difficulties that arise.... Though these considerations may not be strong enough to establish the absolute inutility of consuls, they may make us less anxious to extend their privileges and jurisdictions.... That the government [of France] thinks them useful is sufficient reason for us to give them all the functions and faculties which our circumstances will admit." [56]

In August, 1786, Jay had written Jefferson, "The consular convention is now, as it has long been, under the consideration of Congress, and I have reason to hope they will soon enable me to send you full instructions on the subject." [57] This he was able to do on the third of October with the observation that "these papers will possess you fully of the whole business. I am persuaded that it will appear to you, as it does to Congress, to be a delicate one, and require delicate management." [58] Jefferson had promised, the following January, to "do the best I can for the reformation of the consular convention, being persuaded that our states would be very unwilling to conform their laws either to the convention or to the scheme; but it is too difficult and too delicate to form sanguine hopes." He then asks for special powers "in which there shall be no reference to the scheme." [59] These were granted him in May, and Congress agreed to "ratify and confirm whatever conventions shall in virtue of this commission be by you so concluded, provided the duration of the same be limited to a period of 12 years." [60]

Congress' instructions did not reach Jefferson until the nineteenth of December, 1787. Being then "much engaged in getting forward the *arrêt* which came on the twenty-ninth of December, and willing to have some interval between that act and the solicitation of a reconsideration of our consular convention, I had declined mentioning it for some time, and was just about to bring it on the carpet, when it became necessary for me to go to Amsterdam. Immediately on my return, which was about the last of April, I introduced the subject to the Count de Montmorin, and have followed it unremittingly from that time." [61]

It was a year before the actual negotiations began.

On June 20, 1788, Jefferson wrote Montmorin, "conformably to the desire you expressed," a long letter detailing the objection of the United States to the various articles in the convention as proposed by Vergennes and Franklin. "This, Sir," he says in conclusion, "is a general sketch of the alterations which our laws and our manner of thinking render necessary in this convention, before the faith of our country is engaged for its execution. Some of its articles, in their present form, could not be executed, and others would produce embarrassments and ill humor, to which it would not be prudent for our government to commit itself." [62] On September 16 Jefferson submitted to Rayneval, to be handed to Montmorin, his "observations on the alteration proposed in the consular convention," along with a "draught, on the basis of the one you were pleased to give me, altered so as to reconcile it to the spirit of our laws." [63]

Two months later, on the fourteenth of November, the "convention between his most Christian Majesty and the United States of America for the purpose of defining and establishing the functions and privileges of their respective consuls and vice consuls" was signed. [64] It remained substantially the same into modern times. The most important changes from Franklin's convention were, according to Jefferson: "(1) The clauses of the convention of 1784, clothing consuls with the privileges of the laws of nations, were struck out, and they were expressly subjected, in their persons and property, to the laws of the land; (2) The giving of right of sanctuary to their houses was reduced to a protection of their chancery room and its papers; (3) Their coercive powers over passengers were taken away, and those whom they might have termed deserters of their nation, were restrained to deserted seamen only; (4) The clause allowing them to arrest and send back vessels was struck out and instead of it they were allowed to exercise a police over the ships of their nation generally; (5) So was that which declared the indelibility of the character of subject, and the explanation and extension of the eleventh article of the treaty of amity; (6) The innovations in the laws of evidence were done away; and the convention from being perpetual was limited to twelve years.

"Although strong endeavors were made to do away with some other disagreeable articles, yet it was found that more could not be done without disturbing the good humor which Congress wished so much to preserve, and the limitations obtained for the continuance of the convention insured our finally getting rid of the whole. Congress, therefore, satisfied with having so far amended their situation, ratified the convention." [65] This body did more than that. It went out of its way, through Jay, to inform Jefferson that his conduct of the negotiations was "greatly and deservedly commended." [66]

It would not be in place in a work of this scope to follow the seesaw of negotiations between Jefferson, Montmorin, Lambert, the controller-general who succeeded Calonne, Necker, the minister of finance, and Luzerne, the minister of marine, concerning other questions of consequence to the two countries. These were chiefly concerned with the importation and duties on whale oil and the various by-products of that creature, the importance of which in this day of electricity we tend to forget, as well as on flour, wheat, and other grains, particularly rice. They followed much the same pattern as those discussed concerning the tobacco trade. That Jefferson was an ardent and assiduous advocate of the products of his country is proven by the many "observations," usually of extended length, which he indited and had printed for the various ministers, "finding it necessary to give them information on the whale fishery [or whatever might be the subject under discussion] of which they knew little." [67] The success of his endeavors is attested by the various *arrêts* of the King's Council of State designed to encourage commerce between the United States and France, some of which have already been discussed. Nothing, no effort, no investigation, no amount of correspondence was too much trouble or presented too many obstacles to this man, who was almost superhuman in his ability to conquer details and his determination to make his country one of the elect of the nations of the world.[68]

Jefferson's task had not been an easy one. The position of American minister, as has already been observed, was one of minuscule importance at court. As Gouverneur Morris says of his own presentation to

Montmorin, "he is very civil, but the English of it seems to be that he had already more trouble than he desires with strangers." [69] Although Jefferson seems to have enjoyed the confidence and respect of Vergennes, particularly of Calonne, of Montmorin and Necker, Luzerne, brother of the Chevalier de la Luzerne who had succeeded Gérard as French minister to the United States, was frankly hostile —perhaps from a surfeit of democracy. He "receives me with a degree of hauteur I never before experienced," [70] Morris writes. Jefferson fared even worse at his hands. "He speaks of Jefferson with much contempt as a statesman," Morris continues, "and as one who is better formed for the interior of Virginia than to influence the operations of a great people. I own I am rather surprised at this sentiment," Morris adds, "because Mr. Jefferson has in general excited favorable ideas of his intellectual faculties." [71]

That Luzerne's estimate was far from widespread but due, rather, to individual caprice, Morris affirms on another occasion in speaking of the position Jefferson occupied in Paris. "The French, who pique themselves on possessing the graces," he writes, "very readily excuse in others the want of them; and to be an *étranger* (like charity) covers a multitude of sins. On the whole, therefore, I incline to think that an American Minister at this court gains more than he loses by preserving his originality." [72]

IV. The World of Art

JEFFERSON'S ACTIVITIES IN Paris were by no means to be confined to the traditional ministerial duties we have just been discussing. He was to be the first to play a large part in promoting the cultural relations between the United States and France, bringing to his own country examples of the arts that his fellow citizens may have read and heard about, but that few had ever seen.

On June 24, 1784, the Virginia Assembly had passed a resolution requesting the Executive "to take measures for procuring a statue of General Washington to be of the finest marble, the best workmanship," and dictating the inscription that was to be carved upon the pedestal.[1] There was some anxiety among the legislators that the likeness might not be a happy one. They determined to make certain of it by having the collaboration of a portrait painter. On July 1, Benjamin Harrison, the governor of Virginia, wrote the celebrated Philadelphian Charles Willson Peale concerning the proposal, adding, "that I may be enabled to discharge the pleasing trust reposed in me in the most perfect manner possible, I have to request the favor of you to draw a full-length picture of him immediately, and, as soon as it is sufficiently dry, to have it packed up in the most secure manner and shipped in the first ship bound for France to the address of the honorable Thomas Jefferson." [2]

On August 15 Peale replied that he had "begun a whole length portrait of our late most worthy commander-in-chief, General Washington, and will make all the dispatch I can." On October 30 he wrote Harrison again that the picture was finished and would be sent on the first ship bound for France.[3] The following April 15, 1785, Jefferson informed the Governor of Virginia that "the picture of General Washington is come safely to hand." [4]

Before leaving America Jefferson, who was, of course, aware of the sentiment in the Virginia legislature and who may have had an inkling that he might be called upon to recommend a sculptor, as none was available in the United States, had, as we have seen, taken the precaution of having Washington's portrait painted by Joseph Wright.[5] There were thus two portraits available in Paris for the use of a sculptor.

Meanwhile the burden had lain heavily on the sturdy shoulders of Harrison, accustomed as he was to affairs of the plantation rather than of the arts. On the twentieth of July he had turned his troubles over to his friend Thomas Jefferson, informing him of the action of the Assembly and enclosing the resolution. "You will observe," he writes, with a furrowed brow, "they have only provided for one side of the pedestal, and that the others, with the dress, etc., are left to the genius of the Executive. This would be a very pleasing employment for us if we had ever turned our thoughts that way, or were adepts in the science of devices, emblems, etc. But as we are not, we have unanimously fixed on you and my friend Dr. Franklin, who, we all know, are fully competent to the task.... The intent of the Assembly is that the statue should be the work of the most masterly hand. I shall therefore leave it to you to find out the best in any of the European states." [6]

Harrison's letter did not reach Jefferson until the twenty-ninth of November, 1784. On the twelfth of January, 1785, he replied persuasively and at length: "There could be no question raised as to the sculptor who should be employed, the reputation of Mons. Houdon, of this city, being unrivalled in Europe.... Of course no statue of General Washington which might be a true evidence of his figure to posterity could be made from his picture. Statues are made every day from portraits, but if the person be living they are always condemned by those who know him for want of resemblance." He goes on to say that Houdon is "so anxious to be the person who should hand down the figure of the general to future ages" that he has offered "to leave the statues of Kings" [7] unfinished and will embark for America in the April packet. He does not mention Houdon's main motive for undertaking the trip—the hope that he might, in addition, secure the commission of modeling the equestrian figure of Washington voted by Congress in 1783, an ambition he failed to realize.

Meanwhile, it had been necessary to send another persuasive letter to Washington, acquainting him with the necessary details. This Jefferson did on December 10. "I find that a Monsieur Houdon, of this place, possesses the reputation of being the first statuary in the world," he writes. "I sent for him and had some conversation with him on the subject. He thinks it cannot be perfectly done from a picture, and is so enthusiastically fond of being the executor of this work, that he offers to go to America for the purpose of forming your bust from the life, leaving all his business here in the meantime. He thinks that being there three weeks with you would suffice to make his model in plaster, with which he will return here, and the work will employ him three years. . . . Monsieur Houdon," he adds in conclusion and by way of recommendation, "is at present engaged in making a statue of the King of France. A bust of Voltaire executed by him is said to be the finest in the world." [8]

Both Washington and the Virginia legislature readily agreed to Houdon's employment, indeed Richard Henry Lee wrote that he considered it "very happy for America that events of such high importance should have taken place here as to invite artists of Mr. Houdon's great reputation to visit us." [9] The matter of Houdon's fee appears to have been left for Jefferson to arrange. In his first letter to Harrison, Jefferson, in taking up the matter of expense, had written, "We believe from his character that he will not propose any very considerable sum for making this journey, probably two or three hundred guineas, as he must necessarily be absent three or four months, and his expenses will make at least a hundred guineas of the money." Virginia was to find, however, that the financial path she was to tread with the sculptor was, as always, to be strewn with many thorns. The first intimation of this was in Houdon's demand that his life be insured "between his departure from Paris and his return to it" to the extent of 20,000 livres. "This latter proposition was disagreeable to us," Jefferson writes. "But he has a father, mother and sisters who have no other resource but in his labors, and he is himself one of the best men in the world. He therefore made it a *sine qua non*, without which all would have been off." [10] In haste Jefferson wrote Adams on July 7, 1785,"to enquire what it will cost to ensure that sum on his life in London, and to give me as early an answer as possible." [11] As things turned out Houdon arrived in America with no such safeguard, and on September 24 we find Jefferson still asking Adams, "Is insurance made on Houdon's life? I am uneasy about it, lest we should hear of any accident." [12] It was not until November 19, on the very eve of Houdon's departure from America on the return journey, that Jefferson could thank Adams for his efforts and send him the 32 pounds, 11 shillings the insurance had cost.[13]

On July 12, 1785, shortly before Houdon's embarkation, Jefferson addressed a letter to the Virginia delegates in Congress asking them to favor the sculptor with their "patronage and counsels" and saying frankly that nothing but the expectation of making the equestrian statue "could have engaged him to undertake the voyage, as the pedestrian statue for Virginia will not make it worth the business he loses by absenting himself. I was therefore obliged to assure him of my recommendation of this greater work. Having acted for this in the state, you will, I hope, think yourselves in some measure bound to patronize and urge his being employed by Congress. I would not have done this myself," he adds, "nor asked you to do it, did I not see that it would be better for Congress to put this business into his hands than those of any other person living, for these reasons," and he goes on to summarize them. "The pedestrian statue in marble is to take three years. The equestrian, of course, much more. Therefore the sooner it is begun, the better." [14]

In a subsequent letter to Jay, after the return of Houdon to France, Jefferson again urges the employment of Houdon and encloses the sculptor's terms for making such a statue, along with a "description of the cost of several bronze statues and the names of the artists who executed them" designed to show Jefferson and Congress that his demands were very modest.[15] According to this, Falconet was to receive 25,000 livres a year in addition to expenses, and other commissions from the Empress Catherine for modeling the statue of Peter the Great. Bouchardon, who began an equestrian figure of Louis XV, received a pension of 15,000 livres per annum during the fifteen years he was at work on it, and Sully was rewarded by the astronomical sum of 3,000,000 livres for the nineteen years he devoted to one of Frederick V at Copenhagen.[16] Houdon asked what he considered a modest "600,000 livres and the term of ten years from the present instant . . . in case the bargain should be signed by both parties in the course of the present year." A second proposal from the sculptor decreased the necessary time to eight years and increased the fee to 1,000,000 livres.

Meanwhile, on July 15, 1785, Jefferson had been writing Patrick Henry, newly elected governor of Virginia, about his troubles of another sort. "We had hoped from first conversation with him," he says, "that it would be easy to make our terms, and that the cost of the statue and the expense of sending him would be but about a thousand guineas. But when we came to settle this precisely, he thought himself obliged to ask vastly more, insomuch that one moment we thought our treaty at an end. But, unwilling to commit such a work to an inferior hand, we made him an ultimate proposition on our part. He was as much mortified at the prospect of not being the executor of such a work, as we were not to have it done by such a hand." The equestrian statue still beckoned, and Houdon "acceeded to our terms," which were "25,000 livres or 1,000 English guineas . . . for the statue and pedestal," though, as Jefferson observed, "we are satisfied he will be a considerable loser." In addition, the state was "to pay his expenses going and returning, which we expect will be between four and five thousand livres. If he dies on the journey, we pay his family 10,000 livres." Franklin, it seems, "was disposed to give 250 guineas more, which would have split the difference between the actual terms and Mr. Houdon's demands." Jefferson urges that at the conclusion of Houdon's work the state "agree to give him this much more, because I am persuaded he will be the loser, which I am sure their generosity would not wish."[17]

Houdon had been unable to take the April packet. He was stricken with a serious illness that almost cost him his life. It thus came about that he made the long journey to America in the company of Franklin, sailing from Havre on July 20. The story of his lost luggage and sculptor's equipment, of how the passengers on the ship took up a collection of shirts and socks for the sculptor and his assistants, and of how he was obliged to pay "the tailor for four persons," besides the hatter, the shoemaker, stockings and linen, is well known. He finally arrived at Mount Vernon on Sunday, October 2, "after we were in bed," Washington writes, "about eleven o'clock in the evening." [18] His stay was not long. On the nineteenth Washington again notes, "Mr. Houdon, having finished his business which brought him hither, went upon Monday [the seventeenth] with his people, work and implements, in my barge, to Alexandria, to take passage in the stage for Philadelphia the next morning." [19]

The artist had accomplished a phenomenal amount during his short stay at Mount Vernon. He seems to have spent the first several days forming his impressions of his subject and preparing to work, for it was not until the sixth of October that Washington, as he tells us, sat "for Mr. Houdon to form my bust." [20] Aside from making this bust, which is of terra cotta and which may still be seen at Mount Vernon, he made a life mask of his sitter to guide him in the statue he was to make for Virginia, and recorded the General's measurements. Casts of the bust were likewise made at Mount Vernon, one of which, now lost, seems to have been given Franklin.[21] Astute diplomat that he was, Franklin suggested that Houdon take this bust with him to New York "in order to show Congress what he is capable of doing, and thereby obtaining the preference in being employed to make the equestrian statue voted long since." [22] This Houdon did, and Congress seems to have been properly impressed. Indeed, Charles Thomson, the secretary, was so enthusiastic that he wrote Jefferson on November 2, "It appears to me to be executed in a masterly manner.... The artist, by elevating the chin and countenance, has given the air of one looking forward into futurity." [23]

Houdon returned to Paris on Christmas Day, 1785. He brought with him, as Jefferson wrote Washington a few days later, "the mould of the face only, having left the other parts of his work with his workmen to come by some other conveyance." [24] On February 8, 1786, Lafayette, in announcing the sculptor's arrival, remarked to Washington, he "had not yet brought your bust, which he expects by water from London." [25] The bust Lafayette referred to was, of course, a cast of the one Houdon had left at Mount Vernon. By May 7 it had reached Paris, and Jefferson reported to Temple Franklin that "it meets the approbation of those who know the original." [26]

Now that Houdon was prepared to start work on the statue for Virginia, the question arose as to the dress in which Washington should be shown and the inscription that should appear on the pedestal. In the letter to Washington just mentioned, Jefferson had raised the first question by asking "whether there is any particular dress, or any particular attitude, which you would rather wish to be adopted." [27] Washington, modest and considerate as always, answered that he did not "desire to dictate in the matter. On the contrary, I shall be perfectly satisfied with whatever may be judged decent and proper." He then suggests that "perhaps a servile adherence to the garb of antiquity might not be altogether so expedient as some little deviation in favor of the modern costume." [28]

Despite a natural inclination toward the classical, Jefferson was frankly delighted with Washington's decision. He had been in London during the spring of 1786, where he was in contact with the artistic world, and had talked the matter over. "I am happy to find," he writes the General, "that the modern dress for your statue would meet your approbation. I found it strongly the sentiment of West, Copley, Trumbull, and Brown, after which it would be ridiculous to add, that it was my own. I think a modern in antique dress as just an object of ridicule, as a Hercules or Marius with a periwig and a *chapeau bras*." [29]

Nevertheless, the matter was not so easily settled. Houdon is known to have made one or more models or sketches for the figure before he reached his final version. One, in particular, is of interest, as certain previous suggestions were retained. This, oddly enough, represented Washington as the protector of agriculture, rather than as a soldier. He is said to have been "clothed in the plain and noble habiliments appropriate to a man of rural pursuits . . . sandals on the feet, with a cloak fastened across the chest and enveloping the back and shoulders, suggesting protection to the agriculturist against bad weather. One hand rests upon a walking stick, the other is placed upon the republican fasces, crowned by a liberty cap. At his feet stands a plough." [30]

In Houdon's final version the walking stick, the fasces, and the plow have been retained, a sword added. The cloak has been discarded—it lies thrown over the fasces—and Washington stands before us in the uniform of a revolutionary officer, a noble, life-size figure, elevated upon a pedestal five feet in height.

Shortly after his return from America, Houdon called on Jefferson "to remonstrate against the inscription proposed" for the statue by the Virginia Assembly. It had been written by James Madison, in the best eighteenth-century Virginia style and, to our taste, seems rather overwhelming. It read: "The General Assembly of the Commonwealth of Virginia have caused this statue to be erected as a monument of affection and gratitude to George Washington, who, uniting to the endowments of the hero the virtues of the patriot, and exerting both in establishing the liberties of his country, has rendered his name dear to his fellow citizens, and given the world an immortal example of true glory." [31]

Houdon complained about the length. Jefferson replied that he was "not at liberty to permit any alteration, but I would represent his objection to a friend, who could judge of its validity, and whether a change could be authorized." The inscription became the subject of conversation among Jefferson and his friends. At length he proposed one as "best" to Madison, which, it must be said, put the efforts of the Virginia Assembly to shame. On one side the following words were to be inscribed: "Behold, Reader, the form of George Washington. For his worth ask History, that will tell it, when this stone shall have yielded to the decays of time. His country erects this monument; Houdon makes it.... On the second, represent the evacuation of Boston with the motto: '*Hostibus primum fugatis.*' On the third, the capture of the Hessians, with '*Hostibus iterum devictis.*' On the fourth, the surrender of York, with '*Hostibus ultimum debellatis.*' This is seizing the foremost brilliant actions of his military life." [32]

Jefferson concluded his remarks with the suggestion that "by giving out here, a wish of receiving mottos for this statue, we might have thousands offered, from which still better might be chosen." [33] Luckily, this was apparently not done. When it was finally shipped to America, in January, 1796, long after Jefferson's departure, it bore no inscription upon the pedestal, only the name "George Washington" on the base upon which it stands. In 1814 the original inscription was at last carved upon the pedestal.

The figure of Washington was not the only one with which Jefferson was charged. As early as December, 1781, when the glow of Lafayette's victory over Lord Cornwallis was still strongly felt, the Virginia legislature had "resolved unanimously that a bust of the Marquis de Lafayette be directed to be made, in Paris, of the best marble employed for such purpose, and presented to the Marquis." An inscription of some length was determined upon and it was further resolved that "the commercial agent be directed to employ a proper person in Paris to make the above bust." [34] This was, of course, a very advanced step for the state to take. Gratitude on the part of the various states, at this period, was to take the form of gifts of land to their benefactors rather than sculptural representation. Indeed, with four notable exceptions—the figure of Lord Botetourt, which stood in the capitol at Williamsburg, and the statues of Pitt, commissioned by the states of New York and South Carolina at the time of the repeal of the Stamp Act, as well as the equestrian figure of George III that adorned the Bowling Green in New York—sculpture was not only a rarity but nonexistent in America. The question inevitably arises whether Jefferson with his early study and appreciation of the arts, as we have seen, stimulated his friends in the Virginia legislature to this act and subsequently to the one for a statue of Washington. There is no written document to substantiate this. It can only be a hypothesis that remains not beyond the bounds of possibility.

A copy of the resolution was sent Lafayette, but no steps were taken toward its execution. The Assembly had failed to direct the Governor to carry it out, and the commercial agent had already resigned. When two years had passed without his having "received the intended compliment," Lafayette, who, as is well known, panted not only for glory but for any appreciation of his services, expressed his disgruntlement to Washington. The latter, in replying, stated that he would "not be unmindful of what you have written about the bust," and would "endeavor to have matters respecting it placed on their proper basis." [35] On April 5, 1784, Benjamin Harrison, then governor of Virginia, who had had the matter brought to his attention during a visit to Mount Vernon a few days before, laid it before the Council. As a result of the action of that body, he wrote the same day to Thomas Barclay, the American commissioner for settling public accounts and consul at Nantes. He enclosed the resolution of the Assembly and directed Barclay to have it "carried into immediate execution, and by one of the best artists that can be procured." More important, he sent "a bill of exchange of Wm. Alexander & Co. for one hundred and sixty pounds sterling, which you will apply in the first instance to the above purpose of paying for the bust, and the remainder to the credit of the state with yourself." [36]

Before Barclay had a chance to carry out Harrison's directions, the Virginia Assembly appears to have had a change of heart. On December 1, 1784, it most surprisingly passed another resolution directing that the bust be given not to Lafayette, but "be presented in the name of the Commonwealth, to the city of Paris, with a request that the same may be accepted and preserved in some public place of the said city." Not content with this, they also resolved that "as a further mark of the lasting esteem of this Commonwealth for the illustrious qualities and services of the Marquis de Lafayette", a second bust be procured and "fixed in such public place at the seat of government as may hereafter be appointed for the erection of the statue voted by the General Assembly to General Washington." [37]

By this time Jefferson was in Paris. In June, 1785, Patrick Henry, governor at that time, sent a copy of the act to him, as well as to Barclay, saying "the enclosed resolution will inform you of the change which has taken place respecting the bust formerly voted to the Marquis de Lafayette." The astonished Marquis was informed "that the gratitude of those who claim you as their fellow citizen may be as conspicuous as the merit it wishes to perpetuate, the bust which was to have been presented to yourself is now to be erected in the city of Paris, and as we cannot have the happiness of your personal residence, another is to grace our Capitol." [38] Lafayette could not take umbrage at that. Far from it, indeed. He wrote Washington of his pleasure at being placed "within the Capitol of the State [where] I shall be eternally by the side of, and paying an everlasting homage to the statue of my beloved general."[39]

On receipt of Harrison's letter of April, 1784, Barclay had taken steps to have the bust executed. He had turned to Houdon. On August 23, 1785, he writes the Governor, "Mr. Houdon, who embarked for America with Dr. Franklin, made a considerable progress in executing the first bust that was ordered, but, the Marquis being at present in Prussia, the matter must rest until he and M. Houdon return. I think it will be better that the same person complete both busts; the more so as he is at the top of his profession. The cost of each will be 3000 livres, and I have paid 50 louis d'or for the purchase of the marble of the first."[40]

As the sculptor had been chosen—and he would have made the same choice—Jefferson considered the assignment Barclay's affair. Nevertheless he wrote the Governor, "I shall render cheerfully any services I can, in aid of Mr. Barclay, for carrying this resolution into effect. The Marquis de Lafayette being to pass into Germany and Prussia, it was thought proper to take the model of his bust in plaster before his departure. Monsieur Houdon was engaged to do it, and did it accordingly. So far Mr. Barclay had authorized himself to go in consequence of orders formerly received. There is due to M. Houdon for the model of the busts . . . in plaster, I imagine, about 750.0.0."[41]

This time there was no long discussion about dress or other details. That was, doubtless, decided in conversation. In January, after Houdon's return to Paris, Jefferson wrote the Governor, "The first of the Marquis's busts will be finished next month. I shall present that one to the city of Paris, because the delay has been noticed by some. I hope to be able to send another to Virginia in the course of the summer."[42] The bust was duly completed by late spring. It shows Lafayette in military uniform, terminating in drapery. The features are bold and imperious, the pose proud, if not haughty. His contemporaries found the face "rather simple than ingenuous."[43]

To Jefferson, very naturally, fell the task of arranging for the presentation of the bust. This proved to be no simple matter. For a while it seemed to be impossible. "No instance of similar proposition from a foreign power had occurred in their history,"[44] Jefferson wrote the Governor. A new question of propriety had been raised. Jefferson laid the matter before Rayneval in a letter of May 16, 1786, saying he had been informed he should take the matter up with the *prévôt des marchands et échevins de Paris,* in other words, the Mayor of the City of Paris. Before doing so, however, he wanted to ask whether "the respect due to the King and his Ministers, would require from him a previous reference of the subject to them." [45] He found that this was very much the case and negotiations of the most intricate character were entered into, which it is not necessary to detail here.

It was not until September that permission was finally obtained to place the bust "so as to do honor to the Marquis de Lafayette." On the twenty-seventh of that month Jefferson wrote the *prévôt des marchands* to solicit "on behalf of the city, their acceptance of a bust of this gallant officer," and requested that "they will be pleased to place it where, doing most honor to him, it will most gratify the feelings of an allied nation." [46] Arrangements had already been made to put the bust in the great hall of the Hôtel de Ville. A grand ceremony was made of the occasion. The Mayor of Paris presided. The chief recorder, M. Veytard, read the resolutions of the Virginia Assembly as well as Jefferson's letter of the day before. This, in the true French manner, contained a eulogy of the Marquis, expressing Jefferson's pleasure "in obeying the call of that Commonwealth to render just homage to a character so great in its first developments [Lafayette was only 29 years old at this time] that they would honor the close of any other." [47] Mr. de Corny, the attorney-general and husband of Jefferson's great friend, who had been in America during the revolution and was a member of the Cincinnati, responded, music sounded, and the bust was put in place. Only Jefferson was absent. He was still suffering acutely from the fall in which his wrist was dislocated, and could not leave his room. William Short, his secretary, "a citizen of the State of Virginia, and heretofore a member of its Council of State," [48] did the honors.

Jefferson's association with Houdon led to the modeling of his own bust, a thoughtful, sensitive representation of the man in his prime. Although Jefferson was often at Houdon's studio and saw him frequently otherwise, he has left no record of posing for the sculptor.

We do not know when the bust was begun, but we do know it was completed by 1789, as it was exhibited in plaster in the Paris *salon* of that year as *M. Jefferson, envoyé des Etats de la Virginie.*[49] Baron Grimm says of it, "Noteworthy among the pieces of sculpture exhibited this year, are a large number of busts remarkable for their perfect likeness.... Some complain that certain of his portraits are cold and meager in their execution, but is it not a proof of the artist's talent that in the angular features of M. Jefferson he has embodied the interest and the grace which distinguish those of Mlle. Olivier?"[50]

Early in the revolutionary war and from time to time thereafter, while enthusiasm was still high, Congress had voted medals and swords for the leaders of various outstanding actions. An essay into another realm of the artistic world was undertaken by Jefferson in this regard. A committee had been appointed, which had turned the matter over to Robert Morris. He, learning that David Humphreys was to go to Europe as secretary to the commissioners, wrote him, in June, 1784, that "the medals and swords can best be executed in Europe, and therefore I am now to request that you would as speedily as may be, cause them to be made."[51] Humphreys remained in Paris less than two years. He, apparently, first took care of the swords, for in February, 1787, Jefferson wrote Jay, "The swords were finished in time for him to carry them back to the United States. The medals not being finished, he desired me to attend to them."[52] There were ten men who were to receive the medals, outstanding among them being Washington, Franklin, John Paul Jones, Nathanael Greene, and Horatio Gates.

Humphreys had addressed a letter to the "Royal Academy of Inscriptions and Letters," as was requisite, and they furnished him with a device and inscription for Washington's medal. He seems also to have concerned himself with the medal for Gates, as on December 5, 1785, Jefferson wrote him questioning the fact that Gates is shown with the insignia of the Cincinnati, "which did not exist at that date." There was another reason for its not being appropriate, Congress having "studiously avoided giving to the public their sense of this institution ... I am of the opinion that it would be very disagreeable to them to be placed under the necessity of making this declaration."[53]

When the task of procuring the rest of the medals was turned over to him, Jefferson, in his usual methodical manner, made a list in French and English of the persons for whom they were intended, the date of the act of Congress, the size of the medal, the design of each, and the inscription.[54] The latter were produced by the Academy of Belles Lettres on the basis of the material furnished them. According to the taste of today, or what we consider the best classical examples of the art of the medalist, these seem rather fussy, overcrowded, and sententious. However, they were in the best tradition of the time. The men employed were Gatteaux (or Gateau), Dupré, and Duvivier, names very likely suggested by someone in the artistic circle in which Jefferson moved. As secretary of state, he subsequently recommended these men when it became necessary "to determine on a present proper to be given to diplomatic characters on their taking leave of us," and he decided on "a medal and chain of gold." [55]

When Greene's medal was delivered to him, in February, 1787, Jefferson requested Jay "to ask the pleasure of Congress as to the number they would choose to have struck. Perhaps," he suggests, "they might be willing to deposit one of each person in every college of the United States. Perhaps they might choose to give a series of them to each of the crowned heads of Europe, which would be an acceptable present to them. They will be pleased to decide." Jay presented a report to Congress embodying these suggestions with the observation that "he presumes Mr. Jefferson does not mean that any should be presented to the King of Great Britain, for that would not be delicate. Nor that by crowned heads he meant to exclude free states from the compliment, for to make a discrimination would give offence." [56] He concluded that, "as these medals were directed to be struck in order to signalize and commemorate certain interesting events and conspicuous characters, the distribution of them should, in his opinion, be such as may best conduce to that end."

It was ultimately decided, and Jefferson received instructions "to deliver one of gold or silver—as the case may be—to the person who is the subject; to send one of silver to every sovereign and one of copper to every University of Europe (Great Britain excepted), two hundred copies to Congress, and one apiece to Lafayette, Rochambeau, Destaing and Degrasse. I am at liberty to deliver no others. Not even at the orders and expense of the persons who are the subjects of the medals. But your wish—" he is writing to John Paul Jones— "will be fulfilled as to the Empress [of Russia], because I shall send her a suite of the whole medals under the general order." [57]

While governor of Virginia, Jefferson had, as we have seen, been one of the prime movers in having the capital of the state removed from its original situation in Williamsburg to the new town of Richmond at the falls of the James River. This had occurred in April, 1780, only four years before he was to go to France. It was the first step toward the realization of a dream to withdraw his country, as he still called Virginia, from colonial provincialism and establish it in a dignity suitable to its new station as one of the thirteen independent yet united states. To this end he had early caused to be introduced into the legislature two bills, the one of October 14, 1776, providing for the erection of the public buildings to adorn the new seat of government. These were to be a house for the use of the General Assembly, to be called the Capitol, "which sd. Capitol shall contain two apartments for the use of the Senate and their clerk, two others for the use of the House of Delegates and their clerk, and others for the purposes of conferences, committees and a lobby." In addition there was to be erected another building to be called the Halls of Justice, "which shall contain two apartments for the use of the Court of Appeals and its clerk, two others for the use of the High Court of Chancery and its clerk, two others for the General Court and its clerk, two others for the use of the Court of Admiralty and its clerk, and others for the uses of grand and petty juries. . . . The said houses," the bill continues, and we hear the voice of Jefferson, "shall be built in a handsome manner, with walls of brick or stone and porticos where the same may be convenient or ornamental, with pillars and pavements of stone." [58] It was an ambitious scheme for a hamlet with a population of only a few hundred.

To insure the carrying out of these plans and to supervise the design and construction of the buildings, a second bill was introduced into the Assembly on May 29, 1779, providing for the election of five men to be called "the directors of the public buildings." They "or any three of them shall have power . . . to agree on plans for the said buildings, to employ proper workmen to erect the same, to superintend them, to secure the necessary materials," etc.[59] A year later the number of directors was increased by the Assembly to nine. Jefferson, then governor, was included among them.

These proposals were completely revolutionary. Nowhere yet in the old world, to say nothing of the new, had separate buildings for the legislative, judicial, and executive branches of the government been envisaged. Jefferson had leaped far ahead of his time in proposing such a scheme. Yet, however ideal it may have been, whatever the enthusiasm for it among Jefferson's associates, it was destined not to be realized at this period—largely because of lack of sufficient funds. In October, 1784, with the persuasive and revolutionary Jefferson safely in France, the legislature voted "that it shall be in the discretion of the said directors to cause apartments to be provided for the uses aforesaid under one and the same roof, any law to the contrary notwithstanding." [60] Jefferson's governmental village was thus, alas, not to come into existence. It was not until some forty years later, when he was planning and building his academical village, which came to be known as the University of Virginia, that this vision came true.

Jefferson was, of course, not satisfied with merely introducing and promoting bills in the Assembly. He did not wait for some one else to carry out his ideas. Indeed, there was no one capable of doing so. All the time he had had in his mind a clear picture of how, as he confided to Madison, he wanted to form the taste of his countrymen in this "beautiful art of architecture" by using every occasion when public buildings were to be erected of "presenting to them models for their study and imitation," of giving them "the satisfaction of seeing an object and proof of national good taste," rather than "the regret and mortification of erecting a monument of our barbarism." [61] To this end he had early undertaken to make drawings for the proposed buildings himself. It was, of course, not his first attempt. We have already seen how, as early as 1767 he had begun calculations and drawings for his own Monticello, subsequently a plan, at the request of Lord Dunmore, with a view to enlarging the College of William and Mary. There has, furthermore, recently been discovered a "Design of a chapel the model the temple of Vesta," an octagonal structure, with a surrounding peristyle, concentric benches, and a central altar, which is believed to have been drawn in 1770 for erection in Williamsburg.[62]

Jefferson's plans for the government buildings at Richmond likewise still exist among his papers. Among them is to be found a small sketch for the Halls of Justice—a plain, rectangular building 90 by 68 feet, the interior arrangement of which follows, in most respects, the provisions of the Removal Act. There are likewise drawings for a *villa rotunda*, a favorite scheme of Jefferson, with two four-column porticoes at front and rear, and balancing outbuildings connected by short, double colonnades with the main building which was doubtless intended for the Governor's Mansion, also provided for in the same act. It is believed that these drawings were made about 1780.[63]

The most important of these designs were those Jefferson made for the capitol of Virginia. They have only recently come to light. It had hitherto not been known that Jefferson had made drawings for this edifice before going to Europe. The evidence of the paper on which they are drawn, along with a study of his occupations and duties at the period, leads to the conclusion that they were made in 1780. In them Jefferson made the wholly revolutionary proposal, not only for America but for Europe as well, of using the form of a rectangular temple for a building intended for practical use, with monumental porticoes at either end eight columns wide, the full breadth of the structure. This was Jefferson's first and determined attempt, as he wrote in his autobiography, "of introducing into the state an example of architecture in the classic style of antiquity,"[64] and it was to be realized within a few years by the building of the capitol in Richmond very much along the lines he had laid down.

When Jefferson sailed for France, he had, apparently, very little idea that the erection of the capitol would be undertaken in the near future. He appears either to have taken his drawings for the building with him or left them at home among his papers at Monticello. Certain it is that he did not turn them over to the Directors of the Public Building in Richmond—indeed, in view of the subsequent correspondence, it is questionable whether they were even aware of the existence of such plans. Jefferson had scarcely left America when William

Short, who had been elected a member of the Council of the State of Virginia in 1783 and who was presently to follow him to Europe, wrote from Richmond, on July 28, 1784, "The Assembly voted at the last session the sale of the public property here, in order to begin the buildings on the hill. The Directors have contracted with an undertaker [contractor] and Roy Randolph is to draw the plan." After observing that he had urged them to "send to some part of Italy for a design and workmen," Short concludes with the discouraging remark that "I do not think the Directors believe it possible to build a more magnificent house than the Williamsburg Capitol. It seems impossible to extend their ideas of architecture beyond it." [65]

Nothing further was heard of these schemes until June, 1785, when Jefferson received a letter, written the preceding March, from James Buchanan and William Hay on behalf of the Directors. Short's urgings to seek the benefit of European skill and experience had apparently borne fruit. "The active part which you took before your departure from Virginia as a director of the public buildings," they write, "leads us to believe that it will not be now unacceptable to you, to cooperate with us, as far as your engagements will permit. . . . We must entreat you to consult an able architect on a plan fit for a Capitol, and to assist him with the information of which you are possessed." After expressing their fear that "the Assembly would not countenance us in giving sufficient magnificence to distinct buildings," they announce that they have "obtained leave to consolidate the whole under one roof, if it should seem advisable. The enclosed draught will show that we wish to avail ourselves of this license. But, although it contains many particulars, it is not intended to confine the architect except as to the number and area of the rooms."

After telling Jefferson that the site he preferred is still the favored one, they add that "the Legislature have not limited us to any sum, nor can we, as yet at least, resolve to limit ourselves to a precise amount. But we wish to unite economy with elegance and dignity—at present the only funds submitted to our order are nearly about £10,000 Virginia currency." In urging haste they inform Jefferson that one Edward Voss of Culpeper has already been engaged to lay 1500 thousand bricks, and they presume "he may commence his undertaking by the beginning of August. . . . This circumstance renders us anxious for expedition in fixing the plan; especially, too, as the foundation of the Capitol will silence the enemies of Richmond in the next October session." They conclude this letter with a request for "a draught for the Governor's house and a prison. But we hope that the Capitol will be first drawn and forwarded to us, as there is no hurry for the other buildings." [66]

Jefferson was stunned by the demand for speed. He wrote the Directors on the fifteenth of June, the day after receiving their letter, that "between that date and the 1st of August it would be impossible to procure and put into your hands the draughts you desired." [67] Two months later, on the thirteenth of August, he again wrote, "I did hope indeed to have had them prepared before this, but it will yet be some time before they are in readiness. I flatter myself, however, they will give you satisfaction when you receive them and that you will think the object will not have lost by the delay." He goes on to say that it took "considerable time before I could find an architect whose taste had been formed on a study of the ancient models of this art. . . . I at length heard of one, to whom I immediately addressed myself, and who perfectly fulfills my wishes. He has studied 20 years in Rome, and has given proofs of his skill and taste by a publication of some antiquities of this country." [68]

The architect selected by Jefferson was Charles Louis Clérisseau, once a pensioner of the Academy at Rome, who had spent some twenty years making drawings of the remains of ancient architecture. When the Empress Catherine II of Russia planned to build herself a palace on the model of those of the Roman emperors, she appealed to the French Academy for an architect, and Clérisseau was recommended. It is small wonder Jefferson thought him suitable for the Virginia project. Although architectural interiors comprise the bulk, if not all, of his executed work, there is not the least doubt that he was a competent architect.

With laymen, a combination such as this, of statesman and professional architect, the question always arises as to who contributed what. We have already had proof of Jefferson's architectural abilities. His own statements in his autobiography and his contemporary letters to his associates leave us in no doubt that it was he who selected the model for the building, as well as determined the arrangement of the interior and fixed every principal dimension, both inside and out, after the most painstaking studies and elaborate calculations. There exist among his papers a number of sheets, hitherto unobserved, that bear testimony to this. They are too technical to analyze in detail here. He compares the dimensions of various temples, such as the Erechtheum in Athens, the temple of Balbec, and that of Mars in Rome, with the "Ionic from Palladio," which he was determined to use on the exterior of his building. The entablature for the two large rooms below was to be Doric. Two pages are devoted to the disposition of the rooms, the dimensions, and the architectural elements. These notes were then translated into French and handed to Clérisseau as *Explications des plans du Capitole pour l'état de la Virginie.*[69]

A final proof, if any were needed, of Clérisseau's rôle as consultant, rather than designer of the building, is to be found in three documents. One is the payment made on June 2, 1786, to "Clérisseault for his assistants in drawing the plans of the Capitol and Prison, 288 livres," which appears in Jefferson's account with the Commonwealth of Virginia under the date of December 9, 1789. The second is a letter from Clérisseau to Jefferson, dated June 2, 1786, in which he says, "*Je suis entièrement satisfait lorsque je suis assuré, que vous êtes satisfait du zèle avec le quel j'ai secondé vos intentions,*" and, finally, still another entry in Jefferson's account with the state in which he notes paying, on June 3, 1789, Odiot, a Paris silversmith "for coffee pot as a present to Clérissault for his trouble with the drawings, etc., of public buildings, 423 livres." [70]

The plans were finally completed, and on January 18, 1786, Jefferson was able to write Dr. Currie, "I send by this conveyance designs for the Capitol. They are simple and sublime, more cannot be said. They are not the brat of a whimsical conception never before brought to light, but copied from the most precious, the most perfect model of ancient architecture remaining on earth, one which has received the approbation of nearly 2000 years, and which is sufficiently remarkable to have been visited by all travellers." [71]

The Directors were pleased with Jefferson's efforts. On October 18 they wrote thanking him and assuring him that his ideas were "perfectly corresponding to those of the Directors, respecting the style and ornaments proper for such a work, and we trust the plans will be designed in conformity thereto." They then broke the devastating news that "from the anxiety of the public to have the work begun" it had actually been started, without benefit "of a more perfect plan from you." They therefore deemed it proper to inform Jefferson "what has been done, that you may judge how far we shall be able to adopt the plan you transmit us." In the next sentence Jefferson learned that "the foundation of the Capitol is laid, of the following dimensions, 148 by 118 feet, in which are about 400 M bricks; the centre of the building of 75 by 35 to be lighted from above, is designed for the Delegates; the rest is divided in such a manner as to answer every purpose directed by the Assembly. The foundation of the four porticoes are not laid, tho' the end and side walls are contrived to receive them. . . . We hope we shall be able to avail ourselves of your assistance," they conclude, "without incurring much expense." [72] If Jefferson's heart sank, he gave no indication of it—except more doggedly to pursue his scheme and ultimately to assure the Directors that the whole of the work begun "need not be taken to pieces, and of what shall be taken to pieces the bricks will do for inner work, mortar never becomes so hard and adhesive to the bricks in a few months but that it may easily be chipped off." [73]

On January 26, Jefferson sent "the ground plan, the elevation of the front, and the elevation of the side . . . knowing that this was all which would be necessary in the beginning." These were accompanied by a long letter to the Directors in which he explained and, to some extent, justified his course. "Two methods of proceeding presented themselves to my mind," he writes. "The one was to leave to some architect to draw an external according to his fancy, in which way experience shows that about once in a thousand times a pleasing form is hit upon. The other was to take some model already devised and approved by the general suffrage of the world. I had no hesitation in deciding that the latter was best, nor after the decision was there any doubt what model to take."

He goes on to acquaint the Directors, solid Richmond burghers and worthy planters, whose fancies had never flown beyond the confines of Virginia, with the beauties and charms of the Maison Carrée, a small Roman temple at Nîmes, "erected in the time of the Caesars, and which is allowed without contradiction to be the most perfect and precious remain of antiquity in existence.... I determined, therefore to adopt this model and to have all its proportions justly drewed." Well aware that no foreigner could know "what number and sizes of apartments could suit the different corps of our government," Jefferson himself drew the plans for the interior of the building. These he handed to Clérisseau, who shared Jefferson's enthusiasm. "He was too well acquainted with the merit of that building," Jefferson observes, "to find himself restrained by my injunctions not to depart from his model. In one instance only he persuaded me to admit of this. That was to make the portico two columns deep instead of three, as the original is. His reason was that this latter depth would too much darken the apartments. Economy might be added as a second reason. I consented to it to satisfy him, and the plans are so drawn," Jefferson admits. The man who could scarcely find even economy a valid reason for his deviation, comforted himself with the reflection that "I knew that it would still be easy to execute the building with a depth of three columns, and it is what I would certainly recommend." [74]

In order to insure a more perfect execution of the project than he believed possible by workmen who had never seen a Roman temple and who were not very expert in their art, Jefferson determined to have a plaster model made. He wrote the Directors that it would add to the expense as "it would cost 15 guineas, and I would not have incurred it but that I was sensible of its necessity." Part of this extra cost would be made up by the fact that "the body of this building covers an area of but two fifths of that which is proposed and begun," and "of course it will take but about one half the bricks," which he is sensible "will enlist all the workmen and the people of the art against the plan." A final argument in favor of the economy of his scheme was that there would be only one portico instead of the four shown on the builder's plan.

The model was finally finished in May, 1786. It had been made, Jefferson tells us, under Clérisseau's direction "by an artist who had been employed many years in Greece, by the Count de Choiseul, Ambassador of France at Constantinople, in making models of the most celebrated remains of ancient architecture in that country." [75] A note in Jefferson's account book reveals that on May 22 he "pd. Fouquet for the State of Virginia for model of the capitol in plaster, 372 fr." On the thirteenth of June he paid Marc, one of his servants, for "State of Virginia duties and postage on the model of the Capitol, 25 fr 18," and it was sent "down the Seine to Havre, it being necessary that it should go by water." It safely withstood the long voyage across the Atlantic and today may still be seen in the capitol at Richmond, a miniature of the building the Duc de la Rochefoucauld-Liancourt called "beyond comparison the most beautiful, the most noble, and the greatest in all America" [76]—a monument of Jefferson's devotion to his country.

V. The Circle of Literati

One of the things to which Jefferson most looked forward in going to France was the opportunity of associating with what he called "the society of literati," and he was not to be disappointed. This no longer meant what it had a few years before in the middle of the century, the heyday of that brilliant assemblage of fearless thinkers and sharp wits, the philosophers, whose convictions found expression largely in the famed and influential *Encyclopédie*. The great figures, who had so thoroughly laid the foundation of the revolution that even then was in process of germination, had passed on. Voltaire and Rousseau had died in 1778, Turgot, the "gigantic stature" of whose mind Jefferson so greatly admired, in 1781, Diderot the year Jefferson came to Paris, Helvétius and Quesnay a good ten years or more before. Even the celebrated Madame Geoffrin, Madame du Deffand, and Mademoiselle de Lespinasse, whose *salons* had been the delight and ornament of their day, were no longer on the scene.

Jefferson was not to find a world denuded, however. The circle of literati into which he was to be received, and of which he was to become a part, was composed, with one or two exceptions, of men and women of his own generation, who represented newer ideas. Indeed, two of the leading members, the Duc de la Rochefoucauld and the Marquis de Condorcet, were born in the same year as Jefferson. It was bound together, primarily, by the advanced political views its members shared. Since the middle of the century, as the philosophers persistently and surely destroyed all faith in the monarchy and in religion, the concept of the republic had become its ideal. This at first, of course, meant the republic of Rome. With the outbreak of the American Revolution, however, the enthusiasm of the French was transferred from the ancient world to the new. The spectacle of a new nation fighting for existence and for the freedom of which the French were forever talking, enthralled them. As Patrick Henry remarked at about this time, "America has lighted the candle to all the world." [1]

Lafayette, supremely conscious of this, wrote Washington, "The spirit of liberty is prevailing in this country at a great rate. Liberal ideas are cantering about from one end of the kingdom to the other." [2] On his return from Germany in 1786, where he had visited Frederick the Great, he reported enthusiastically to Jay, "Wherever I went, America was, of course, a topic of conversation. Her efforts during the contest are universally admired, and in the transactions which have so gloriously taken place, there is a large field of enthusiasm for the soldier, of wonder and applause for the politician, and to the philosopher and philanthropist they are a matter of unspeakable delight." [3] And Jefferson, in giving the Marquis de Valadée a letter of introduction on his impending trip to America, described him as "a gentleman of distinguished family in this country. A genuine love of liberty, a desire of freeing himself from the shackles which the laws and manners of Europe impose, and a predilection for our country, tempt him to pay it a visit. You will find him well informed, sensible, honest, and plain as a republican." [4]

The enormous influence of the American Revolution and the stimulation supplied by the alliance between France and America to the dissemination of these ideas is nowhere better expressed than by Jefferson, who was to write, "Celebrated writers of France and England had already sketched good principles on the subject of government, yet the American Revolution seems first to have awakened the thinking part of the French nation in general, from the sleep of despotism in which they were sunk. The officers, too, who had been to America, were mostly young men, less shackled by habit and prejudice, and more ready to assent to the suggestions of common sense, and feeling of common regrets, than others. They came back with new ideas and impressions." [5]

How new and how utterly foreign to their thought and training were the ideas which these young men imbibed in the new world, and how idealistic became their outlook, we may gather from the first letter the twenty-year-old Lafayette wrote his wife on his arrival in Charleston in 1777. "I shall now speak to you, my love," he says, "about the country and its inhabitants, who are as agreeable as my enthusiasm had led me to imagine. Simplicity of manner, kindness of heart, love of country and of liberty, and a delightful state of equality are met with universally. The richest and the poorest man are completely on a level; and, although there are some immense fortunes in this country, I may challenge anyone to point out the slightest difference in their respective manner toward each other.... What gives me the most pleasure is to see how completely the citizens are all brethren of one family. In America there are none poor, and none even that can be called peasants, each citizen has some property, and all citizens have the same rights as the richest individual or landed proprietor in the country." [6]

Other influences in spreading these new and revolutionary ideas, Jefferson continues, were "the press, notwithstanding its shackles.... Politics became the theme of all societies, male and female, and a very extensive and zealous party was formed which acquired the appellation of the Patriotic party, who, sensible of the abusive government under which they lived, sighed for occasions of reforming it. This party comprehended all the honesty of the Kingdom, sufficiently at leisure to think, the men of letters, the easy bourgois, the young nobility, partly from reflection, partly from mode; for these sentiments became matter of mode, and as such, united most of the young women to the party." [7]

This, then, was the circle to which Jefferson was introduced and in which he was to take a worthy place. "Words cannot express to you how much I am pleased with Mr. Jefferson's conduct," Lafayette wrote Washington when Jefferson had been in Paris nearly a year and when his qualities were beginning to be known. "He unites every ability that can recommend him with the ministers and at the same time possesses accomplishments of the mind and of the heart which cannot but give him many friends." [8]

Paris was, indeed, prepared to like Jefferson. The way had been paved for him by his venerable predecessor, Benjamin Franklin, who had come to France in December, 1776, when he was in his seventy-first year. He was already one of the most celebrated and most discussed men in the world. What Franklin's sponsorship meant we see as early as 1769 when Benjamin Rush, then a young man, set out for Paris. Franklin gave him letters to Diderot and the Marquis de Mirabeau. He "kept a coterie once a week at his house, to which I was invited," Rush tells us. "Upon my entering his room, which was large and filled with ladies and gentlemen of the first literary characters in Paris, Dr. Dubourg [a botanist friend of Franklin] announced me in the following words: '*Voilà! Un ami de Monsieur Franklin.*' The Marquis ran towards the door and took me by the hand, saying at the same time, '*C'est assez.*' The subjects of conversation," he concludes, "were economics, liberty and government." [9]

In the eight years that had passed between Franklin's arrival in France and that of Jefferson, he had come to be idolized not only by this circle of patriots and literati but by all Paris. Adams declared, "His name was familiar to government and people, to kings, courtiers, nobility, clergy and philosophers, as well as plebians, to such a degree that there was scarcely a peasant or a citizen . . . who was not familiar with it, and who did not consider him as a friend to human kind. . . . They seemed to think he was to restore the golden age." [10]

Such was the formidable heritage to which the new American minister, wise in his heart, yet untried in the ways of the great world, succeeded. It is small wonder he was led to observe that "the succession to Dr. Franklin at the court of France was an excellent school of humility" and followed this by his famous remark that no one could replace Franklin, only succeed him.[11] Although Jefferson had no such reputation as a scientist, in an age that was awakening to the wonders of it, although he did not wear the halo of a homespun philosopher, and although he lacked a certain warmth of nature and an endearing touch of charlatanism, he was of that rare and fashionable species, an American, a symbol of a new way of life—and the French took him to their hearts.

As in all old societies, this group of intellectually and politically minded persons was a small one at the time of Jefferson's arrival. It was dominated on the one hand by that most ardent liberal, the Duc de la Rochefoucauld, and his remarkable mother the Duchesse d'Anville, by their most intimate friend the Marquis de Condorcet, and, a little later, by Lafayette. The distinguished Abbés Morellet, Arnauld, Chalut, de Mably, Barthelmy, and the Papal Nuncio, Comte Dugnani, with whom Jefferson kept up relations until the Cardinal's death in 1820, were what might be called the theorizers of this group in contrast to the men of action. Closely allied with them, with interests more purely literary and artistic, was the celebrated Baron de Grimm, and the well-known writer, Marmontel, who, Jefferson says, dined with him "every Thursday for a long time, and I think told some of the most agreeable stories I ever heard in my life. After his death, I found almost all of them in his memoirs, and I dare say he told them so well because he had written them before in his book." [12]

Louis-Alexandre, Duc de la Rochefoucauld, had just passed forty when Jefferson met him. At nineteen he had married Louise-Pauline de Montmorency, who was killed in 1771 by a fall from her horse. Some years later he married again, this time his niece, the lovely Alexandrine de Rohan-Chabot, known familiarly as Rosalie, who was twenty years his junior. With her, and with his widowed mother, he lived in the elegance befitting his means and his station in a handsome *hôtel* situated in an elaborate garden bounded by the rue des Petits Augustins and the rue de Seine, or at his fortresslike château on the river Seine, La Roche-Guyon, which had its beginnings as far back as the year 998. He enjoyed the distinction of being a peer of France as well as head of an illustrious family, which had given two cardinals to France. By temperament and education he was of a liberal turn of mind. He was likewise a patron of the arts and of science, and numbered among his friends many of the contemporary philosophers.

Jefferson seems to have met the Duke not long after his arrival, probably through Franklin. Among his papers is a letter dated New York, July 15, 1784, from that remarkable Frenchman, Crèvecoeur, who after a self-imposed exile of twenty-one years had returned to his native country in 1781 and been immediately inducted into this circle by Madame d'Houdetot. The letter reads, "I beg you put Mr. Franklin in mind of introducing you to the good Duke de la Rochefoucauld. He is the pearl of all dukes, a good man and a most able chemist. His house is the centre of reunion where men of genius and abilities often meet. You have, therefore, a great right to share his friendship. He honors me with his esteem and friendship. I write to him by this packet to announce you to him. . . . I wish you health and plenty of friends. I hope you'll be pleased with our social scene, which is the shining side of our nation." [13]

Franklin had been in touch with the Duke within a month of his arrival in Paris. On January 29, 1777, he had written his friend Mary Hewson, "Yesterday we dined at the Duke de la Rochefoucauld's, where there were three duchesses and a countess." [14] Like the rest of the French, the Rochefoucauld family and its satellites were prepared to take to their hearts this figure of "an old man, with grey hair appearing under a martin fur cap," so remarkable "among the powdered heads of Paris," [15] as Franklin described himself. From that time on, every American of distinction was welcomed to this citadel of aristocracy and liberalism.

So interested in America and its new experiment in government and so well-versed in English was the Duke that, at Franklin's suggestion, he undertook to translate the constitutions of the thirteen states into French. Franklin first mentions that he had done so in a letter to Robert R. Livingston, secretary of foreign affairs, in July, 1783.[16] The following December he recounts, in his forthright manner, the reasons that led to it. "The extravagant misrepresentations of our political state in foreign countries," he writes, "made it appear necessary to give them better information, which I thought could not be better or more authentically done, than by publishing a translation into French, now the most general language in Europe, of the book of constitutions, which had been printed by order of Congress. This I accordingly got well done, and presented two copies, handsomely bound, to every foreign minister, one for himself, the other more elegant for his sovereign. It has been well taken, and has afforded matter of surprise to many, who had conceived mean ideas of the state of civilization in America, and could not have expected so much political knowledge and sagacity had existed in our wilderness." [17]

Preceding Jefferson as a friend of the Rochefoucauld family was John Adams. As early as 1778, much impressed by the distinguished company of "dukes, abbotts, etc. etc. etc.," he writes, "The Duchess d'Anville and her son, the great friends of Turgot, were said to have great influence with the Royal Academy of Sciences, to make members at pleasure, and the *Secrétaire Perpétuel,* M. d'Alembert, was said to have been of their creation, as was M. Condorcet afterwards. . . . Their family was beloved in France, and had a reputation for patriotism, that is, of such a kind of patriotism as was allowed to exist and be esteemed in that kingdom, where no man, as Montesquieu says, must esteem himself or his country too much." [18]

In December, 1782, Adams notes that "the Duke de la Rochefoucauld made me a visit today and desired me to explain to him some passages in the Connecticut Constitution, which I did." [19] There seems to have been much further conversation on constitutions and government between the two men at the "convivial dinners" that Adams says they attended together, and at other times. Adams had brought with him to France "a printed copy of the report of the Grand Committee of the Massachusetts Convention which I had drawn up, and this became an object of speculation. Mr. Turgot, the Duke de la Rochefoucauld and Mr. Condorcet and others, admired Mr. Franklin's constitution and reprobated mine." [20] To defend it, he adds, "cost me three volumes."

This attack upon his ideas was, seemingly, to influence Adams' ultimate opinion of the Duke and his activities. The final impression he carried with him was to be expressed many years later in his irascible old age and must be read with the proverbial grain of salt. He says of Turgot, Condorcet, and Rochefoucauld that "they were as amiable, as learned and as honest men as any in France. But such was their inexperience in all that relates to free government, so superficial their reading in the science of government, and so obstinate their confidence in their own great characters for science and literature, that I should trust the most ignorant of our honest town meeting orators to make a constitution sooner than any or all of them." [21]

Jefferson's association with the Duke proved to be one of the closest and most stimulating of any he had in France. Through the accident that the young Duchess and William Short, Jefferson's secretary and protégé, to whom he felt and acted as a father, entertained tender feelings for each other, the relationship became even more intimate. The two men were frequently asked either to the family's Paris *hôtel* or to La Roche-Guyon by the Duke's understanding mother, who was the virtual head of the family. The Duke, wholly engrossed in the revolutionary movement, found Jefferson a sympathetic companion. The Duchess discovered similar qualities in Short, but for other reasons.[22] It is our misfortune that, to use Jefferson's words, we have such "a wonderful scarcity of knowledge" as to what actually passed between Rochefoucauld and Jefferson—who held for this opinion, who for that, who argued which side of what question. That they were Attic conversations, as on a famous occasion earlier in Jefferson's life, we cannot doubt.

We have, however, just one informal glimpse of a meeting of these men of kindred interests and ambitions. This occurs in the *Memoirs* of Philip Mazzei, that amazing Italian adventurer who dabbled in agriculture, economics, and politics and who became a friend of kings and princes and philosophers—and of Jefferson. Unfortunately, as is always the case with Mazzei, his remarks are centered largely on Mazzei. He is speaking of a time in 1788 shortly before he published his *Recherches historiques et politiques sur les Etats-Unis de l'Amérique septentrionale* in answer to two works on America by the famous Abbés Mably and Raynal. "When I had finished my work," he writes, "Jefferson, Short and I went to Rocheguyon, the magnificent château of the Duchesse d'Anville, on the border of Normandy. There we met several persons we were in the habit of seeing at the Hôtel de la Rochefoucauld in Paris, among them the Marquis Condorcet, who had promised to examine my work.

"After the establishment of the American republic," he continues, "many wished to see a complete and impartial description of that interesting country. As yet, no one who had written of it deserved to be taken seriously. The Duke de la Rochefoucauld and his friends, the most intimate of whom was the Marquis de Condorcet, were especially interested. The Duke had spoken to Jefferson of this more than once, but always in vain, and, as he repeatedly asked questions, Jefferson told him that he would give him all the information he wanted, taking each question separately, provided he would write out his questions, and provided his inquiries confined themselves only to the state of Virginia." [23] Mazzei, whose memory was often confused in writing his *Memoirs*, considers this the origin of Jefferson's *Notes on Virginia*, in which he is, of course, mistaken.[24]

How highly Jefferson thought of the Duc de la Rochefoucauld is revealed in the farewell letter he sent the Duke after his return to America, the only piece of correspondence between the two men that, so far as the writer has been able to learn, is preserved.[25] After saying that circumstances oblige him to "abandon the expectation of paying my respects to you in person, in Paris," he continues, "though removed to a greater distance in future, and deprived of the pleasure and advantages of your conversation and society, which contributed so much to render my residence in Paris agreeable, I shall not be the less anxious for your health and happiness, and for the prosperous issues of the great revolution in which you have taken so zealous and distinguished a part.... Accept, Sir, my sincere thanks for all your kindnesses, permit me to place here those which I owe Madame la Duchesse de la Rochefoucauld, and which I render with the greatest cordiality. Were her system of ethics and of government the system of everyone, we should have no occasion for government at all." [26]

One of the most remarkable members of this circle was the Duchesse d'Anville,[27] mother of the Duc de la Rochefoucauld, whom Franklin, along with all who met her, describes as "a lady of uncommon intelligence and merit." [28] She was the widow of the well-known naval officer, the Duc d'Anville, of whom his biographer says, "In an exacting service where roughness is too often united with courage, he was able to retain his taste for letters, and the elegance of manner and customs which characterized his illustrious family." [29] In 1745 he had led an armada of forty vessels into American waters in an attempt to recapture Louisburg, a stronghold fortified by the French on Cape Breton. "A mighty impression was made upon my little head," writes John Adams, who was only ten years old at the time, "... on the approach of the Duke d'Anville's armament against Boston." [30] The fleet was largely destroyed in a violent storm. The ships that were not wrecked fell into the hands of the enemy and the Duc d'Anville came to his end on the wild coast of Nova Scotia.

Adams, who first met the Duchess in 1778, recalls this event in his

THE CHÂTEAU DE LA ROCHE-GUYON

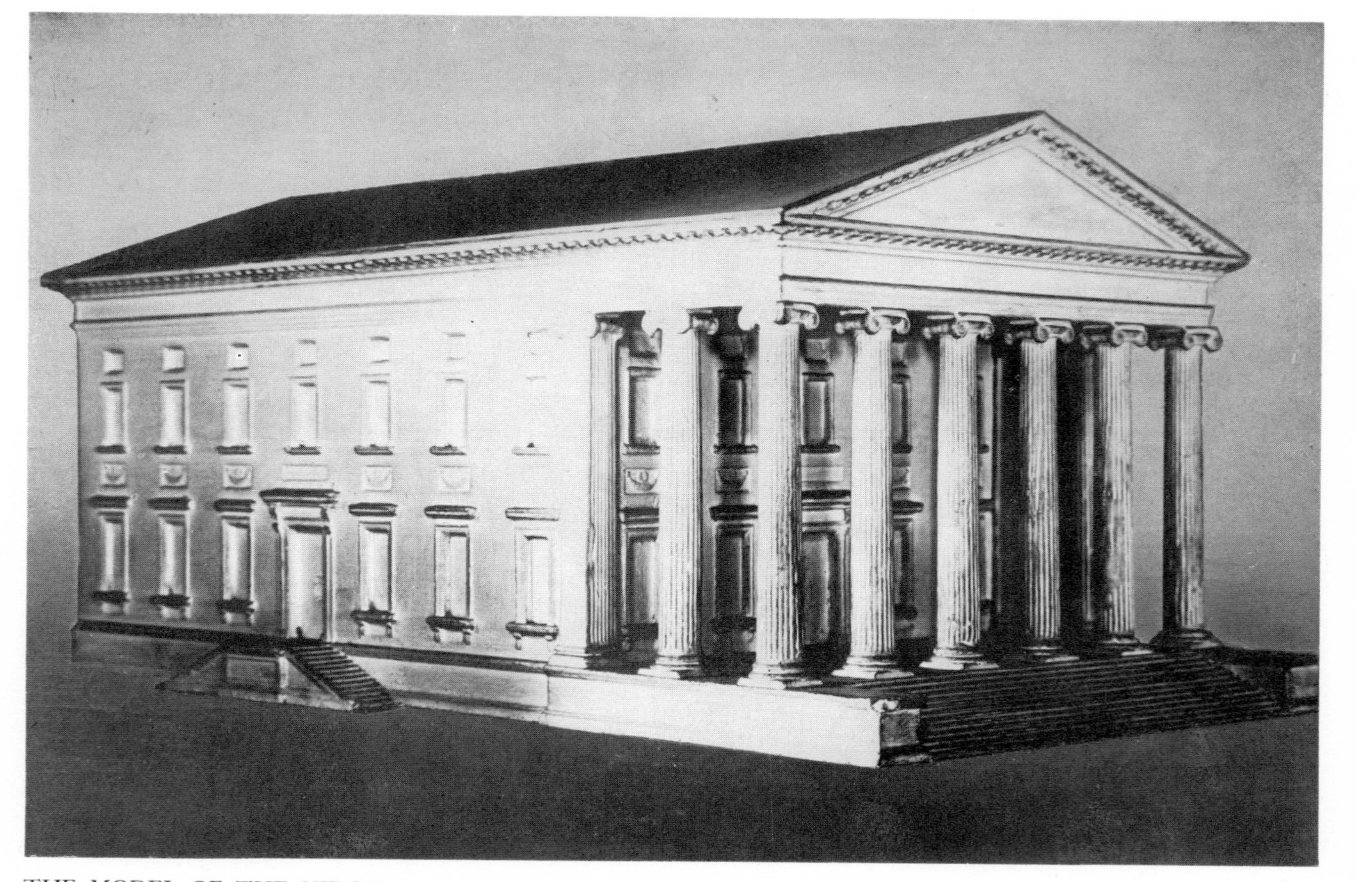

THE MODEL OF THE VIRGINIA CAPITOL. (*Courtesy of the Commonwealth of Virginia*)

comment upon the occasion of a dinner to which she invited him and Franklin, along with "twenty of the great people of France. I thought it odd," he observes, "that the first lady I should dine with in France, should happen to be the widow of our great enemy, who commanded a kind of armada against us, within my memory, but I was not the less pleased with her conversation for that. She appeared to be venerable for her years, and several of her observations at table, full, as I thought, of bold, masculine and original sense, were translated to me. It is in vain," he adds, "to attempt a description of the magnificence of the house, gardens, library, furniture, or the entertainment of the table." [31] It was the first glimpse for the New England Spartan into the splendor and luxury characteristic of the life of the great nobles of the period.

Mrs. Adams has left a picture of the Duchess at the time Jefferson met her. "We found the old lady," she writes, describing a call paid upon her, "sitting in an easy chair; around her sat a circle of Academicians, and by her side a young lady. [This was, without doubt, the young wife of the Duke, who was devoted to her.] Your uncle [Mr. Adams] presented us, and the old lady rose, and, as usual, gave us a salute. As she had no paint, I could put up with it, but when she approached your cousin, I could think of nothing but Death taking hold of Hebe. The Duchess is near eighty, very tall and lean.[32] She was dressed in a silk chemise, with very large sleeves coming halfway down her arm, a large cape, no stays, a black velvet girdle round her waist, some very rich lace in her chemise, round her neck and in her sleeves; but the lace was not sufficient to cover the upper part of her neck," the chatty and censorious Abigail adds, "which old Time had harrowed. She had no cap on, but a little black gauze bonnet, which did not reach her ears, and tied under her chin; her venerable white hairs in full view.... The old lady has all the vivacity of a young one. She is the most learned woman in France, her house is the resort of all men of literature, with whom she converses upon the most abstruse subjects. She is of one of the most ancient, as well as richest families in the Kingdom." [33]

Except for a few dinner invitations and a farewell note to Jefferson written on September 7, 1789, we have no correspondence between him and the Duchess until after his return to the United States. From a letter dated April 2, 1790, we can see in what high regard he held this great and distinguished lady and what a delight his association with her must have been to him. "I assure you, Madam," he writes, "that I consider yourself personally as with the foremost of your nation in every virtue. It is not flattery; my heart knows not that; it is a homage to sacred truth, it is a tribute I pay with cordiality to a character in which I saw but one error: it was that of treating me with a degree of favor I did not merit. Be assured I shall always retain a lively sense of your goodness to me, which was a circumstance of principal happiness to me during my stay in Paris."

The Duchess shared her son's, and Jefferson's, passionate interest in the revolution then commencing in France. There is small doubt but that this was frequently discussed among them, as we may gather from the latter part of this letter. "I hope by this time," Jefferson continues, "you have seen that my prognostications of a successful issue to your revolution have been verified. I feared for you during a short interval, but after the declaration of the army, though there might be episodes of distress, the denouement was out of the question. Heaven send that the glorious example of your country may be but the beginning of the history of European liberty, and that you may live many years in health and happiness to see at length that Heaven did not make man in its wrath." [34]

Jefferson little knew how much he did have to fear for his friend. As the revolution advanced, her son, true to his convictions, took an increasingly prominent part. Such a course was bound to be hazardous among a people whose apparent sturdiness masked a highly volatile temperament. In June, 1792, as president of the Department of Paris, Rochefoucauld had signed the decree suspending Péthion and Manuel from office for their participation in the assault on the Tuileries on the twentieth of that month. Harassed by all factions, he was obliged to resign his post and retire to La Roche-Guyon, where he remained in seclusion with his family.

On the eighteenth of August the Duke, with his wife, his mother, and a close friend, Madame d'Astorg, set out on a trip to Eaux Forges, a small watering place to the north, that had been made fashionable years before by Anne of Austria. On a Sunday early in September the Duke and Duchess were at dinner with friends when word was brought that their house was surrounded. In an unpublished letter, Madame d'Astorg, who was present, has told the story of the tragic events that followed and given a first-hand picture of the horrors of the revolution. "A moment afterwards," she writes, "people told me of the arrival of the commissionaires. You know that we were taking the waters very quietly. Two days earlier he [the Duc de la Rochefoucauld] had come to join us. We began to fear nothing further, and we rejoiced at being reunited. On Sunday he was at luncheon with Madame de Tracy. I had just left their house, when someone came to find me and tell me that Forges was surrounded, their house was discovered, and that no one knew what was going to happen. Imagine my terror! A moment afterwards people told me of the arrival of commissionaires who went into many houses, which still left doubt for some time as to their misfortune. But the certainty came all too soon. The commissionaires arrived at [the Duke's] house, and gave the order of arrest. He kissed his wife goodby and proceeded to the town hall.

"Sentinels were placed at all our doors, and we were guarded, with permission for all to insult us. I remained in a separate house with his mother, who learned this horrible event from the sentinels who surrounded her room, no one having been able to get to her in advance. People came to rummage in our papers, to place seals upon them, and also upon mine, for having been stupid enough to tear up some paper and throw it out of the window. Finally they allowed us to reassemble with his mother; he was brought back from the town hall to her house, and we remained all together with three sentinels in our room. The Commissionaire told us that we would leave the next day at four o'clock in the morning for Vernon. We made preparations to be ready at that hour. Other affairs occupied the Commissionaire in the neighborhood so that he did not come back until three hours after dinner, and did not have us start until that time in the afternoon. Surrounded by *gendarmes nationales*, by guards, and by a great number of idlers, we arrived at Gournay at midnight, where other guards took charge of us and we were conducted to the inn, dead with fatigue. The carriage was made up of the Commissionaire, M. R., Mde. R., the mother, and me; a cabriole followed with the maid and a very tall, thin gentleman.

"On our arrival, the same sentry, and prohibition to speak low. They left us women below, however, and without guards. We were not under arrest. We were told that we would leave again at four in the morning in order to avoid the market, which is very crowded. This hope was dashed. We did not start until nine o'clock, in the midst of the outcries of the great number which such a cortège astonished. We reached Gisors at noon. Scarcely had we arrived when some *fédérés* who appeared surrounded our house, and began to make us fear for our safety. The Commissionaire came back and told us that he had just received a reinforcement of gendarmes sent by M. Santerre to protect our passage. He told him [the Duke] to show himself at the window as the crowd demanded, with great outcry. He appeared there and they had us go back into the rear of the house to escape the horrible cries that were constantly to be heard. Finally the hubbub became so much worse that they had us leave at once, as the people threatened to burn the house. The Commissionaire requisitioned the city armed guard and said to us that he would answer for him with his head. He demanded that we should enter the carriage without him [the Duc de la Rochefoucauld]. He made him go on foot surrounded by the city guard. His cabriole came next, and then we followed immediately. We passed in single file in the midst of the most ghastly outcry and threats. We had mud thrown at us, and all the insults of a misguided populace. Ten minutes after our departure I heard, in the midst of the shouts, 'C'est fait!' and I saw him carried past the carriage, lifeless.... They [his wife and mother] did not know of their loss until the next day. Fear, terror, had prevented them from seeing all that had happened." [35]

It was the last day of December before the stricken Duchess could pull herself together and write her old friend of the virtual extinction of her family, for Charles, Comte de Chabot, her grandson and brother of the Duchesse de la Rochefoucauld had likewise come to an unhappy end. This letter from a torn heart reflects not only her admiration for Jefferson but her trust in him and the comfort she had derived from his words in hard days that had preceded these. "You may recall, my dear friend," she writes, "how your rare judgement, your noble spirit and your profound sagacity calmed my fears at the beginning of our revolution. I was too far removed at that time to foresee the disastrous consequences of which my daughter-in-law and I are now the unfortunate victims. You know my son's sentiments; no sacrifice was too great for him that would bring about the well-being and happiness of his country. His reward was assassination before our very eyes. This catastrophe has extinguished all my happiness and all my delight in life. He was as fine a son as he was a citizen; I may say that he possessed every virtue.

"But this was not sufficient to drive us to complete despair! Two days later my grandson, Charles, was killed in cold blood in the prison where he had deported himself with the courage born of innocence. Both perished without fear and without remorse, as we know it in this world. I am the most unhappy of mothers. My daughter-in-law, widow of one and sister of the other, is utterly desolated. This tender young woman, who possesses every most estimable and most amiable quality, adds to my terrible sorrow. Only a noble spirit such as yours, Monsieur, can help assuage our grief. . . . I beg your pardon, Monsieur," she concludes, "for entering upon the details of my cruel sorrow." Then, with the gesture of the great lady whose despair has led her inadvertently to expose her heart, she adds, "the great kindness which you showed my son, and the friendship with which you have always honored me, have, perhaps, caused me to be indiscreet." [36]

Closely associated with the Rochefoucauld family, so closely, indeed, that he was more like a son to the venerable Duchess than a friend, was the Marquis de Condorcet, the famous mathematician, who was also a philosopher and a figure of the first importance in politics. His brilliant mind elicited the admiration, as well as the friendship, of most of the illustrious men of his day. John Adams, who had encountered him in the spring of 1778 at a dinner given by the Duchesse d'Anville, describes him as "having a face as pale, or rather as white, as a sheet of paper. I suppose from hard study." [37] A cold and reserved exterior did, indeed, mask his natural exuberance and enthusiasm to such an extent that his friend D'Alembert referred to him as a volcano covered with snow. As he approached middle age he had followed in the Duke's footsteps by marrying a woman some twenty years younger than he, Sophie de Grouchy, sister of the future marshal, who was renowned alike for her great beauty and her intelligence. Together they lived at the stately Hôtel des Monnaies (Condorcet held the official post of inspector of the mint), where the leading figures in this new circle of literati gathered about them.

Jefferson early met Condorcet through the Rochefoucauld family. He has, alas, as in the case of most of his living contemporaries, left no account of their relationship or of such conversations and discussions as they may have had. It would seem inevitable that they were on terms of close friendship for they shared the same liberal and humanitarian ideas and the same enthusiasm for democracy. Early in the American Revolution Condorcet had written in favor of independence of the colonies and had gone so far as to discuss freedom for the Negroes. He was as ardently antimonarchical as Jefferson and was one of the first French liberals to advocate a republic. In 1792 he prepared the document which led to the suspension of the King and the summoning of the National Convention. He subsequently drew up a constitution for his country and presented it to the Convention in February of the following year, but it was not adopted.

A man of his independent spirit could not hope to survive the Terror. It was not long before he was accused of being an enemy of the republic, condemned and declared *hors la loi.* While in hiding, before his untimely death, he undertook his most celebrated work, the *Esquisse d'un tableau historique des progrès de l'esprit humain.* The idealism and the high hopes for humanity that Condorcet shared with Jefferson and la Rochefoucauld are sublimated in this work, which seeks to demonstrate the continuous progress of the human race from barbarism to ultimate perfection, largely through popular education. The last part of the work, the tenth epoch of history, as it is usually called, which deals with the future as Condorcet saw it, is a paean to freedom, to a deep conviction of the ultimate equality and freedom of all nations and all individuals. Although this book was published posthumously, the ideas and convictions it expresses are so much in line with those held by Jefferson and already advanced by him somewhat differently and in quite another connection in his revisal of the laws of Virginia, as well as in his *Notes,* that it is impossible to think they were not discussed between them.

Gouverneur Morris tells of dining at Jefferson's house in Paris, in the small company of Condorcet, the Duc de la Rochefoucauld, who "comes from the States-General," and Lafayette, but unfortunately he does not report any of the conversation beyond Lafayette's observation that "some of the troops under his command were about to march tomorrow to Versailles to urge the decisions of the States-General.... I ask him if his troops will obey him. He says they will not mount guard when it rains, but he thinks they would readily follow him in action." [38] Such philosophical speculation as there may have been was beyond the interest or the knowledge of Mr. Morris.

In a letter written to Condorcet after his return to the United States, Jefferson bids his friend farewell and expresses his high hopes for the success of the revolution in which he had played so important a part. "I am looking ardently to the completion of the glorious work in which your country is engaged," he writes. "I view the general condition of Europe as hanging on the success or failure of France. Having set such an example of philosophical arrangement within, I hope it will be extended without your limits also, to your dependents and to your friends in every part of the earth." [39]

The fourth man of what might be called this practical group—those who sought to transform their theories and their beliefs into action—was the youthful Lafayette, who was fired with a passion for the cause of liberty. His idealistic adventure in behalf of the revolting English colonies, undertaken when he was a hot youth of only nineteen, substantiated his later statement that "when I first learned the subject of this quarrel, my heart espoused warmly the cause of it." [40] Adams wrote of him in 1778 as "a youth of the finest accomplishments, and most amiable disposition, panting for glory, and ardent to distinguish himself in military service.... All France pronounced it [*i.e.,* taking up arms for the colonists] to be the first page in the history of a great man." [41]

Jefferson had known Lafayette since the hard days of his governorship in the spring of 1781, when he expressed his gratitude and that of the state "to a nobleman who has already so much endeared himself to the citizens of these states by his past exertions." [42] In renewing their acquaintanceship in February, 1785, on Lafayette's return from his third trip to America, Jefferson found a much more mature man. His unquenched enthusiasm for liberty was now flaming with equal ardor for his own country, or, as Jefferson put it, "he proved himself equally zealous for the friendship and welfare of both nations." [43] Jefferson, in his work as ambassador, with the numerous delicate problems it entailed, was, to use his own words, to be "powerfully aided by all the influence and the energies" of this extraordinary man. In return, Lafayette was to attempt to transmit many of Jefferson's ideas to his own people, as will be discussed later.

It is impossible to overvalue Lafayette's influence at court or among the more enlightened nobility, allied as he was through his wife to one of the greatest families of France. At sixteen he had married thirteen-year-old Marie Adrienne de Noailles, daughter of the Duc d'Ayen and granddaughter of the Duc de Noailles. Adams, who dined with the Noailles' in 1778, observed that they "lived in all the splendor and magnificence of a viceroy, which is little inferior to that of a king." In one of his rare bursts of French he adds, *"La maison, le jardin, les promenades, les tableaux, les garnitures, sont très magnifiques."* [44] But Adams, as well as Jefferson, was not impressed merely by the wealth and magnificence of this family; indeed that was not what was stressed. "I was told," he says of them, "by some of the most intelligent men of France, ecclesiastics as well as others, that there were no less than six marshals of France in this family . . . that the family had been remarkable for ages, for their harmony with one another, and for doing nothing of any consequence, without a previous council and concert; that when the American revolution commenced, a family council had been called to deliberate upon that great event, and determine what part they should take in it, or what conduct they should hold toward it." [45]

The young Marquise de Lafayette entered loyally and wholeheartedly into her husband's enthusiasms. Scarcely more than a girl herself, she had taken young Patsy Jefferson under her wing and had been influential in securing her the opportunity of attending the convent of Panthemont, as we have seen. Mrs. Adams describes her as "a very agreeable lady," who "speaks English with tolerable ease.... She is a middle-sized lady, sprightly and agreeable, and professes herself strongly attached to Americans. She supports an amiable character, is fond of her children, and very attentive to them, which is not the general character of ladies of high rank in Europe." [46]

Lafayette's devotion to his second country, his pride in his American citizenship, the bestowal of American names on his progeny, who are described by Mrs. Adams as speaking English and "behaving very prettily," [47] are too well known to merit comment. It is small wonder that David Humphreys should write after a visit to this family, "There was something at the Marquis de Lafayette's which put one in mind of the freedom of investigation in America. It was an assemblage of such friends of America as these, the Duc de Rochefoucauld, the Marquis de Condorcet and Chastellux, Messrs. Metza, Crèvecoeur, etc. to hear a discussion on American politics and commerce by a M. Warville; the tendency of whose performance is good, some of the observations new, many of them ingenious; but perhaps, there is too much declamation blended with them." [48]

Distinguished in the circle in which Jefferson moved as what might be called the theoretical members rather than the men of action, was that group of secular ecclesiastics known in France as abbés. Outstanding among them was the Abbé Morellet, friend of Turgot, Diderot, and D'Alembert, and himself one of the last of the *philosophes*. At the time Jefferson made his acquaintance he was a man of about fifty-eight who had recently been elected an immortal by the *Académie Française*. He was a person of solid and excellent education, having made the best use of five years at the Sorbonne and a prolonged sojourn in Rome. He was known as a great wit—"*une conversation à-la-fois solide et maligne, sans être caustique, une humeur enjouée,*" his biographer says of him [49]—so much so that Voltaire labeled him "*L'Abbé Mord-les.*" On his return to France he was taken under the wing of the celebrated Madame Geoffrin, who at that time drew all persons of literary or artistic talent to her *salon*. Morellet was not long in winning his place in this much vaunted society he adored, and where he loved to display his Socratic wit.

Early in his career, Morellet, like so many of his contemporaries, experienced the first stirrings of the revolution that was to come. He interested himself in the rights of man and sought, as his biographer tells us, "*s'éclairer sur les éléments de la richesse et du bonheur des nations.*" It was natural that he should become an ardent follower of the revolution in America. In 1781, he undertook a work on the American colonies, which he submitted to Franklin.[50] While on a mission to England in 1772, where he was warmly received by Shelburne, later the Marquis of Lansdowne, he had first met Franklin. The two men were immediately attracted to each other. To Morellet, as to so many other Frenchmen, Franklin was the living symbol of the new age of which they dreamed, a representative of an Utopia based upon freedom and justice. When Franklin came to France, Morellet was one of those who drew him into the gay, intimate circle so charmingly described by Madame Brillon, with whom he dined twice a week and took tea on several mornings. "My fat husband will make us laugh," she writes of one of these tea parties, "our children will laugh together, our big neighbor will quiz, the Abbés La Roche and Morellet will eat all the butter . . . Père Pagin will play 'God of Love' on his violin, I the march on the piano, and you 'Petits Oiseaux' on the harmonica." [51]

Morellet lived with his sister and his niece, who was married to Marmontel, in a handsome apartment overlooking the gardens of the Tuileries. From his windows, into which shone the noonday sun, the guests who frequented the Abbé's famous *matinées* looked down upon "the most celebrated walk in Paris" with "the six large gates by which you may enter." Mrs. Adams further describes them as being "adorned with noble rows of trees, straight, large and tall, which form a most beautiful shade. . . . Upon one side of this garden is the castle of the Tuileries, which is an immense pile of building, very ancient. . . . Upon the terrace which borders this château, are six statues and two vases. These vases are large, circular spots of water conveyed there from the Seine. . . . Round the great vase, which is in the midst of the *parterre,* are four groups of white marble." Although two of them represented "a rape" and "a ravishment," Abigail, who was affronted by so much in French life, considered them "*very pretty* ornaments for a garden." [52]

After viewing this scene, the guests, who represented the elite in letters, art, and society, assembled in the *salon* and the library, which, says the Duchesse d'Abrantès, was one of the largest and best selected in all Paris. "There, in the midst of perfect quiet and with peace in one's heart and soul," she writes, "one listened to the most ravishing music, or to discussions of the latest poetry and prose." [53]

It was shortly before Jefferson's arrival in Paris that the celebrated controversy arose between Piccinni, the Italian composer, and Gluck. The director of the *Opéra* persuaded the two composers to write a work based on the same subject, *Iphigénie en Taurîde*. Parisian society immediately became divided into two camps, the Gluckists and Piccinnists, and many friendships of a lifetime were wrecked in these discussions. The *matinées* of the Abbé Morellet were no exception. The tones of music eventually gave way to the quarreling of the protagonists, and in the end the Abbé felt it necessary to abandon these *réunions* where, as our informant remarks, "men of unusual gifts brought the tribute of their talents to enrich the life of this sage." [54]

It is pleasant to think of Jefferson in this great, sunny library, discussing his *Notes on Virginia* with the Abbé. With his command of several languages, Morellet was an avid translator—he was later to translate into French the eulogies on Franklin's death. He now proposed to Jefferson that they publish a French edition of the *Notes*. In his *Mémoires* he speaks of them as "*une livre, utile pour la connaissance de ce pays, livre intéressant, varié, enrichi d'observations philosophiques, pleins de justesse et de raison*." [55] Many conferences between the author and the translator took place during the two years the men worked on the French edition. This is attested by a series of letters from 1786 to 1788 concerning corrections and the inclusion of the famous map of Virginia, which caused Jefferson many a heartache.[56]

Whether Morellet's impatience with the slowness of the map and Jefferson's seven pages of "Errors in the Abbé Morellet's translation . . . the correction of which is indispensable," ultimately caused a certain coolness between the two friends is one of those questions about which we can only surmise. It is striking, however, that in the "*liste des personnes de quelque nom que j'ai connus, et avec lesquelles j'ai eu des rélations,*" which Morellet included in his *Mémoires*, the name of Jefferson is not included.[57] Franklin, however, merits a paragraph. It was thus not without reason that Franklin had written the Abbé de la Roche on his return to America, "I hope soon to be in a situation where I can write largely and fully to my friends in France. . . . At present I can only tell you that I am well, that I esteem you and l'Abbé Morellet and M. Cabanis, and love dear Mme. Helvétius." [58]

The Abbés Arnauld and Chalut, whose names are always linked, were two other members of this society with whom Jefferson, and John Adams before him, were on intimate terms. Abigail Adams speaks of Arnauld as "about fifty, a fine sprightly man, who takes great pleasure in obliging his friends." Chalut was seventy-five.[59] John Adams had met the two Abbés on his first visit to France, in 1778, and has left us the best picture of them and their activities.

"Two abbés," he writes, "de Chalut and Arnauld, the former a brother of the farmer-general of that name, and himself a Knight of Malta, as well as the order of St. Louis, and both of them learned men, came early to visit me. They had a house in the city and another in the country at Passy, in our neighborhood, where they resided in summer. Whether they were spies of the court, or not, I know not, but I should have no objection to such spies, for they were always my friends, always instructive and agreeable in conversation. They were upon so good terms, however, with the courtiers, that if they had seen anything in my conduct, or heard anything in my conversation that was dangerous or very exceptional, I doubt not they would have thought it their duty to give information of it. They were totally destitute of the English language; but by one means or another they found a way of making me understand them, and sometimes by calling an interpreter, and sometimes by gibbering something like French, I made them understand me." [60]

Jefferson appears to have encountered the Abbés shortly after his arrival. As early as July, 1785, he was writing Mrs. Adams, then in London, that the settlement of the affairs of the learned Abbé Mably "is likely to detain his friends Arnauld and Chalut in Paris the greatest part of the summer. It is a fortunate circumstance for me, as I have much society with them."[61] It was not intrigue that linked Jefferson to these men but, as he remarked to the Reverend James Madison of William and Mary College, "the crumbs of science on which we are subsisting here," and of which he sends Madison an account. The Abbé to whom he refers as having "shaken, if not destroyed, the theory of de Dominis, Descartes and Newton, for explaining the phenomenon of the rainbow," is generally supposed to have been one of these men. Jefferson adds his own reflections and observations on this phenomenon and concludes that "it appears to me that these facts demolish the Newtonian hypothesis, but they do not support that erected by the abbé. . . . The result is that we are wiser than we were, by having an error the less in our catalogue; but the blank occasioned by it must remain for some happier hypothesis to fill up."[62]

Discussions on the new scientific theories that were in the air filled many an evening. John Quincy Adams reports one on "animal magnetism," which was "very strenuously defended" in the home of the Abbés.[63] In the spring of 1787, when Jefferson made his tour of southern France, the pleasure of his stay at Nîmes was enhanced by meeting Arnauld there, when they discussed not only Roman antiquities but questions of agriculture as well. A letter to the Abbé, written not long after Jefferson's return to Paris, describes a certain type of grist mill used in America, which the Abbé apparently found novel, with diagrams for its construction. On another occasion the American theory of government and more particularly the participation of the people in the enforcement of the law was under discussion, if we may judge from a letter from Jefferson to Arnauld discussing this and enclosing "a catalogue of all the books I recollect on the subject of juries."[64] Even after Jefferson's return to America, the discussions were continued in letters, as when the Abbés sent him a seven-page discussion of the French constitution.

In bidding these friends farewell, Jefferson reveals how much he had in common with these good and learned men and how much he felt indebted to them. "Instead of the pleasure, my dear friends, of meeting you again in Paris, of recounting to you our revolution and enquiring of you the details of yours," he writes, "I have now to write you a letter of adieu. Receive my sincere thanks for the kindnesses beyond number which you rendered me while in Paris, and my regrets that I am now to be cut off from the pleasure of your society and conversation. I shall never cease to recollect the multiplied proofs of your friendship to me, and of your patriotism towards your own country, or rather I may say towards the whole world. I hope your love of mankind in general will now be fully gratified by seeing a rational liberty established in your own country, and extended to others. My new situation would have been less unacceptable but for the friendships from which it has withdrawn me. Among these yours was of the most valued." [65]

Jefferson's old friend Mazzei has given us the best picture we have of a day in Jefferson's full and busy life. It was in the summer of 1785. Mazzei had just returned from America and "went immediately to look for Jefferson. He was living in that charming little villa with a pretty garden at the end of the Champs Elysées, within gunshot of the stockade through which one must pass on the way to Versailles. I had informed him of my arrival . . . so that he was expecting me daily. Nevertheless our meeting was very touching to both of us. . . . I learned that in my haste to have my letters for friends in Paris reach him in Boston before he sailed, I had forgotten de Marmontel. We agreed to call on him the following morning." Mazzei duly called for his friend, and one of the memorable friendships of Jefferson's life began. "When we arrived," Mazzei continues, "Marmontel was just going out, but he insisted on turning back. That morning Jefferson had to go to various other places; nonetheless, our chat lasted about two hours. They had much to tell and more to ask each other. Jefferson remarked, among other things, that he did not understand why the ministers of foreign powers made a mystery out of entirely trivial matters, and Marmontel replied: 'That's true, they always padlock their lips, but if you take the padlock off, you'll see the trunk is empty.' As we were about to leave, the Abbé Morellet, the foremost logician of France, appeared. He was the maternal uncle of Marmontel's wife and lived in the same house. We had to stay another hour to talk to him, after which we went to Lavoisier's, to Condorcet's, to the Duke de la Rochefoucauld's and then home." [66] It had, indeed, been a day to fulfill the happiest of dreams.

Jefferson's experience in Paris would have been incomplete, indeed unthinkable, without an introduction to the *salons* for which the eighteenth century was famous. The *matinées* of the Abbé Morellet were essentially that. As a rule, however, these occasions were conducted by women, such as the Marquise de Condorcet, Madame Helvétius and various others, who had risen to a position of eminence through their wit, their charm, and their intellectual ability, or a combination of these various qualities. These gatherings, presumably of persons of similar tastes, took place on a given day each week. At the time of Jefferson's arrival the tone of the *salon* was undergoing a definite change. It was no longer primarily a *bureau d'esprit*. A passion for politics had superseded the passion for the fine arts that had ruled supreme for many years. The revolution was taking over in this field, as in every other.

One of the most influential women at this period was the Comtesse d'Houdetot, the celebrated Julie of Rousseau's *Confessions*. Gouverneur Morris describes her as "the ugliest woman I ever saw, even without her squint, which is the worst kind." [67] She was now an "old woman of 55" and had retired to her country seat at Sannois, some ten miles from Paris. Here she lived amicably with her husband and her lover, St. Lambert, the poet and philosopher, and held court. Her *salon* was rivaled in importance only by those of the well-known Madame Helvétius, the widow of the philosopher and the adored of Franklin, and of Madame Necker, wife of the financier and statesman, whom Jefferson admired. Here he met her brilliant daughter, Madame de Staël, with whom he exchanged letters on European affairs for years.

On the twenty-first of June, 1785, Jefferson wrote his good friend, Abigail Adams, "I took a trip yesterday to Sannois and commenced an acquaintance with the old Countess Houdetot. I received much pleasure from it and hope it has opened a door of admission for me to the circle of literati with which she is environed." [68] He was to be well rewarded. Years later he observed to a visitor at Monticello, "Madame Houdetot's society was one of the most agreeable in Paris when I was there. She inherited the materials of which it was composed from Madame de Terrier and Madame Geoffrin. St. Lambert was always there, and it was generally believed that every evening on his return home he wrote down the substance of the conversations he had held there with D'Alembert, Diderot, and the other distinguished persons who frequented her house. From these conversations he made his books." [69]

With this new interest in the affairs of the world supplanting those of the head and the heart, it pleased Madame d'Houdetot to welcome to her circle two leading exponents of it, the Americans Franklin and Jefferson. Franklin's first visit in April, 1781, when he was received with open arms and poetry and when he planted an *acacie de Virginie* in the garden at Sannois to commemorate the occasion, have been duly recorded.[70] No such fanfare greeted Jefferson. He humbly records, on his second visit, "lost at lotto at Sannois, 18[3]." [71]

Jefferson and the Countess entered into a correspondence that lasted for some years. It started with Jefferson sending her news of their mutual friend Franklin, after he had returned to America, then drifted inevitably to politics. Jefferson, apologizing for a neglect of several weeks, writes her the news of the signing of a treaty between Prussia and England and of the possibility of war being started by Sweden. She congratulates him on the adoption of the constitution by the United States, and "as a citizen of your country," (the freedom of the city of New Haven had been conferred upon her, and others, in May, 1785, which she interprets as citizenship) she writes, "I have a right to share in this happiness." Being no stranger to the art of flattery, she admires the "spirit, the wisdom, the reason, the humanity and the enlightenment" characteristic of the heads of the new states and assures Jefferson that if she were to return to this life there would be only two countries in which she would care to live, Switzerland and the United States.

As the time of his own departure for America approached, Jefferson suggested paying his respects a last time. In indicating a day, she takes occasion to express her unbounded admiration for "those two great men for whom even antiquity can offer no model, Washington and Franklin," and then adds a word as to the virtues of her correspondent. "If I were to see them," she writes, "I should talk of you, Monsieur, of the wise and humane spirit which animates you, of a character that is worthy of them, in short I should speak of this man so learned, so accomplished, so amiable, of whom I have seen all too little, and whose company is so precious to me. He is one of that very small number of persons whom one is happy to see and to know, and who makes one content with one's species and with society." [72]

This noble tribute could not have failed to please Jefferson. One of the half-dozen notes of farewell he wrote his French friends from New York, after his appointment as secretary of state, was addressed to the Comtesse d'Houdetot, with whom he felt a particular kinship. It stressed not only his appreciation of her favors to him, socially, but touched upon their great common interest, politics. "Accept, I pray, grateful acknowledgements for the manifold kindnesses by which you added so much to the happiness of my stay in Paris. I have found here a philosophic revolution, philosophically effected. Yours, though a little more turbulent has, I hope by this time issued in success and peace. Nobody prays for it more sincerely than I do, and nobody will do more to cherish a union with a nation dear to us through many ties, and now more approximated by the change of its government." [73]

A *salon* of no less importance than that of Madame d'Houdetot, in fact even more fashionable at this time, was the one of Madame Necker, whose husband, after a brilliant career and subsequent banishment from Paris, was recalled as minister of finance while Jefferson was there. Every writer of memoirs of the period describes Madame Necker, and scarcely anyone has a good word for her. She was intelligent and had had a superb education, but she had no nobility of spirit. As the Baroness Oberkirch observed, "She lacks the art of ingratiating herself. She can neither laugh nor cry." [74] Prudish to a degree, at a time when laxity of speech and of conduct were anything but extraordinary, her detractors are reported to have heard her remark that she found the manner of procreating the species objectionable, and that she had vowed to find another method. Young lovers were reputedly in a frenzy for fear her prayers would be heard and the hallowed laws of nature overthrown. Jefferson says of her that she was "a very sincere and excellent woman, but she was not very pleasant in conversation, for she was subject to what in Virginia we call the 'budge,' that is, she was very nervous and fidgety. She could rarely remain long in the same place, or converse long on the same subject. I have known her to get up from table five or six times in the course of the dinner, and walk up and down her saloon to compose herself." [75]

Nevertheless, although all who were there had something to say against her, the chief leaders of the literary, political, and financial worlds thronged her *salon.* Her Fridays—she had been obliged to select this day of fasting as all other days of the week had been pre-empted by the other *salonières*—became as celebrated and as much frequented as the Mondays of Madame Geoffrin and the Wednesdays of Madame Helvétius. The leading Encyclopedists were her friends and were always to be seen there. The company, according to the long account of these evenings by Duchesse d'Abrantès, sat about a large round table covered with green velvet bordered with gold fringe. Upon this stood a silver candelabrum of twelve branches, surmounted by a shade. Gathered around the table were, among others, M. de la Harpe, the well-known critic, the Marquis de Chastellux, M. de St. Lambert, Baron de Grimm, the great naturalist the Comte de Buffon, Marmontel, the Abbé Morellet, and, we may assume, Jefferson. Madame Necker, Madame de Staël, the beautiful Princess of Monaco, the Comtesse de Tessé, and other ladies completed the circle. Chit-chat, bantering, the reading of poems, occupied the first part of the evening. With the announcement of supper, the somewhat constrained and solemn atmosphere that had heretofore prevailed was relaxed. Madame Necker chatted with each person at table until she had made the rounds, conversation then became general, politics and literature were discussed at length. It is to be regretted that the Duchess, in reporting remarks of various members of the company, fails to include any made by Mr. Jefferson.[76]

Jefferson's particular friends in this group, aside from those already discussed, were those two diversely extraordinary characters, the Baron de Grimm and the Comtesse de Tessé. At the time of Jefferson's residence in Paris, Grimm had been the minister to France from the duchy of Saxe-Gotha for some ten years. He had first come to Paris in 1748 when a young man of twenty-five, and became closely allied with the Encyclopedists. Diderot, D'Alembert, Helvétius and Holbach were his friends. Following in the footsteps of the Abbé Raynal he began, in 1754, his famous *Correspondence littéraire*, letters addressed to a few chosen correspondents, the Empress Catherine of Russia, Frederick the Great, the Duke of Saxe-Gotha, the Grand Duke of Tuscany, and certain others. In the beginning he was satisfied to give his views on art and literature, but gradually he included nearly every phase of French cultural life, politics, religion, and society as well as literature and art. It has been well said of him that he was the father of modern literary criticism.

Although Jefferson speaks of Grimm as "the oracle of taste at Paris in sculpture, painting and the other fine arts,"[77] his importance as an exponent and interpreter of French life and literature was not realized until years after his death when his *Memoirs* were published. Shortly after that, in response to an enthusiastic letter from John Adams in praise of them, Jefferson wrote: "Did I know Baron Grimm while at Paris? Yes, most intimately. He was the pleasantest and most conversable member of the diplomatic corps while I was there; a man of good fancy, acuteness, irony, cunning and egoism. No heart, not much of any science, yet enough of every one to speak its language; his forte was belles-lettres, painting and sculpture. In these he was the oracle of society, and as such, was the Empress Catharine's private correspondent and factor, in all things not diplomatic. . . . Although I never heard Grimm express the opinion directly, yet I always supposed him to be of the school of d'Alembert, d'Holbach."[78]

This and the observation that Grimm "came often to my house in Paris while Colonel Trumbull was with me to see his paintings" and "gave him the decided preference" over other contemporary artists is all the reticent Jefferson has to say of their association. It is to be regretted that the Baron has maintained complete silence in regard to his American colleague.

The Comtesse de Tessé may well be called Jefferson's spiritual affinity. She shared his humanity and his passion for freedom, as well as his love of the arts, particularly architecture and gardening. She was a member of the great Noailles family, an aunt of the Marquise de Lafayette, not so much older but that her famous nephew-in-law called her his cousin. At court she occupied the position of *dame d'honneur de la reine*. Madame de Tessé lived with her husband, a Spanish grandee, and a friend, Madame de Tott, who was likewise an artist of some distinction, at Chaville. This property, once appended to the Grand Dauphin's seat of Meudon, stood at the left of the high road from Paris to Versailles. The château itself was a handsome box approached by a broad *allée* from the forecourt, flanked itself by the stables, orangery, and chapel. The grounds were extensive. In certain sectors about the house, a formal arrangement still persisted in parterres, bosquets, and orchard, but the new informality from England had invaded other areas. Thus, below the fountains of the terrace, irregular clumps of trees bordered the vista to the north; on the east was an extensive *jardin anglais* with an extravagantly winding "river" and meandering paths through woodland and meadow. This garden was adorned by various romantic structures, the adjuncts of every true English garden of the period, such as a kiosk, a battlemented tower rising beside a stone bridge, and a group of granite columns against a background of somber trees. Many of the exotics that Jefferson had sent over from Virginia and the Carolinas were destined to enhance this garden. Here we can think of Jefferson and his hostess—he dined with the Tessés at least once a week—as strolling while they inspected plantations and he expounded his philosophy that "botany is the school of patience and its amateurs learn resignation from their daily disappointments." [79]

Gouverneur Morris, whose supposedly aristocratical tendencies are well known, dined with Madame de Tessé very shortly after his arrival in Paris. He speaks of her as "a very sensible woman" who "has formed her ideas of government in a manner not suited (I think) either to the situation, the circumstances or the dispositions of France." [80] He describes her friends at this dinner party as "republicans of the first feather," and relates on another occasion how these politically minded ladies "became at length animated to the utmost bounds of politeness." [81] The friendship between the Countess and Jefferson, however, was based not so much on the community of their political views as on the identity of their artistic tastes. This is displayed in a series of twenty-one letters extending over a period of thirty years, from the first little notes of their early acquaintance, hoping that Mr. Jefferson's affairs may take him to Versailles and thus to Chaville, or presenting him with "an altar for the woods at Monticello," to Jefferson's last farewell to his "very dear and ancient friend" in the spring of 1817, which arrived, alas, too late for her to read. These reflect, to a great degree, "the happy hours and animated conversations at Chaville," as Lafayette wrote Jefferson in announcing her end. "You know what a woman has been lost to society, what a friend to me," he says. "How far from us those times, and those of the venerable Hôtel de la Rochefoucauld. And we who still number among the living," he adds in wistful retrospect, "do we not chiefly belong to what is no more?" [82]

VI. The Elysian Fields

THE HÔTEL DE LANDRON, on the cul-de-sac Taitbout, in which Jefferson had established himself in October, 1784, proved inadequate for his needs. As with every house in which he lived, he could not resist the temptation of making alterations. A plan for certain minor ones exists,[1] and his account book indicates that he paid a joiner for "beaufets and book shelves," as well as "necessary changes in the house," along with a *serrurier* "for iron work done." During the year he lived there, he was chiefly concerned, however, with starting the formation of his collection of paintings and sculpture and with buying the fabrics, the damask, and *toile de Jouy,* for window and bed hangings that, after use in his various establishments in Paris and Philadelphia, were ultimately to adorn Monticello. Within less than a month of his moving into the house David Humphreys was writing home that Jefferson had "furnished a very elegant Hôtel, where letters will find me."[2]

Convenient as the house was, and near many of his friends, the nature-loving Jefferson could never long be happy in the heart of a great city. He also came to realize that his establishment was far too modest in relation to those of the ministers from other countries. When, in March, 1785, he was appointed minister to France and could look forward to a longer stay in that country than was implied by his original commission of two years, he determined to look around for a house on the outskirts of the city. He was shortly rewarded. On September 4, 1785, he wrote Mr. Adams, "I have at length procured a house in a situation much more pleasant to me than my present. . . . It suits me in every circumstance but the price, being dearer than the one I am now in. It has a clever garden to it."[3] This was the beautiful Hôtel de Langeac at the corner of the Champs-Elysées and the rue de Berri.

Jefferson signed the lease on the eighth of September, and on the third of October he paid the Comte de Langeac "the last six months rent, 3750 livres." He moved in on the seventeenth of the month, just one year after he had taken over the Hôtel de Landron.

The new house was at the Grille de Chaillot, the massive iron gate that crossed the Champs-Elysées at this point, and where customs duties were collected by the city from the farmers, wine merchants, and other purveyors who brought their goods to town. Although within the city limits, Jefferson had the advantage of being only a few miles from Passy, Auteuil, and Neuilly, at that time rural villages clustered about the great heart of France.

Aside from having the country at his doorstep, Jefferson was fortunate not only in having a garden of his own but in being surrounded by those of his neighbors. Opposite him on the Champs-Elysées was, as a contemporary guide book says, "an interesting garden designed by an Englishman, Mr. Jansen, in the style of those of his country." [4] Nearby was a similar one belonging to M. Tronchin, the minister from Geneva. The length of the street one could observe "numerous handsome houses with a charming view." [5] The Champs-Elysées, or Grand Cours as it was often called at the time, which Jefferson's house and garden overlooked, was much as we know it today, except for the part that has long since been taken over by commerce, which is, alas, the section where he lived. The regular plantation of trees, with which we are familiar, had been made in 1765, and they were already full sized in Jefferson's time. Lemonade vendors and purveyors of other refreshments had already constructed their kiosks. The broad space between the avenues of trees was given over to games. On Sundays and holidays the fashionable world promenaded along the avenue, careful, as our guide book says, to remain "in the section which adjoins the gardens of the superb *hôtels* of the Faubourg St. Honoré." [6]

The Hôtel de Langeac had been designed by the noted architect, Chalgrin. He had also designed the recently finished Church of Saint-Phillipe-du-Roule on the rue du Faubourg Saint-Honoré, as well as the northern tower of the church of Saint-Sulpice. His greatest work was to be the Arc de Triomphe de l'Etoile. The house Jefferson leased was intended as a residence for the Marquise de Langeac, mistress of the Comte de Saint-Florentin, and had been begun in 1768. On the accession of Louis XVI, six years later, she was exiled from Paris and building was temporarily suspended. In 1778 her son, the Comte de Langeac, from whom Jefferson rented the place, acquired possession of it, and the work once more went forward. It had not long been finished, and the financially embarrassed Count had already been obliged to sell a portion of the property when the new American Minister started looking for a suitable dwelling.

The house was characterized by the refinement and elegance we associate with the *style Louis Seize*. It was of three stories, noble in proportion, with a circular bay toward the garden, the *entresol* of which was adorned with classic bas-reliefs. The visitor entered the establishment through a large court on the rue de Berri, screened from the street by a grille. To the left were the stables and coach house, to the right the *hôtel*. The ground floor, or *rez-de-chaussée* as the French call it, consisted of an entrance hall opening into a *salle ronde* with a dome. Leading off from this was the large oval *salon*, or drawing room, its ceiling embellished with a painting of the rising sun by Berthelmy, a well-known painter of historical and mythological subjects. Steps led from the *salon* to the garden. On the side of the house toward the Champs-Elysées, likewise accessible from the *salon ronde*, were the *petit salon* and another room used as a dining room.

Jefferson's living quarters were on the top floor above an *entresol* or mezzanine, of which no complete plan exists but which doubtless contained minor suites. Jefferson made drawings for remodeling a section of the *entresol*,[7] but whether it was executed, we do not know, as the only plans of the house extant are dated 1817.[8] The interior might well have been remodeled several times, as is frequent in French houses, between Jefferson's occupancy and the later date. A monumental stairway led to the second floor where there was a *grand antichambre*, which opened into the oval *salon* overlooking the garden. This floor contained three suites, each complete, in the French manner, with a bedroom, study, and dressing room. The presence of *lieux à l'anglaise* indicates that the house was very up to date with modern plumbing.

The English influence seems likewise to have been felt in the garden. The existing plans show that a formal parterre, in the old manner, was retained along one side; elsewhere the garden was developed along the newer lines, which were the height of fashion in the seventeen-eighties, with winding walks and a spiral maze. Among the Jefferson papers[9] are three designs for this garden. Whether the one shown in the plans of 1817 was executed according to his ideas or whether it pre-existed, it is impossible to know.

No description of the interior of Jefferson's *hôtel* has been preserved in any of the countless letters and memoirs of the period. We can, however, gain a very good idea of the furnishings and works of art that adorned it, and of the manner in which he lived, by a glance at the contents of the eighty-six packing cases he had shipped to the United States on leaving France.[10] As is usual in any household, chairs formed the largest number of items, fifty-nine in all. They were mostly of the familiar Louis Seize type with gilt, or gray and gold, frames. As late as 1815 an inventory of the furnishings of Monticello lists "6 sophas with gold leaf" and "44 chairs gold leaf." They were the traditional French types *fauteuil*, *bergère*, and *chaise*, the two former being different varieties of the armchair. The seats and backs were covered with blue or crimson damask, as the case might be; with *velours d'Utrecht*, a velvet with a small raised pattern; and others with red morocco.

There was one group of chairs in mahogany that represented the very latest word in fashion. At the time of Jefferson's residence in Paris, chairs of this wood, designed along classical lines by the famous cabinetmaker Jacob, had begun to make their appearance. It was a revolutionary step in a world that had been seated for generations on gold chairs, but it was destined to triumph in the Directoire and Empire styles that followed the Louis Seize. Jefferson, who was a great admirer and proponent of the classical tendency, had Jacob make some for him. The two now preserved at Monticello, signed by Jacob, are thus the earliest-known examples of this classical type and prove Jefferson once more to have been of the advance guard in still another field.

Aside from the chairs, there were sofas of varying types, mahogany tables with marble tops, others bound in brass, reading tables, mahogany buffets, consoles, and commodes, largely, if we may judge from surviving examples, of the late Louis Seize style, verging on the Directoire, such as were made in great numbers by Jacob. There were likewise mirrors, paintings, statuary, a "large vase ornamented with three female heads, surrounded with *perles* and a bouquet of flowers," and quantities of silver and china—in short, that infinite variety of practical and ornamental objects that go to make up a great establishment. Some of these, such as a black marble clock in his study, still running for one of his descendants, and a silver tea urn, now standing in the dining room at Monticello, were after his own design.

We know, too, that on Jefferson's dining table was that most French of ornaments, a *surtout de table*, or *plâteau de dessert* as it is also called. This consisted of an oval mirror of several sections, surrounded by a gilt or silver balustrade, or gallery as the term is today, an inch or so high. Candelabra, mythological figures of biscuit or gilt bronze, and small decorative baskets to hold flowers and fruit were used in conjunction with it. On her arrival in London Mrs. Adams apparently wanted to add a note of elegance to the ministerial table and commissioned Jefferson to get a *surtout* for her. On September 25 he informed her that he had secured one with a silvered balustrade and four biscuit figures. "With respect to the figures," he writes with the utmost gallantry, "I could only find three of those you named matched in size. These were Minerva, Diana, and Apollo. I was obliged to add a fourth, unguided by your choice. They offered me a fine Venus, but I thought it out of taste to have two at table at the same time. Paris and Helen were represented. I conceived it would be cruel to remove them from their peculiar shrine. When they shall pass the Atlantic, it will be to sing a requiem over our freedom and happiness. At length a fine Mars was offered, calm, bold, his falchion not drawn but ready to be drawn. This will do, thinks I, for the table of the American Minister in London, where those whom it may concern may look and learn that though Wisdom is our guide, and the Song and Chase our supreme delight, yet we offer adoration to that tutelar God also who rocked the cradle of our birth, who has accepted our infant offerings and has shown himself the patron of our rights and the avenger of our wrongs." [11]

Jefferson has left no such description of his own *plâteau*. Whether it was on the order of Mrs. Adams' we can only conjecture. We know that he paid 264 livres for hers and 422 for his own, from the same maker, Bazin, and it is not unreasonable to suppose that his was either more elaborate or the figures more costly.

Other pieces of furniture that Jefferson had made according to his designs were various small tables and dumbwaiters, looking like what is today called a muffin stand. Trumbull tells us that the latter were new and fashionable adjuncts to a dinner table while he was in Paris. One was placed between each two guests and the servants were dismissed for the remainder of that course. It was a custom to which Jefferson, ever a friend of undisturbed conversation, became addicted at this time and one that he was later to introduce at the White House. Following his instructions to dispose of "portables of common wood," these tables were not shipped to America when Jefferson left France. Thus only his drawing of them survives.[12]

It is significant how closely Jefferson conformed to the prevailing French fashion in furnishing his house and how few provincial ideas he sought to impose. Item by item the invoice of his things corresponds with contemporary descriptions of the necessary and proper furniture for a household of fashion. Thus we learn that his drawing room, aside from the chairs and sofas, was furnished with "three gaming tables with marble tops, four tables, marble tops, with gilt borders, four mirrors with gilt frames and borders," along with chandeliers, girandoles, vases of white porcelain, and groups of porcelain figures. Five busts in marble and plaster completed the ensemble.

For the draperies and upholstery of his Paris house Jefferson spent well over five thousand francs, a considerable sum for that time. From the inventory, as well as from notations in his account books, it would appear that crimson and blue damask predominated. We can assume that his bedroom was hung with blue damask, for he notes that he paid twenty-four francs, three centimes for three pairs of blue damask window curtains, and nine francs for blue damask bed curtains.[13] The inventory likewise shows a chaise longue in blue damask. In choosing these colors for his hangings Jefferson seems to have made a compromise between the old and the new in fashion. The aristocrats, we are told by a writer of the period, remained faithful to the classical crimson damask draperies, divided vertically and horizontally by bands of gold. Occasionally they employed a golden yellow damask. But when bankers and the bourgoisie redecorated in the latest style, "the hanging and curtains of crimson or yellow damask have been taken down, and sky blue now adorns the walls." [14] Certain of Jefferson's rooms were hung with *toile de Jouy,* the copperplate print with classical masks and temples, or French pastoral scenes, that was the height of fashion at this moment. He bought quantities of it in red and white, and some was still hanging at Monticello at the time of his death.

We have seen how among Jefferson's earliest ambitions was his eagerness to embellish Monticello with suitable paintings and pieces of sculpture.[15] Now, in Paris, he had for the first time not only the opportunity to extend his knowledge of the fine arts but to gratify his desire of owning some examples. He still cherished the idea of acquiring copies of famous paintings of the great masters, an idea that today would be regarded with contempt but that was entirely in harmony with the taste of his time. The walls of the finest houses and many palaces were hung from floor to ceiling with copies of famous works rather than with originals. This was the case with his friends the Cosways. The paintings in their London house would have rivaled the treasures of the Louvre and several other museums, had those which decorated the "saloon," the "eating room," and eight other apartments—attributed to such artists as Poussin, Van Dyck, Giorgone, and Rubens—been the actual work of the masters whose names they bore.[16]

Just how fully Jefferson succeeded in realizing this ideal, we can gather from a list of his paintings sold at the time of his death. We learn that, among others, he bought copies of Raphael's "Holy Family," which still hangs in the parlor at Monticello, Leonardo's "St. John," Van Dyck's "Descent from the Cross" and "Crucifixion," as well as Rubens' "Diogenes and His Lantern."

On October 16–19, 1784, there occurred the sale of the pictures of Monsieur de Billy, recently deceased, who had been the *premier valet de garderobe du roi.* Jefferson had moved into the Hôtel de Landron at this very moment, and he attended the sale, which contained some sixty-six pictures, and twenty-three pieces of sculpture, beside other objects of art.[17] On the nineteenth Jefferson notes paying for "2 small laughing busts 21 livres, 2 pictures of heads, 7 livres 4, d° half lengths, viz. an ecce homo and another 18 livres." On the twenty-sixth he bought "a Hercules in plaister" and on the twenty-ninth "five paintings (heads)."

One of the paintings he purchased was item number 21 in the sale, described as a "*Vièrge représentée à mi-corps, les yeux levés vers le ciel*," by Carlo Maratti. The identity of the other purchases has not been established. In February of the following year, Jefferson was one of those who crowded the great *vente* of Monsieur Dupille de Saint-Séverin. Four items, according to the catalogue, went to *l'envoié d'Amérique*—numbers 36, 59, 248, and 306. They were "St. Peter Weeping for his Offence," by Guido Reni, a "Magdalen Penitent," by Ribera, "Herodiade Bearing the Head of St. John on a Platter," attributed to Vouët and still preserved at Monticello, and "The Prodigal Son," "*maître inconnu*."[18]

From the provincial who wistfully wrote of "countries whose improvements in science, in arts and in civilization it has been my fortune to admire at a distance, but never to see," Jefferson was not long in becoming one of the "society of literati of the first order," as we have seen. Inevitably his association with these personages, his visits to the various collections, both royal and private, as well as his intimacy with certain artists, stimulated Jefferson's interest in art and influenced his critical judgment.

It was at this period that a definite plan for forming a collection of works by living masters, as opposed to buying pictures and sculpture as so much household furniture, seems to have been formed in Jefferson's mind. This was to assemble portraits and busts of his distinguished contemporaries and friends. The first step in this direction had been taken in May, 1784, as we have seen, when Jefferson, who was on his way to Boston to embark for Europe, commissioned Joseph Wright the well-known artist, to paint a portrait of General Washington for him.[19] "I could only allow Wright time to finish the head and face and sketch the outlines of the body," he writes. "These and the drapery were afterwards finished at Paris by Trumbull." [20] Another portrait of Washington, the one painted by Charles Willson Peale at the instance of the state of Virginia and intended for Houdon's use in modeling his statue of Washington, likewise hung in Jefferson's *hôtel.*

A further impetus to the idea came through Jefferson's association with Houdon. Jefferson became such an admirer of the man whose chisel, he observed, seemed "destined to consecrate to immortality illustrious men in every walk of life," that he gradually acquired seven of Houdon's portrait busts—the famous head of Voltaire, the Turgot, and Lafayette, Franklin, Washington, and John Paul Jones. The latter was a gift from Jones. Jefferson likewise acquired his own bust in plaster, as has been observed, and, on his return to the United States, carried with him three copies of it.

To supplement his sculpture Jefferson set out to acquire portraits of the men with whom he had worked in forming the United States. Next after Washington, Adams and Jefferson himself were added to the collection. When in London, in the spring of 1786, Jefferson, who had been introduced into the circle of the American artists, West, Copley, and Trumbull, had sat for his portrait for the first time, so far as is known. It was executed by a young American, Mather Brown. Jefferson paid ten pounds for it. It shows him as an alert and obviously thoughtful man, rather young for his years, with a ruddy complexion. His hair is powdered and brushed off the face, with rolls over the ears. He is wearing a dark coat, a waistcoat, and revers of a striped, reddish brown fabric, and lace, or mull and lace, stock and ruffles at the wrists. A classical female figure with a staff crowned by a Phrygian cap, presumably a statue of liberty, fills the background at the right.

The picture was not delivered to Jefferson for more than two years, although an item in the *New York Packet* for October 19, 1786, states that it may be seen in Brown's room in London "among pictures of near one hundred Americans." [21] Meanwhile, on October 22, Jefferson had written to Colonel William Stephens Smith, "Will you undertake to prevail on Mr. Adams to set for his picture, and on Mr. Brown to draw it for me? I wish to add it to those of other principal American characters which I have or shall have, and I rather it would be an original than a copy," [22] a remark that indicates Jefferson's advance in artistic matters. The following year he ordered still a third portrait by Brown, whose work he must have liked. On October 4 he asked Trumbull to "execute another commission for me. It is to ask Mr. Brown to draw a picture for me of Mr. Paine, author of Common Sense, now in London. I asked his permission, and it will be necessary to do it immediately lest he should quit London, something he expects. I would wish it to be the size of the one he drew of myself." [23]

Brown was as slow about the Adams and Paine portraits as about Jefferson's. Indeed, he appears to have been somewhat reluctant about the former, for on February 2, 1788, Jefferson once more wrote Smith, "With respect to Mr. Adams's picture, I must again press it to be done by Brown, because Trumbull does not paint of the size of life, and could not be asked to hazard himself on it." [24] Brown was ultimately won over, and a receipt in Trumbull's hand, dated July 2, 1788, indicates that Jefferson paid ten pounds for the Adams portrait on that date.

The following March Trumbull, who was acting as Jefferson's agent in artistic matters in London, wrote that the pictures would be forwarded soon. "Mr. Adams is like," he observes. "Yours I do not think so well of." Obviously upset and surprised, Jefferson replied, "You say mine does not resemble. Is it a copy? Because he agreed that the original should be mine, and it was that I paid him for." To which Trumbull answered, "I believe what he means to send you of yourself to be the copy, and that of Mr. Adams thus the original." [25] Whether or not Jefferson finally received the original is not certain. Artists had a way of making substitutions in those days, as since, and the Brown portrait that Jefferson owned has long since disappeared. The one believed to be a replica is, however, still in the possession of the Adams family.

Jefferson, who always had a liking for gifted young men, had taken a particular fancy to Trumbull and invited him to stay at the Hôtel de Langeac while he was making a study of the art treasures of Paris. This Trumbull did the summer after their meeting. In August of that year Jefferson wrote Ezra Stiles, the president of Yale College, "another countryman of yours, Mr. Trumbull has paid us a visit here and brought with him two pictures which are the admiration of the connoisseurs. His natural talents for this art seem almost unparalleled." [26]

Already in 1785, Trumbull tells us, he had begun to meditate seriously "the subjects of national history, of events of the Revolution, which have since been the great objects of my professional life." [27] He had painted his "Battle of Bunker's Hill" and "Battle of Quebec," before going to Paris. Jefferson "highly approved of my intention of preparing myself for the accomplishment of a national work," [28] Trumbull observes, and "under the kind protection of Jefferson's hospitable roof at Chaillot" the two men planned the composition of the picture of the Declaration.[29] On Trumbull's return to London in November, 1786, he "arranged carefully the composition for the 'Declaration of Independence' and prepared it for receiving the portraits, as I might meet the distinguished men who were present at that illustrious scene." [30] In the fall of 1787 he again visited Paris, "where I painted the portrait of Mr. Jefferson in the original small 'Declaration of Independence'...and the French officers in the 'Surrender of Lord Cornwallis'....I regard these as the best of my small portraits." [31]

Although, of course, this painting did not hang in the Hôtel de Langeac, the figure of Jefferson in it is of particular interest as having been painted from life during his residence there.[32] It seems the most sensitive of all the Jefferson portraits. In the eyes and in the aspect of the face, the artist has caught the visionary that was Jefferson at this period of his life. He wears a dark coat, a red waistcoat with gold buttons, and a white stock. The powder, characteristic of the time, had been brushed from his hair, revealing its natural, reddish hue. The cheeks are highly colored, as family tradition tells us they were. Jefferson towers straight and strong above the other signers. It is one of only two portraits, the second being by Sully when the subject was an old man, showing Jefferson in full length.

At the time he painted Jefferson into the "Declaration," Trumbull appears to have executed an oil miniature, a modified replica of the "Declaration" head, to leave with his host as a memento. This came down in Jefferson's family through the Trist line and still belongs to the estate of one of Jefferson's descendants.[33]

A portrait of Franklin was, of course, a necessity in any gallery of

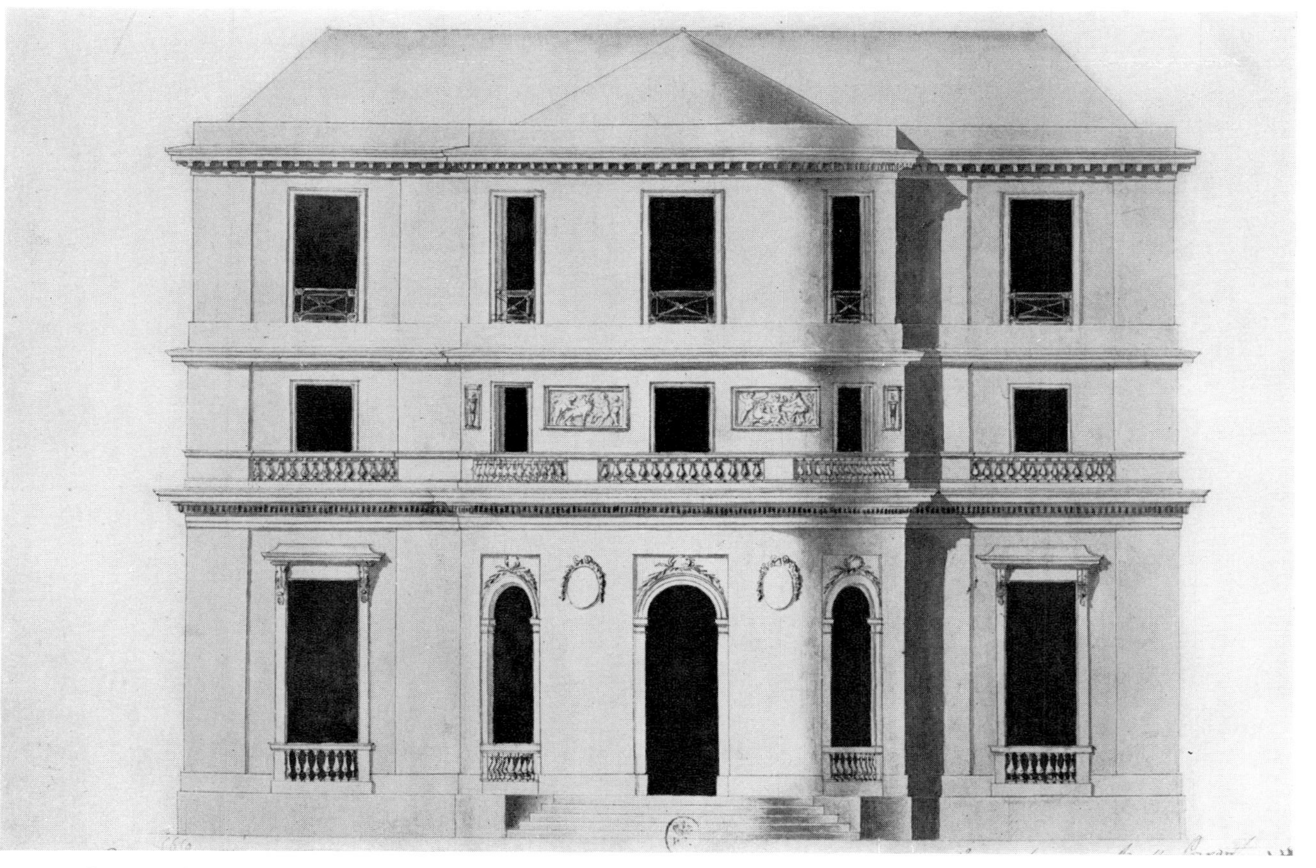

THE HÔTEL DE LANGEAC. (*Courtesy of the Bibliothèque Nationale*)

PONT DE NEUILLY WITH MONT VALÉRIEN. (*Courtesy of the Musée Condé, Chantilly*)

American worthies. Jefferson's catalogue bears the notation, "Dr. Franklin, an original, drawn for the Abbé Very, by Greuze." It is a thoughtful and dignified likeness, which now hangs in the Boston Museum of Fine Arts, a gift from one of Jefferson's descendants.

In April, 1790, after his return to America, Jefferson wrote William Short, who was in charge of his affairs, "My pictures of American [characters?] will be absolutely incomplete without one of Lafayette." To Short was given the task of selecting a painter and of inducing the Marquis to sit. In August Short reported a complete lack of success. Lafayette "always says he will do it but never keeps his word, and indeed he has not time—not even one moment to spare. Still, if it is possible, it shall be done." [34] The impossible was accomplished within a month. The elusive Marquis sat for Joseph Boze, a popular *peintre du roi* and well-known miniaturist, who promptly presented his bill for 486 livres.[35]

Aside from his contemporaries, Jefferson wanted likenesses of the great figures of the distant American past. "I considered it even of some public concern," he wrote, "that our country should not be without the portraits of its first discoverers." [36] On September 17, 1787, he wrote a long letter to Mazzei, who was then in Italy, asking his help in securing these pictures. The letter begins with a description, in Italian, of those he wanted. "By these passages," he continues, "it would seem that the pictures of Americus Vespucius, of Columbus, of Magellan and Cortez exist in Florence. I should wish extremely to obtain copies of the two first, and even of the last two, also, if not too expensive. Painters of high reputation are either above copying or ask extravagant prices. But there are always men of good talents who, being kept in obscurity by untoward circumstances, work cheap and work well. Copies by such hands as these might probably be obtained at prices as I would be willing to pay. But how to find out those good hands, covered by the veil of obscurity? Can Mr. Mazzei put me on a method of knowing whether these portraits still exist? Whether permission can be obtained to copy them? If a painter such as above described can be found? What he would ask for half length copies, of the size of life?" [37]

Mazzei lost no time in making arrangements and in having the pictures copied from originals in the collections of the Medici in Florence. They arrived in Paris in February, 1789, in time to hang in the Hôtel de Langeac during the last months of Jefferson's residence there. On February 16 he notes paying 145 livres, 10 sous for them. He describes the portrait of Columbus as being "the size of life . . . It has the aspect of a man of thirty-five, still smooth-faced and in the vigor of life, which would place its date about 1477." [38]

Meanwhile Jefferson had written Trumbull, who was again in London, to secure for him copies of portraits of what he called his "trinity," the philosophers Bacon, Locke, and Newton. On March 15, 1789, Trumbull replied, "I have made enquiries about the pictures of which you enquire. . . . A young man I know and who will do the copies as well as most copyists, undertakes to do them for three guineas each. . . . I do not think tolerable copies can be secured for less. The busts in plaster of Newton, Locke, Bacon and Shakespeare may be had for 23 s. to 30 each, the size of life." [39] Ten days later Jefferson instructed Trumbull to have the portraits copied, and they were shortly added to the collection at the Hôtel de Langeac.

Like all important collectors, Jefferson started to make a catalogue of his paintings, but it was never finished. It lists fifty-eight canvases. The date at which it was made cannot be determined as the paper on which it is written has no watermark. The sheets appear to have been torn from a book. It was obviously after 1790 as a portrait of Madison by Pine of that date is mentioned. On the other hand, certain pictures that were hanging in Monticello at the time of Jefferson's death are not listed, indicating that it was not complete. Many, if not most of the subjects, were of a religious character, but they are varied by a few "landscapes of canvas," a "Danae Visited by Jupiter," and an "Aeneas Bearing off Anchises on His Shoulders," and certain others of a similar nature. In the best tradition of catalogues, each picture is carefully analyzed and opposite the description is given the appropriate Biblical or classical quotation.[40]

As Jefferson's third year in Paris drew to a close, such was the pressure of business and society that he determined to find a place where he could work undisturbed. In his many walks to the Pont de Neuilly or his drives in the Bois de Boulogne, Mont Valérien, the highest of the hills surrounding Paris, loomed on the west bank of the Seine, towering above the little village of Suresnes and beckoning him like another Monticello.

In 1620 a community of hermits had settled on top of this mountain. They were not priests and took no vows, but were lay brothers. Mont Valérien, or Mont Calvaire as it was also called in the eighteenth century, with its three great crosses surmounting the summit, became a popular place of pilgrimage, partly for religious purposes, partly for those who wished for some reason or another to escape the world. There were numerous permanent as well as temporary guests. To accommodate the increasing number of people anxious to *"s'occuper serieusement du salut de leur âme,"* [41] large buildings were erected. They were arranged in groups near the original primitive cells, close to the *maison des prêtres* at the summit of the mountain. They were two stories high, divided into cells furnished with only a bed, a table, and a chair. To make up for this Spartanism, we are told that the meals were of unusual excellence! The rooms on the ground floors of these buildings were devoted to manufacturing the silk hosiery for which the brothers were famous. It was here that Jefferson was in the habit of buying these articles for Mr. and Mrs. Adams, as well as for himself.

For how long a time Jefferson had contemplated retreating to Mont Valérien, we do not know. During July and August of 1787 he notes paying small sums there or ferriage at Suresnes, when he presumably went out just for the day. On September 5 we find the following entry in his account book: "Took possession of apartments at Mont Calvaire, paid dinner, 6 fr." And on October 12, "Pd. at Mont Calvaire 60 f. viz. @ 2 f 10 for myself, and 1 f. for my horse." A similar payment, but in full, as he expected soon to return home, was made in October, 1788. The first payment is substantiated by an entry in the account book of the *Ermites du Mont Valérien* preserved in the *Archives de la Seine*, on the page for October, 1787: *"Avoir reçu de Mr. Jeffersonne Ambassadeur de l'Amérique pour dix jours qu'il a passe a l'hermitage depuis le* 7.7^{bre}*, avec son cheval,* 60/—." [42]

On moving into the Hôtel de Langeac, Jefferson, fully aware that at the court of Versailles respect could not be commanded without a certain amount of display, completely changed his style of living to be more in line with that of the ministers from other countries. The Baron de Staël, ambassador from Sweden, who was shortly to marry the brilliant, unattractive, and enormously rich daughter of Necker, set the style for the other ministers according to Abigail Adams. "He lives in a grand hotel," she writes, "and his suite of apartments, his furniture and his table are the most elegant of anything I have seen. Although you dine upon plate in every noble house in France, I cannot say you may see your face in it; but here the whole furniture of the table was burnished, and shone with regal splendor. Seventy thousand livres in plate will make no small figure; and that is what His Majesty gave him. The dessert was served in the richest china, with knives, forks, and spoons of gold. As you enter his apartments, you pass through files of servants, into his antichamber, in which is a throne covered with green velvet, upon which is a chair of state, over which hangs the picture of his royal master. These thrones are common to all ambassadors of the first order, as they are the immediate representatives of the king. Through this anti-chamber you pass into the grand saloon, which is elegantly adorned with architecture; a beautiful lustre hanging from the middle. Settees, chairs, and hangings of the richest silk, embroidered with gold; marble slabs upon fluted pillars, round which wreaths of artificial flowers in gold intwine. . . . The dining room is equally beautiful being hung with Gobelin tapestry, the colors and figures of which resemble the most elegant painting." [43]

Jefferson had, indeed, much to live up to, but he was wise enough not to attempt ostentation, for which he was temperamentally unfitted and for which his country was ill prepared. Symbolic were the two sturdy portraits of Washington in their simple frames, which adorned his *hôtel* and which so truly represented the man who was the father of his country and not its master. They were a long way from the elaborate and heavily gilded eighteenth-century confections that portrayed the sovereigns of other countries in the various embassies. Although aware that other governments "provide a service of plate and a fixed sum for all other articles, which sum is in no case lower than a year's salary," Jefferson writes that he desires "no service of plate, having no ambition for splendor. My furniture, carriage and apparel are all plain, yet they have cost me more than a year's salary." [44]

Realizing that, aside from his house, a proper equipage was of first importance, Jefferson set about acquiring one. The Virginia phaeton, which had aroused so much interest on his arrival, was shortly abandoned except for certain private occasions. Until he was able to secure one, Jefferson hired a chariot, a vehicle suitable for a gentleman and an ambassador, from one Goujon, for which he paid 384 francs a month. In March, 1785, he bought a chariot of his own, which he had painted and upholstered in green morocco. The following November he purchased a cabriolet for 1,000 francs, and in 1788 he ordered another and more elegant chariot in London through Trumbull. He continued to pay Goujon 300 francs a month for horses, although in June and August, 1786, he notes buying a horse, the second one for riding, which before that, he says he could not afford. When his servant Petit brought his little daughter Polly from England in the fall of the year, horses were also brought along.

In the Hôtel de Landron Jefferson had lived with a modest staff of four menservants headed by a maître d'hôtel, named Marc. Mrs. Adams who was "loth to submit to such an unnecessary number of domestics," was "thankful that we are able to make eight do for us." [45] Meals were sent in by a nearby *traiteur*, or restaurateur as we should say today. Now, with his move, he was obliged to add a gardener to his staff, as well as an assistant to the *frotteur*. In December, 1785, he engaged a cook. He agreed to give her 300 francs a year wages, 100 francs for wine, and 180 francs for supper.[46] There is no record of any change in this department while Jefferson remained in Paris, and from this unknown artist he doubtless acquired the recipes he was ultimately to bring back to Monticello and that are still found in his papers.[47]

The question of paying for his establishment was one that had worried Jefferson from the time of his arrival, as we have seen, and he had asked his friends to sound out Congress on the matter. In November, 1782, that body had appointed Thomas Barclay commissioner to "liquidate and finally settle the accounts of all the servants of the United States who have been entrusted with the expenditure of public moneys in Europe."[48] He had, as Jefferson says, "settled those of Doctor Franklin and Mr. Adams, and it was intended between us that he should settle mine. But as what may be done at any time is often put off to the last, this settlement had been made to give way to others."[49] Barclay was sent on a mission to Morocco. He subsequently and unexpectedly returned to the United States.

In May, 1788, when four years had passed since his appointment, during which the Commissioners of the Treasury had taken no steps to reimburse him or to make funds available, and when a new federal government was about to be installed, Jefferson reluctantly decided to take up the matter of his outfit, as he called it, with John Jay, the secretary of foreign affairs.[50] On Jefferson's first appointment as minister plenipotentiary to negotiate treaties of commerce, he was by resolution of Congress to receive a salary of nine thousand dollars a year, more than two thousand dollars less than ministers at foreign courts had hitherto been paid. "My appointment being temporary," he writes Jay, "for two years only, and not as of a resident Minister, the article of outfit did not come into question. I asked an advance of six months' salary that I might be in cash to meet the first expenses, which was ordered. The year following I was appointed to succeed Dr. Franklin at this court. This was the first appointment of a Minister resident since the original ones, under which all expenses were to be paid. So much of the ancient regulation as respected *annual expenses* had been altered to a sum certain, so much of it as respected *first expenses or outfit* remained unaltered; and I might, therefore, expect that the actual expenses for outfit were to be paid.

"Supposing, therefore," he continues, "that mine being the first case, Congress would make a precedent of it, and prefer a fixed sum for the outfit as well as the salary, I have charged it in my account at a year's salary, presuming there can be no question that an outfit is a reasonable charge.... It is a usage here (and I suppose at all courts) that a Minister resident shall establish his house in the first instant.... It is the universal practice, therefore, that all nations allow the outfit as a separate article from the salary....

"It is not more certain to me that the sun will rise tomorrow," he continues, "than that our government must allow the outfit on their future appointment of foreign Ministers, and it would be hard on me to stand between the discontinuance of a former rule, and institution of a future one as to have the benefit of neither. I know I have so long known the character of our federal head, in its present form, that I have the most unlimited confidence in the justice of its decisions....

"Not knowing the circumstances under which Congress may exist and act at the moment you receive this," he concludes, "I am unable to judge what should be done on this subject. It is, therefore, that I ask the aid of your friendship and that of Mr. Madison, that you will do for me in this regard what you think it is right should be done, and what it would be right for me to do were I on the spot, or were I apprized of all existing circumstances. Indeed, were you two to think my claim an improper one, I would wish it to be suppressed, as I have so much confidence in your judgment that I should suspect my own in any case where it varied from yours, and more especially in one when it is liable to be warped by feelings." [51]

In the accompanying letter to Madison he included certain supplementary details "not proper for me to state to Mr. Jay." These consisted of a résumé of the allowances made by the government to Jay while minister to Madrid, to Adams both at the Hague and in London, and to Franklin. When Congress reduced the latter's salary from 2,500 to 2,000 guineas "he refused to accede to it and asked his recall. ... He lived plain, but as decently as his salary would allow.... To him I have succeeded," Jefferson continues. "He had established a certain style of living. The same was expected from *me*, and there were 500 guineas less a year to do it on. It has been arrived at, however, as far as was practicable. This rendered it constantly necessary to step neither to the right nor to the left to incur any expense which could possibly be avoided, and it called for an almost womanly attention to the details of the household, equally perplexing, disgusting and inconsistent with business." [52]

Jefferson's letter did not receive the reply it would seem to have merited. It may well have been too straightforward. Jay wrote him on September 23 with the reserve characteristic of those in high station. He was not hopeful. "I... think it best," he says, "to postpone details for the present, as well as the private letter, which you have reason to expect from me on the subject. You also hinted to Mr. Madison, with whom I have conferred, respecting it. There is a reluctance in some to adopt the idea it suggests, and I apprehend that others will prefer delay to a decision upon it." [53]

Madison was in a position to write more freely and did so. He had a conference with Jay in which the latter "agreed to suggest the matter to Congress." This was done, and it was referred to the inevitable committee. "I had discovered," Madison says, "that he [Jay] was not struck with the particularities of your case even when insinuated to him. How far the committee will be so is more than I can yet say. In general I have no doubt that both it and Congress are well disposed." [54]

Less than a month later, on October 17, Madison again reported. "Nothing has been done on the subject of the outfit," he writes, "there not having been a Congress of nine states for some time, nor even of seven for the last week. It is pretty certain that there will not again be a quorum of either number within the present year, and by no means certain that there will be one at all under the old Confederation. The Committee, finding that nothing could be done, have neglected to make a report as yet. I have spoken with a member of it in order to get one made, that the case may fall of course and in favorable shape within the attention of the new government. The fear of a precedent will probably lead to an allowance for a limited time of the salary as enjoyed originally by foreign ministers in preference to a separate allowance for outfit. One of the members of the treasury board," he adds ominously, and his reference has always been considered as indicating Arthur Lee, "who ought, if certain facts have not escaped his memory, to witness the reasonableness of your calculations, takes occasion, I find, to impress a contrary idea." [55]

This letter sounded the death knell of Jefferson's hopes. He was not, like Franklin, "to save nothing, but avoid debt." [56] His situation was even more grave than that of the Adams', where "a deficit in their accounts appeared in their winding up." In serving his country as minister to France, he laid the cornerstone to the debts that were eventually to ruin him and leave him insolvent in his old age.

VII. England and Its Gardens

On the twenty-seventh of February, 1786, a young man arrived in great haste at the Grille de Chaillot. He was William Stephens Smith, late aide to General Washington and recently appointed secretary of legation at London. He carried an important letter from John Adams, American minister to the Court of St. James, urging Jefferson to come to the British capital at once. The Ambassador from Tripoli had called upon Adams and stated that "he had much at heart a treaty between the Barbary and American States" and "wished it might be soon... The time was critical and the sooner peace was made the better; for from what passed before he left home, he was convinced if the treaty shall be delayed another year, it will, after that, be difficult to make it." [1] Adams was frankly delighted and hopeful. Recently he had written Jay that "there are not wanting persons in England who will find means to stimulate this African to stir up his countrymen against American vessels." [2] He now informed the Secretary of Foreign Affairs that it was "apparent that his principal business here was to treat with the United States, and that no harm could be done by dealing frankly with him." He even, adds Adams, " 'called God to witness,' that is to say he swore by his beard, which is a sacred oath with them, 'that his motive for this earnestness for peace, although it might be of some benefit to himself, was the desire of doing good.' " [3]

Knowing the uncertain character of the people with whom he had to deal, Adams did not fail to play the proper part, as we learn from his daughter Abigail. "Pappa made a visit this eve to the ambassador from Tripoli," she writes. "By a little Italian and French, and some lingua Franca, they got into conversation and understood each other wondrously. A servant soon brought two long pipes, with two cups of coffee. Pappa took both; and smoked away, taking a sip of coffee, and a whiff at his pipe; the ambassador did the same. At last one of the secretaries cried out in ecstasy to Pappa: '*Monsieur, vous êtes un véritable Turk.*'"[4] After a return visit during which, however, "Pappa could not offer him a long pipe," the young lady observes that "something favorable may arise from these conferences, but we are not at liberty to say what."[5]

At the same time the Chevalier de Pinto, the ambassador from Portugal, a country with which the United States was eager to treat, informed Adams that "he had written to Lisbon for explanation from his Court upon certain points, that he expected an answer in a few days, and that as soon as he should receive it, he would call upon me, and proceed in the negotiation."[6]

It was these circumstances that led to the unheralded arrival of Colonel Smith in Paris. The letter he handed Jefferson read, "I have desired Colonel Smith to go express to Paris to entreat you to come here without loss of time. The Portugese Minister has received his instructions from his Court and we may here together conduct and finish the negotiation with him, I suppose in three weeks. But there is another motive more important. There is here a Tripolitan ambassador with whom I have had three conferences. The substance of what passed Colonel Smith will explain to you. Your visit here will be imputed to curiosity to take a look at England and pay your respects at Court and to the Corps Diplomatique. There is nothing to be done in Europe of half the importance of this and I dare not communicate to Congress what has passed without your concurrence. What has been already done and expended will be absolutely thrown away and we shall be involved in a universal and horrible war with these Barbary States, which will last many years, unless more is done immediately. I am so impressed and distressed with this affair that I will go to New York or to Algiers, or first to one and then to the other, if you think it necessary, rather than it should not be brought to a conclusion. Somebody of us must go to New York, one of us, or Humphreys or Smith, in order to persuade Congress of the necessity of doing more. Then somebody must go to Holland to obtain the means, and then somebody perhaps to Algiers to make use of them. The Tripolitan might be persuaded to go with him. I refer you to the bearer for all other particulars." [7]

It did not take Jefferson long to make up his mind. Although he had an aversion to going to England and more than an aversion to the British—he had recently reiterated it in a letter to Mrs. Adams, "I fancy it must be the quantity of animal food eaten by the English, which renders their character unsusceptible of civilization. I suspect it is in their kitchens, and not in their churches that their reformation must be worked, and that missionaries from hence would avail more than those who should endeavor to tame them by precepts of religion or philosophy—" [8] he was ready to leave Paris within less than a week. First, however, he wrote the Comte de Vergennes that "circumstances of public duty calling me suddenly to London, I take the liberty of mentioning it to your Excellency, and of asking a few minutes' audience of you at as early a day and hour as will be convenient to you, and that you will be so good as to indicate them to me. . . . I shall be happy to be the bearer of any commands your Excellency may have for that place, and will faithfully execute them." [9] He seems to have received an immediate appointment for he wrote Jay: "I went immediately to Versailles . . . arranged with him [Vergennes] some matters, and set out with Colonel Smith for this place." [10]

Accompanied by Petit, his *valet de chambre*, and another servant named John, the two men left Paris early on the morning of March 6 in the bad weather typical of that season. They traveled in a cabriolet, for the hire of which Jefferson paid seventy-two francs, and used post horses. Ever one to make the most of an opportunity, Jefferson profited by this one to take the road through the lovely forest of Chantilly to the château of the same name. He had not yet been there, and it had been warmly recommended by the Adams family. They had taken this same route in the late summer of 1784 when John Adams had brought his wife and daughter from London to Paris. Jefferson notes that he paid twelve francs at Chantilly for the usual "seeing things," and there can be no doubt he enjoyed the very scenes so enthusiastically described by Abby. "At Chantilly," she writes, "we visited the seat of the Prince of Condé. First to the kennel of dogs, two hundred or more, which the Prince keeps for hunting. There were more than two hundred horses with their names over each manger.... I am told the Prince sometimes sups with his horses and passes two or three hours with his dogs; rather an uncivilized taste, I think."

After describing the theater in which the Prince and his daughter were amused to act, she speaks of the gardens "about 20 acres, a canal full of fish, groves and arbours, walks and windings, fountains playing, statues, flowers. Here was the car of Venus drawn by doves; the statue of Cupid, with a motto in French, representing the pursuit of love ineffectual.... The furniture was of chintz, chairs, settees and curtains [a fashion Jefferson was later to adopt in the White House]. There were four fountains in the room... and a number of paintings, but they were not in a style that pleased me.... We next visited the English garden, as it is called. In one part there was a representative of a cottage, a mill with a plough, and every utensil for a farmer; another building, they told us, was the barn. It had the appearance, on the outside, of a little dirty place, with old windows and little doors, when, to our surprise, we were shown into an elegant apartment, with pictures and paintings; the furniture of pink silk, trimmed with a deep, rich silver fringe and tassels.... We were also shown some buildings in the Chinese style. The whole was exceedingly beautiful." [11]

The road to Calais was nearly two hundred miles, with suitable stopping places few and far between. The Adams' had been obliged to drive fourteen posts, or eighty-seven miles in one day, to find a place where they could be accommodated. Jefferson and Smith spent the first night at Breteuil, an inconsequential hamlet some sixty miles from Paris. The second day they reached Abbeville, the ancient fortified town girdled by ramparts, which was destroyed in the late war. If Jefferson took a look at the fine old church, he does not mention it. On the eighth the party spent the night at Montreuil, a hill town with old fortifications and citadel made famous by Sterne in his *Sentimental Journey*. It was only forty miles to Calais, that now utterly desolate port, which looks across the channel toward England. Here Jefferson put up at the well-known inn of Monsieur Dessein, likewise immortalized by Sterne. The Adams' had also stayed there, much to Abby's delight, as she mentions in her journal. "Here is the very monk," she writes, "that gave benefaction to our writer, and who has just passed my window to present himself to Pappa. I do not think he is quite so respectable a figure as the one that accosted Yorick." [12]

The weather was so inclement that Jefferson and his companion remained a day and a half in the dreary port. It was probably made reasonably tolerable by the inn, which, according to Thomas Blaikie, a Scotch gardener who had stopped there in 1785 on his way to Versailles, was "the largest in Europe. There is to be found in this inn everything necessary, all sorts of merchandise and carriages for travelling; there is in this hotel shoemakers, tailors, and all sorts of mechanicks, beside a playhouse furnished with good actors, a table de hotte and every thing tolerable raisonable." [13]

On the evening of the eleventh, after a passage of nine and a half hours,[14] Jefferson and his companion finally reached London. Jefferson took up lodgings with Mrs. Connor at No. 14 Golden Square, on the south side next to the house formerly occupied by Angelica Kauffmann the artist, on the outskirts of the fashionable West End. It is described in a contemporary guide book as "a very neat but small square, containing about two acres. A large space on the inside adorned with grass plats and gravel walks, was till lately surrounded with wooden rails, but these have been removed, and handsome iron ones placed in their room." [15] A diminutive statue of George II still stands in the center of the square.

Jefferson went at once to see Adams, as he tells us, and the following day there was another long conference. The agenda for the meetings with the various ambassadors were prepared, as we may judge from Jefferson's papers, which contain countless drafts and memoranda for treaties, not only with the powers concerned in the present negotiations, but with numerous others. The business in hand did not proceed as smoothly as had been hoped. Despite his avowals and despite his beard, the Tripolitan ambassador, one Abdrahaman, proved to be a hard-headed and practical man. "He asked us thirty thousand guineas for a peace with his Court," Jefferson writes, "and as much for Tunis, for which he said he could answer. What we were authorized to offer being to this but a drop in the bucket, our conferences were repeated only for the purpose of information. If the demands of Algiers and Morocco should be proportioned to this according to their superior power," he adds, "it is easy to foresee that the United States will not buy peace with money." [16] The negotiations were long drawn out. It was not until January 3, 1797, that a treaty between the United States and Tripoli was actually concluded and signed.

The Chevalier de Pinto was ill when Jefferson arrived in London. In consequence of this and of the inability of the two powers to see eye to eye, the conferences continued for six weeks. "The only article of difficulty between us," writes Jefferson, "was a stipulation that our bread stuff should be received in Portugal in the form of flour as well as grain. He approved of it himself, but observed that several nobles of great influence at their court, were the owners of windmills in the neighborhood of Lisbon, which depended much for their profits on manufacturing our wheat, and that this stipulation would endanger the whole treaty." [17] Despite these objections and despite Jefferson's disappointment at not securing "some privileges in their American possessions," he and Adams signed the treaty on the twenty-fifth of April.[18] "Its fate," Jefferson remarks, "was what he had candidly portended." [19]

Adams appears at this time to have been persuaded that he was not without influence at the British court. As his wife had recently written Jefferson, "You will find by the public papers what favorites we are at court. The Prince of Wales supping with us. Mr. Adams holding frequent conferences with His Majesty, and yesterday going to Windsor for the same purpose. It is said by some that these are ministerial manoeuvres to keep up the stocks. A paragraph of this kind has certainly been attended with that effect. Others say it is to feel out the minds of the people in respect to a treaty with America, of which if I dared to give an opinion I should say that some symptoms have lately appeared tending to that point. But this is said in confidence, Sir, as I must not betray secrets." [20]

Jefferson's arrival now furnished an "occasion to renew our overtures to the court of London." Adams promptly sent a note to the Marquis of Carmarthen, the British minister of foreign affairs, acquainting "his Lordship that Mr. Jefferson, Minister Plenipotentiary at the Court of Versailles, is now here, and as they have something to communicate to his Lordship, relative to the affairs of the United States, they request a time when they may have the honour to pay their respects to his Lordship, before the levee on Wednesday." [21]

The Marquis appears to have received the two Ministers, but, says Jefferson, "these overtures were not attended to . . . and I suppose this the last offer of friendship which will ever be made on our part. . . . I think the king, ministers, and nation are more bitterly hostile to us at present than at any period of the late war. . . . Our enemies (for such they are, in fact,) have, for twelve years past, followed but one uniform rule, that of doing exactly the contrary of what reason points out. Having early, during our contest, observed this in the British conduct, I governed myself by it in all prognostications of their measures. And I can say with truth, it never failed me but in the circumstance of their making peace with us." [22]

In a report to John Jay, dated April 25, the futile attempt to find a basis of negotiation with Great Britain is rehearsed by Adams and Jefferson. "His Lordship, after harping a little on the old string," they write, "the insufficiency of the powers of Congress to treat and compel compliance with treaties, said he would lay the matter before the Ministry and the King. In a few days his Lordship meeting one of us, proposed . . . that as the project already communicated contained many political regulations, we should propose a project of a treaty merely commercial." [23] Proposals and counterproposals were entertained until the exasperated commissioners were forced to report, "There is no party nor individual here in favor of a treaty, but upon the principle that the United States will retaliate if there is not one. All agree that if America will suffer England to *pocket* (that is the expression) all her navigation, England would be unwise not to avail herself of the advantage." [24] In a private letter to Jay, Jefferson speaks of a "small band of friends," including the Marquis of Lansdowne and Dr. Richard Price, a friend of America and intimate of Pitt, that "favorable as it is, does not pretend to say one word in public on our subject." [25]

Jefferson was not satisfied to treat only with the officials of the government. He conferred with "some of the most distinguished mercantile characters," whom he found at once reasonable and sympathetic.

"Our conferences were intended as preparatory to some arrangement," he writes. "It is uncertain how far we should have been able to accommodate our opinions. But the absolute aversion of the government to enter into any arrangement, prevented the object from being pursued. Each country is left to do justice to itself and to the other, according to its own ideas as to what is past, and to scramble for the future as well as they can, to regulate their commerce by duties and prohibitions, and perhaps by cannons and mortars—in which event we must abandon the ocean, where we are weak." [26]

The snub that the British Ministers, particularly Carmarthen, inflicted upon Jefferson and thus upon the United States, was dealt with in greater detail and much bitterness in his report to Jay.[27] It rankled in his heart until the very end of his life. In his old age he wrote in his autobiography, "On the first conference with the Marquis of Carmarthen . . . the distance and disinclination which he betrayed in his conversation, the vagueness and evasions of his answers to us, confirmed me in the belief of their aversion to have anything to do with us. We delivered him, however, our *projet*, Mr. Adams not despairing as much as I did of its effect. We afterwards, by one or more notes, requested his appointment of an interview and conference, which, without directly declining, he evaded, by pretences of other pressing occupation for the moment." [28] Small wonder Jefferson was led to exclaim that "of all nations on earth, they [the British] require to be treated with the utmost hauteur. They require to be kicked into good common manners." [29]

Despite his aversion to the British and his distaste for the ceremonies in which he was obliged to take part, despite the fact that only ten short years ago he had immortalized their monarch in one of the most scathing indictments known to history, Jefferson was duly presented at court on the seventeenth of March. In announcing his arrival in London, *The Gazetteer* states that on Wednesday he "was introduced to the King at St. James by his Excellency, John Adams, and on Thursday to the Queen. It is conjectured by those that pretend to be wise," the paper adds, "that Mr. Jefferson's visiting England is on the subject of an American treaty." From the same source we learn that the levee at which he was presented was "very thin of nobility," whereas "Their Majesties, the Princes and Princesses, all the foreign ministers, the great officers of state, with several others of the nobility of both sexes," had attended the drawing room of the preceding day.[30]

The meeting with this monster of oppression was seemingly so incidental an occasion to Jefferson that he does not mention it in any of his letters written immediately after or report in detail on the ceremonies and his reaction, as did John Adams to Jay when he had been received the previous year.[31] Jefferson merely notes in his account book that he "pd. porters at St. James on my being presented, 42." [32] He leaves us in no doubt, however, that the occasion was no more felicitous than the meetings with Carmarthen. In his autobiography he observes that "on my presentation, as usual, to the King and Queen, at their levees, it was impossible for anything to be more ungracious, than their notice of Mr. Adams and myself. I saw at once that the ulcerations of mind in that quarter, left nothing to be expected on the subject of my attendance." [33] Charles Francis Adams, John Adams' grandson, goes so far as to say, "The King turned his back upon our American commissioners, a hint, which of course, was not lost upon the circle of his subjects in attendance." In any case, there was no "air of familiarity," or "air of gayety" such as Adams reported on his reception, no statement that "I have no attachment but to my own country," and no royal rejoinder "as quick as lightning, 'an honest man will never have any other.'" [34] Both men were aware who had written the Declaration of Independence.

While in England, Jefferson naturally availed himself of many of the pleasures and many of the opportunities offered by the greatest city in the world—its theaters, its music, its shops. His taste for the theater was noteworthy from the earliest days, whenever there was a chance to attend. It is thus not surprising to find that he was scarcely settled in London before he went to Drury Lane, on the evening of the thirteenth. It was the third performance by the famous Mrs. Siddons in a new tragedy, *The Captives*, with an epilogue spoken by her. An additional attraction was *The Gentle Shepherd*, and at the end of the first act highland reels were danced. Jefferson seems to have been as great an admirer of her art as were the majority of his contemporaries and attended her performances whenever possible. Thus on the twentieth of April he saw her play Portia in *The Merchant of Venice*, and two evenings later, Lady Macbeth. On the nineteenth of April he tried Covent Garden, where *The Mourning Bride* and *The Two Misers*[35] were the attractions, but this is the only time he records going there.

Jefferson also went only once to the opera, on March 18. It was a command performance at the King's Theatre in the Haymarket, opera in all its glitter and glory. The advertisement tells us that it was "a new comic opera, *La Scuola de Gelosi*, the music entirely new by the celebrated Signor Saliari, music master to His Imperial Majesty." At the end of the opera a *divertissement* "entirely new" was presented. From the newspapers we learn that Their Majesties with the two eldest Princesses were there "for the first time these several years... They were welcomed by one of the most splendid and brilliant audiences that ever graced the King's Theatre. The opera was performed admirably in all its parts.... The Prince of Wales honoured the theatre with his presence; His Royal Highness was most elegantly dressed in a maroon colored velvet, the buttons of which were ornamented with steel, which produced the brilliant effect of diamonds." [36]

There were two other diversions Jefferson permitted himself, one was to see "the learned pig" for which he paid a shilling and of which no account seems available. The second, a visit to two famous places of amusement. The first was the Pantheon which had been opened in 1771 and had been largely given over to balls and masquerades. It was now devoted principally to music. On March 23, the evening Jefferson attended, the newspapers printed the announcement: "The nobility and gentry are respectfully acquainted that there will be a concert at this place this evening in which will be introduced some glees. The principal vocal parts by Mrs. Barthalemen and Mr. Arrowsmith." [37] Nearly a month later, on the eighteenth of April, Jefferson sought amusement at Astleys, a noted place of entertainment for more than two centuries on Westminster Bridge road. *The Gazetteer* tells us of this place that "everyone without exception, speaks much in praise of Astley's, and christening it the 'Royal Grove' [a new name recently bestowed] was a good thought for a summer place of amusement. Astley has shown himself a wise general in many instances, particularly in setting up his place to represent a grove and selecting the best performers to put therein. In the military phrase, he leads the Vanguard, for to our certain knowledge box, pit, and galleries overflow every evening." [38]

On the twenty-second of March Jefferson hired a carriage and horses and drove the twenty-three miles along the Thames to Windsor Castle, that most noble and romantic of royal residences towering above the village of the same name. The Adams', who often accompanied him on such trips, were not with him on this occasion but followed his footsteps a few months later and spent a day and a half there. It is from Mrs. Adams rather than from Jefferson that we view the scene which met his eye, before the taste of the nineteenth century had vulgarized the monument. "The most luxuriant fancy cannot exceed the beauties of this place," she writes. "I do not wonder that Pope styled it the seat of the Muses . . . this place, as in former days, is the retreat of the monarch. The royal family reside here nine months of the year, not in the castle, as that would require the attendance of ministers, etc. . . . the family resides here with as little parade as that of a private gentleman . . . [The castle] is situated upon a high hill . . . in front is a wide and extensive vale, adorned with fields and meadows, with groves on either side, and the calm, smooth water of the Thames running through them. Behind it are hills covered with forests, as if designed by nature for hunting. The terrace round the castle is a noble walk covered with fine gravel. It is raised on a steep declivity of a hill, and overlooks the whole town. Here the King and royal family walk on Sunday afternoons, in order to show themselves to their subjects who choose to repair to Windsor for that purpose. In fine weather the terrace is generally thronged. . . . To describe to you the apartments, the paintings and decorations within this castle would require a volume instead of a letter." [39] However, she cannot resist closing her letter with a description of the Queen's bed chamber and "the room of beauties" designed to dazzle her New England correspondent.

The Queen and two princesses arrived at Windsor from London on the day of Jefferson's visit, *The Gazetteer* tells us, "and in about two hours the King came down to the castle. The public apartments are now having their annual beautifying before the Royal Family will take up their constant residence here again." Mrs. Adams remarks that the "Queen has a neat lodge here, close to the castle, and there is another, a few rods distant, for the Princesses. His Majesty is a visitor to the Queen. . . . The castle," she observes, not without humor, "is one of the strongest places in Europe, as it is said, and a safe retreat for the family in case any more revolutions should shake this Kingdom." [40] That spring was not yet on the way and that the country did not present the smiling aspect of June during Jefferson's visit, we learn from the statement that "there are large quantities of snow still undissolved in many parts of the Great Park, as well as in the forest." [41]

Jefferson had been enthralled and delighted, as we have seen, with the artistic treasures of Paris and the opportunity to form the collection of which he had so long dreamed. Now, in England, he was equally captivated by what he called the mechanical arts, which, he declared, were "carried to a wonderful perfection." [42] He used the occasion to buy himself numerous instruments, which we find listed in detail in his accounts, from thermometers, hydrometers, a circular draw pen, a compound microscope, and pocket dividers to "a little electrical machine," most of them now far more outmoded than the works of art he purchased in the French capital. Although he said he could write "volumes on the improvements, which I find made and making here, in this field," he confined himself largely to sending accounts to interested friends in America of "one which deserves particular notice, because it is simple, great and likely to have extensive consequences. It is the application of steam, as an agent for working grist mills. . . . I hear you are applying the same agent in America to navigate boats, and I have little doubt, but that it will be applied generally to machines. . . . We know that steam is one of the most powerful engines we can employ, and in America, fuel is abundant." [43]

For years Jefferson had found his vast correspondence a great burden, especially the copying of letters. Before leaving America he seems to have had some sort of copying machine for, in a farewell letter written to Robert Morris on July 2, 1784, he notes, "He may take copying machine if he wants it." [44] Shortlv after his arrival in Paris he "put in the hands of W. T. Franklin to buy copying press and books in London, 16½ guineas,"[45] and a few weeks later wrote enthusiastically to Madison, "Have you a copying press? If you have not, you should get one. . . . I would give ten times that sum [its cost] to have had it from the date of the Stamp Act."[46]

These machines appear to have been of a large, cumbersome nature. Jefferson, as he says, "having a great desire to have a portable copying machine, and being satisfied, from some experiments, that the principle of the large machine might be applied in a small one, I planned one while in England and had it made. It answers perfectly. I have since set a workman to making them here, and they are in such demand that he has his hands full."[47]

The first one, we learn from a letter of John Paradise to Jefferson on May 23, 1786, was completed at that time by one Cavallo and turned over to William Stephens Smith for shipment to Jefferson. It cost five guineas.[48] Jefferson's design for this is still preserved, it is on the order and about the size of an ordinary clothes wringer. He employed a man named Goldsmith and another named Charpentier in Paris to make them, and there was scarcely one of his circle who did not benefit by them from Madison in Virginia and Carmichael in Spain to Lafayette, Chastellux, the Portuguese Ambassador and the Papal Nuncio in Paris.

During his stay in London Jefferson was entertained to some extent by the Americans who, according to Abigail Adams, had "essentially injured themselves by running here in shoals after the peace."[49] No account has come to light of his appearance at any of the great London houses. In a letter to R. H. Lee he speaks of having "dined the other day in a company of the ministerial party"[50] and rehearses some of the conversation, but there is no further indication where it was.

As had been the case in Paris, he dined often with the Adams family and their circle. Thus not long after his arrival he was one of a large dinner party given by Mr. and Mrs. Paradise, friends of the American Minister. Mrs. Paradise was the former Lucy Ludwell of Virginia, who had gone to England as a girl and married that fantastic character, partly Greek, partly English, John Paradise. On this occasion, aside from the British and American Ministers, there were present the

Russian Ambassador, Count Woronzow, and his lady, the Venetian Minister, Count Soderini, the Prussian Minister, that dubious American Dr. Bancroft, and Colonel Smith, the faithful attendant of young Abigail. At eight o'clock, Mrs. Adams tells us, the guests returned to their various homes to dress "for the ball at the French Ambassador's."

The Gazetteer had duly informed the public that "The French Ambassador's Sunday evening rout is continued with its usual brilliancy and splendor. His Excellency does not as formerly send out cards, those only of the ton are expected whose visits have been returned. Chit-chat, French wines, vive la bagalette and the Faro tables form the amusements of this elegant lounge."

Mrs. Adams was properly enthusiastic in writing home about the event. "The Hotel de France," she says, "is beautifully situated fronting St. James' Park, one end of the house standing upon Hyde Park. It is a most superb building. About half past nine we went and found some company collected. Many very brilliant ladies of the first distinction were present. The dancing commenced about ten and the rooms were soon filled. The room which he had built for this purpose is large enough for five or six hundred persons. It is most elegantly decorated, hung with a gold tissue, ornamented with twelve brilliant cut lustres, each containing twenty-four candles. At one end there are two large arches. These were adorned with wreaths and bunches of artificial flowers upon the walls; in the alcoves were cornucopiae loaded with oranges, sweetmeats, etc. . . . In the other rooms card tables and a large faro table were set. . . . The whole style of the house and furniture is such as becomes the ambassador from one of the first monarchies of Europe." [51]

John Adams recounts that he met the Marquis of Lansdowne and the Earl of Harcourt on this occasion. Still impressed by a title, as have been so many of his compatriots since that time, and still uncertain of his new democracy in this glittering world so far removed from the farmhouse at Quincy, and still protesting a bit too vigorously, he continues, "These two noblemen ventured to enter into conversation with me. So did Sir George Young. But there is an awkward timidity in general. This people cannot look me in the face; there is conscious guilt and shame in their countenances when they look at me. They feel that they have behaved ill, and that I am sensible of it."[52]

Jefferson had expected to remain in England but a short time. As the negotiations with Portugal dragged out and those with England had reached the point where, Jefferson felt, the "government not only has it not in contemplation at present to make any, but that they do not conceive that any circumstances will arise which shall render it expedient for them to have any political connection with us,"[53] he determined to fulfill certain private ambitions. He had early interested himself in gardens and gardening, as we have noted.[54] His own youthful and romantic plans for the development of the grounds of Monticello were based not on actual examples he had seen, but on the books he had been able to procure in Virginia, notably Thomas Whately's *Observations on Modern Gardening*. Now, fifteen years later, his interest unabated, he eagerly seized the opportunity of visualizing his dreams. In company with John Adams, he set off on the second of April "into the country to some of the most celebrated gardens."[55] What they saw staggered the two men, accustomed as they were to the simplicity and provincial character of the American scene.

"The gentlemen's seats were the highest entertainment we met with," Adams writes of this trip, "architecture, painting, statuary, poetry are all employed in the embellishment of these residences of greatness and luxury.... It will be long, I hope, before riding parks, pleasure grounds, gardens and ornamented farms grow so much in fashion in America." Coming to the defense of his own country, he concludes that "nature has done greater things and furnished nobler materials there; the oceans, islands, rivers, mountains, valleys are all laid out on a greater scale."[56] Disregarding the evidences of luxury and concentrating on the main purpose of his tour—"my inquiries were directed chiefly to such practical things as might enable me to estimate the expense of making and maintaining a garden in that style"—Jefferson summed up his impressions in a letter to John Page shortly after his return to Paris. It was written in the terse style he often employed when deeply pleased. "The gardening in that country," he remarks, "is the article in which it surpasses all the earth. I mean their pleasure gardening. This, indeed, went far beyond my ideas."[57]

The gardens that Jefferson and Adams visited lay along the Thames or its tributaries in a westerly direction from London. Although now largely embraced in the suburbs, they were at that time in the open country. With a copy of Whately in his hand, and with the energy and determination characteristic of the American tourist of all times, the two gentlemen, traveling in a post chaise with Petit and John, their servants, paid their respects to no less than six country seats on the first day. It was perhaps no accident that they started with Chiswick, the magnificent Palladian villa built by Lord Burlington and owned, in Jefferson's day, by the Duke of Devonshire, "which, for elegance of taste, surpasses everything of its kind in England",[58] as a contemporary guide book truly tells us. The casino, for such it was, with a *piano nobile* of eight communicating rooms designed rather for reception rooms than for everyday living, must have embodied for Jefferson a great deal that he hoped to achieve at Monticello, although with a sumptuousness of decoration that exceeded his wildest imaginings. Perhaps the austere Virginian was somewhat repelled by this display of reckless luxury, perhaps there was the merest twinge of envy at things not yet achieved—for Monticello had still to acquire its final form—when he wrote, "the octagonal dome has an ill effect both within and without."[59]

The superb gardens, neglected today but retaining their original form and ornaments, were "laid out in the finest taste." They contained various features similar to those Jefferson had planned for his own. Aside from the statuary that adorned them and a so-called wilderness with a Palladian wooden bridge, we are informed that the lawn leading down to the river was planted with "clumps of evergreens, with agreeable breaks, between which the water is seen; and at the farther end is an opening into an inclosure, where are a Roman temple, and an obelisk . . . and in the middle a circular piece of water."[60] Jefferson merely commented, "An obelisk of very ill effect; another in the middle of the pond, useless."[61]

Pope's garden at Twickenham, "a pleasant village in Middlesex situated on the Thames," next lured the travelers. "The elegant gothic seat called Strawberry Hill, belonging to the Honourable Mr. Walpole," [62] which they passed, was completely ignored by them. Much as he admired Pope, and much as he may have pondered over the poet's theories on gardening, first expressed nearly seventy-five years before and executed at Twickenham after 1719, Jefferson's comments on the place are as noncommittal as usual—a brief and objective record of the size of the garden and location of the house, a mention of the noted grotto, the mound, and the rookery. This time the obelisk at the bottom of the garden, with an inscription to Pope's mother, draws forth no unfavorable comment.[63]

Hampton Court, the largest of the royal palaces and the handsomest, lay next on Jefferson's route. It was so greatly admired in the eighteenth century that it inspired the learned philosopher Grotius to exclaim, "E'er a Briton what is wealth don't know; let him repair to Hampton Court, and there view all the palaces of the earth, where he will say, 'Those are the residence of Kings, but this of the Gods!' " [64] The edifice combines the mellow red brick of Cardinal Wolsey, who built the original palace in 1515, and the academism of Sir Christopher Wren, who was commanded by William III to remodel the palace after the one at Versailles. Although a guide book of the period describes the gardens, which are maintained to this day, as "not in the present natural style, but in that which prevailed some years ago, when mathematical figures were preferred to natural forms," [65] Jefferson paid four shillings, sixpence to see them and observed, "Old fashioned. Clipt yews grown wild." [66]

Some four miles south of Hampton, on the river Mole, lay Esher Place, enthusiastically described by Whately as "a place wherein to tarry with secure delight, or saunter with perpetual amusement." [67] The house had once been the palace of Cardinal Wolsey but had subsequently been remodeled except for two Gothic towers. It lay "in a bottom near the river," Jefferson tells us, and the gardens were distinguished by "heights rising one beyond and above another, with clumps of trees," [68] as well as by a temple or "fine summer house built upon a hill on the left as you enter, which commands the view of the house, park, and country round on both sides of the Thames for many miles." [69] Jefferson was especially enthusiastic about the clumps of trees that "on each hand balance finely—a most lovely mixture of concave and convex." [70] Esher has now, alas, been engulfed in a modern suburb. Even the house that Jefferson saw was replaced some fifty years ago by one on what he describes as "the heights," and only one of Cardinal Wolsey's towers still stands guard in the distance. There is no longer a trace of the magnificent estate "where Kent and nature vied for Pelham's love."

Almost contiguous with Esher Place was Claremont, once the seat of the Duke of Newcastle, who had employed Vanbrugh to build a great house "in a whimsical style of architecture," and to develop the gardens, which were almost as celebrated as those of Stowe. Lord Clive had subsequently bought the property, torn down the house, and built the large, somewhat formidable mansion with the portico that Jefferson saw and that remains today. The park, according to our guide book, "is distinguished by its noble woods, lawn, walks, mounts, prospects, etc." [71] Vanbrugh's walled garden, which we find so picturesque, and that curious structure known as the Belvedere, its situation "singularly romantic" with "a prodigious fine prospect of the Thames and adjacent villas," were there for Jefferson to admire, as they are for the traveler of the present. Jefferson, however, dismissed the place with the words, "Nothing remarkable."

From Claremont his road led to Painshill. This had almost everything that would appeal to Jefferson, from the manner of its planting to an ingenious water wheel. Whately devotes ten pages to a description of the place, to praising "the boldness of design and a happiness of execution, which attend the wonderful efforts which art has there made a rival to nature." [72] "The whole place," we learn, "is about five miles round; it is laid out in the modern taste, and planted with a beautiful variety of trees, plants and flowers. The fine inequalities of the ground give a perpetual variety to the prospects, especially on the side next the river Mole, which river, though it lies lower than the gardens by twenty feet, is brought into them by means of a wheel curiously contrived, which is turned by the river." Thus, "by the joint assistance of nature and art, it is formed into a winding lake or piece of water, with an island on it, planted and laid out in walks, with bridges over it of the most simple contrivance, and the whole surrounded with rising grounds, clumps of trees, and hanging woods, in as romantic and picturesque manner as imagination can conceive." [73]

These improvements had been made by 1761 by the Honourable Charles Hamilton, to whom the place belonged at that period. By the time of Jefferson's visit, it had been sold to a Mr. Hopkins who built himself a house that Jefferson describes as "ill-situated," unfinished, and its architecture "incorrect." However, there was "a Doric temple, beautiful." [74] As in the case of Claremont, nothing now remains of its former grandeur. The gardens have been reduced to uncultivated fields. There is no trace of earlier buildings. Everything, except a Victorian gatehouse, has fallen into decay and been eradicated.

Jefferson, Adams, and Colonel Smith, who was one of the party, spent the first night away from London at Weybridge, a village in Surrey about four miles southwest of Hampton. Early the next morning, as was the custom in those days, the travelers set out to explore the neighborhood. Grouped about the village within a few miles of each other were three great country seats: Oatlands, that of the Earl of Lincoln, "whose majestic grandeur, and the beautiful landscape it commands, words cannot describe nor the pencil delineate";[75] Ham Farm belonging to the Earl of Portmore, situated at the junction of the Thames and the Wye, with "a fine command of water";[76] and adjoining it, Woburn Farm, "the seat of the late Phillip Southgate, now belonging to Lord Peters." It was to this place, so highly praised by Whately, that Jefferson gave most of his attention. "'Tis what the French call a *ferme ornée*," the guide book says, reflecting the common opinion, "but perhaps it is too much ornamented for the simple plainness of a farm." [77]

In his *Observations on Modern Gardening*, Whately philosophizes on the subject, and on the motives that led those captives of grandeur, from an English lord to a French queen, to seek release from parade and restraint in what they almost convinced themselves in believing was the simple life of a farm. He devotes one section to a discussion of the four forms of a farm—a pastoral farm, an ancient one, a simple farm, and an ornamented one. "The simple farm may undoubtedly be delightful," he observes. "It will be particularly acceptable to the owner if it be close to his park or garden. The objects which constantly remind him of his rank, impose a kind of constraint, and he feels himself relieved, by retiring sometimes from the splendor of a seat into the simplicity of a farm. It is more than a variety of scene; it is a temporary change of situation in life, which has all the charms of novelty, ease, and tranquillity, to recommend it. A place, therefore, can hardly be deemed perfect, which is not provided with such a retreat." [78] Jefferson was in a sense eventually to achieve such a retreat at Poplar Forest, to which he fled with increasing frequency during his presidency and afterward. It did not fulfill the condition of being contiguous to his seat, Monticello, but was in Bedford County some eighty miles distant.

The ornamented farm, according to Whately, involves "bringing every rural circumstance within the verge of a garden." Woburn farm he considered the most perfect execution of this idea, and it is obvious that Jefferson agreed, for he returned the following day to go over it again. "The place," says Whately, "contains a hundred and fifty acres, of which near five and thirty are adorned to the highest degree, of the rest about two thirds are in pasture, and the remainder is in tillage. The decorations are, however, communicated to every part." [79] He gives a detailed description of the walk, with appendages, which "forms a broad belt round the grazing grounds, and is continued... through the arable. This walk is properly garden; all within it is farm." After discussing the cornfields and the pastures and speaking of the clumps and the single trees, which are of greatest importance in a garden of this type, he comments on the buildings that adorn it: "On the top of the hill is a large, octagon structure, and not far from it the ruin of a chapel.... The lawn is further embellished by a neat Gothic building, the former by the house, and the lodge at the entrance, and in both, other objects of less consequence, little seats, alcoves and bridges continually occur." [80]

The walk, on which so much emphasis was laid, was "shut out from the country... by a thick and lofty hedge row, which is enriched with woodbine, jassamine, and every odiferous plant whose tendrils will entwine with the thicket." [81] Then comes the significant feature that Jefferson was to carry in his mind during the years until he made the final plans for his western garden in 1808, where it was embodied. It was recreated in the restoration of the gardens in 1940. "A path, generally of sand or gravel, is conducted in a waving line, sometimes close under the hedge, sometimes a little distance from it [Jefferson did not employ a hedge but used the natural boundary or hedge of a hilltop]. And the turf on either hand is diversified with little groups of shrubs, of firs, or the smallest trees, and often with beds of flowers . . . in some parts the walk is carried between larger clumps of evergreens, thickets of deciduous shrubs, or still more considerable open plantations." [82] Another feature characteristic of Woburn was to be adopted by Jefferson at Monticello. "The country has . . . been searched for plants new in a garden," Whately tells us, "and the shrubs and flowers which used to be deemed peculiar to the one, have been liberally transferred to the other, while their number seems multiplied by their arrangement in so many and such different dispositions." [83] Anyone familiar with Jefferson's activities as a gardener will know that he searched not one country but many for exotic plants, trees, and shrubs and that he carried on a lifelong correspondence as well as an exchange of seeds and plants with other devoted amateurs.

Jefferson's own comments on Woburn are brief. He depended on Whately's full description to recall details of its actual appearance. As usual, he noted the practical details. "Four people to the farm, four to the pleasure garden, four to the kitchen garden. All are intermixed, the pleasure garden being merely a highly ornamented walk through and round the divisions of the farm and kitchen garden." [84]

From Woburn the party turned back toward London and spent the night of the third of April there. The next day they were off again, stopping once more at Woburn on the way. Caversham, not long since sold by Lord Cadogan to a Major Marsac, was their first objective. John Adams describes the place, along with Woburn and the Leasowes, by the simple word "beautiful." Jefferson seems not to have found the place so satisfactory. "A straight, broad gravel walk passes before the front and parallel to it," he writes, "terminated on the right by a Doric temple, and opening at the other end on a fine prospect. This straight walk has an ill effect." However, he found compensation in "the lawn in front, which is pasture, well disposed with clumps of trees." [85] From Caversham it was but a short distance to

Reading, an ancient town on the Thames and still a favorite stopping place for oarsmen on that river, where the travelers passed the night.

The next two days were spent viewing the properties of the Marquis of Buckingham, first Wotton, characterized by Adams as "both great and elegant though neglected," then that most princely of country places, Stowe. The extended use of water in the development of the gardens was the outstanding feature at Wotton. Jefferson tells us there were no less than seventy-two acres of it. This mass, according to Whately, was divided into four principal parts, "all of them great in style and in dimensions, and differing from each other both in character and situation." There was "a reach of a river, about a third of a mile in length, and of a competent breadth, flowing through a lovely mead, open in some places to views of beautiful hills in the country, and adorned in others with clumps of trees so large that their branches ... form a high arch over the water. The next seems to have been once a formal basin, encompassed with plantations ... and out of it issue two broad collateral streams winding towards a large river.... The river is the third great division and a lake into which it falls is the fourth." [86] A romantic island, the ground irregularly broken, thickets hanging on the side, had been created near the junction of the waters. "Towards the top is placed an Ionic portico, which commands a noble extent of water, not less than a mile in circumference, bounded on one side with wood, and open on the other to two sloping lawns." Other features were a Tuscan portico close to the great basin, an "elegant bridge with a colonade upon it," an "octagon building," and a "Chinese room." Whately ends his enthusiastic description with the observation that "however interrupted, however varied, they still appear to be parts of one whole, which has all the intricacy of number, all the greatness of unity; the variety of a stream, and the quantity of a lake; the solemnity of a wood, and the animation of water." [87]

Jefferson's comments again were brief. After describing the obvious features in a few sentences, he remarks that "but two hands [are employed] to keep the pleasure grounds in order; much neglected. The water affords two thousand brace of carp a year. There is a Palladian bridge, of which, I think, Whately does not speak." [88]

The sixth of April was dedicated to visiting the two places that represent the greatest extremes it is possible to imagine—the palatial magnificence of Stowe and Shakespeare's humble birthplace. The gardens at Stowe were probably the most celebrated in Georgian England. Despite their faded glory, they remain so today. A road two miles in length led from the nearby village of Buckingham to "a large Corinthian arch or gateway, 60 feet high and 60 feet wide, decorated on each side with a large military column, from whence appears the garden front of his Lordship's house, proudly standing on the summit of a verdant hill, and encompassed by the garden and park. The road to the house leads through the arch and is beautifully diversified with hill, valley, lawn, river, and a perpetual change of scene, arising from the numerous buildings intermixed with wood, and 'bosomed high in tufted trees,' which strike the eye with a most picturesque and ever varying magnificence." [89] Jefferson differed with most of his contemporaries in finding "the straight approach very ill. The Corinthian arch has a very useless appearance, inasmuch as it has no pretension to any destination. Instead of being an object from the house, it is an obstacle to a very pleasing distant prospect." [90]

The extensive gardens, the delight of every amateur of that art, contained no less than twenty-three architectural elements dispensed through the park. Among other features there were a circular Temple of Ancient Virtue and a Temple of Venus erected by Kent, as well as one of Concord and Victory by the same artist, on the model of Jefferson's adored Maison Carrée at Nîmes. The famous Rotundo with a statue of Bacchus was designed by Vanbrugh. Artificial ruins "covered with evergreens and adorned with statues of fawns, satyrs and river-gods" and embellished with a cascade that "falls in three sheets from the upper water into the lake, along with an hermitage, a grotto, and a Gothic temple 70 feet high adorned with . . . a very fine collection of old painted glass consisting of sacred subjects and . . . armorial bearings," [91] catered to the romantic taste of the time. There were also numerous sculptured features, such as a Doric arch leading into the Elysian Fields, standing "on an eminence accompanied by the statues of Apollo and the nine Muses," and a curious monument to Congreve, likewise designed by Kent.

It was not far to Stratford on Avon, where Jefferson notes he paid one shilling "for seeing house where Shakspeare was born" and another for "seeing his tombstone." Adams was more vocal about the experience. He allows that Stratford is "interesting, as it is the scene of the birth, death and sepulture of Shakspeare. Three doors from the inn is the house where he was born, as small and mean as you can conceive. They showed us an old wooden chair in the chimney corner where he sat." Succumbing like most tourists to lurking temptation, the two men "cut off a chip" of the chair, which both justify by the phrase "according to custom." Adams continues, "The house where he died has been taken down, and the spot is now only yard or garden. ... There is nothing preserved of his great genius, which is worth knowing; nothing which might inform us what education, what company, what accident turned his mind to letters and the drama. His name is not even on his gravestone." [92]

The secret delight of this trip northward was the prospect of visiting the Leasowes, one of the earliest landscape gardens in England. As we have seen, it had been of great influence in the development of Jefferson's early design for Monticello.[93] Whately treats it under the heading of a farm, more particularly what he calls a pastoral farm, and devotes some ten pages to a lyrical description of it. The place had been developed by William Shenstone, the poet, and perhaps not inappropriately, it was adorned with numerous inscriptions. Whately speaks of them as a "striking peculiarity" of the gardens and observes that "the elegance of the poetry and the aptness of the quotations atone for their length and their number. ... They are, indeed, among the principal ornaments of the place, for the buildings are mostly mere seats, or little root-houses. A ruin of a priory is the largest ... Every natural advantage of the place within itself has been discovered, applied, contrasted, and carried to the utmost in the purest taste, and with inexhaustible perfect fancy." [94]

That the place had suffered in the twenty years since Jefferson had first heard of it, and that he was somewhat disappointed in what he saw is readily observed from his own comments. "The waters small," he writes. "This is not even an ornamented farm—it is only a grazing farm with a path around it, here and there a seat of board, rarely anything better. Architecture has contributed nothing. The obelisk is of

THE TEMPLE AND OBELISK AT CHISWICK. *Copyright* Country Life.

THE TEMPLE OF CONCORD AND VICTORY AT STOWE. From the engraving by T. Medland.

brick. Shenstone had but three hundred pounds a year, and ruined himself by what he did to this farm.... The walk through the wood is umbrageous and pleasing.... Many of the inscriptions are lost." [95]

The party now turned back in the general direction of London, stopping in Birmingham to view "a manufactory of paintings upon paper," as Adams tells us. On the eighth they visited Hagley Park, the magnificent estate in Worcestershire belonging at the time to Lord Wescot, which contained the first Greek temple to adorn an English garden. Although Horace Walpole writes of it, "You might draw, but I can't describe the enchanting scenes of the park.... I wore out my eyes with gazing, my feet with climbing, and my tongue and vocabulary with praising," Jefferson displays no such enthusiasm. His mentor Whately considers it "equally elegant and noble." Jefferson emphasizes what struck him as the shortcomings, disregards the famous temple, and concludes, "The ponds yield a great deal of trout. The walks are scarcely gravelled." [96]

The following day was noteworthy, first for a visit to Blenheim, that "truly princely habitation" as Whately calls it, and then to Oxford, concerning which Jefferson makes no comment except to note that he paid the "doorkeepers of colleges" five shillings. "The prodigious pile of building" that constitutes the famous castle at Blenheim interested Jefferson less than the gardens. Whately in hand, as usual, he traversed them and jotted down a few practical observations, such as the number of acres in garden, water, and park, the number of people employed to keep it in order—an impressive two hundred.

"The water here," he writes, "is very beautiful, and very grand. The cascade from the lake, a fine one; except this the garden has no great beauties. It is not laid out in fine lawns and woods, but the trees are scattered thinly over the ground, and every here and there small thickets of shrubs, in oval raised beds, cultivated, and flowers among the shrubs"—an idea that was subsequently to be incorporated at Monticello. "The gravelled walks are broad," he concludes, "art appears too much." [97]

Mrs. Adams, who visited Blenheim the next year, was more appreciative and, with one or two exceptions, gives an excellent picture of the palace as it still exists today. "The castle is upon the grandest scale of anything I have yet seen," she writes. "We enter the park through a spacious and elegant portal, of the Corinthian order, from whence a noble prospect is opened to the palace, the bridge [a Palladian bridge was a feature of many of the great gardens], the lake, with its valley, and other beautiful scenes. The front of this noble edifice, which is of stone, is 348 feet from wing to wing." Declaring it would take a week to view the palace and a volume to describe it, she devotes two pages to the mansion before taking up the gardens. "Here I am lost," she says, "not in confusion, but amidst scenes of grandeur, magnificence and beauty. They are spacious and include a great variety of ground. The plain, or as artists term it, the lawn, before the palace . . . is as smooth as the surface of a looking glass. . . . From this lawn is a gradual descent to the water, and you pass through spacious gravel walks, not in straight lines . . . but pleasing intricacies intervene. Through the winding paths, and every step, open new objects of beauty which diversified nature affords of hill, valley, water, and woods. The gardens finally are lost in the park, amidst a profusion of venerable oaks. . . . The gardens are four miles round, which I walked, and the park is eleven. There is a magnificent bridge consisting of three arches; the water it covers is formed into a spacious lake." The gardens had lately been improved, she adds, "by the addition of some well-placed ornaments, particularly the temple of Diana and a noble cascade, round which are four river gods." [98] She concludes her remarks with a description of the famous column erected by Sarah, Duchess of Marborough, to her husband.

There were only two more stops before London, Enfield Chase, built by Lord Chatham, where Jefferson particularly admired the water, and Moor Park, that superb Palladian mansion in Hertfordshire, designed by the Venetian architect Leoni, a protégé of Lord Burlington. The house represented almost everything Jefferson most admired and he was moved to remark, "The building superb." The gardens, some thirty acres to the southeast, had been laid out by the well-known landscape gardener Brown in a lawn with a broad walk from the house that led to rising terraces, thence to a pool with an Ionic garden temple dedicated to "The Winds." Nevertheless, Jefferson felt the place "wants water." There is unfortunately no trace left of Enfield Chase. It has been absorbed in greater London.

The tenth of April found Jefferson back at his lodgings in Golden Square. His taste for sight-seeing had been whetted, however, and he made one or two short excursions to nearby points of interest. One was to the famed Tower of London, an ancient fortress, another to Kew, at that time a little village in Surrey on the Thames about six miles from Hyde Park Corner. "Here the late Mr. Molyneux, Secretary to his present Majesty, when Prince of Wales, had a very fine seat on the Green, the gardens of which are said to produce the best fruit in England," [99] our guide book tells us. The gardens established by this gentleman and the previous owner, Lord Capel, had been greatly increased and improved after they came into the possession of the royal family. Sir William Chambers, an authority on Oriental gardening, was engaged to transform the existing grounds into the so-called picturesque style. The result was the sort of thing Jefferson had envisioned years ago for his own Monticello, a pagoda of eight stories in the Chinese style, a mosque, a Moorish building called the Alhambra, a Roman ruin, and a row of Greek temples. However, what really intrigued Jefferson this time was a screw for raising water, designed on the principle established by Archimedes and of which Jefferson made a drawing.

Buckingham House, the residence of the Queen, likewise drew Jefferson to see it. This mansion had been erected in 1721 and was purchased by George III from the Duke of Buckingham. The house, situated at the west end of St. James Park, had little resemblance to the Buckingham Palace of today, which it was to become. It was built of brick with stone pilasters, and on each side of the building were colonnades with Ionic columns, crowned with a balustrade and vases. The colonnades connected with the offices, each of which was surmounted by a small turret supporting a weathercock. The general effect was that of a simplicity not unlike certain early buildings in the American colonies, except for the court toward the front, which was enclosed with iron rails. Behind the house, the parterres of former times had been replaced by spacious gardens in the new manner.

On the twentieth of April, in the height of the luscious English spring, Jefferson joined the Adams family in a pilgrimage to Osterley Park and Syon House in Middlesex, those two great monuments to the genius of the brothers Adam. It was not to see the gardens that they went, for they were relatively undistinguished, but the interior of the mansions themselves. At the time of Jefferson's visit they represented the last word in fashion and elegance in the internal decoration and furniture. Behind the square mass of battlements, walks, and towers of Syon House, whose history dates from the early fifteenth century, was concealed a great suite of state apartments containing some of the earliest of Adam's delicate stucco work in the antique taste he had made his own. Osterley Park, which had been rebuilt for the banker Child from 1761 onward, was similar in character. Although the opulence of these establishments far exceeded Jefferson's dreams, a faint echo of what he had there seen for the first time was to be realized, many years later, in the ornaments of the mantels, the frieze in the hall, and the curtain cornices at Monticello.

No one has given a better description of the magnificence of Osterley than Horace Walpole in writing his friend the Countess of Upper Ossory. "On Friday we went to see—oh the palace of palaces—and yet a palace sans crown, sans coronet, but such expense! such taste! such profusion! . . . The old house I have often seen . . . but it is so improved and enriched, that all the Percies and Seymours of Sion must die of envy. There is a double portico that fills the space between the towers in front, and is as noble as the Propyleum at Athens. There is a hall, library, breakfast room, eating room, all chefs d'oeuvre of Adam, a gallery 130 feet long and a drawing room worthy of Eve before the Fall. Mrs. Child's dressing room is full of pictures, gold filigree, china and from afar so is all the house. . . . There are Salvators, Gaspar Poussins, and to a beautiful staircase, a ceiling by Rubens. . . . Then, in the drawing room I mentioned, there are doorcases, and a crimson and gold frieze, that I believe was borrowed from the Palace of the Sun."[100]

Jefferson does not mention Osterley or Syon in his memorandum on English Gardens or in his letters. It is only from his account book that we learn he "gave servants at Osterly and Sion house 7/." John Adams was more voluble. After briefly describing the exterior appearance of Osterley, finding the lovely semicircular conservatory curious, and commenting on the hothouse with its "blowing-roses, ripe strawberries, cherries, plums, etc." (Child is reputed to have spent £1,400 a year on his kitchen gardens) he finds the pleasure grounds disappointing. They "were only an undulating gravel walk, between two borders of trees and shrubs; all the evergreens, trees, and shrubs were here.... The verdure is charming; the music of the birds pleasant; but the ground is too level."

"This farm," he continues, "is watered by a rivulet drawn by an artificial canal of the Thames. A repetition of winding walks, gloomy evergreens, sheets of water, clumps of trees, green-houses, hot-houses, etc." The celebrated "lacework gateway" facing the Great West Road, which aroused so much controversy in its time and which Walpole considered "most improper to be exposed in the high road to Brentford," was the one object that pleased Adams. He considered it "a beautiful thing, and lays open to the view of the traveller a very beautiful green lawn, interspersed with clumps and scattered trees." Summing up his impression of the great country seats he had seen, he concludes in his forthright New England manner, "The beauty, convenience and utility of these country seats are not enjoyed by their owners. They are mere ostentation of vanity; races, cocking, gambling, draw away their attention." [101]

Less than a week after this excursion Jefferson was taking leave of London, which he was never again to see. The long-drawn-out conferences with the Portuguese Ambassador had finally come to an end. The impossibility of accomplishing anything with the British was obvious to all. Jefferson's commission was to expire momentarily. He was free to depart. His last days were filled with countless errands such as last days always are. With perfect punctiliousness, he sent a note to the Minister of Foreign Affairs informing him that he had "the honor of presenting his respects to the right honourable, the Marquis of Carmarthen; he had that of calling at his house to take leave on his departure for Paris; from which place the arrangements he had taken do not permit his longer absence. He shall be happy if he can be useful to his Lordship in being the bearer of his commands for that capital." [102] He answered that he had none, as Jefferson says in the autobiography, "and wishing me a pleasant journey, I left London the 26th." John Paradise, whom Jefferson found a stimulating companion and who shared his interest in scientific matters, traveled with him as far as Greenwich. Together they inspected the famous observatory and the even more famous naval hospital, once a royal palace, given by King William III for the use of disabled seamen and "for the widows and children of such as were slain in fighting at sea against the enemies of their country." [103] Surprisingly enough, he makes no mention of that magnificent monument, the Queen's House, the first Palladian masterpiece of Inigo Jones.

Continuing through the fertile Kent countryside, Jefferson passed through the ancient towns of Rochester and Canterbury to Dover, where he arrived shortly before midnight, as he wrote Paradise. The weather was bad with unfavorable winds, and he was detained for a day and a half. Meanwhile, as we learn from his account book, he took occasion to visit the famous Dover Castle, originally built by the Romans and subsequently enlarged and strengthened by the Saxons and Normans, which rises on a height to the east of the town. From this height, as had Adams before him, Jefferson viewed "the whole channel, the whole town and harbor of Dover. The harbor is but a basin, and the town but a village.... It has not the appearance of a place of any business at all. No manufacture, no commerce, no fishery of any consequence here... The channel between this and Calais is full of vessels, French and English, fishing for herrings." [104]

At length, on the twenty-eighth, Jefferson tells us he had "an excellent passage of three hours only" to Calais. He notes that he "gave the successor of Sterne's monk at Calais, 1 f, 4" and paid the famous rascal, Dessein, the innkeeper, 14 fr., 10 for entertainment. Then he and Petit were off for Paris, through St. Ouen, Roye, and Bourget, "through one of the most lovely countries imaginable" in the blossoming of late spring. Pegasus must have loaned him wings, for within forty-eight hours of leaving Calais he was miraculously back in Paris.

To what extent Jefferson's visit to England and his contact with the British on their own soil affected his opinion of his former countrymen is a question that naturally arises. The answer is, not at all. His experiences with the Duke of Dorset, the Marquis of Carmarthen, and with

George III could not have altered his position. He could still speak of the British with the same contempt as "our natural enemies, and as the only nation on earth who wish us ill from the bottom of their souls. And I am satisfied that were our continent to be swallowed up by the ocean, Great Britain would be in a bonfire from one end to the other." [105] When France appointed the Comte de Moustier French minister to the United States, Jefferson took occasion to write him that he would "find the affections of Americans with France, but their habits with England. Chained to that country by circumstances, embracing what they loathe, they realize the fable of the living and the dead bound together." [106]

A few days after his return to Paris, Jefferson sat down to write his impression of England to his old friend John Page, with whom he had once hoped to visit it. "I traversed that country much," he writes, "and both town and country fell short of my expectations. Comparing it with this, I found a much greater proportion of barrens, a soil, in other parts, not naturally so good as this, not better cultivated, but better manured, and, therefore, more productive.... The laboring people here are poorer than in England. They pay about one half their produce in rent, the English, in general, about a third." London he did not find "so handsome as Philadelphia." English architecture he considered "in the most wretched style I ever saw, not meaning to except America, where it is bad, or even Virginia, where it is worse than in any other part of America which I have seen." [107]

It was for Madame de Corny, however, that most understanding of friends, who was a light in the circle in which Jefferson and Lafayette moved, that he summed up his estimate of the character of the two European countries with which he was so far acquainted. "And how do you like England, Madame?" he inquired on the occasion of her first visit there. "I know your taste for the works of art gives you a little disposition to Anglo-mania. Their mechanics certainly exceed all others in some lines. But be just to your own nation. They have not patience, it is true, to set rubbing a piece of steel from morning till night, as a lethargic Englishman will do full charged with porter. But do not their benevolence, their cheerfulness, their amiability, when compared with the glowering temper and manners of the people among whom you are, compensate their want of patience? I am in hopes that when the splendor of their shops, which is all that is worth looking at in London, shall have lost their charm of novelty, you will turn a wistful eye to the people of Paris, and find that you cannot be so happy with any others." [108]

To these sentiments Jefferson said a fervent amen.

VIII. A Last Romance

THE YEAR 1786 brought Jefferson one of the most momentous experiences of his life. It was something that, at the secure age of forty-three, he had no reason to expect.

The summer of that year was brightened for him by the arrival in Paris of John Trumbull. He was a young man of thirty, a friend and fellow New Englander of John Adams, who had seen distinguished service in the revolutionary war. In 1784 he had come to London to study under Benjamin West, the well-known artist. Jefferson had met Trumbull during his visit to London and, as the latter says, "kindly invited me to come to Paris, to see and study the fine works there, and to make his house my home, during my stay." [1] This he proceeded to do. He arrived in August with a letter from Mrs. Adams which she "would not refuse him" as it gave her "an opportunity of paying my respects to a gentleman for whom I entertain the highest esteem and whose portrait dignifies a part of my room." [2] Shortly after Jefferson wrote David Humphreys, "Your friend, Mr. Trumbull, is here at present. He brought his 'Bunker's Hill' and 'Death of Montgomery,' to have them engraved here. He was yesterday to see the King's collection of paintings at Versailles, and confesses it surpasses everything of which he ever had even an idea. I persuaded him to stay and study here, and then proceed to Rome." [3]

Trumbull soon made an acquaintance of the leading French artists, "David in particular," he writes, "became and continued my very warm and affectionate friend." [4] David, with whom Jefferson, the art lover, was so much in harmony that he was led to confess, "I do not feel an interest in any pencil but that of David." [5] There was also Houdon, with whom Jefferson had long been in touch, as we have seen, and who had recently acquired a pretty young wife. Other members of the group were Belisard, *architecte du roi*; two talented amateurs, the Marquis Trotti, the Marquis de Vaudreuil; Madame Le Brun, the celebrated portrait painter, and Monsieur d'Hancarville, a friend of the arts who had published a series of works on Etruscan, Greek, and Roman antiquities. "At the same time," writes Trumbull, "Mr. and Mrs. Cosway of London were in Paris. He (then the admired miniature painter of the day), had been invited by the Duke of Orleans to paint the duchess and her children. I became acquainted and intimate with them," [6] as is usual with residents of a city who meet on foreign soil. It was thus through his protégé that Jefferson came to know this celebrated couple, and thus that he became a member of this happy company of artists and amateurs whose delight it was to explore the treasures of Paris.

Richard Cosway was a man of Jefferson's age. In 1781 he had married Maria Hadfield, a girl of twenty-two. She had been born in Florence of English parents who kept a large boardinghouse there much frequented by tourists from their native country. When four years old the child had been placed in a convent and, as she says, "I was immediately put to learn music.... At eight years I began drawing, having seen a young lady draw. I took a passion for it more than I had for music." [7] Her studies were continued in Florence and in Rome until interrupted by the death of her father, about 1779. Mrs. Hadfield then determined to return to England with her family, and Maria, as she tells us, "had letters from Lady Rivers for all the first people of fashion: Sir Joshua Reynolds, Cipriani, Bartolozzi, Angelica Kauffmann." [8] The latter now became the sponsor of the beautiful and talented Maria in the world of art as well as that of society. Within two years she was married to Richard Cosway, the most popular miniature painter of his day, when the miniature was one of the most prized forms of art. Personally he appears to have been an eccentric dandy, a funny little man who, his contemporaries claimed, had an uncanny resemblance to an ape—but he knew how to please his public. By the time of his marriage he had made a fortune, and for some years thereafter he and his wife lived in the utmost luxury and extravagance. Their popularity knew no bounds, and they entertained at their house on Pall Mall in a princely manner. Georgiana, the beautiful duchess of

Devonshire, was an intimate, and the Prince of Wales is said to have paid more than passing attention to the lovely Mrs. Cosway.

There is no evidence that Jefferson met the Cosways in London, as some have claimed. Their social orbit was not the one in which he moved. Trumbull states definitely that the meeting took place in Paris. In speaking of those late summer days of 1786 he says, "I distinctly recollect, however, that this time was occupied with the same industry in examining and reviewing whatever related to the arts, and that Mr. Jefferson joined our party almost daily. And here commenced his acquaintance with Mrs. Cosway, of whom very respectful mention is made in his published correspondence." [9]

Jefferson seems to have been swept completely off his feet by the beautiful Maria. He speaks of her "modesty, beauty, and that softness of disposition which is the ornament of her sex and charm of ours." [10] Her contemporaries described her as being "a golden-haired, languishing Anglo-Italian, graceful to affectation, and highly accomplished, especially in music." [11] Her various portraits attest to the deep blue of her eyes, her fair skin, to an imperiousness and a dainty voluptuousness that could not but be beguiling. From these sources, as well as from her letters, we see that she was the essence of femininity. An occasional saucy pout, the soft trace of a foreign accent—English was not her native language, and she wrote it with some difficulty—were completely devastating to her admirers. And Jefferson was no exception.

During the month of August Jefferson was regularly a member of these excursions to various points of interest. Thus on the fifth the party went to Suresnes near St. Cloud, at that time a charming village, to see a local celebration—the crowning of the *rosière*. "Every year the most amiable, industrious, and virtuous poor girl of the parish is elected, who is received by all the village, and a crowd of strangers in the church, with great solemnity," Trumbull tells us. "The rosière of the year, with the preceding candidate, is arranged on the right of the bishop—their parents and friends with them. The crown of flowers is placed by a little girl, daughter of the seigneur of the parish, with the *benedicte* of the bishop, and accompanied by music. The rosière is then conducted home, attended by the clergy, music and company, when she receives three hundred livres." [12]

After this picturesque ceremony the party "returned to Paris on foot, over the Pont de Neuilly, a very beautiful bridge over the Seine ... of seven arches which have a beautiful degree of lightness." [13] It was a favorite of Jefferson and his companions.

Another day, this "charming coterie," as Jefferson fondly called it in later years, masking its seriousness with a mantle of gaiety, "went with M. and Madame Houdon to the *Salon* on the Boulevards to see his little Diana in marble, a very beautiful figure ... a dignity worthy the chastity and virtues of the goddess." [14] They visited the studios of lesser sculptors, Pajou and Girardon. They went to Versailles, to the Louvre, the Palais Royal, the Bibliothèque du Roi, the Luxembourg, the "new church of St. Geneviève," now known as the Pantheon, and numerous other public buildings and private collections. There was hardly a day without its tour, without breakfasting or dining together. What this informal association with artists, this opportunity of looking at works of art through the eyes of professionals, meant to Jefferson, we can only surmise.

Perhaps the day that stood out most in Jefferson's mind, and which he immortalized in his *Dialogue of the Head and Heart,* is the one on which he took this congenial and merry company to see the famous Halle aux Blés. This building, circular in form and noble in proportions, had been recently executed. The most remarkable feature about it was the dome newly added by Legrand and Molinos. This vault, the largest in France, was 120 feet in diameter and rose 100 feet. It was built on wooden ribs, permitting radiating, glazed openings of almost the entire length to flood the interior with light—a scheme that Jefferson was later to adopt in the Capitol at Washington. Jefferson, as he says, doubtless with slight exaggeration, considered it "the most superb thing on earth," worth all he had yet seen in Paris. The problem of such a dome was one that had long challenged him and now, occupied as he was with the public buildings for the new capital of Virginia, it had a particular significance. "My visit to Legrand and Molinos," his head excuses itself to his heart, "had public utility for its object. A market is to be built in Richmond. What

MARIA COSWAY. Miniature by Richard Cosway. (*Courtesy of the Henry E. Huntington Art Gallery*)

RUGGIERI'S VAUXHALL. From a contemporary drawing. (*Courtesy of the Musée Carnavalet*)

a commodious plan is that of Legrand and Molinos, especially if we put on it the noble dome of the Halle aux Blés." [15] This grand scheme was, alas, never to be executed.

Entranced with each other's society, intoxicated by artistic fervor, the company found it impossible to part. Although, as Jefferson tells us, every soul had an engagement for the day, "lying messengers were to be despatched into every quarter of the city with apologies for your breach of engagements." He himself "had the effrontery to send word to the Duchesse d'Anville, that on the moment we were setting out to dine with her, despatches came to hand, which required immediate attention." [16] Instead, the party dined together, then drove to the lovely park of St. Cloud, with its deep-shaded allées and its joyous cascades tumbling from marble fountains toward the Seine. They stopped to see the famous gallery of the palace, with murals by Mignard, the piers decorated with pictures of the royal châteaux, the ceiling and walls adorned with mythological scenes. Back in Paris, they went to the rue St. Lazare to see the *Spectacle Pyrrhique des Sieurs Ruggieri.* This was a sort of Vauxhall or pleasure garden kept by two Italians, known for its beautiful illumination and for the brilliant display of fireworks. But even this glimpse of fairyland failed to satisfy their romantic cravings. This deliriously happy day was brought to a close by listening to the sadly sweet music of Julie Krumpfholz, the renowned harpist. Truly, as Jefferson remarked in retrospect, "if the day had been as long as a Lapland summer day, you would still have contrived means among you to fill it." [17]

On the ninth of September Trumbull left Paris for Germany, his "brain half turned by the attention which had been paid to my paintings in Paris, and by the multitude of fine things which I had seen." [18] The artistic pilgrimages came to an end. For some time, however, they had been superseded for Jefferson by others more intimate in character. Every few days his phaeton would stop before Mrs. Cosway's door in the rue Coqhéron, not far from the Halle aux Blés, and his former residence in the cul-de-sac Taitbout, and as he says, they would "hie away to the Bois de Boulogne, St. Cloud, Marly, St. Germain, etc." [19] There was no spot in that lovely country along the Seine, no monument in that royal playground they failed to visit. "Every moment," Jefferson writes, "was filled with something agreeable. The wheels of time moved on with a rapidity, of which those of our carriage gave but a faint idea. And yet, in the evening, when one took a retrospect of the day, what a mass of happiness had we travelled over." [20] That, like a youth of twenty, he was tampering with the proverbial fire he well knew, but he was deaf to all warnings. "Thou art the most incorrigible of all the beings that ever sinned!" his reason cried out. "I reminded you of the follies of the first day, intending to deduce from thence some useful lessons for you; but instead of listening to them, you kindle at the recollection, you retrace the whole series with a fondness which shows you want nothing, but the opportunity, to act it all over again. I often told you, during its course, that you were imprudently engaging your affections under circumstances that must have cost you a great deal of pain... that you rack our whole system when you are parted from those you love, complaining that such a separation is worse than death, inasmuch as this ends our sufferings, whereas that only begins them." [21] But Jefferson did not listen.

The high point of this romantic vagabonding, if so it may be called, occurred during the first two weeks of September, before a pitiless fate stepped in and caused an accident that was to cripple Jefferson for weeks and months to come. Trumbull, who had unconsciously been the leader, was leaving. Cosway seems to have been busy with his miniatures. It was no longer a question of parties. Jefferson and his "vastly pleasant" companion, as Gouverneur Morris called her, now made the excursions together. On the fifth they started off as usual through the Bois, stopping first at Bagatelle, that elegant little casino built by the Comte d'Artois, brother of the King, on a wager with the Queen that it could not be accomplished in sixty days. The gardens, in the *genre pittoresque*, were such as would have completely captivated Jefferson. A little further on, he and his companion halted at Madrid, a curious château built by Francis I after his return from imprisonment in Spain. A semicircle of huge trees formed a royal esplanade before the building. Its most striking feature and one that attracted many visitors was the decoration of varnished terra cotta, which sparkled in the sunlight in a truly dazzling manner. From the castle there was a superb view of the Seine and surrounding country, with the much admired Pont de Neuilly on one hand, on the other, the heights of Mont Valérien where Jefferson was soon to have his retreat.

Two days later a longer excursion was undertaken. As a lovesick youth might have done, Jefferson led his beloved—for surely she reigned as such in his heart—on a pilgrimage to his favorite haunts in the environs of Paris. It proved a day never to be forgotten. "Be a kind comforter," he subsequently adjured his head in the well-known *Dialogue*, "and paint to me the day we went to St. Germain. How beautiful was every object!" And he takes us with him over the Pont de Neuilly, along the wooded hills of the Seine to Marly, where he points out the rainbows created by the many wheels of the fabulous machine as they churned the water of the river in the sun. From there the road turned up the hills, as it does today, toward St. Germain-en-Laye, that noble eminence some three miles distant, which has seen so much of the history of France since the first fortress was built there in the twelfth century. The formidable château that adorned it in Jefferson's day as well as ours dates from the time of Francis I. The noble esplanade or terrace, which is the most notable feature of the site, with its unrivaled view of the Seine and distant Paris, was, however, built for Louis XIV by that greatest designer of gardens, André Le Nôtre.

There was another feature at St. Germain that may well have lured Jefferson and his companion. This was "a very curious gardin", as Thomas Blaikie, the Scotch gardener who visited it in 1784, tells us. It belonged to the "Marichal de Noel [Noailles]" and was "laid out in what they call the English way, which is rather a confusion of walks and crooked turnings. Some little mountains, or rather molehills; but what is most curious is the variety of exotic plants and many of them very old and strong. The only thing that was tolerably well made was a rock who formed a cascade which formed the beginning of the river. This water comes from the fountain of the town which is not always clean." [22]

From St. Germain the couple drove back to Marly, the retreat of Louis XIV, described in Jefferson's guide book as a château "the most beautifully situated and the most pleasant in all France." [23] This palace, which consisted of a large, isolated pavilion of the utmost elegance, with six small pavilions on each side leading up to it, was later not to be without influence on Jefferson's design for the University of Virginia.

Blaikie likewise undertakes to describe this secluded, yet dazzling retreat. Every feature, every virtue was foreign to him, yet his comments, unsophisticated as they are, give us an idea of how such a complex of buildings and gardens must have struck the untutored eye. "This is one of the King's palais's," he writes, "and stands in a bottom hid on every side, the grounds are all laid out in that regular style, cut in lines; statues of all the gods and demigods that have ever existed in the imagination; there is some of them exceedingly fine. There are two groups of men and horses stands upon the top of a basin by the roadside which is esteemed a chef-d'oeuvre; to the right of this, upon the top of the hill, stands the reservoir of the Machine de Marly which is an astonishing building and furnishes the water for the gardens at Versailles." [24] Madame Le Brun, the well-known artist, has given us a more sympathetic picture of this dazzling scene. "We went to Marly-le-Roi, and there I found a more beautiful spot than any I had seen in my life. On each side of the magnificent palace were six summer houses communicating with one another by walks embowered with jessamine and honeysuckle. Water fell in cascades from the top of a hill behind the castle, and formed a large channel on which a number of swans floated. The handsome trees and carpets of green, the flowers, the fountains, one of which spouted up so high that it was lost from sight—it was all grand, all regal; it all spoke of Louis XIV. One morning I met Queen Marie Antoinette walking in the park with several of the ladies of her court. They were all in white dresses, and so young and pretty that for a moment I thought I was in a dream. I was with my mother and was turning away when the Queen was kind enough to stop me, and invited me to continue in any direction I might prefer." [25]

After a tour of these magnificent gardens, Jefferson and Mrs. Cosway repaired to a nearby inn—the tiny village still boasts of a Trois-Couronnes—where Petit had had supper laid out for them. There was one more stop before returning to Paris—at Louveciennes, the charming casino built in 1772 by Louis XV for Madame du Barry. It is situated nearly opposite Marly. Here again it was the gardens that Jefferson took his enchantress to see. They were among the earliest of the so-called *jardins anglais* in France. The two circular colonnaded garden temples, along the lines of those at Stowe and Kew, were a great novelty at the time. Indeed, they were the first of the sort to be built on the Continent.

On the sixteenth of September Jefferson and Mrs. Cosway set out on an excursion neither of them was ever to forget. It was to the *Désert de Retz*, a garden in the *style anglo-chinois*, situated about four miles from St. Germain. It had recently been created by Monsieur de Monville, a wealthy engineer, and he had quite outdone the professional gardeners. Contemporary guide books speak of it with the greatest admiration, and plates showing the various unusual features appear in all the important books on gardening. Here indeed was brought to life everything Jefferson had dreamed of for his own garden, and more than his fancy ever beheld. Even now in its sad decay we still sense its ancient grandeur.

At the entrance was a sort of grotto, on the order of the one still in existence near Les Cascades, a café in the Bois on the way to Longchamps. The outstanding feature of the place, however, is the ruined column (it was built as such) sixty-five feet in diameter, in which are situated the living quarters. There are four floors, with four rooms on each, connected by a spiral staircase in a circular stair hall, which rises the height of the four stories. The windows, now taken over by wild vines and most of the glass shattered, were placed in the flutes of the column. The interior detail, of which much still remains, was in the delicate style of Louis XVI. Small wonder Jefferson exclaimed, in recalling the scene to Mrs. Cosway, "How grand the idea excited by the remains of such a column!" [26] And that a contemporary remarked *"On c'est extasié sur un pareil tour de force, on regarde cette idée comme neuve et hardie."* [27]

The gardens contained no less than twenty-six buildings such as a ruined Gothic church, a Chinese *orangerie*, a *temple de répose*, an *isle de bonheur*, a *laiterie*, an *obelisque*, some of which still remain. The lovely *temple au dieu Pan* collapsed only recently under the shelling of St. Cyr, the French Military Academy not far distant, and the enchanting *maison chinoise*, with its unbelievably delicate tracery, knew the last of its glory when American soldiers decided to use the funny old shack as a target for pistol practice. Only the *glacière*, in the form of a pyramid, still remains, stolid, defiant, and untouched.

On the eighteenth of September Jefferson met with an accident that put an end to his romantic wanderings. A letter from Franklin's friend Le Veillard, written to Temple Franklin on September 20, tells us that "the day before yesterday Mr. Jefferson dislocated his right wrist in trying to leap over a large kettle in the small court yard. His wrist has been set, but he is suffering greatly, and I do not see how he can write before a month." [28] We are not told where the accident occurred, but it is reasonable to suppose that the *petit cour* mentioned was in his own establishment. The nearest Jefferson ever came to describing his misfortune was in a letter to William Stephens Smith to whom he wrote a month or more later: "How the right hand became disabled would be a long story for the left to tell. It was by one of those follies from which good cannot come, but ill may." [29] Two surgeons were sent for but their attempts to set the injured wrist were unsuccessful, to say the least. Twenty subsequent visits brought no relief.

Word of the accident reached Mrs. Cosway. She did not fly to her friend. She did not send a servant to inquire. At length she sent a fluttery little note with too many excuses. In this first letter to her admirer she reveals herself for what she essentially was, a spoiled, egocentric young woman, with a very limited emotional capacity. "You don't always judge by appearances," she writes, "or it would be much to my disadvantage this day, without deserving it. . . . I meant to have seen you twice, and I have appeared a monster for not having sent to know how you were the whole day. I have been more uneasy than I can express. This morning my husband killed my project I had proposed to him by burying himself among pictures and forgetting the hours. Though we were near your house, coming to see you, we were obliged to come back, the time being much past that we were to be at St. Cloud, to dine with the Duchess of Kingston. Nothing was to hinder us from coming in the evening, but alas! my good intentions proved only a disturbance to your neighbors, and just late enough to break the rest of all your servants, and perhaps yourself. . . . We will come to see you tomorrow morning, if nothing happens to prevent it." Then, feeling, very likely, that a little cajoling would be in order, she adds, "Oh, I wish you were well enough to come to us tomorrow for dinner, and stay the evening. I won't tell you what I shall have. . . . I would serve you and help you at dinner, and divert your pain after with good music." [30] It is perhaps just as well that Jefferson was unable to accept this invitation, for Gouverneur Morris later remarks of a similar occasion at Mrs. Cosway's London house, "We dine *en italien*. The soup and ragouts are mixed with cheese, and that none of the newest." [31]

With the accident, this late summer idyl drew to a close. Jefferson was house bound and the Cosways were to leave Paris any day. One last excursion together seems to have been attempted, despite all, as the following letters indicate. On the Thursday after his misfortune—it occurred on a Monday [32]—Jefferson wrote the first of the many letters he was to write Mrs. Cosway. It is in the trembling script of his left hand, which he was already training himself to use. "I have passed the night in so much pain," he says, "that I have not closed my eyes. It is with infinite regret, therefore, that I must relinquish your charming company for that of the surgeon whom I have sent for to examine into the cause of this change. I am in hopes it is only the having rattled a little too freely over the pavement yesterday. If you do not go today, I shall still have the pleasure of seeing you again. If you do go, God bless you wherever you go. . . . Addio. Addio. Let me know if you do not go today." [33]

Apparently in reply to this, Mrs. Cosway sent another letter to her friend, accusing herself of having caused him more suffering, "I am very sorry indeed and blame myself for having been the cause of your pains in the wrist. Why would you go, and why was I not more friendly to you, and less so to myself by preventing your giving me the pleasure of your company? You repeatedly said it would do you no harm. I felt interested and did not resist. We shall go, I believe, this morning. Nothing seems ready, but Mr. Cosway seems more disposed than I have seen him all this time. I shall write you from England; it is impossible to be wanting to a person who has been so excessively obliging. I don't attempt to make compliments—there can be none for you," and she asks him to send her a line to Antwerp with news of his wrist.[34]

It was the fifth of October before the Cosways were finally ready to leave Paris. Jefferson hired a cabriolet and, taking along Monsieur d'Hancarville, accompanied his friends through the noble Porte St. Denis, along the broad, tree-lined avenue leading out of Paris, as far as the village of that name. There, in the shadow of the abbey that houses the mortal remains of most of the kings of France, the friends shared a last meal at the Pavilion St. Denis. Then, in Jefferson's words, "having performed the last sad office of handing you into your carriage . . . and seen the wheels get actually into motion, I turned on my heel and walked, more dead than alive, to the opposite door where my own was waiting. . . . We were crammed into the carriage like recruits for the Bastille, and, not having soul enough to give orders to the coachman, he presumed Paris our destination, and drove off." [35]

Seated at his fireside, solitary and sad as he says, Jefferson proceeded to write one of the most amazing love letters ever penned, the famous *Dialogue of the Head and Heart.* He calls it a sermon, and in many ways it is one. He makes no attempt to conceal his misery in this "history of the evening I parted from you." No Werther ever expressed himself with more romantic fervor. "I am indeed the most wretched of all earthly beings," he cries. "Overwhelmed with grief, every fibre of my frame distended beyond its natural powers to bear, I would willingly meet whatever catastrophe should leave me no more to feel, or to fear. . . . I am rent into fragments by the force of my grief. If you have any balm," he adjures his head, "pour it into my wounds; if none, do not harrow them by new torments. Spare me this awful moment!"

"Harsh, therefore, as the medicine may be," his head reminds him, "it is my office to administer it. You will be pleased to remember that, when our friend Trumbull used to be telling us of the merits and talents of these good people, I never ceased whispering to you that we had no occasion for new acquaintances; that the greater their merits and talents, the more dangerous their friendship to our tranquillity, because the regret at parting would be greater."

THE COLUMN AT THE DÉSERT DE RETZ. Photograph by Lionel Friedman. (*Courtesy of Howard C. Rice, Jr.*)

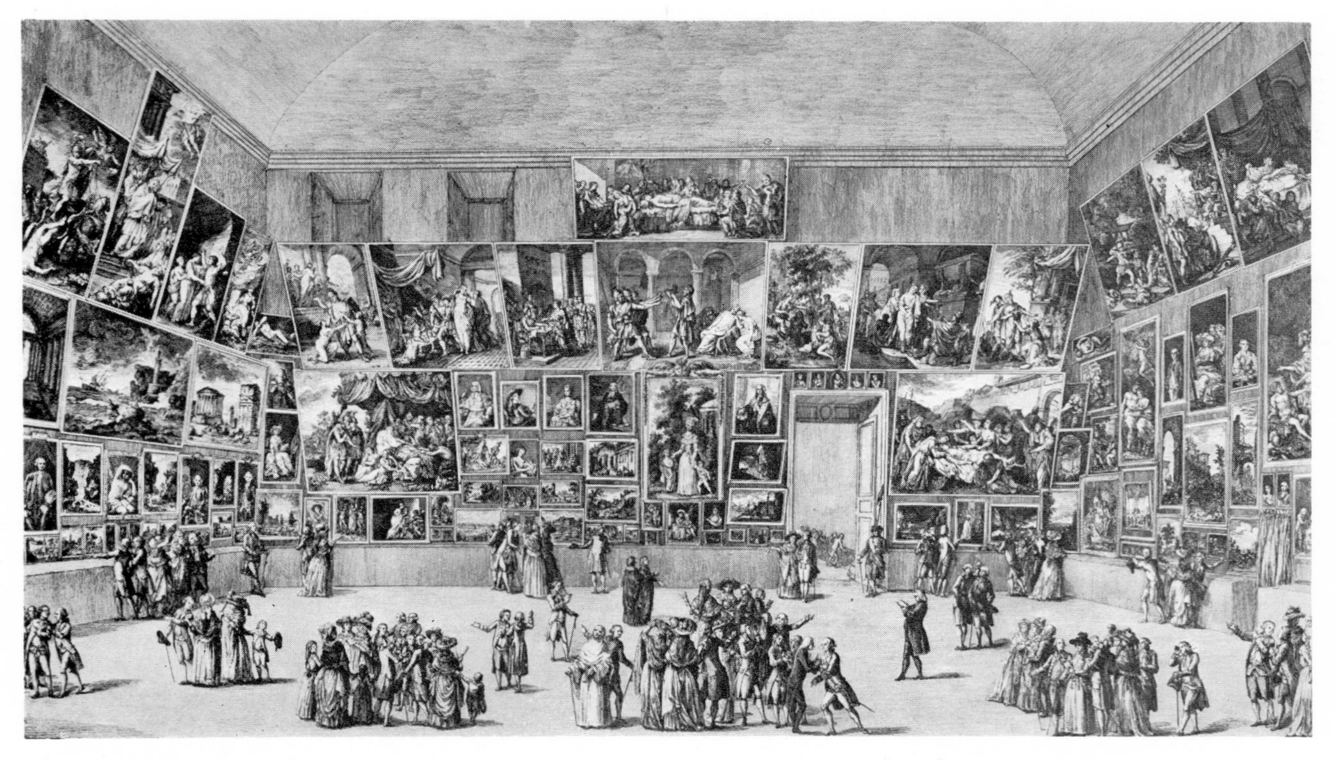

THE SALON OF 1785. From the engraving by Bornet. (*Courtesy of the Metropolitan Museum of Art*)

The head continues to counsel the heart at length, pouring out the wisdom accumulated during his forty-three years by the man who said of himself, "Deeply practiced in the school of affliction, the human heart knows no joy which I have not lost, no sorrow of which I have not drunk! Fortune can present no grief of unknown form to me!"

Persistently the head continues, "I wish to make you sensible how imprudent it is to place your affections, without reserve, on objects you must so soon lose, and whose loss, when it comes, must cost you such severe pangs.... Do not bite at the bait of pleasure till you know there is no hook beneath it. The art of life is the art of avoiding pain. ... The most effectual means of being secure against pain, is to retire within ourselves, and to suffice for our own happiness. Those which depend on ourselves are the only pleasures a wise man will count on; for nothing is ours which another may deprive us of. Hence the inestimable value of intellectual pleasures. Ever in our power, always leading us to something new, never cloying, we ride serene and sublime above the concerns of this mortal world." And this was how, after the death of his wife, Jefferson had arranged his life until he met Maria Cosway.

The heart, however, was to have the last word in this dialogue. "You confess," it observes, "that in the present case I could not have made a worthier choice [of friends]. You only object, that I was to lose them so soon. We are not immortal ourselves, my friend; how can we expect our enjoyments to be so? We have no rose without its thorn, no pleasure without alloy. It is the law of our existence, and we must acquiesce. It is the condition annexed to all our pleasures not by us who receive, but by him who gives them. True, this condition is pressing cruelly on me at this moment. I feel more fit for death than life. But when I look back on the pleasures of which it is the consequence, I am conscious that they were worth the price I am paying."

The heart concludes on a note of hope, even though the head was ultimately to win. "Notwithstanding your endeavours, too, to damp my hopes," it continues, "I comfort myself with expectations of their promised return. Hope is sweeter than despair; and they were too good to mean to deceive me. 'In the summer,' said the gentleman; but 'in the spring,' said the lady; and I should love her forever, were it only for that!"

At this point Jefferson decided, as he says, "to rest the issue of the dialogue." He promises not to write so formidable a letter again and even agrees "to express but half my esteem for you, for fear of cloying you with too full a dose. But on your part," he begs Mrs. Cosway, "no curtailing. If your letters are as long as the Bible, they will appear short to me. Only let them be brimfull of affection, I shall read them with the dispositions with which Arlequin, in *Les deux billets*, spelt the words '*je t'aime*' and wished that the whole alphabet had entered into their composition." [36]

Before Jefferson had sent his letter, he received one from Antwerp in the hand he had been looking for. Again the lady fell short of his expectations. "I prepared myself for a feast," he writes. "I read two or three sentences, looked again at the signature to see if I had not mistaken it. It was visibly yours. Read a sentence or two more. Diable! Spelt your name distinctly. There was not a letter of it omitted. Began to read again. In fine, after reading a little and examining the signature alternately, half a dozen times, I found that your name was to four lines only, instead of four pages." He forgave her, however—how could he do otherwise?—and enclosed with this letter "the history of the evening I parted with you," along with a song he had promised her. "Bring me in return its subject," he pleads, "*Jours heureux!* Were I a songster I should sing it all to these words: *Dans ces lieux qu'elle tarde à se rendre!*" [37]

How eagerly Jefferson waited for Mrs. Cosway's response to his effusion, how he longed for something more than a miserable four lines, it is not difficult to imagine. She did reward him with a four-page letter, but to anyone not infatuated with her charm and beauty it seems singularly unsatisfactory—certainly no adequate response to what he had laid at her feet. Maria Cosway continued to be more interested in Maria Cosway than in anyone else. The letter begins with a few sentences in English, only a meager word or two of which can be deciphered, as the manuscript has been mutilated, but we learn that she is "ready to burst with all the variety of sentiments" that she is "sensible of my loss in separating from the friends I left, I have hardly time to indulge in a melancholy tribute, but my thoughts must be contrasted with the joy of meeting my friends in London, it is an excess which must tear to pieces the human mind when felt. You seem to be a master on this subject that whatever I may say will appear trifling, not well expressed, faintly represented, etc., but felt." She tells Jefferson that his "letter could employ me for some time, an hour to consider every word. To every sentence I could write a volume, but I wish that my selfishness was not reproaching me, for with difficulty do I find a line but, after having admired it, I recollect some part concerns me. Why do you say so many kind things? Why present so many opportunities for my feeling undeserving of them? Why not leave me a free consolation in admiring a friend?"

She then lapses into Italian. "But, foolish thing! Why write so much English when I could write my own language and make myself a little less confused. I did not know what I was doing; I shall have to rewrite it. But no! You would wish me to send the first sheet, the first lines I wrote on my arrival in London, let the consequences be what they may. Oh Heavens! If my letters were worthy of yours, how perfect they would be. I can only express my gratitude for your friendship."

After speaking at length of her trip, the weather, the gloominess of London, and the melancholy that so often assailed her, she asks Jefferson, "In the long winter evenings when you have an unoccupied moment, sacrifice it to me, to give me news of you. I long to receive a letter from your right hand. It must be very inconvenient to write with the left. . . . I shall never forget your kindness and attention to us. Sometime we shall talk of the tour for next year, whether in Paris or Italy. Many things could prevent me from carrying it out, but many more impossible things have come true." [38] With this ray of hope she sent her oddly childish letter on its way.

The correspondence which Jefferson so greatly desired was carried on with the utmost difficulty. "My letters, which pass through the post offices either of this country or of England being all opened," he writes Mrs. Cosway, "I send through that channel only such as are very indifferent in their nature. This is not the character, my dear Madam, of those I write to you. The breathings of pure affection would be profaned by a *commis* of the *poste.* I am obliged, then, to wait for private conveyances. . . . Could I write by the post, I should trouble you too often, for I am never happier than when I commit myself into dialogue with you, though but in imagination." [39]

Travelers between London and Paris were not too numerous, and letters entrusted to individuals were as likely to be forgotten or put in pockets in Jefferson's day as in ours. In her femininity, Maria Cosway seems to have overlooked this. When she wanted a letter, she expected it to be forthcoming. Excuses were not in order. Thus the letters she sent Jefferson during this fall were likely to contain that most fatal of all devices—reproaches. In November she writes, "I have written twice without receiving a letter from you after the first one which I found on my arrival here, and which promised me the pleasure of a more frequent correspondence. Every post-day I have waited with great concern, I fear that your arm may be worse, but even this would not prevent you from writing me. I take this occasion to send you two lines in order to ask you whether you have received my letters and beg you to send me news about you." [40]

And again, "What does this silence mean? I await the post with so much anxiety and when each time it arrives without bringing me a single letter from Paris, I am truly uneasy. I suppose you must be ill, and that your arm is worse. I think of a thousand things at once—aside from my friends having already forgotten me. If you are planning to make me another present of a long letter, I beg you to send me shorter ones but more frequent. I have no patience to wait longer, and have resolved to take up my pen without being sure if I should complain, if I should implore patience, or if I should express my mortification and anxiety at this disappointment." [41] She adds a postscript: "I receive at this moment two letters from Paris, but not from you."

Meanwhile Jefferson had not forgotten his absent friend. Six weeks after her departure he paid her homage by inscribing to her the first letter with his right hand. "But I write with pain, and it must be short," he says. "This is good news for you, for were the hand able to follow the effusions of the heart, that would cease to write only when this shall cease to beat." [42] Ten days later he sent another, trusting this one to the post office "disguising my seal and superscription." He was back on the topic that would leave him no peace. "Heaven has submitted our being to unkind laws," he writes. "When those charming moments were present which I passed with you, they were clouded with the prospect that I was soon to lose you, and now, when I pass the same moments in review, I recollect nothing but the agreeable passages, and they fill me with regret.... I am determined when you come next not to admit the idea that we are ever to part again. But are you to come again? I dread the answer to this question, and that my poor heart has been duped by the fondness of its wishes. What a triumph for the head! God bless you! Write to me often, write affectionately and freely, as I do to you. Say many kind things and say them without reserve. They will be the food for my soul." [43]

The letters of adoration continue, and those of a "Lady in a Passion," who finds her correspondent's long silence unpardonable and who proposes "only to say *nothing*, to send a blank sheet of paper" [44] regularly found their way across the channel. On Christmas Eve Jefferson sat down by his fire to spend an hour with his friend, as he had done on the day of her departure. "If I cannot be with you in reality," he writes, "I will be in imagination. But you say nothing of coming to Paris. Yet you were to come in the spring and here it is winter. It is time therefore you should be making your arrangements, packing your baggage, etc., unless you really mean to disappoint us. If you do, I am determined not to suppose I am never to see you again. I will believe you intend to go to America, to draw the Natural Bridge, the Peaks of Otter, etc., that I shall meet you there and visit with you all these grand scenes. I had rather be deceived, than live without hope. It is so sweet.... Think of me much and warmly. Place me in your breast with those who love you most, and comfort me with your letters. *Addio la mia cara ed amabile amica!*" [45]

Almost at the same time, on New Year's Day, Mrs. Cosway put on paper her version of a love letter, or at least what she must have thought would charm her distant friend. "I have waited with great eagerness and anxiety," she writes, "for the long letters which will explain to me my disgrace and tell me for what offence I must suffer the anguish of Tantalus. Each day I expect it, but it has never come. In your last letter of a century ago you tell me of having received *one* of my letters. I have written three in all. . . . But the loss is mine since it deprives me of those moments that you sacrifice to read my letters, those moments that recall me for an instant to your mind."

Her long and rambling letter complains of the severe London winter, of the melancholy aspect of the country, until she comes to the realization that Jefferson might like a word about herself. Even then what she had to say could hardly have been satisfying to an admirer. "I am surrounded by lovable people," she writes, "friends and all that is attractive. I spend most of the time in the house, and I may say that pleasures come to me since I do not go searching them elsewhere. All day I paint and exercise my fancy on such things as suggest themselves. Great is the pleasure of painting when one has the liberty of pursuing it only when desire is the inspiration. The evening, generally is passed in practicing music, and an amiable society makes the harmony perfect. Both unite to produce a truly happy time. But I have written all this when I began with the intention of setting down only two words to confess the truth—I want to hold myself to your example." [46] With this tribute, she brings her letter to a close.

The correspondence gradually fell off. On February 23 Jefferson wrote Trumbull, who was in London, "Tell Mrs. Cosway she is inconstant. She was to have been in Paris long ago, but she deceived us. The first evening that I find myself seated in a comfortable inn, solitary and pensive, I will invite her to sup, and will commit our conversation to writing. It will be a very scolding one on my part. In the meantime, lay all my affection at her feet." [47] No imaginary dialogue resulted this time, however.

Five days later Jefferson set off on a journey to the South of France and Northern Italy. It was not until he was back in Paris, and he found that she had not come as planned, that he wrote her again. It was a letter to make the heart soar, but Mrs. Cosway replied with "a scold." "You conclude from my long silence, Madame," he writes, "that I am gone to the other world. Nothing else would have prevented my writing to you so long. I have not thought of you the less, but I took a peep into Elysium. I entered it at one door and came out at another, having seen, as I passed, only Turin, Milan and Genoa. I calculated the hours it would have taken to carry me on to Rome, but they were exactly so many more than I had to spare. Was not this provoking? In thirty hours from Milan I could have been at the espousal of the Doge and the Adriatic, but I am born to lose everything I love.

"Why were you not with me?" he asks. "So many enchanting scenes which wanted only your pencil to consecrate them to fame.... But have your pallet and pencil ready," he adds, conjuring before the eyes the fairyland of the Col de Tende he so admired, "for you will be sure to stop in the passage, at the château de Saorgio. Imagine to yourself, Madame, a castle and village hanging to a cloud in front, on one hand a mountain cloven through to let pass a gurgling stream, on the other, a river, over which is thrown a magnificent bridge; the whole formed into a basin, its sides shagged with rocks, olive trees, vines, herds, etc. I insist on your painting it."

And again the question, when are you coming here? "If not at all, what did you ever come for? Only to make people miserable at losing you." Once more he cries, calling up scenes never to be forgotten, "Come then, my dear Madam, and we will breakfast every day *à l'anglais*, hie away to the Désert, dine under the bowers of Marly, and forget that we are ever to part again." [48]

Mrs. Cosway's response to this outpouring was, alas, far from gracious or understanding. She was only aware that Jefferson had, apparently, neglected her for some time. The poetry of a scene she had never witnessed entirely escaped her. "Do you deserve a long letter, my dear friend? No, certainly not, and to avoid temptation I have a small sheet of paper.... How long do you like to keep your friends in anxiety! How many months was you without writing to me? And you felt no remorse? I was glad to know you was well, sure of your being much engaged and diverted, and had only to lament I was not a castle hanging to a cloud, a stream, a village, a stone on the pavement of Turin, Milan, and Genoa, etc. NO! I entered into the calculation of hours that prevented you from visiting Rome. I am not sure if I had any share in the *provoking* part. Oh, if I had been a shadow of this *Elysium* of yours! How you would have been tormented!" [49]

The time was approaching for Mrs. Cosway to make the promised visit to Paris. It appears that she was not accompanied by her husband this time. On August 28, Trumbull wrote Jefferson from London, asking what would be the best time to come to Paris so as to be able to sketch the various French officers who had been present at the surrender at Yorktown. "Before this reaches you," he concludes, "Mrs. Cosway will be with you. I am very sorry I cannot be there at the same time. The salon would be doubly interesting seen in such company." [50]

On the thirtieth, before this letter had reached him, Jefferson was already urging Trumbull to come to Paris again. There is no doubt that, in his heart, he hoped to recreate the happy days of the year before. As Mephistopheles tempted Faust with a beautiful woman, so Jefferson dangled the *Salon,* which had opened a few days previously, before the eyes of his young friend. "I enclose you a list of its treasures," he writes. "The best thing is the Death of Socrates by David, and a superb one it is. A crucifixion by Roland in imitation of relief, is as perfect as it can be. Five pieces of antiquities by Robert are also among the foremost. Many portraits by Madame Le Brun are exhibited and much approved. There are abundance of things in the style of mediocrity. Upon the whole it is well worth your coming to see. You have only to get in the diligence," he urges, "and in four days you are here . . . and as it happens but once in two years, you should not miss it. Come and take your bed here. You will see Mrs. Cosway, who arrived two days ago." [51] Thus we learn when she actually reached Paris.

We know very little about this second Paris visit. Jefferson did not ruminate over it at its close, as he had the preceding October in the *Dialogue.* His account book, which usually has so much to tell about his activities, reveals next to nothing. There was a trip to St. Germain on September 12 and one to Versailles on the eighteenth, but the sums paid were not adequate for two people. The one occasion when there seems to have been a larger gathering was on the twenty-fifth of October when Jefferson notes paying twenty-four francs for dinner at the Palais Royal. It may well have been at this time that Mrs. Cosway, who apparently had been asked to include some of her friends, wrote him, "My dear Sir, why will you make such great dinner? I had told the Princess of the pleasure I intended myself tomorrow. She seemed very glad to go with me, but had not thought of anybody else. To begin by Mr. d'Hancarville, he is very sorry not to be able to wait on you as he has been particularly engaged for some time past. Mr. St. André, I shall see this evening. Mr. Niemsewicz accepts with pleasure your kind invitation. Count Btorki is not here, but I shall deliver to him your invitation." [52] It was, indeed, a gala party.

There were two circumstances, aside from the inevitable one that no idyl can ever be repeated, in which these autumn days of 1787 differed from those of the preceding year. In the first place, Mrs. Cosway seems to have been determined to establish a position in Paris for herself similar to the one she held in London. She appears to have stayed with her intimate friend, the Princess Lubomirski,[53] in a section of the city remote from the Grille de Chaillot and inconvenient to it. Jefferson complained later that he saw her "only by scraps." The time before, he says, "we were half days and whole days together, and I found this too little." [54] If we may believe a contemporary, her residence in Paris this time "became the resort of all the English of talent, as well as many of the French of the same description. She held a court like the fair Aspasia of old, and Fiat stamped honour on every work she condescended to approve." [55]

She had, furthermore, surrounded herself by an entourage that made the carefree, Bohemian existence of the last visit out of the question. "Your mere domestic cortege was so numerous," Jefferson wrote after her departure, "*et si imposante*, that one could not approach you quite at their ease, nor could you so unpremeditately mount into the phaeton and hie away to the Bois de Boulogne, St. Cloud, Marly, St. Germain, etc. Add to this the distance at which you were placed from me. When you come again you must be nearer, move more extempore." [56]

Jefferson, on his part, had chosen this month of September to take possession of his apartments at Mont Valérien, and we find him frequently spending a night or two there, as we have seen. It is thus not surprising that both felt something had gone out of their relationship and that Mrs. Cosway, always quick to blame, should have written Jefferson, "If my inclination had been your law, I should have had the pleasure of seeing you more than I have. I have felt the loss with displeasure." [57]

With the coming of winter, apparently early in December, Mrs.

Cosway returned to London. She had asked Jefferson to a *déjeuner à l'anglais*, of which he speaks on the morning of her departure. But the hostess was absent. She had sent him a little note the evening before, seemingly after they had parted, which did not reach him in time. "I cannot breakfast with you tomorrow," it reads. "To bid you adieu once is sufficiently painful, for I leave you with very melancholy ideas." [58] This is, perhaps, the nearest she ever came to writing a love letter.

That her action had been precipitate, that it might have seemed harsh to her admirer, seems gradually to have come over her. In two letters written from London, on the twentieth of December and again on Christmas Day, and which are almost identical in wording, she exclaims, "You promised to come to breakfast with me the morning of my departure, and to accompany me part of the way. Did you go? I left Paris with much regret, indeed, I could not bear to take leave anymore. I was confused and distracted. You must have thought me so when you saw me in the evening. Why is it my misfortune to find amiable people where I go, and why am I obliged to part with them! It is very cruel." And again, "You came to the invitation of my breakfast the morning of my departure! And what did you think of me? I did it to avoid the last taking leave. I went too early for anybody to see me. I cannot express how miserable I was in leaving Paris. How I regretted not having seen more of you. And I cannot have even the satisfaction to unburden my displeasure by loading you with reproaches." And then this cryptic sentence, "Your reasons must be sufficient, and my forcing you would have been unkind and unfriendly as it would be cruel to pretend [*i.e.*, insist] on what is totally disagreeable to you." [59]

If Jefferson was hurt, he concealed it in his reply. His infatuation had not diminished. "I went to breakfast with you according to promise," he writes, "and you had gone off at 5 o'clock in the morning. This spared me, indeed, the pain of parting, but it deprives me of the comfort of recollecting that pain." After speaking of various friends, he continues, "But in your case it was not any fault, unless it be a fault to love my friends so dearly as to wish to enjoy their company in the only way it yields enjoyment, that is, *en petit comité*. You make everybody love you," he adds. "You are sought and surrounded therefore by all." [60]

Through the many letters they exchanged following this visit, there rings the same cry that echoes through all those this couple were destined to write each other: "When you come again!" In the spring of 1788 Mrs. Cosway wrote, "Oh, I wish, my dear friend, I could announce to you our return to Paris. I am afraid to question my lord and master on this subject, he may not think or like to refuse, and a disappointed promise of this kind would be too much for me. I cannot bear it." [61]

Jefferson, on his part, kept urging her to come to enjoy the artistic triumph that was hers. Her engraving of "The Hours Crowning Love," in the gently sentimental style of the period, had been an instant success in Paris. As Jefferson writes: "Your Hours, my dear friend, are no longer your own. Everybody now demands them, and were it possible for me to want a memorandum of you, it is presented me in every street in Paris. Come, then, to see what triumph time is giving you. Come and see everybody stopping to admire the Hours, suspended against the walls of the Quai des Augustins, the Boulevards, the Palais Royal, etc. with a 'Maria Cosway, delin.' at the bottom. But you triumph everywhere, so, if you came here, it will be, not to see your triumphs but your friends, and to make them happy with your presence." [62]

There was no visit to Paris this year, however. Jefferson had applied for leave to go home—which was not granted until 1789—and his eyes were fixed beyond the sea. Mrs. Cosway planned a trip to the scenes of her childhood. "I am going to America, and you to Italy," he wrote her in September. "One of us is going the wrong way, for the way will ever be wrong which leads us farther apart." And, as so often before, he talked of her coming to the United States as though that could be a possibility, as indeed it might this time have been. "But why go to Italy?" he asks. "You have seen it, all the world has seen it, and ransacked it thousands of times. Rather join our good friend Mrs. Church in her trip to America. There you will find original scenes, scenes worthy of your pencil.... I should find excuses for being sometimes of your parties. Think of this, my friend... and let us all embark together at Havre." [63]

Meanwhile Mrs. Cosway had been begging Trumbull to give her a portrait of her friend, a copy of the head of Jefferson he had painted into his "Declaration of Independence" while staying with him in Paris. On March 6 Mrs. Cosway asked Jefferson, "Will you give Mr. Trumbull leave to make a copy of a certain portrait he painted in Paris? It is a person that hates you that requests this favor." [64] On the same day Trumbull was writing his patron, "Mrs. Cosway's love to you, and his, too. She is angry, yet she teases me every day for a copy of your little portrait—that she may scold it, no doubt." [65] That the scolding and complaints contained in each letter became a little monotonous can readily be imagined. That her admirer felt this we may gather from a subsequent letter from Jefferson, written on his return from Germany in July. "Cease to chide me," he writes. "It is hard to have been chained to a writing table, drudging over business daily from morning to night ever since my return to Paris. It will be a cruel exaggeration if I am to lose my friends into the bargain. The only letter of private friendship I wrote on my return, and before entering on business, was to you. The first I wrote on getting through my budget was to you.... I am incapable of forgetting or neglecting you, my dear friend.... Of voluntary faults to you I can never be guilty, and you are too good not to pardon the involuntary. Chide me then no more, be to me what you have been, and give me without measure the comfort of your friendship." [66]

Jefferson had charged Trumbull to "kneel to Mrs. Cosway for me and lay my soul in her lap." Now, as he believed the time of his departure was approaching, he wrote her again to perform this office himself and to say, "We are so apt to believe what we wish that I almost believe I shall meet you in America, and that we shall make together the tour of the curiosities of that country. Be this as it may, let us be together in spirit. Preserve for me always a little corner of your affection in exchange for the spacious part you occupy in mine." [67] To which the lady replied, "You are going to America, and you think I am going with you. I thank you for the flattering compliment. I deserve it for I shall certainly be with you in spirit," and

THE PONT DU GARD. By Hubert Robert. (*Courtesy of the Musée du Louvre*)

A GALLERY AT DÜSSELDORF. From *Pigage*, Galerie Electorale. (*Courtesy of the Philadelphia Museum of Art*)

she adds in her tantalizing way, "I shall walk through the beautiful scenes you will describe to me by letter." The letters at last took on a value in her eyes, she saw in them something more than their failure to arrive. "When I read [them]," she says, "you seem to say so much in so few words, that I forget the little number of the syllables for the beauty of the expression and the elegant style." [68] This was, perhaps, the only compliment she ever paid him.

Jefferson's leave finally arrived and on the twenty-sixth of September, 1789, he left Paris. While he waited at Cowes for favorable winds, Mrs. Cosway sent him a little note, by Trumbull, "to put you in mind of me in those still more distant parts of the globe where your friends, perhaps all your heart and sentiments are. . . . I was very near coming to see you when Trumbull told me you was to be at the Ile of White, but I have been very ill with a most violent cold, the weather is very bad and every difficulty opposes my desire of surprising you with a visit." Once more she reverts to the imperious Maria, the one Jefferson so well knew. "Why don't you come?" she demands. "It would be so easy, so short, such a pleasure to us. I think I could be angry with you for not coming. But perhaps you cannot. You may have your reasons. Therefore shall say no more." [69]

Jefferson wrote his letter of farewell from Cowes. "I am here, my dear friend," he says, "waiting the arrival of a ship to take my flight from this side of the Atlantic and as we think last of those we love most, I profit of the latest moment to bid you a short but affectionate adieu. . . . Under the present circumstances, aggravated as you will read them in the English papers, we cannot hope to see you in France. But a return of quiet and order may remove that bug bear, and the ensuing spring might give us a meeting at Paris with the first swallow. So be it, my dear friend, and adieu under the hope which springs naturally out of what we wish. Once and again, then, farewell, remember me and love me."

As his ship weighed anchor at daylight from Yarmouth, Jefferson handed the pilot a letter with a shilling for postage. It is not difficult to believe that this was his last farewell to Maria Cosway.

IX. The Remains of Roman Grandeur

HIS DISLOCATED WRIST, which refused to mend but kept plaguing him day and night, led Jefferson to embark upon one of the most soul-satisfying experiences of his European sojourn—his journey to the south of France and to Italy. A new world was to open up before him, a world of which he had dreamed as a youth. The sparkling blue waters of the Mediterranean, the glory of the Alps, the wonders of Roman antiquity were to become realities and pass in a pageant before his eyes. Something of this is expressed in a letter he wrote James Madison urging him to come to Europe and assuring him that for the slight cost of the trip "you will have purchased the knowledge of another world." [1] More of it was expressed in the glowing lines inscribed to Lafayette: "From the first olive fields of Pierrelatte to the orangeries of Hyères has been continued rapture to me." [2]

Nearly five months after the accident, Jefferson again wrote Madison, "In a former letter I mentioned the dislocation of my wrist. I can make not the least use of it, except for the single article of writing. I have great anxieties lest I should never recover any considerable use of it. I shall, by the advice of my surgeons, set out in a fortnight for the waters of Aix, in Provence. I chose these out of several they proposed to me, because, if they fail to be effectual, my journey will not be useless altogether. It will give me an opportunity to examine the canal at Languedoc, and of acquiring knowledge of that species of navigation which may be useful hereafter; but, more immediately, it will enable me to make the tour of the ports concerned in commerce with us, to examine on the spot the defects of the late regulations respecting our commerce, to learn the further improvements which may be made in it, and on my return to get this business finished. I shall be absent between two and three months." [3]

It was, indeed, to be no mere pleasure trip. As always, Jefferson improved the shining moment to a degree that has hardly been realized. "I am constantly roving about to see what I have never seen before and shall never see again," he writes Lafayette from Nice, one of the garden spots of the Côte d'Azur. "In the great cities I go to see what travelers think alone worthy of being seen, but I make a job of it, and generally gulp it all down in a day. On the other hand I am never satiated with rambling through the fields and farms, examining the culture and the cultivators with a degree of curiosity which makes some take me to be a fool, and others to be much wiser than I am.

"To do it most effectually," he adds, and the picture Jefferson now draws for us seems strangely out of line with the reserve and dignity we tend to associate with him, "you must be absolutely incognito, you must ferret the people out of their hovels, as I have done, delve into their kettles, eat their bread, loll on their beds under pretense of resting yourself, but in fact to find if they are soft. You will find a sublime pleasure in the course of this investigation, and a sublimer one hereafter when you shall be able to apply your knowledge to the softening of their beds, or the throwing of a morsel of meat into their kettles of vegetables." [4]

On the twenty-eighth of February, 1787, as gloomy and damp a season as Paris has to offer, Jefferson set out. From the moment of starting he was "pelted," as he said, "with rain, hail and snow. Now and then a few gleamings of sunshine to cheer me by the way." [5] This continued during the first part of his journey until he came within sight of the sunny Riviera. He traveled alone, not even accompanied by the usual servant. "I was quite determined to be a master of my own secret," he wrote William Short, "and therefore to take a servant who should not know me. At Fontainebleau I could not get one, but at Dijon I got a very excellent one, who will probably go through the journey with me." [6] He made the trip in his own carriage and used post horses. His road lay to the southeast through Melun, through the great forest of Fontainebleau, on to the town itself, where he arrived toward evening and spent two days.

On the second of March he was on his way again as far as the ancient city of Sens. Here he spent the night and, like many an American since, visited the Cathedral of Saint-Étienne, which dates from the twelfth century. Jefferson makes no comment on it, however, other than to enter in his account book that he paid two francs, four for "seeing church." From Sens he continued along the lovely, languid river Yonne through Joigny, Auxerre, Vermanton to Lucy-le-bois, where he arrived on the third. "The face of the country is in large hills," he writes on leaving Sens, "not too steep for the plough, somewhat resembling the Elk Hill and Beaver-dam hills of Virginia.... There are a few apple trees, but none of any other kind, and no inclosures, no cattle, sheep or swine, fine mules. Few chateaux; no farm houses, all the people being gathered in villages.... The people are illy clothed. Perhaps they have put on their worst clothes at this moment, as it is raining." [7]

For the first time Jefferson seems to have encountered a spectacle he could never understand and against which he railed whenever it came to his attention. "I observe women and children carrying heavy burdens and laboring with the hoe. This is an unequivocal indication of extreme poverty. Men in a civilized country never expose their wives and children to labor above their force and sex, as long as their own labor can protect them from it." [8] Already the American woman was seated upon her throne.

The journey through Burgundy continued with a two-day stop at the Hôtel de Condé at Dijon. He writes vividly of this country in the memoranda he made of the trip. "Here the hills become mountains, larger than those of Champagne. More abrupt, more red and stony. I passed through about one hundred eighty miles of Burgundy. It resembles extremely our red, mountainous country, but is rather more stony. All in corn [9] and wine. I mounted a videt, put a peasant on another and rambled through their most celebrated vineyards....The same in Beaujolais, where nature has spread its richest gifts in profusion. On the right we had fine mountain sides lying in easy slopes, in corn and vine, and on the left the rich, extensive plains of the Saône in corn and pasture. This is the richest country I have ever beheld." [10]

On the ninth of March, on his way south from Mâcon to Lyon, Jefferson arrived at the Château de L'Aye-Epinaye, which lies in the hills not far distant from Villefranche, "a seignory of about

15,000 acres in vine, corn, pasture and wood, a rich and beautiful scene." Jefferson had been introduced to the family by friends in Paris, the Abbés Chalut and Arnauld. Although Monsieur de L'Aye was detained in Paris a good part of the year, his wife received Jefferson, as he tells us, "with a hospitality, a goodness and an ease which were charming, and I left with regret." [11] While there, to use his own words, he fell deeply in love. The object of his affection was this time no mere mortal of flesh and bones but "a delicious morsel of sculpture" by M. A. Slodtz, a chaste Diana and an Endymion. "The group," he writes, "carries the perfection of the chisel to a degree of which I had no conception. It is the only thing in sculpture which I have seen in my journey worthy of notice." [12]

Jefferson reached Lyon on the evening of the eleventh and spent three days there at the Hôtel du Palais Royal. Although he notes spending more than ten francs for "seeing things," his only observation on them is that "there are some feeble remains here, of an amphitheatre of two hundred feet in diameter, and of an aqueduct in brick. The Pont d'Ainay has nine arches of forty feet from center to center. The piers are of six feet." [13] He took time at Lyon to write Short a long letter discussing affairs at the ministry in Paris and describing his travels. "Six or seven hundred leagues still before me," he concludes, "and, circumscribed in time, I am obliged to hasten my movements. I have not visited all the manufactures of this place: because a knowledge of them would be useless, and would extrude from memory other things more worth retaining. Architecture, painting, sculpture, antiquities, agriculture, the condition of the laboring poor fill all my moments. Hitherto I have derived as much satisfaction and delight from my journey as I could propose to myself. The plan of having servants who know nothing of me, places me perfectly at my ease." [14]

After concluding a morning of business on the fifteenth, Jefferson set out again, south along the Rhone. The stormy scenery of Dauphiné quite swept him off his feet. "Nature never formed a country of more savage aspect than that on both sides of the Rhone," he recorded in his travel notes. "A huge torrent rushes like an arrow between high precipices, often of massive rock, at other times of loose stone with but little earth. Yet has the hand of man subdued this savage scene, by planting corn where there is little fertility, trees where there is still less, and vines where there is none. On the whole it assumes a romantic, picturesque and pleasing air. The hills on the opposite side of the river, being high, steep and laid up in terraces, are of a singular appearance. . . . The high mountains of Dauphiné and Languedoc are now covered with snow. The almond is in general bloom and the willow putting out its leaf." [15]

Some thirty kilometers from Lyon, Jefferson reached the town of Vienne, picturesquely situated on a hillside surrounded by mountains. "The hills come in precipices to the river," Jefferson writes, "resembling thus very much our Susquehanna and its hills, except that the Susquehanna is ten times as wide as the Rhone." [16] He neglected to state, however, that the Rhone is ten times as rapid as the Susquehanna. At Vienne Jefferson was to have his introduction to the world of Rome, a world he had long known and admired in books. He at once walked out to view the famous temple of Augustus and Livia built by the Emperor Claudius, the curious Plan d'Aiguille, or "sepulchral pyramid," as Jefferson called it, and the last traces of the ramparts of the old Roman city.

The following day he engaged guides to take him to the Côte-Rôtie and its celebrated vineyards, which lie a few kilometers to the south of Vienne, on the opposite side of the river. "It is a string of broken hills," Jefferson writes, "extending a league on the river, from the village of Ampuys to the town of Coudrieux. The soil is white, tinged a little sometimes with yellow, sometimes with red, stony, poor and laid up in terraces. Those parts of the hills only which look to the sun at midday, or the earlier hours of the afternoon, produce wines of the first quality." [17]

On leaving Vienne Jefferson drove along the beautiful valley of the Rhone toward Tain, through country he described as "delicious." On both banks of the river were mountains with vineyards and orchards bursting into bloom. The rugged Pilat range formed a picturesque background. At Tain, a village of a thousand souls, sheltered under the mountain known as the Ermitage, Jefferson paused overnight to study the "wine called Hermitage, so justly celebrated." "Go up to the hermitage on the top of the hill," he was to write his young friends

Rutledge and Shippen, "for the sake of the sublime prospect from thence." But he warns them, "do not go to the tavern of the Post house, the master of which is a most unconscionable rascal." [18]

From Valence, quite some distance farther on, Jefferson's road led through Orange and Avignon to his destination, Aix-en-Provence. Instead of following this, however, he stopped at Orange to view the Roman ruins at that place, then turned southwestward to Nîmes. A secret mission that he had confided to no one took him there. That he was to fall in love with the place and find it difficult to tear himself away after five days among its antiquities, its *medailleurs,* and its book shops was something he had not anticipated when he went out of his way to visit this ancient town. Nîmes enjoys the distinction of possessing more monuments of Roman antiquity than any other place in France, and here Jefferson indeed lost his heart. Here he penned his famous love letter to a Roman temple, addressed to his old friend Madame de Tessé. "Here I sit, Madame, gazing whole hours at the Maison Carrée, like a lover at his mistress. From Lyon to Nîmes I have been nourished on the remains of Roman grandeur.... At Vienne I thought of you. But I am glad you were not there; for you would have seen me more angry than, I hope, you will ever see me. The Praetorian Palace, as it is called, comparable for its fine proportions to the Maison Carrée, defaced by the barbarians who have converted it to its present purpose, its beautiful Corinthian columns cut out, in part, to make space for Gothic windows, and hewed down, in the residue, to the plane of the building, was enough, you must admit, to disturb my composure. At Orange, too, I thought of you. I was sure you had seen with pleasure, the sublime triumphal arch of Marius at the entrance to that city. I went then to the arena... I thought of you again, and I was then in great good humor, at the Pont du Gard, a sublime antiquity and well preserved. But most of all here, where Roman taste, genius and magnificence excite ideas analogous to yours at every step.... I am immersed in antiquities from morning to night. For me the city of Rome is actually existing in all the splendor of its empire." [19]

In a letter written to John Jay from Marseille on the fourth of May, 1787, Jefferson revealed the real reason for his going to Nîmes and asked that the information he was sending be laid before Congress. It had to do with a matter of rebellion, in which Jefferson confesses he was always interested. The preceding October he had received a letter from a foreign gentleman who announced that he had a matter of great consequence to impart to Jefferson, and inquired how it might safely be done. Jefferson replied that he would be going to the south of France and "that I would go off my road as far as Nîmes under the pretext of seeing the antiquities of that place, if he would meet me there." The rendezvous was arranged, and the foreigner proved to be a Brazilian, one of the first of a long line of revolutionists, seeking aid and comfort for his country. After summing up the conditions in Brazil as outlined by the emissary, which included a potential backing of some twenty-six millions of dollars for the "little rebellion," Jefferson concluded, "In short, as to the question of revolution, there is but one mind in that country. But there appears no person capable of conducting a revolution, or willing to venture himself at its head, without the aid of some powerful nation, as the people of their own might fail them. They consider the North American Revolution as a precedent for theirs. They look to the United States as most likely to give them honest support, and from a variety of considerations, have the strongest prejudices in our favor. . . . They would want cannon, ammunition, ships, sailors, soldiers and officers, for which they are disposed to look to the United States, it always being understood that every service and furniture will be well paid.

"I took care," Jefferson continues, "to impress on him through the whole of our conversation, that I had neither instructions nor authority to say a word to anybody on this subject, and that I could only give him my own ideas, as a single individual; which were that we were not in a condition at present to meddle nationally in any war . . . yet a successful revolution in Brazil could not be uninteresting to us.

"I trouble Congress with these details," he concludes, with the almost prophetic insight that often characterized him, "because, however distant we may be both in conditions and dispositions, from taking an active part in any commotions in that country, nature has placed it too near us, to make its movements altogether indifferent to our interests, or to our curiosity." [20]

Jefferson left Nîmes on the twenty-fourth and went on to St. Remy, where he spent the night. His road lay through Arles with its many Roman monuments, which were a renewed source of delight. "At an ancient church in the suburbs of Arles," he notes, "are some hundred of ancient stone coffins, along the roadside. The ground is thence called les champs elysées. In a vault in a church are some curiously wrought, and in a back yard are many ancient statues, inscriptions etc. ... But the principal monument here is an amphitheatre, the external portico of which is tolerably complete. How many porticos there were cannot be seen; but at one of the principal gates, there are still five. ... The whole of the upper entablature is gone, and of the attic, if there was one. Not a single seat of the internal is visible. The whole of the inside and nearly the whole of the outside, is masked by buildings. It is supposed there are one thousand inhabitants within the amphitheatre.[21] The walls are more entire and firm than those of the amphitheatre at Nîmes. I suspect its plan and distribution to have been very different from that." [22]

The following evening Jefferson arrived at Aix-en-Provence. It seemed as though he had, indeed, reached Elysian fields. In an exultant letter to Short he writes, "I am now in the land of corn, vine, oil and sunshine. What more can a man ask of heaven? If I should happen to die in Paris, I will beg of you to send me here, and have me exposed to the sun. I am sure it will bring me to life again." He then proceeds to give a description of the physical aspect of this earthly paradise. "This city is one of the cleanest and neatest I have seen in any country. The streets are straight, from 20 to 100 feet wide and as clean as a parlour floor. Where they are of a width sufficient, they have 1, 2, or 4 rows of elms from 100 to 150 years old, which make delicious walks. There are no porte cochères, so that the buildings show themselves advantageously on the streets. It is in a valley just where it begins to open towards the mouth of the Rhone, forming in that direction a boundless plain which is an entire grove of olive trees, and is, moreover, in corn, lucerne or vines, for the happiness of the olive tree is that it interferes with no superficial production. It takes well in every soil, but best where it is poorest, or where there is none. ... In the long chain of causes and effects, it is droll sometimes to seize the distant links and to present the one as the consequence of the other. Of this nature are these propositions. The want of dung prevents the progress of luxury in Aix. The poverty of the soil makes its streets clean. These are legitimate consequences of the following chain. The preciousness of the soil prevents its being employed in grass. Therefore, no cattle, no dung. Hence the dung gatherers (a numerous calling here) hunt it as eagerly in the streets as they would diamonds. Everyone, therefore, can walk cleanly and commodiously. Hence few carriages, hence few assemblies, routs and other occasions for the display of dress." [23]

Despite the beauty of the place, despite having made the long journey for the benefit of the waters, Jefferson stayed in Aix only four days. Each day he dutifully tried the prescribed treatment, as his account book tells us, with its entries, "douches, 2 fr. 8" or "douches, 3 fr." Yet he wrote Short, "You enquire kindly the effect of the waters on my wrist. None at all. But time is doing slowly what they cannot do." [24] Between treatments he amused himself taking in the sights and going to the theater. He writes of the latter, "We were last night treated with Alexis and Justine and Mazet, in which the most celebrated actress from Marseille came to bear a part for the advantage of her friend whose benefit night it was. She is in the style of Mme. Dugazon, has ear, voice, taste and action. She is, moreover, young and handsome and has the advantage over Mme. Dugazon and some other of the celebrated ones of Paris, in being clear of that dreadful wheeze, or rather whistle in respiration, which resembles the agonizing struggles for breath of a dying person." [25]

On the twenty-ninth of March, after being at Aix "long enough to prove the inefficacy of the waters," Jefferson wrote John Jay, "I came on to this place [Marseille] for the purpose of informing myself here, as I mean to do at the other seaport towns, of whatever may be interesting to our commerce." [26] He remained in the great Mediterranean seaport for a whole week. Although there were few remains of Roman civilization to interest him, he was enchanted by the lovely situation of the city, in a vast amphitheater of hills, green nearby and with "high mountains of naked rock, distant two or three leagues." Most of his time, however, was given over to the constant pursuit of studying things, largely of an agricultural nature, which would be of benefit to his own country. He comments on the unusual wine cellar of Monsieur de Bergasse, on the pumps worked by the wind at the Château Borelli, keeps a record of the daily mean and maximum temperatures, notes that on the "2nd of April young figs are formed, the 4th we have Windsor beans . . . the 5th I see strawberries and the Guelder rose in bloom," and tells us "I measured a mule, not the largest, five feet and two inches high." [27] Nothing escaped his attention.

From Marseille he wrote Mazzei that a mutual friend had "promised to make me acquainted with a well-informed gardener whom I expect to find among the most precious of my acquaintances. From men of that class I have derived the most satisfactory information in the course of my journey and have sought their acquaintance with as much industry as I have avoided that of others who would have made me waste my time [in] good society. For these objects one need not leave Paris. I find here several interesting articles of culture; the best [illegible] grapes for drying, a smaller [illegible] the same purposes without a seed, from Smyrna, olives, capers, pistachio nuts, almonds. All of these articles may succeed on or southward of the Chesapeake." [28]

"Among other objects of inquiry," he had written Jay, "this was the place to learn something more certain on the subject of rice, as it is a great emporium for most of the Levant and of Italy. I wished particularly to know whether it was the use of a different machine for cleaning which brought European rice to market less broken than ours, as had been represented to me by those who deal in that article in Paris. I found several persons who had passed through the rice country of Italy, but not one who could explain to me the nature of the machine. But I was given to believe that I might see it myself on entering Piedmont. As this would require but about three weeks, I determined to go and ascertain this point, as the chance only of placing our rice above all rivalship in quality as it is in color, by the introduction of a better machine, if a better existed, seemed to justify the application of that much time to it." [29]

Thus on the sixth of April, Jefferson settled his bill for entertainment at the Hôtel des Princes and started toward Italy, the land of his dreams. It is a pity that, as he says, "my time allowed me to go no further than Turin, Milan and Genoa: consequently I scarcely got into classical ground.... In architecture, painting, sculpture I found much amusement: but more than all in their agriculture, many objects of which might be adopted with us to great advantage." [30] He did, however, pass through one of the garden spots of this earth, that enchanting strip of coast known as the Riviera, from Hyères to Genoa, where bold promontories alternate with gentle wooded hills and curving white beaches, where the azure of the Mediterranean animates the picture, and where the exotic vegetation transports the traveler to another world.

From Toulon, where he spent two days viewing the animated commerce, questioning the peasants about the planting of capers, the yield of fig, olive, and apricot trees, and, as always in a city, visiting the theater, Jefferson went on to Hyères, the oldest winter resort on the Mediterranean, with its extensive olive groves and orange orchards. He visited the famous gardens of Monsieur Fille, in which were to be found more than fifteen thousand orange trees. "They are blossoming and bearing all the year, flowers and fruit in every stage at the same time." He describes Hyères and its "delicious" environs as "a village of about five thousand inhabitants at the foot of a mountain which covers it from the north, from which extends a plain of two or three miles to the seashore. It has no port. Here are palm trees twenty or thirty feet high ... the streets in every direction are steep, in steps of stairs, and about eight feet wide. No carriage of any kind can enter it. The wealthiest inhabitants use *chaises au porteurs*. But there are few wealthy, the bulk of the inhabitants being labourers of the earth." [31]

After Hyères Jefferson continued through country that has since become a playground for half the world, through valleys that he considers "tolerable good," over mountains "always barren," past St. Raphael, La Napoule, Cannes, Antibes to Nice, the road "generally near the sea, passing over hills or strings of villages" much as it does today. At Nice, where he found the "climate quite as delightful as it has been represented," he paused four days, enjoying the enchanting country, visiting the orange groves, seeing the King's gardens, pursuing his inquiries as to rice, and writing friends. He lodged, as he tells us, at the Hôtel de York. "It is a fine English tavern, very agreeably situated and the mistress a friendly, agreeable woman." [32] On the twelfth he wrote Short, "To-morrow I set out on my passage over the Alps, being to pursue it ninety-three miles to Coni, on mules, as the snows are not yet enough melted to admit carriages to pass. I leave mine here, therefore, proposing to return by water from Genoa. . . . I am now in the act of putting my baggage into portable form for my bat-mule. . . . I shall not be heard of again in three weeks." [33]

Mounting his mule and followed by others bearing his servant, guides, and luggage, Jefferson set out on what must have seemed a great adventure. Accustomed as he was to the lovely, smiling scenery of his native Albemarle, he was hardly prepared for the grandeur of the Alps. From Nice he headed north through the Alpes Maritimes crossing them at Colle di Tenda, one of the most picturesque spots imaginable. In approaching it he had passed through the beautiful gorge of Saorgio and exclaimed in what were, for him, extraordinarily impassioned words, "Fall down and worship the site of the Château de Saorgio, you never saw, nor will never see such another." In the next sentence he had caught hold of himself, however, and observed dryly, "This road is probably the greatest work of the kind which was ever executed either in ancient or modern times. It did not cost as much as one year's war." [34]

The first Italian city of any size in which Jefferson found himself was Turin, where he arrived on the sixteenth of April and remained until the nineteenth. Two of his three evenings there he attended the comedy, and he likewise visited the cabinet of antiquities, which he describes as worth seeing, but his attention here, as for the next two weeks, was focused chiefly on the culture of rice. He toured the great rice fields that lie between Vercelli and Pavia, talked to the peasants who worked them and interviewed the owners. "There was but one conclusion to be drawn," he writes Edward Rutledge of rice-growing

South Carolina, "to wit, that the rice was of a different species, and I determined to take enough to put you in seed. They informed me, however, that its exportation in the husk was prohibited, so I could only bring off as much as my coat and surtout pockets would hold. I took measures with a muleteer to run a couple of sacks across the Apennines to Genoa, but have not great dependence on its success. The little, therefore, which I brought myself must be relied upon for fear we should get no more." [35]

From Turin Jefferson went toward Milan, through Vercelli, where he spent the night at the Trois Rois, on to Novara with "fields of rice all along the road." At Milan he passed three days, lodging at the Albergo Reale and making various excursions. One was to Rozzano to see Parmesan cheese made, of which he has left a lengthy and detailed description. Another to the celebrated church of Certosa, halfway to Pavia, the plan of which forecasts that of the University of Virginia in its first proposed form. Jefferson speaks of it as "the richest thing I ever saw." In Milan he admired especially the "Casa Roma and Casa Candiani, by Appiani and Casa Belgioiosa by Martin. . . . In the second is a small cabinet, the ceiling of which is in small hexagons, within which are small cameos, and heads painted alternately, no two the same. The salon of the Casa Belgioiosa is superior to anything I have ever seen." [36] If he saw Leonardo's sublime, faded "Last Supper" in the refectory of Santa Maria della Grazie, we do not know it. He remarks, however, that "the Cathedral of Milan is a worthy object of philosophical contemplation, to be placed among the rarest instances of the misuse of money. On viewing the churches of Italy it is evident without calculation that the same expense would have sufficed to throw the Apennines into the Adriatic and thereby render it terra firma from Leghorn to Constantinople." [37] Jefferson cannot be criticized for these opinions as the world had not as yet awakened to an appreciation of the Gothic.

Genoa was Jefferson's final objective in Italy. He spent four days there, visiting the theater and the palaces, making careful notes of everything new that came to his attention. On the twenty-seventh he made an excursion of some fifty kilometers along the beautiful Riviera di Levante through Nervi as far as Sestri. Fortunately for him it was before the day of railroads with their endless tunnels, and he was able to enjoy the magnificent prospect here and there as his carriage rolled along the water's edge. As we have seen, he planned to return to Nice by water from Genoa and duly embarked on the evening of the twenty-eighth, but his ship was becalmed. After two days at sea, "and mortally sick," he landed at the charming little fishing village of Noli, some fifty kilometers distant. He passed the night there and tells us that he spent the next two days "clambering the cliffs of the Apennines, sometimes on foot, sometimes on a mule, according as the path was more or less difficult, and two others traveling through the night as well as day without sleep." [38] Yet all was not bitter. As he walked from Louano to Albenga, the blue sea on his left, snow-covered mountains on his right, he reflected that "if a person wished to retire from his acquaintance, to live absolutely unknown, and yet in the midst of physical enjoyments, it should be in some of the little villages of this coast, where air, water and earth concur to offer what each has most precious. Here are nightingales, beccaficas, ortolans, pheasants, partridges, quails, a superb climate, and the power of changing it at any moment from summer to winter by ascending the mountains. The earth furnishes wine, oil, figs, oranges and every production of the garden, in every season." [39]

The journey back to Paris was a long and arduous one, which took him to almost every section of France he had not yet visited. It was notable for his inspection of public works and of shipping, as well as for the intensive study he made of the wines of France. It was no mere tasting or sampling jaunt, but a profound examination of the soil, the planting of the vines, their spacing, the height of the poles, the dunging, grafting, in short, the infinite number of painstaking steps required to produce a wine of the first quality. This trip through the wine country of France, along with his Rhine journey the following year, undertaken for much the same purpose, made Jefferson a great connoisseur of wines, one whose advice was much sought on his return to the United States. The notes he made during his tour of the wine regions are no longer traveling notes but thorough, competent, and complete discussions of the culture of the vine and the making of wine.

The most agreeable feature of Jefferson's return journey was undoubtedly his trip through the Canal du Midi, or Canal of Languedoc, as it is also known and as he called it. This complicated waterway, uniting the Mediterranean with the Atlantic Ocean, had been dreamed of since the time of the Romans. It had finally been realized in the seventeenth century under the great Louis XIV. The mechanics of it had long tantalized Jefferson's imagination, and he devotes pages of his travel notes to describing it. The more lyrical aspects he recounts in a letter to Short, written on the twenty-first of May. "I have passed through the canal from its entrance into the Mediterranean at Cette to this place," he writes, "and shall be immediately at Toulouse, in the whole 200 American miles by water, having employed, in examining all its details, nine days, one of which was spent in making a tour of forty miles on horseback among the Montagnes Noires, to see the manner in which the water has been collected to supply the canal, the other eight on the canal itself. I dismounted my carriage from its wheels, placed it on the deck of a light bark, and was thus towed on the canal instead of the post road. That I might be perfectly master of all the delays necessary, I hired a bark to myself by the day and have made twenty to thirty-five miles a day, according to circumstances, always sleeping ashore. Of all the methods of travel I have ever tried, this is the pleasantest. I walk the greater part of the way along the banks of the canal, level, and lined with a double row of trees which furnish shade. When fatigued, I take seat in my carriage where, as much at ease as if it were my study, I read, write and observe. My carriage being of glass all round admits a full view of all the varying scenes through which I am shifted, olives, figs, mulberries, vines, corn and pasture, villages and farms. I have had some days of superb weather, enjoying two parts of the Indian's wish, cloudless skies and limpid waters: I have had another luxury which he could not wish since we have driven him from the country of mockingbirds, a double row of nightingales along the banks of the canal in full song. This delicious bird gave me another rich treat at Vaucluse. Arriving there a little fatigued, I sat down to repose myself at the fountain which, in a retired hollow of the mountain, gushes out in a stream sufficient to turn three hundred mills. The ruins of Petrarch's château perched on a rock two hundred feet perpendicular over the fountain, and every tree and bush filled with nightingales in full chorus. I find Mazzei's observation just, that their song is more varied, their tone fuller and stronger than on the banks of the Seine. It explains to me another circumstance, why there never was a poet north of the Alps and why there never will be one. A poet is as much a creature of climate as an orange or a palm tree. What a bird the nightingale would be in the climates of America! We must colonize him thither. You should not think of returning to America without taking the tour which I have taken, extending it further south." [40]

From Toulouse, where he spent two days, Jefferson continued his journey to Bordeaux, passing through the country from which come the most famous white wines of France, the sauternes. From Bordeaux he continued to the other great seaports engaged in commerce with America, as far as Nantes and Lorient in Brittany. As always, every form of vegetation, of agriculture, every variation of soil, every detail of viniculture was given the most careful attention and reflected in the voluminous travel notes. And always there is the refrain of the intolerable lot of the common man. In Brittany he did not see the picturesqueness for which we cross an ocean, but "hilly country with poor, grey soil, half in waste, in furze and broom. The people are mostly in villages, they eat rye bread and are ragged. The villages announce a general poverty, as does every other appearance. Women smite on the anvil, and work with the hoe, and cows are yoked to labor. . . . There are but few châteaux here." [41]

On returning to Nantes from Lorient, on the seventh of June, Jefferson turned inland and set out on the last lap of his long and fatiguing journey. The following day found him at Tours, with an opportunity at hand to settle a question that had vexed him a long time. This was a statement made by Voltaire concerning the spontaneous growth of shells unconnected with animal bodies. It was supposed to have occurred at the Château de Grillemont, about six leagues from Tours, which belonged at that time to Monsieur de la Sauvagière. Jefferson called on M. Gentil, the *premier secrétaire de l'intendance*, with a letter of introduction secured through the good offices of the Marquis de Chastellux. He found, as he tells us, that Gentil was "of all men, the best to whom I could have addressed myself. He told me he had been in correspondence with Voltaire on that very subject and was perfectly acquainted with Monsieur de la Sauvagière and the Falunière where the fact is said to have taken place. . . . He says that de la Sauvagière was a man of truth and might be relied on for whatever facts he stated as of his own observations; but that he was overcharged with imagination which, in matters of opinion and theory, often led him beyond the facts, but as to the fact in question, he believed him." After an hour of discussion and fine French distinction between imagination and fact, Jefferson left with the conclusion that "this question is one of those beyond the investigation of human sagacity" and that he "must wait till further and fuller observations enable him to decide it." [42]

From Tours, which he left on the afternoon of the eighth, it was only two days to Paris and we can well imagine that Jefferson's heart sang with happiness. He was to be reunited with his beloved daughter Martha, and his second little daughter, Polly, whom he had not seen in more than three years, was due to arrive from America any day. Urging his horses on, he drove through Amboise and stopped to see the famous gardens and *pagode* of Chanteloup, the property of the late Duc de Choiseuil, where his widow now lived. Jefferson felt rewarded, for he described it to his young friends Rutledge and Shippen as "well worth seeing and examining." That evening he reached Blois. The following day, hurried though he was, he could not resist the temptation of visiting the beautiful Château of Menars, which had belonged to Madame de Pompadour and, subsequently, to her brother, the Marquis de Marigny. It was he who had developed the superb gardens along the Loire, and Jefferson was no one to resist gardens. They remain today exactly as he saw them, a broad plateau divided into parterres, adorned with espaliered roses, heliotropes, fuschias, and other exotic plants and embellished with classical garden structures by Soufflot. Broad, vine-covered ramps lead to a lower level with the lovely, dreamy *boulingrin*, a canal-like body of water embowered in moss and greenery, again adorned with classical figures, and a mysterious grotto to which Soufflot had lent his genius. Not a word of this in Jefferson, however. He merely notes that he paid three francs for "seeing château of Madame de Pompadour."

Nightfall of the ninth found Jefferson in Orléans. He took time to visit a barber and to have necessary repairs made to his chariot. But he was done with seeing sights. Early the next morning he was on his way again through the "continued plain of corn and St. Foin, sometimes grey, sometimes red," that led to Etampes, then through the rocky, mountainous region around Arpajon to the Seine, and finally back to Paris. As he covered the last leagues he may well have pondered what he had written his friend James Monroe on his first arrival in France, "The pleasure of the trip will be less than you expect but the utility greater. It will make you adore your own country, its soil, its climate, its equality, liberty, laws, people and manners. My God! how little do my countrymen know what precious blessings they are in possession of, and which no other people on earth enjoy. I confess I had no idea of it myself." [43]

X. America's War Debts

A BURDEN THAT was to fall with ever increasing weight upon Jefferson's shoulders was that concerned with the financial relations between his country and the European nations from which it had borrowed, chiefly France and Holland. "Our affairs at Amsterdam press on my mind like a mountain,"[1] he wrote John Adams, and he might well have added, "Those of Paris no less so." There was nothing surprising in this. War debts are a perennial problem, no matter what the nation or what the period in history. The monetary difficulties of the United States went back to its very beginning as an independent nation, and the involvements and consequent ramifications were already very considerable by the time Jefferson reached Europe. The indifference of Congress and its inability to raise money at home to pay the interest on the loans already made was becoming known, and European investors were seriously questioning the credit of the United States. One of Jefferson's early tasks had been to reassure the great Dutch banking firm of Willincks and Van Staphorsts concerning the financial position of the United States at that time. "I must observe to you," he writes, "that the first and great division of our federal debt is into 1, foreign, and 2, domestic. The foreign debt comprehends, 1, the loan from the government of Spain; 2, the loans from the government of France, and from the Farmers-General; 3, the loans negotiated in Holland by order of Congress. This branch of our debt stands absolutely singular; no man in the United States having ever supposed that Congress, or their legislatures, can, in any wise modify or alter it.... But with respect to the domestic debt, they consider Congress as representing both the borrowers and the lenders, and that the modifications which have taken place in this have been necessary to do justice between the two parties.

... The domestic debt comprehends 1, the army debt; 2, the loan office debt; 3, the liquidated debt; and 4, the unliquidated debt. The first term includes debts to the officers and soldiers for pay, bounty and subsistence. The second term means moneys put into the loan office of the United States. The third comprehends all debts contracted by quarter-masters, commissaries, and others duly authorized to procure supplies for the army, and which have been liquidated (that is settled) by commissioners appointed under the resolution of Congress, of June 12, 1780, or by the officer who made the contract. The fourth comprehends the whole mass of debts, described in the preceding article, which have not yet been liquidated. They are in course of liquidation, and are passing over daily into the third class. The debts of this third class, that is the liquidated debt, is the object of your inquiry. No time is fixed for the payment of it, no fund as yet determined, nor any firm provision for the interest in the meantime. The consequence is, that the certificates of these debts sell greatly below par." [2]

Jefferson had previously already assured the bankers that if he were a holder of any of these certificates of domestic debt, he "should not have the least fear of their full payment." Foreigners, however, he admonishes, should "be sure they are well advised, before they meddle with them, or they may suffer. If you will reflect with what degree of success persons actually in America could speculate in the European funds which rise and fall daily," he concludes, "you may judge how far those in Europe may do it in the American funds, which are more variable from a variety of causes." [3]

A fortnight later, in a letter to Jay, he reported a recent conversation with the French Foreign Minister, the Comte de Vergennes, who "had asked me if the condition of our finances was improving. He did not make an application to the question of the arrearage of our interest, though perhaps he meant that I should apply it." Jefferson tactfully avoided a discussion of this by telling him "the impost [tax] still found obstacles, and explained to him the effects I hoped from our land office." [4]

The following year, in September, 1786, Jefferson first transmitted to Jay a new suggestion for the solution of one phase of the difficulties.

"It being known that M. de Calonne, the Minister of Finance, is at his wits' end to raise supplies for the ensuing year," he writes, "a proposition has been made him by a Dutch company to purchase the debt of the United States to this country for seventy millions of livres in hand. His necessities dispose him to accede to the proposition, but a hesitation is produced by the apprehension that it might lessen our credit in Europe, and perhaps be disagreeable to Congress." After reflecting on it, Jefferson came to the conclusion that "if there be a danger that our payments may not be punctual, it might be better that the discontents which would thence arise, should be transferred from a court, of whose good will we have so much need, to the breasts of a private company. But it has occurred to me, that we might find occasion to do what would be grateful to this court, and establish with them a confidence in our honor. I am informed that our credit in Holland is sound. Might it not be possible, then, to borrow the four-and-twenty millions due to this country, and thus pay them their whole debt at once? This would save them from any loss on our account." [5]

Congress appears to have been cool to this suggestion, but it was an idea that persisted in Jefferson's mind as an eminently sensible one. To confirm his own beliefs, he wrote Dumas, the American agent at the Hague, on December 25, 1786, asking for a confidential report as to whether it would be possible for the United States to borrow the necessary sum in Holland.[6] To this Dumas replied in a long letter of January 17, 1787, the essence of which was that "it is impossible to assert positively that a new negotiation could be effected, or to determine what might be the sum and the conditions of it," and adding a few half-digested suggestions of his own. Undismayed, Jefferson continued to urge his point.[7] "Would to heaven they would authorize you to take measures for transferring the debt of this country to Holland, before you leave Europe," he writes Adams not long before the latter's return to the United States. "I have pressed [it] on them ... in order to remove everything which may excite irritations between us and this nation. I wish it may be done before this ministry may receive ill impressions of us. They are at present very well disposed." [8] And again, on August 2, 1787, in urging Madison to use his influence in Congress, he says, "I must press on one subject. Mr. Adams informs me he has borrowed money in Holland, which, if confirmed by Congress, will enable them to pay, not only the interest due here to the foreign officers, but the principal. Let me beseech you to reflect on the expediency of transferring this debt to Holland. All our other debts in Europe do not injure our reputation so much as this. These gentlemen have connections both in and out of office, and these again their connections, so that our default in this article is further known, more blamed and excites worse dispositions against us than you can conceive. If you think as I do, pray try to procure an order for paying off their capital." [9]

It cannot have been pleasant for Jefferson to have been pelted by requests for money from the French officers who had served in America, or their wives, the more so as he was in no position to help them. Each one was conscious that he had a case, and he was not hesitant about making himself heard. The bankers who had financed the loans or bought up blocks of the securities were equally vociferous. Letters from these gentlemen cluttered Jefferson's mail. A letter from the Chevalier de Sigond is typical of the many. He writes saying that the interest was two years in arrears and asks, "Shall it be much longer, and must we forever apply to our friends for the purpose of fulfilling our engagements, when we cannot do it ourselves? After we have exposed our lives for the service of your States, and after we have co-operated in the great work of your independence, is it not natural that we would depend on an income so well acquired? When, during a very long war, we have deprived ourselves of all enjoyments, and when we could not even procure ourselves the absolute necessaries of life, except at our own expense, is it not horrible that the States should be so long in liquidating a debt which they have authentically acknowledged as well as acquired—that they do not pay even the interest?" [10]

There was no answer to such a letter. Even excuses seemed futile. Jefferson's reply is straightforward yet sympathetic. He holds out the only hope there is, the hope of truth. The letter is characteristic of the many that passed across his desk in an endeavor "to quiet, as well as I can, those interested." [11] "I have duly received the letter with which you have been pleased to honor me," he writes, "complaining of the non-payment of interest on the sum due to you from the United States.

I feel with great sensibility the weight of these complaints, but it is neither in my province nor in my power to remedy them. I am noways authorized to interfere with the money matters of the United States in Europe. These rest altogether between the Commissioners of the Treasury of the United States at New York and their bankers in Europe. Being informed, however, from Mr. Grand [a banker] that the funds appropriated to the payment of the foreign officers were exhausted, I took the liberty of representing strongly to the Commissioners the motives which should urge them to furnish new supplies. They assured me in answer, that they would do it at the first moment it should be in their power. I am perfectly persuaded they will. However, I shall immediately forward to them the letter you have been pleased to address to me, and will observe to you that it is to them alone, or to Congress, to whom you can make any future applications with effect." [12]

The situation took an even more ominous turn when the subject of the American debt was discussed in the Assemblée des Notables. Jefferson reports that "hard things were said of us. They were induced, however, in committing us to writing, to smother their ideas a little [something in which the hand of Lafayette is again doubtless to be seen]. In the notes, now gone to be printed, our debt is described in these words: 'The twenty-first article of the account, formed of the interest of the claims of his Majesty on the United States of America, cannot be drawn out for the present, except as a document. The recovery of these claims, as well principal as perhaps even interest, although they appear to rest on the most solid security, may, nevertheless, be long delayed, and should not, consequently, be taken into account in estimating the annual revenue. This article amounts to one million and six hundred thousand livres.'

"Above all things," he continues, "it is desirable to hush the foreign officers by payment.... I hear ... that Mr. Beaumarchais means to make himself heard, if a memorial which he sends by an agent in the present packet is not attended to as he thinks it ought to be. He called on me with it and desired me to recommend his case to a decision, and to note in my dispatch that it was the first time he had spoken to me on the subject. This is true, it being the first time I ever saw him, but my recommendations would be as displaced as unnecessary. I assured him Congress would do in that business, what justice should require, and their means enable them." Once more he urges his sovereign remedy, as he holds out a plum for inducement, "Congress will judge by Mr. Adams' letters," he says, "how far the transferring all our debts to this country, to Holland, is practicable. On the replenishing of their treasury with our principal and interest, I should not be afraid to ask concessions in favor of our West India trade. It would produce a great change of opinion as to us and our affairs." [13]

As was usual with Congress, no immediate action was taken. That body seemed quite oblivious of its obligation to the men who had helped bring salvation in the hard days preceding victory. Shortly before Jefferson went to Amsterdam, in March, 1786, an incident occurred that once again threatened international relations. "The foreign officers," he later wrote the Board of Treasury, "had proposed a meeting, the object of which was, as I heard, to address Congress in terms which would have been very disagreeable, and, at the same time, to present a petition to the King, claiming his interposition. This would have made a great deal of noise and produced very disagreeable effects." The day before his departure Jefferson sought out one of the leaders of the movement, Colonel Gouvion, "and desired him to quiet them till my return, explaining to him that one of the objects of my journey would be to enable you to pay them. I have, since my return, informed them of the prospect of payment, and that your orders for that purpose may be hoped by the end of June." [14]

One great hope of financial salvation and thus of paying these pressing obligations lay, in Jefferson's eyes, in the sale of Western lands. "I turn to this precious resource," he writes his old friend Edward Carrington in December, 1787, when he had just learned of the successful sale of large areas, "as that which will, in every event, liberate us from our domestic debt, and perhaps too, from our foreign one, and this much sooner than I had expected." He did not think, however, "that anything could have been done with them in Europe. Individual speculators and sharpers had duped so many with their unlocated land-warrants, that every offer would have been suspected." [15]

Shortly after this he was reassuring C. W. T. Dumas, the United States agent already mentioned, on the status of the American debt, and commending him for his publications in the Leyden *Gazette* "which will tend to re-establish that credit which the solidity of our affairs deserve. With respect to the sale of lands," he goes on to say, "we know that two sales of five millions and two millions of acres have been made. Another was begun for four millions which, in the course of the negotiation, may have been reduced to three millions, as you mention. I have not heard that this sale is absolutely concluded, but there is reason to presume it. Stating these sales at two-thirds of a dollar the acre, and allowing for 3 or 400,000 acres sold at public sale, and a very high price, we may say they have absorbed seven millions of dollars of the federal debt. The states, by taxation, and otherwise, have absorbed eleven million more, so that debt stands now at about ten millions of dollars, and will probably be all absorbed in the course of the next year. There will remain, then, our foreign debt, between ten and twelve millions, including interest. The sale of lands will then go on for the payment of this. But as this payment must be in cash, not in public effects, the lands must be sold cheaper. The demand will probably be less brisk. So we may suppose this will be longer paying off than the domestic debt." [16]

The close of 1787 brought on a crisis in the financial relations of the United States and its European creditors, which blossomed into a full-blown one by February. In December Jefferson had received word that the principal of a loan of 51,000 florins obtained by the bankers Fiseaux and Co. would be due on the first of the year. He was at first inclined to say that he was "in nowise authorized" to do anything about it, that it rested altogether with the Board of Treasury. "But on consulting with some persons better acquainted with the delicacy of credit in Holland, I found there was reason to fear that a failure to pay that money might not only do essential injury to our credit in general, but even hinder the progress of the loan going on in the hands of Willincks and Van Staphorsts; and that it would be for the interest of that loan itself, to pay this demand out of it, if possible." Jefferson consulted Adams, who agreed, and wrote Willincks and Van Staphorsts. They "answered that they had in their hands money enough to pay the February interest of the former loan . . . but that if they should pay Fiseaux's loan, it would be an advance of their own. They likewise observed, that to pay such a sum without your orders, placed them under an unnecessary responsibility. Upon this I concluded to ask them only to pay this year's interest, now becoming due, to desire Fiseaux to receive this, and with it endeavor to quiet the creditors till your orders could be received." [17]

At almost the same time Willincks and Van Staphorsts were suddenly informed by the Commissioners of the Treasury that they would be unable "to remit them one shilling till the New Government gets into action, and that therefore the sole resource for the payment of the Dutch interest till that period is in the progress of the last loan. Willincks and Van Staphorsts reply that there is not the least probability of raising as much on that loan as will pay the next June interest, and that, if that payment fails one day, it will do an injury to our credit, which a very long time will not wipe out." Jefferson then outlines a scheme of "a Mr. Stanitski, one of our brokers who holds $4,340,000 of our domestic debt" whereby, upon payment of "one year's interest of that debt, he will have the whole of the loan immediately filled up, that is to say he will procure the sum of 622,840 florins still unsubscribed." The bankers claimed "that by this means they can pay Fiseaux's debt, and all the Dutch interest, and our current expenses here, till June, 1789, by which time the new government may be in action. They have proposed this to the Commissioners of the Treasury." [18]

A further complication arose from the speculation by the European bankers of some $840,000 in the domestic debt of the United States. "A year's interest was becoming due on this, and they wished to avail themselves of our want of money for the foreign interest, to obtain payment of the domestic," Jefferson writes Jay.[19] "This circumstance, and the failure to pay off Fiseaux's loan were the sole causes of the stagnation of our late loan. For otherwise our credit would have stood on more hopeful grounds than heretofore. If the transfer of these debts to Europe meet with any encouragement from us," he informs the Commissioners of the Treasury, "we can no more borrow money here, let our necessities be what they will. For who will give ninety-six percent for the foreign obligations of the same nation, whose domestic ones can be bought in the same market for fifty-five percent? The former, too, bearing an interest of only five percent, while the latter yields six. If any discouragements can be honestly thrown on this transfer, it would seem advisable, in order to keep the domestic debt at home." [20] He then proposes a certain measure which, he declares, is not for him to decide but for the Commissioners to take under consideration.

Business of this sort, Jefferson says, was "the most disagreeable to me of all others, and for which I am the most unfit person living. I do not understand bargaining, nor possess the dexterity requisite for that purpose." [21] "Pressed," as he says, "between the danger of failure on the one hand, and an impossible proposition on the other, I heard of Mr. Adams being gone to the Hague to take leave. His knowledge of the subject was too intimate to be neglected under the present difficulty, and it was the last moment of which we could be availed of it." [22] He turned to his old friend who, "while residing at the Hague, had a general authority to borrow what sums might be requisite for ordinary and necessary expenses. Interest on the public debt, and the maintenance of the diplomatic establishment in Europe, had been habitually provided in this way. He was now elected Vice-President of the United States, was soon to return to America, and had referred our bankers to me for future counsel, on our affairs in their hands. But I had no powers, no instructions, no means and no familiarity with the subject." [23] Jefferson thus wrote him, on the sixth of February, to "avail myself of your counsel" before "the decision of this proposition [may be forced] on me at the eleventh hour. . . . Your knowledge of the subject enables you to give the best opinion, and your zeal for the public interest, and, I trust, your friendly disposition towards me will prompt you to assist me with your advice on this question, to wit"—and he gives a formal presentation of the problem,[24] which it is not in place to discuss here.

At the same time he wrote the Commissioners of the Treasury in great detail, remarking that "on these points it is for you to decide" and recalling to mind certain conditions which would have to be met should he "receive your acceptance of the proposition." He concludes his letter with the mournful observation that "the same stagnation attending our passage from the old to the new form of government, which stops the feeble channel of money hitherto flowing towards our treasury, has suspended also what foreign credit we had, so that at this moment we may consider the progress of our loan as stopped. Though much an enemy to the system of borrowing, yet I feel strongly the necessity of preserving the power to borrow. Without this we might be overwhelmed by another nation merely by the force of its credit." [25]

The only solution to this complicated business seemed for Jefferson to meet Adams at the Hague and then proceed with him to Amsterdam, the financial capital. He had offered the Commissioners of the Treasury to do this, in his letter of February 7, but well knowing the time inevitably lost by "the delay of letters coming and going," he determined to make the trip without waiting for official sanction. On the second of March he wrote Adams, "I am so anxious to confer with you on the subject, and to see you and them [the bankers] together, and get some effectual arrangements made in time, that I determine to meet you at the Hague. I will set out the moment some repairs are made to my carriage.... I am sensible how irksome this must be to you in the moment of your departure. But it is a great interest of the United States which is at stake, and I am sure you will sacrifice to that your interest and your feelings." [26] True to his word, Jefferson "set out for Amsterdam" on Tuesday, March 4. It was a hurried journey, for he was anxious to reach his destination as soon as possible, and a monotonous one, as all who have made the journey from Paris to Brussels can testify. It was the same road in Jefferson's time as in ours, through the lovely old town of Senlis, marked by its noble thirteenth-century spire, to the ancient, fortified stronghold of Peronne on the Somme, some ninety-four miles from Paris, where he spent the night at the Grand Cerf. An early start the next day brought him through Valenciennes and Mons to Braine le Comte for the night and Brussels to breakfast the next morning. Whether he did so in the superbly beautiful Grand Place with its gilded gables and balconies gleaming in the morning sun, he does not tell us. Presently he was on his way again, reaching Antwerp in time for dinner that day, Rotterdam the next, and the Hague on the ninth.

From the Hague he wrote Short, "After two days of prosperous journey, I had a good gleam of hope of reaching this place in the night of the third day. In fact, however, I got on the third day only to within eight hours land journeying and the passage of the Moerdyke. Yet this remnant employed me three days and nothing less than [illegible] of God could have shortened this time of torture. I saw the Saturday passing over and, in imagination, the packet sailing and Mr. Adams on board. And it was not till Sunday my anxieties were ended by finding him here.... I was at Rotterdam the evening of the prince's birthday. The illuminations were the most splendid I had ever seen and the roar of joy the most universal I had ever heard. My journey has been little entertaining. A country of corn and pasture affords little interesting to an American who has seen in his own country so much of that, and who travels to see the country and not the cities." [27]

The Amsterdam conference proved successful beyond Jefferson's hopes. He was able to write a triumphant report of it to Jay, as well as to the Board of Treasury. To George Washington, soon to be head of the new government, he sent the most lucid and most penetrating analysis of his mission, without going into confusing technical details. He explains his sudden trip to Holland by pointing out "the danger of our incurring something like a bankruptcy in Holland," and analyzes the situation already discussed here. Although he found it "easier to discover than to remove the causes which obstructed the progress of the loan," he found himself happy to inform Washington that "we were able to set the loan agoing again, and that the evil is at least postponed." There was, however, the bugaboo of Congress and its approval, but Jefferson was "tolerably satisfied that if all the measures we proposed are ratified by Congress, European calls for money (except the French debt) are secure enough till the end of the year 1790, by which time, we calculated, the new government might be able to get money into their treasury.

"Much conversation with the bankers, brokers and moneyholders," he continues, "gave me an insight into the state of national credit there, which I had never before been able satisfactorily to get," and he proceeds to share this knowledge with Washington, to whom in his new nonmilitary rôle, it might be of no little value. "The English credit is the first, because they never open a loan without laying and appropriating the taxes for the payment of the interest, and there has never been an instance of their failing one day in that payment. The Emperor [of Austria] and the Empress [of Russia] have good credit, because they use it very little and have hitherto been very punctual. This country is among the lowest in point of credit. Ours stands on hope only. They consider us as the surest nation on earth for the repayment of the capital, but as the punctual payment of interest is of absolute necessity in their arrangements, we can borrow but with difficulty and disadvantage. The moneyed men, however," he adds, holding out a ray of hope, "look towards our new government with a great degree of partiality and even anxiety. If they see that set out on the English plan, the first degree of credit will be transferred to us.

"The transfer of the French debt, public and private, to Amsterdam is certainly desirable," he continues, again touching on his solution of this festering sore. "An act of the new government, therefore, for opening a loan in Holland for the purpose, laying taxes at the same time for paying annually the interest and a part of the principal, will answer the two valuable purposes of ascertaining the degree of our credit and of removing those causes of bickering and irritation which should never be permitted to subsist with a nation, with which it is so much to our interest to be on cordial terms as with France." He speaks again of the injury done to the United States by not having paid the money due the French officers for three years and concludes, "Borrowing as we have done, 300,000 florins a year to pay our interest in Holland, it would have been worth while to have added 20,000 more to suppress these clamors. I am anxious about everything which may affect our credit. My wish would be to possess it in the highest degree, but use it little." [28]

After Adams left, on the twenty-first, Jefferson stayed on at Amsterdam until the thirtieth of March, "in hopes of seeing the millions of the last year filled up," he writes Jay. "This, however, could not be accomplished on the spot. But the prospect was so good, as to have dissipated all fears." [29] He used the time when the main conferences were over for "seeing things," as he always did, and in making purchases of things not available in Paris or the United States, such as waffle irons, a pound of Hyson's tea, another letter press, and, of course, books. It was the season when the flat and monotonous country between Amsterdam and Haarlem is transformed by the glory of thousands of acres of tulips—yellow, pink, red, purple, the spectrum of the rainbow, and then more. Jefferson took a day to drive to Haarlem, only some fifteen miles from Amsterdam, to see this sight, which is unequaled elsewhere in the world. Here he also visited the handsome mansion of the Dutch banker Hope, just being built, and drew a plan and elevation of it. It was a Palladian villa with double frontispiece of columns, very much on the order of Monticello as Jefferson then intended it to be. "It is said this house will cost four tons of silver or forty thousand pounds sterling," he writes, and his heart may well have sunk. "The separation between the middle building and wings in the upper story has a capricious appearance," he comments, "yet a pleasing one." [30]

In reading over the memoranda Jefferson made at Amsterdam, it would seem as though little in the way of things that were new or unfamiliar to him, had escaped his notice. He observes for instance how the joists of the houses are placed, how the windows open "so that they admit air and not rain." The "manner of fixing a flag staff on the mast of a vessel" is discussed, as well as the local way of making "dining tables letting down with single or double leaves, so as to take the room of their thickness only with a single leaf when open." Diagrams are drawn for all these devices. "A lantern over the street door which gives light equally into the antechamber and the street" receives the same attention as a Dutch wheelbarrow. The aviary of Mr. Ameshoff, merchant at Amsterdam, is singled out as being particularly worthy of comment. Even the four leading banking firms are carefully analyzed.[31] Finally, on the thirtieth of March, after paying "entertainment at the Waping Van Amsterdam, 187 f.," he set off for Utrecht on his way to Germany.

By the middle of May, after his return to Paris, Jefferson was able to write the Board of Treasury, as well as Jay, that the Dutch bankers "had disposed of bonds enough to pay our June interest and to replace the temporary advances made by Mr. Grand, and from a fund placed here by the State of Virginia I have desired them, accordingly, to replace these moneys, which had been lent for the moment only, and in confidence of immediate repayment. They add that the payment of the June interest and the news from America will, as they trust, enable them to replace the remaining bonds of last year's million." [32]

Jefferson's troubles were far from over with the successful termination of the loan. It had still to be ratified by Congress and directions given as to the apportionment of the money. By September 6 he had received word that the former had been accomplished. He felt impelled to write the Board of Treasury on the second point. He and Adams had joined in sending Congress an estimate of the proposed outlay of the funds. "As the necessity of this loan resulted from the estimate made by Mr. Adams and myself," he presumed "that the ratification of the loan implies that of the estimate. One article of this was for the redemption of our captives in Algiers," and he urges the Board to send orders for this to the commissioners of the loans at Amsterdam if it has not already been done. "So also for the foreign officers." At this point he makes a suggestion which would seem to have all the earmarks of common sense. No more cumbersome arrangement could have been contrived than existed in regard to these foreign loans and payments. "If the ratification of the loan has been made by Congress," Jefferson writes, with a view to fulfill the objects of the estimate, "a general order from you to the Commissioners of the loans at Amsterdam, to pay the moneys from time to time, according to that estimate, or to such other as you shall furnish them with, might save the trouble of particular orders on every single occasion, and the disappointments arising from the delay or miscarriage of such orders. But it is for you to decide on this." [33]

Meanwhile Jefferson was to discover that all was not smooth sailing as far as the Dutch bankers were concerned. In February, 1789, he received a letter from Willincks and Van Staphorsts declining to make payments for the medals Congress had ordered, as well as for the release of the Algerine captives, to say nothing of the French soldiers. "They quote a resolution of Congress appropriating the loans of 1787 and 1788 to the payment of interest on Dutch loans till 1790, inclusive, and the residue to salaries and contingencies in Europe. . . . Since I have had occasion to pay attention to the proceedings of those gentlemen . . ." Jefferson remarks to Jay, "I have observed that as soon as a sum of interest is becoming due, they are able to borrow just that and no more, or at least only so much more as may pay our salaries and keep us quiet. . . . I think it possible they may choose to support our credit to a certain point, and let it go no further, but at their will; to keep it so poised, as that it may be at their mercy. By this they will be sure to keep us in their own hands." [34] Jefferson wrote the bankers a letter that would have turned a heart of stone. He sent a copy of their letter and his reply to Jay. For once the Board of Treasury acted with promptness. By May Jefferson was able to inform Jay that orders had arrived which "have now settled this question. The interest of the next month is to be first paid, and after that the money for the captives and foreign officers is to be furnished, before any other payment of interest. . . . My representations to them, on account of the contracts I have entered into for making the medals, have produced from them the money of that object, which is to be lodged in the hands of Mr. Grand." [35]

During the last year or so of his stay in France, Jefferson may well be said to have been as deeply concerned with affairs in America, the adoption of the Constitution, and the forming of the new government as he was with those in France. The necessity of preserving close and friendly relations was constantly in his mind. With the prospect of the new government superseding the old and cumbersome Congress, he gave even more thought than usual to this. "This Government [the French] will expect, I fancy, a very satisfactory provision for the payment of their debt from the new session of Congress," he writes Madison, in November, 1788. "Perhaps, in this matter, as well as in the arrangement of your foreign affairs, I may be able, when on the spot with you, to give some information and suggest some hints, which may render my visit to my native country not altogether useless." Meanwhile, "supposing the funding of the foreign debt will be among the first operations of the new government," he sent two estimates, one by himself, one by "a gentleman infinitely better acquainted with the subject, showing what fund will suffice to discharge the principal and interest, as it shall become due, aided by occasional loans, which the same fund will repay."[36]

In his last letter from Paris to Jay, written on September 19, Jefferson was able to write, "I am well informed that our credit is now the first at that [the Amsterdam] exchange, England not borrowing at present. Our five percent bonds have risen to ninety-seven and ninety-nine. They have been heretofore at ninety-three. There are, at this time, several companies and individuals here, in England and Holland, negotiating to sell large parcels of our liquidated debt. A bargain was concluded by one of these the other day for six hundred thousand dollars. In the present state of our credit, every dollar of this debt will probably be transferred to Europe within a short time."[37]

Although Jefferson may have discounted his own abilities as a financier, he must have felt a certain satisfaction over the outcome of his efforts, and in his heart he must have been able to say, "This was a task well done."

XI. Jefferson's Rhine Journey

WITH HIS BUSINESS in Amsterdam concluded and nothing urgent demanding his immediate return to Paris, Jefferson determined, as he said, to gratify "the desire of seeing what I have not yet seen,"[1] and "return along the banks of the Rhine to Strassburg, and thence strike off to Paris."[2] He was embarking upon something of an adventure. Early in life, as we have seen, he had had the ambition to "visit particularly England, Holland, France, Spain, Italy (where I would buy me a good fiddle) and Egypt."[3] Germany was not included in these tentative plans. This was not surprising, for at that time Germany and the Germans were as remote to the British colonials of Tidewater Virginia as was Tibet. German literature, as we know it, had not yet flowered, and there were few German books to be found on the shelves of colonial libraries. The German philosophers were known either in Latin, in which language they usually wrote, or in French translation. There is no evidence that Jefferson knew German, except for an abortive attempt in his youth.[4] Indeed, as late as 1814, we have his own statement that he was unacquainted with the works of Goethe, the outstanding literary figure of the time.

Unlike his journey to the South of France, which was undertaken primarily for reasons of health, the expenses of this trip, which amounted to 1,228 livres, were charged to the United States. There can be no question but that it was entered upon in part for the study of the agriculture and, more particularly, of the viniculture of Germany. What he had written George Wythe the preceding year on his return to Italy held doubly true of his trip to Germany: "In architecture, painting, sculpture, I found much amusement, but more than all in their agriculture, many objects of which might be adopted with us to great advantage."[5] It remained Jefferson's creed throughout his life that "the greatest service which can be rendered any country is to add an useful plant to its culture." [6]

In making this journey along the Rhine, Jefferson was once more something of a pioneer. The grand tour, as hitherto understood by adventuresome Englishmen of the period and such Americans as visited the Continent, generally included only traveling from England to France and, ultimately, crossing the Alps to Italy. The romantic *Rheinfahrt* as we know it and as it has been known since the spread of romanticism in the early nineteenth century was unheard of in Jefferson's day. The search for the picturesque was a concept alien to the minds of most men of that time. Germany, with its walled cities, its medieval fortifications, its persistent feudal character, to say nothing of the barrier of its language, seldom, if ever, entered the traveler's thoughts. The majority of the persons to be found on a Rhine bateau, aside from local traffic, were people who had been in Switzerland for one reason or another and were now on their way back to Holland or England.

To be sure, at least one of the books on travel that Jefferson owned before this time, Nugent's *Grand Tour,* has the subtitle *Or a Journey through the Netherlands, Germany, Italy and France,*[7] and the author devotes considerable space to a description of Germany, but it is very doubtful whether this book provided the stimulus for Jefferson's going there. It is much more likely that his Rhine journey came about through his friendship with John Trumbull, the painter, whom, as we have seen, he had met in London and who had visited him in Paris in the summer of 1786.

On the ninth of September of that year, Trumbull left Paris for Metz, on his way to Frankfurt-am-Main, where he had an appointment to meet Alexander di Poggi, an Italian artist "of very superior talents as a draughtsman and who had recently commenced the business of publishing." [8] On the advice of his master, Benjamin West, Trumbull had determined to have engraved the first two of his historical pictures, thus, as he says, not only diffusing more widely the knowledge of his talent but receiving "more adequate compensation for my labor." [9] As no suitable engravers were free to assume the task in London at the moment, Poggi undertook to find someone on the

Continent, and Trumbull agreed to meet him in Frankfurt at the moment of the famous *Herbstmesse*, when artists from all over Europe congregated for the sales of pictures that took place at this time.

Trumbull took the road through Metz, Saarbrücken, Mannheim, Worms—where he describes the cathedral as "a very clumsy, heavy Gothic building"—and Oppenheim, "a wretched old Gothic town, once walled, now in decay," to Frankfurt. Here he met Poggi, who was attending the *Herbstmesse*, which drew enormous throngs, and spent three days "running around the town," as he tells us. This included seeing the collections, notably that of "Monsieur Stadle," which was to become the well-known Städel Art Institute. His business concluded, Trumbull set off for Mainz on the twenty-second of September in "a bateau with oars and awning" and proceeded down the Rhine as far as Cologne. There were stops at Bingen, Bacharach, Coblenz and Neuwied, where, owing to very bad weather, he accepted a seat in a chaise with a traveling companion and went on his way to Bonn, Cologne, and Düsseldorf. Here he spent three days visiting the famous collection of paintings belonging to the Elector.

The journal that Trumbull kept of this trip abounds in comment and in vivid description of what he has seen. Being a painter, he could not limit himself to words but enlivened his diary with numerous sketches. There is one of the enchanting village of Dürckheim, with its colored stucco houses that look like the setting for a fairy tale, of Frankenstein with the Rhine Valley opening in the distance, of Bingen with its "ruin of some ancient Gothic castle, overhanging the river and subject country, like the eyrie of an eagle," and of Bacharach, that most romantic of all the towns along the Rhine. There are likewise several sketches of "the entrance to the Highlands of the Rhine," which Trumbull found "picturesque in the highest degree, far superior in grandeur to the highlands of the North River." [10]

When Trumbull reached Amsterdam on the ninth of October, he wrote Jefferson a long letter describing what he had seen on his travels in Germany. We are fortunate that it has been preserved among Jefferson's papers and has hitherto remained unpublished. It was just the sort of letter that would please Jefferson, going into details of soil, climate, population, and whet his desire to know more.

"My little tour," he writes, "has been infinitely more pleasant than I expected. I quitted Paris with regret, and the idea of traveling alone in a country whose language I did not understand was very unpleasant, —but I have been disappointed, in happily finding always some companion who spoke French, and frequently those who spoke English. I have found the distance more considerable and the roads worse in some parts than they were represented, by which means I arrived here only the 6th at night, several days later than I intended. From Paris to Metz my road was thro' a part of the wine country of Champagne, very beautiful, rough and finely cultivated. At Epernay I saw one of the great wine cellars and tasted the finest wine I ever saw. The country soon after sinked to a level sandy plain, covered with corn, but the soil very poor. Entering Lorrain at Clermont, you have again a rough broken country, but fertile; corn, vines, orchards, meadows and woods are intermixed with the most beautiful variety and the people appear to live plentifully and rich. From this to Metz the same style of country and cultivation continues, but with much more poverty both of soil and inhabitants. The situation of Metz is beautiful in a delightful valley, upon the banks of the Moselle, which is navigable for small boats. The town is very strongly fortified and the garrison numerous, but there is no appearance of commerce, manufactures, or industry among the inhabitants. From Metz to Frankfurt the distance is 53 leagues thro' the territory of Deuxponts and part of the Palatinate of the Rhine, the country generally mounts, now poor and thinly inhabited, and the roads a deep heavy sand. At the distance of 6 or 8 leagues from the banks of the Rhine, we leave the mountains and enter one of the most beautiful and fertile valleys of the world. The vines which we had scarcely seen after leaving Metz recommence, and the country is covered with every variety of production, and enrich'd with villages. The villages and inhabitants do not however bear those marks of ease and competency which one would expect even in arbitrary country, from so opulent a soil. The city of Worms is the first on the banks of the River—old, illbuilt, and ruinous —I should have supposed it had suffer'd a siege but a few weeks before

I passed—to Oppenheim where we crossed the river. For 2 leagues on the other side, the road is fine, and the country a perfect garden, from this to very near Frankfurt a dead barren soil, with no trace of cultivation and no production but starved white birch and pine, the roads a deep sand so heavy that I met waggons coming from the fair drawn by 20 horses, and scarce able to proceed even with such a number.

"The situation of Frankfurt is again delightful, the town well built, full of inhabitants and opulent. The fair is rich in the productions of every part of the world; the business which is done during the four weeks which it continues is very considerable, and the number of strangers who are brought together by their affairs or by curiosity very great. The business of all the interior part of Germany for the year is transacted at this time. From Frankfurt to Mayence I went by water, down the Main, in a barge in which were 2 or 300 animals of all ages, ranks, and religions—Jew pedlars, Catholic priests, ladies, market women, beggars, blind fiddlers and German counts. At first entering the boat, I was a little disconcerted—without a companion in such a chaos. I look'd round however, for some one with a good coat and addressed myself to an elderly, decent man, in my best French which, Grace à Dieu, he understood. I found afterwards a lady of Mayence with her daughter, who spoke French also, and passed the day pleasantly. At Mayence (the Maguntium of Caesar) are several remains of Roman power—a tower in the citadel called the monument of Drusus, and ruins of a bridge across the Rhine visible only when the river is very low.—The town is large, well fortified, pretty well built but little commerce, an university, &c. From Mayence I embarked for Cologne, but the weather became bad, the wind contrary, and I was oblig'd to leave the water at Unternach 20 leagues above Cologne. The country through which the river takes its course is for 8 leagues level, fertile and rich. It then meets a chain of mountains similar to those on the North River, becomes contracted, the current broken by rocks and small rapids, which render the navigation somewhat dangerous. The shores are picturesque in the highest degree, precipices of rock, mountains, sometimes barren, again cover'd with vines, and the summits of those which are least accessible cover'd with the ruins of ancient Gothic châteaux, ruins of barbarism which one contemplates with pleasure, as they are so many monuments of the advances of civilization and happiness. The river was really dangerous before we quitted it, and even then we left it with reluctance, so great were its beauties. Rode post all night through Bonn and Cologne, and therefore, know little of the country or towns, except that the latter is large and very ill built. The country from this to Düsseldorf is flat, beautiful, highly cultivated. Düsseldorf is a pleasant little town, remarkable for nothing but the Electoral palace and gallery—but such a gallery as would well repay the trouble of a much longer and less pleasant journey. The works of Rubens, which are the finest part of the collection, are wonderful—much beyond all that I had imagin'd, but an attempt at description would be ridiculous. I stayed here three days, and then took the German post wagon for Aix la Chapelle." [11]

When Trumbull again visited Jefferson in Paris the following year and showed his sketches, there can be little doubt that the two men discussed this journey, so unusual for a foreigner at the time, and that Jefferson then and there determined to retrace the footsteps of his friend at the first opportunity.

Aside from his pocket account book of this period, Jefferson has left us two documents as memorials of his Rhine journey. One, entitled "Memorandum on a Tour from Paris to Amsterdam, Strassburg and back to Paris," is a matter-of-fact record of his tour with emphasis on the curiosities he encountered, whether of an agricultural, mechanical, or architectural nature. He lists the cities through which he passed, comments on the condition of the country and its inhabitants, and goes into considerable detail concerning the wines of the Moselle and the Rhine. Indeed, he follows very much the scheme employed by Nugent in his *Grand Tour*. Except for a phrase or two, it is bare of any description of the scenery, or of any emotional or aesthetic reaction either to nature or to art. He passed through all the great cathedral towns of the Rhine without a word of what he saw. It is almost as though we saw engraved upon his mind the words Goethe had written in Strassburg in 1772: "The first time I visited the cathedral my head was full of all sorts of ideas concerning good taste. Because of hearsay, I paid homage to the harmony of mass and purity of form. I was a sworn enemy of the confused arbitrariness of Gothic decoration. Under the ruberic *Gothic,* as in the headings of a dictionary, I grouped all synonymous misunderstandings which had ever crossed my mind, concerning what is vague, unorganized, unnatural, patched up, revamped and overloaded. No more intelligent than a people which calls the world it does not know, barbaric, I called everything *Gothic* which did not fit into my system . . . and thus I shuddered at the sight of an ill-formed, frizzled, bristly monstrosity." [12]

For natural beauty, however, Jefferson was inevitably prepared. Not in vain had he been born in the beneficent shadow of the Blue Ridge Mountains. Neither did he blindly elect to build his own house on the summit of a mountain commanding a magnificent panorama of the surrounding country. None of this creeps into his "Memorandum," however. Indeed, in the many letters he wrote to his family and friends during his European travels, only two lyric passages may be said to occur, the poem to a Roman temple addressed to Madame de Tessé already mentioned, and a letter to his daughter Martha, written from the canal of Languedoc. It must be remembered, however, that Jefferson was of a reserved nature and that he was not in the habit of freely expressing his feelings on any subject that lay close to his heart.

The second record of his Rhine journey is in the form of "Traveling Notes for Mr. Rutledge and Mr. Shippen" which will be discussed presently.

On March 26, in anticipation of his Rhine journey, Jefferson purchased "Koops 10 Maps of the Rhine, the Mass and the Scheldt, Gr. format," [13] for which he paid five florins, six stivers. Four days later he left Amsterdam and proceeded to Utrecht by boat. At that period three draw-boats a day made the run, the first leaving at eight in the morning, and were the favored method of making this trip. "Go in the track scout (*i.e.,* drag scow)," Jefferson advised his young friends taking the same trip, "on account of the remarkable pleasantness of the canal. You can have the principal cabin to yourselves for 52 stivers." [14]

Accompanied only by his servant Espagnol, as he believed that "one travels more usefully when alone, because he reflects more," Jefferson went on his way. "To Utrecht nothing but plains are seen," he writes, "... almost entirely in grass; few or no farm houses.... The Canal is lined with country houses which bespeak the wealth and cleanliness of the country: but generally in an uncouth state and exhibiting no regular architecture. After passing Utrecht, the hills northeast of the Rhine come into view." Disembarking at Utrecht and using his own chariot with post horses, he proceeded along the road that has since become so familiar to many of us on our journeys to the Rhine, through Kress, where he found the view from the hill "sublime," on to Nijmegen, crowning an amphitheater of seven hills, where he was equally enthusiastic over the prospect up and down the river Waal from the tower of the Bellevue. At this town, Jefferson observes, you must bribe your hostler "to put as few horses to your carriage as you think you can travel with. Because with whatever number of horses you arrive at the first post house in Germany, with that they will oblige you to go through the whole Empire. I paid the price of four horses on condition they would put but three to my chariot." [15]

From Nijmegen Jefferson drove on through those ancient towns rich in Germanic lore: Kleve, with its Schwanenburg and Schwanen-Turm, the legendary seat of Wagner's hero Lohengrin; Xanten, which is mentioned in the Nibelungenlied as the birthplace of Siegfried; Rheinberg; and Duisburg, once a Roman port. The first day of traveling in Germany must have been more or less of a disappointment to Jefferson. A storm of alternate rain and snow began at Kleve and continued intermittently for five days. "The transition from ease and opulence to extreme poverty," Jefferson notes, giving his first impressions of the country, "is remarkable on crossing the line between the Dutch and Prussian territories. The soil and climate are the same, the governments alone differ. With the poverty, the fear also of slaves is visible in the faces of the Prussian subjects. There is an improvement, however, in the physiognomy, especially could it be a little brightened up.

"The road," he continues, "leads generally over the hills, but sometimes through skirts of the plains of the Rhine. These are always extensive and good. They want manure, being visibly worn down. The hills are almost always sandy, barren, uncultivated, and insusceptible of culture, covered with broom and moss, here and there a little indifferent forest, which is sometimes of beech.... There are no châteaux, nor houses that bespeak the existence of even a middle class. Universal and equal poverty overspreads the whole.... The cultivators seem to live on their farms. The farm-houses are of mud, the better sort of brick; all covered over with thatch."

At Duisburg Jefferson was due for another surprise. In fact, he was quite unprepared for what we may call the medieval character of the country, which persisted in many places until very recent years. "Duisburg," he writes, "is but a village in fact, walled in; the buildings mostly of brick. No new ones, which indicate a thriving state." And now Jefferson was to regret that he had been so remiss in his study of German. "I had understood," he adds, "that near that were remains of the encampment of Varus, in which he and his legions fell by the arms of Arminius (in the time of Tiberius I think it was), but there was not a person to be found in Duisburg who could understand either English, French, Italian or Latin. So I could make no inquiry." [16] How disappointed he was we gather in his observation to Rutledge and Shippen. "I missed my object, therefore, tho' I had taken the road on purpose." To fail in something he had set out to do was a circumstance to which Jefferson found it difficult to reconcile himself.

Düsseldorf was the first city of any size encountered in Germany by Jefferson. Here he lodged, as he tells us, at the "Zwei Brücken Hof, chez Zimmerman, the best tavern I saw on my whole journey." [17] The chief attraction for him, however, was the famous art gallery, which he describes as sublime. It was the same one that Goethe had visited on his tour of the Rhine in 1774 and concerning which he had written Betty Jacobi, "I came from the gallery, which melted the hardness of my heart, strengthened it and thus steeled it." [18]

This Academy of Art had been founded in 1767, only twenty-one years before Jefferson's visit, by the art-loving Elector Karl Theodor. In the galleries of his imposing palace he had assembled the superb collection of Italian and Flemish masters that he and his predecessors had gathered. Most notable was the gallery of Rubens,[19] containing many of his finest creations, and "magnificently worthy of him," as Trumbull remarked. It was not these pictures, however, that attracted Jefferson—the man who wrote, "I do not feel an interest in any pencil except that of David," [20] could not find it in his heart to be truly appreciative of Rubens' magnificent sensuality—but those of a minor seventeenth-century Dutch painter, Adriaan Van der Werff. Jefferson was, alas, quite carried away by their cold and sterile beauty. He went so far, indeed, as to say that the gallery "is as great in merit as anything in the whole world, particularly the room of Van der Werff." [21] This extravagant admiration, as great as that shown by the Elector Johann Wilhelm, who brought the artist to Düsseldorf in 1697, was not shared by Jefferson's mentor Trumbull. "Of all the celebrated pictures I have ever seen," he wrote, "[these] appear to me to be the very worst—mere monuments of labor, patience, and want of genius." [22] This has been the judgment of posterity.

On the third of April, after two visits to the gallery, Jefferson left Düsseldorf for Cologne, where he passed the night at the "Holy Ghost, chez Ingal." En route, a little off the direct road but not far from Cologne, was the famous palace at Bensberg, likewise belonging to the Elector. It is described by one of Goethe's companions, on a similar tour, as "an Italian palace, filled with pictures, standing upon a high mountain. It probably commands the finest view in Germany and its situation is undoubtedly the most beautiful." [23] Jefferson knew of this château, as he calls it, and recommended it to the attention of Rutledge and Shippen, but he himself did not take the time to go there. In passing the boundaries of the property, however, he paused long enough to make a sketch of an unusual gate and incorporate this in his notes.

Of his visit to Cologne Jefferson might well echo the words of Victor Hugo, who exclaimed concerning his Rhine journey in 1838, "I passed through Cologne like a barbarian. . . . I left Agrippa's town behind me and I did not look at the old pictures in Sainte-Marie-au-Capitole, nor the crypt paved with mosaics from Saint-Gereon, nor the crucifixion of Saint Peter, painted by Rubens for the old half-Roman church of St. Peter, where he was baptized," and he continues with a list of the other sights he had missed. "I did not stop to look at any of these things," he concludes. "It is ridiculous, but it is true." [24]

Cologne was at this time one of the largest cities in Germany and one of the handsomest. It was "surrounded with a wall, and a dry ditch, with towers, and some bastions. . . . 'Tis very rare to see so many steeples any where at once, as appear to travelers approaching this city," writes one of them. "There are twenty-four gates, thirteen to the land, and eleven on the Rhine. . . . A very considerable part of the town is taken up with churches and monasteries. . . . The cathedral dedicated to St. Peter is a large and magnificent structure, but not finished." [25]

To all this Jefferson paid no attention. What did attract his interest, however, was the extensive commerce of the city. "A good deal is carried to America," he notes, and "its quai resembles, for the number of vessels, a seaport town." [26] The agriculture of the country was of no less consequence, in his eyes. "I observe," he remarks, "the hog of this country [Westphalia], of which the celebrated ham is made, is tall, gaunt, and with heavy lop ears. . . . Their principal food is acorns. . . . It is smoked in a room which has no chimney. Well-informed people here tell me there is no other part of the world where the bacon is smoked. They do not know that we do it," [27] he concludes, a little smugly.

At Cologne, he continues, referring to a subject that had interested him for a long time, "the vines begin, and it is the most northern spot on the earth on which wine is made. Their first grapes came from Orléans, since that from Alsace, Champagne, etc. It is thirty-two years only since the first vines were sent from Cassel, near Mayence, to the Cape of Good Hope, of which the Cape wine is now made. . . . That I suppose is the most southern spot on the globe where wine is made and it is singular that the same vine should have furnished two wines as much opposed to each other in quality as in situation." [28]

On the fourth of April Jefferson set off early from Cologne and reached Bonn, some twenty-five kilometers distant, in time to breakfast there. About halfway between the two places, only a few miles off the road, is situated the beautiful palace of Brühl built as a country seat by the Elector Clement Augustus in 1725. With its handsome rococo decoration and its splendid garden laid out on lines reminiscent of that of Versailles although, of course, on a smaller scale, it is one of the outstanding monuments of the electoral period. Again Jefferson did not stop here, either because he did not know it, which seems improbable, or because he was in too great haste. His whole trip, indeed, had something of the whirlwind character that has ever distinguished Americans traveling on the Continent.

Jefferson makes no comment on the historic town of Bonn, which was originally one of the fifty fortresses built along the Rhine in the year 10 B.C. by Drusus, the commander of the Roman legions. He tells his protégés that "the palace here is to be seen" (it is the palace of the Elector, which since housed the University of Bonn), but he does not describe it or express any opinion about it. The chief objects that attracted his attention were again agricultural, the number of walnut trees growing in the open fields and the beginning of the extensive culture of the grapevine. "These are planted in rows two or three feet apart both ways," he writes. "The vine is left six or eight feet high, and stuck with poles ten or twelve feet high. To these poles they are tied in two places, at the height of about two and four feet. They are now performing this operation. The hills are generally excessively steep, a great proportion of them barren; the rest in vines, principally, sometimes small patches of corn. In the plains, though rich, I observed they dung their vines plentifully; and it is observed here, as elsewhere, that the plains yield much wine, but bad. The good is furnished from the hills." [29]

From Cologne on, Jefferson's travel notes become practically a treatise on viniculture. It was a subject which had absorbed him for many years. As early as 1772, when Philip Mazzei had arrived in Virginia with the intention of introducing the art of making wine into the New World, Jefferson had taken a lively interest in it. He had persuaded Mazzei to settle on land adjoining his in Albemarle County, as we have seen,[30] had raised a fund of two thousand pounds sterling to assist him, and had watched with avidity each step in the clearing of the land and the planting of the vineyards. Then had come the revolutionary war: Mazzei was dispatched on a mission to Europe, his vignerons enlisted or became gardeners for the local gentry, his property was rented to General von Riedesel, "whose horses in one week," Jefferson tells us, "destroyed the whole labor of three or four years; and thus ended an experiment which, from every appearance, would in a year or two more have established the practicability of that branch of culture in America."[31]

Jefferson employed his trip to the South of France in 1787 as well as his Rhine journey to make an intensive study of wine—what were the best sort of grapes, under what conditions was the best wine produced, and so on. On his return from the former, he wrote William Drayton of South Carolina, who was quite as much interested as he in the promotion of all forms of agriculture, "I was induced, in the course of my journey through the south of France, to pay very particular attention to the objects of their culture, because the resemblance of their climate to that of the southern parts of the United States, authorizes us to presume we may adopt any of their articles of culture, which we would wish for. We should not wish for their wines, though they are good and abundant. The culture of the vine is not desirable in lands capable of producing anything else. . . . Wine, too, is so cheap in these countries, that a laborer with us, employed in the culture of any other article, may exchange it for wine, more and better than he could raise himself. It is a resource for a country, the whole of whose good soil is otherwise employed, and which still has some barren spots and surplus of population to employ on them."[32]

Jefferson's travels along the Rhine, his observation of the intensive, scientific culture of wine grapes, seems to have shaken the opinion expressed to Drayton. He was later to write, "We could, in the United States, make as great a variety of wines as are made in Europe, not exactly of the same kinds, but doubtless as good."[33] He even went so far as to advise Jean Baptiste Say, who wanted to remove to Virginia, that "both soil and climate are admirably adapted to the vine which is the abundant natural production of our forests, and you cannot bring a more valuable laborer than one acquainted with both its culture and manipulation into wine."[34]

On the evening of the fourth, Jefferson reached Coblenz and put up at L'Homme Sauvage, which he recommends as "a very good tavern." He was particularly struck by the bread. "Remarkably fine bread here," he writes Shippen and Rutledge, "particularly the rolls for breakfast, from which the Philadelphians derive what they call the French roll, which does not exist in France, but has been carried over by the Germans from Coblenz."

The morning after his arrival he visited the imposing palace of the Elector Clemens Wenceslaus, which had been completed only two years before. Disregarding the tapestries and paintings, the garden with its "statues, waterworks and charming orangery and bower, more than 3000 feet in length by the side of the Rhine," [35] Jefferson concentrated his attention on what was a great innovation at the time. This was a method of heating the rooms of the palace without stoves, something on the order of the modern hot-air heating system. He noted that the large rooms were "very well warmed by warm air conveyed from an oven below." [36]

At Coblenz Jefferson left the Rhine and started up the Lahn, through Nassau, Schwalbach, Wiesbaden, and Hochheim to Frankfurt. Here he had a rendezvous with Baron de Geismar, the former aide-de-camp of General von Riedesel, and an old friend of revolutionary days, when the General and his aide, as prisoners of war, were living at Colle on land adjoining Monticello. "The road from Nassau to Schwalbach," Jefferson wrote, "is over hills, or rather mountains, both high and steep; always poor, and above half of them barren in beech and oak. . . . Between Schwalbach and Wiesbaden we come in sight of the plains of the Rhine, which are very extensive. From hence the lands, both high and low, are very fine, in corn, vines and fruit trees. The country has the appearance of wealth, especially in the approach to Frankfurt." [37]

At Frankfurt Jefferson and Geismar met, according to plan, and Geismar, he tells us, acted "as my cicerone." Jefferson remained at Frankfurt four days, staying at the inn Zum Roten Haus. He took advantage of this large and flourishing city to buy some books, a surtout coat and to have another one made, to make some minor purchases and, above all, to indulge in his favorite pastime, visiting the comedy, which he did on the evenings of the sixth and seventh. He could not have been there at a more auspicious time. "It happens," he writes on the ninth to William Short, "to be the moment of the fair at Frankfurt, which is very great. Yesterday," he continues, "we made an excursion up the Main to Hanau, passing the ground where the battle of Bergen was fought in the war before the last. Tomorrow we shall go to the vineyards of Hochheim and perhaps Rudesheim and Johannisberg, where the most celebrated wines are made." [38]

About a dozen miles east of Frankfurt, at Hanau, "one of the neatest and most regular towns in Germany, where the drum and fife are all that is heard," Baron de Geismar was in garrison. Here, writes Jefferson, "I met with many old acquaintances. The officers who had been stationed in Albemarle with the captivity... But what I have met with the most wonderful in nature," he adds, with one of his rare flashes of humor, "is a set of men absolutely incorruptible by money, by fair words or by foul; and that this should, of all others, be the class of postillions. This, however, is the real character of German postillions, whom nothing on earth can induce to go out of a walk. This has retarded me not a little; so that I shall need to be delivered over to the great jack boots." [39]

A few miles from Hanau, at Wilhelmsbad, was situated the country seat of the Landgraf of Hessen. Geismar took Jefferson to see it and its park, which was still a favorite excursion with the inhabitants of Frankfurt, well into the twentieth century. The Landgraf was among the first in Germany to introduce the *Englischer Garten* and as a feature of it had caused to be erected a ruin which Jefferson describes as "clever" and of which he made a drawing. It represented the remains of an old castle, likewise a hermitage "in which is a good figure of an hermit in plaster, colored to the life, with a table and book before him, in the attitude of reading and contemplation. In a little cell is his bed; in another his books, some tools, etc., in another his little provision of firewood, etc." First and last the Landgraf's contemporaries considered that his "apartments were nobly furnished and the gardens laid out in a grand taste."

After four days rich in pleasure and in experience, and making countless observations on "things worth noting," Jefferson bade farewell to Frankfurt and to his hosts, the *Herren Dick, Vater and Sohn*, who were, as he says, great wine merchants as well as proprietors of Zum Roten Haus. The son, to Jefferson's great delight, spoke French and English, in addition to his native German, and had lived some time in London. He introduced Jefferson to the wine cellars for which he and his father were famous, and here Jefferson sampled "genuine Hock, and of the oldest." [40] At the same tavern Jefferson likewise found one Armand, an exceptional *valet de place* whom he describes as "sensible, active and obliging." Jefferson promptly engaged Armand to travel with him the next few days while he made a little tour to study the wines of the Rheingau. This is that short section of the Rhine, about fifteen miles in length, which produces the most superlative wines. It extends roughly from Rüdesheim to Johannisberg, or a little beyond. "Though they begin to make wine," Jefferson observes, "at Cologne, and continue it up the river indefinitely, yet it is only at Rüdesheim to Hochheim that wines of the first quality are made. The river here happens to run due east and west, so as to give its hills on that side a southern aspect, and even in this canton it is only Hochheim, Johannisberg and Rüdesheim that are considered of the very first quality." [41]

After leaving Frankfurt Jefferson stopped first at Hochheim, on the Main, home of the famous Hock, as the English, and half the world, call the wine of this region. "The spot whereon the good wine is made," Jefferson writes in his notes, "is the hill side from the church down the plain, a gentle slope of about a quarter of a mile wide, and extending half a mile towards Mayence. It is of southwestern aspect, very poor, sometimes grey, sometimes mulatto, with moderate mixture of broken stone. The vines are planted three feet apart, and stuck with sticks about six feet high. They are dunged once in three years.... They begin to yield a little at three years old and continue to one hundred years, unless sooner killed by a cold winter." [42] The agriculturalist in Jefferson could not resist the temptation. He bought one hundred vines for two florins, fifteen stivers,[43] which he later wrote Geismar "succeed to admiration." [44] He then went on to nearby Mainz, where he crossed the Rhine, he tells us, on a bridge one thousand eight hundred and forty feet long, supported by forty-seven boats.

Leaving his horses, he took passage on a bateau to go down the river as far as the famous Marco-Brunnen vineyard between Haltenheim and Erbach. "The women here do everything," he again observes with a certain indignation, for although a Joseph, Jefferson was an admirer of the fair sex. "They dig the earth, plow, saw, cut and split wood, row, tow the bateaux etc. In a small but dull kind of bateau," he continues, "with two hands rowing with a kind of large paddle, and a spare sail, but scarcely a breath of wind, we went down the river at the rate of five miles an hour, making it in three and a half hours to Rüdesheim." [45]

Here Jefferson stopped, not so much to look at the lovely village at the foot of the Niederwald, which marks the upper end of the narrowest section of the Rhine Valley, but to examine the vineyards. The famous white wine grown here claims a longer pedigree than that of any other section. Tradition has it that, from the window of his palace at Ingelheim, only a few miles distant, the observant Charlemagne noted that the first snow to melt was always on the Rüdesheimer Berg, to the west of the present town. He is said to have been the first who caused vines to be planted here. Determined to try his luck, Jefferson bought fifty vines here for two florins, fifteen stivers. "Its fine wines," he writes of Rüdesheim, "are made on the hills about a mile below the village, which looks to the south, and in the middle and lower parts of these they are terraced. The soil is grey, about one-half of slate and rotten stone, the other half barren clay, excessively steep. . . . The vignerons of Rüdesheim dung their vines about once in five or six years, putting a one horse tumbrel load of dung on every twelve feet square." [46]

Jefferson did not go beyond the Marco-Brunnen vineyards, which lie in a range of hills some three miles above Johannisberg. He does not seem to have esteemed the bouquet of this heady wine as much as has posterity, for he describes it as "of the second quality." However, he advises Rutledge and Shippen to be sure to go to the "Abbaye of Johannisberg to examine their vineyards and wine. The latter is the best made on the Rhine, without comparison, and is about double the price of the oldest Hock." Content with what he had seen, he hired horses to drive back to Mainz, where he spent the night. Thus it came about, partly because of the physical difficulties, for there was no road along that part of the river, and partly because of the haste that seems to have prodded him like an evil spirit on this trip, that Jefferson never saw that most famous and most picturesque section of the Rhine, from Bingen to Coblenz, with its magnificent struggle between the river and the cliffs. How much he later regretted this we learn from the travel notes for Rutledge and Shippen. "Were I to pass again," he writes, "I would hire horses to carry me along the Rhine as far as a practicable road is to be found. Then I would embark my carriage on a boat to be drawn by a horse or horses till you pass the cliffs which intercept the land communication. This would be only for a few miles, say half a dozen or a dozen. You will see what I am told are the most picturesque scenes in the world, and which travellers go express to see, and you may be landed at the first village on the North East side of the river after passing the cliffs. And from thence hire horses to Mayence." [47]

On the twelfth of April, after having duly settled his account at the Hotel de Mayence and paid off Armand, Jefferson started out for Oppenheim, Worms, and Mannheim. He passed through the old city of Worms, perhaps richer in history and legend than any other town on the Rhine, without a word in regard to it other than that the surrounding plains were "sandy, poor, and often covered only with small pine." The great cathedral was to him, as to most of his contemporaries, apparently nothing more than a monstrosity. He does not mention the famous wine grown in the vicinity, "to which they have given an odd name, viz., 'Our Lady's Milk,' " but hurried on to Mannheim. This was not sleeping in the past; there was an abundance of modern life on the streets and in the harbor. Even the guide book noted that "the people of this town are very sociable and civil to strangers. There is a company of French comedians who act three times a week." [48] This was just to Jefferson's taste. After putting up at the Cour du Palatin, where he spent three days, he proceeded to go to the theater and, as usual, to "see things," to the extent of seven florins. "At Mannheim," he subsequently wrote his protégés, "you must purpose to make some stay. Buy the pamphlet which mentions the curiosities of the town and country. The gallery of paintings is more considerable than that at Düsseldorf, but has not so many precious things. The Observatory is worth seeing." [49]

From Mannheim Jefferson made a side trip to Heidelberg, which seems to have been one of the high spots of his journey. It is not surprising that this man, who lived in one of the garden spots of America, should experience an indescribable pleasure as he ascended the steep hill on which the castle stands and found it embowered in the glory of an April day. "This château is the most noble ruin I have ever seen," he exclaimed. "The situation is romantic and pleasing beyond expression. It is on a great scale much like the situation of Petrarch's château, at Vaucluse, on a small one. The climate, too, is like that of Italy. The apple, the pear, cherry, peach, apricot and almond, are all in bloom." [50] So carefree and happy was our traveler on this spring day that he even tried "the station in the garden to which the château re-echoes distinctly four syllables."

From Heidelberg Jefferson went to Schwetzingen to see the famous gardens surrounding the Elector's palace. They had been laid out in the middle of the eighteenth century by the Elector Karl Theodor in the manner made familiar by the great French designer, Le Nôtre. Statues, temples, and ruins adorned them. Within a quarter of a century, however, they were regarded as hopelessly old-fashioned. About 1770 there was added to them a so-called "English garden," which Jefferson favored. "The gardens at Schwetzingen," he wrote in condemnation of the old part, "show how much money may be laid out to make an ugly thing. What is called the English quarter, however, relieves the eye from the straight rows of trees, round and square basins, which constitute the great mass of the garden. There are some tolerable morsels of Grecian architecture," he adds and, something to which he never objected, "a good ruin." [51]

After three delightful days in Mannheim and its environs, Jefferson set off again for Karlsruhe. He drove, of course, through Speyer where, he observes, "there is nothing remarkable." If he gave more than a passing glance at the imposing cathedral in which lie the mortal remains of eight emperors of the Holy Roman Empire, we do not know it. It was midafternoon when he arrived in Karlsruhe, which lies six miles off the Rhine. The simple, harmonious buildings of the early nineteenth century that distinguish Karlsruhe for us did not, of course, exist at this time, but the unique fan-shaped plan of the town, with streets radiating from the palace and with the tower of the palace visible at every crossing, was just the same. The first thing Jefferson did was to buy a map of the city, and he subsequently paid five florins for his favorite diversion of "seeing things."

Karlsruhe was at this time the seat of the Markgraf of Baden. "His château," Jefferson tells us, "is built in the midst of a natural forest of several leagues diameter, and of the best trees I have seen in these countries: they are mostly oak, and would be deemed but indifferent in America. A great deal of money has been spent to do more harm than good to the ground—cutting a number of straight alleys through the forest."[52] Then came the features that warmed Jefferson's heart, for he had attempted something similar in his own park at Monticello. "He has a pheasantry of the gold and silver kind, the latter very tame, but the former excessively shy. A little inclosure of stone, two and a half feet high and thirty feet diameter, in which are two tamed beavers. There is a pond of fifteen feet diameter in the centre, and at each end a little cell for them to retire into, which is stowed with bows and twigs with leaves on them. . . . Some cerfs of a peculiar kind, spotted like fawns . . . eight angora goats—beautiful animals—all white."[53] It is not surprising that he advised his young friends to "visit the gardens minutely" when they should reach Karlsruhe.

After one night spent at Au Prince Héréditaire, Jefferson was on his way again toward Strassburg, some sixty-five kilometers distant. It was a beautiful spring day. The grapevines were in blossom as well as all the fruit trees that dotted the broad valley of the Rhine. The distant mountains of the Bergstrasse and the Vosges across the river were covered with snow. Small wonder Jefferson found it a smiling country and was high in his praise of the Markgraf of Baden, whose territory this was. "I see no beggars since I entered his Government," Jefferson writes, "nor is the traveller obliged to ransom himself every moment by *Chausséegeld*. The roads are excellent and made so, I presume, out of the coffers of the Prince. From Cleves till I enter the Margravate of Baden, the roads have been strung with beggars—in Hesse the most, and the road tax very heavy. We pay it cheerfully, however, through the territory of Frankfurt and thence up the Rhine, because fine gravelled roads are kept up; but through the Prussian, and other parts of the road below Frankfurt"—and he must have thought of his native Virginia—"the roads are made only by the carriages, there not appearing to have been ever a day's work employed on them." [54]

Jefferson reached Strassburg late on the sixteenth and spent three days there at the tavern A l'Esprit. Except for Frankfurt, it was the most important city he had encountered on his Rhine journey, and he took full advantage of it. He was able to indulge in the greatest hobby of his lifetime, the purchase of books. "Koenig, book seller here," he wrote Rutledge and Shippen, "has the best shop of classical books I ever saw. Baskerville's types I think are in this town, [blank] of Voltaire are printing here." [55] Jefferson spent no less than 244 livres at Koenig's, buying Plato, Aristotle, and Menander, and other authors, and 36 livres at other shops.

In his own journal Jefferson makes no note of having visited any of the sights of Strassburg, but we learn from his account book that once more he paid 7 livres 16 for "seeing things." These included, as the travel notes for his young friends tell us, the famous palace of the Cardinal de Rohan and the more famous cathedral. "The Cathedral, dedicated to Our Lady," his guide book said, "is perhaps the finest Gothic building in Europe. The portal is quite magnificent, and the high altar, built by Cardinal Fürstemberg, is extremely beautiful. The tower, reckoned by some the highest in the whole world, is built in the form of a pyramid. It is 574 feet high, curiously built of carved stone, and has 662 steps from bottom to top. But that which is most admired, is the great clock, finished in 1573, by the famous Habrecht, remarkable for shewing the motions of the planets, the increase and decrease of the moon, with the motion of the sun through the signs of the zodiac." [56]

Jefferson did not balk at the six hundred-odd steps. Diligently he climbed every one of them, to the top of the tower. "But let it be the last operation of the day," he advises young Rutledge and Shippen, "as you will need a long rest after it." He does not mention the famous clock, but some faint recollection of it may perhaps have inspired the one he later installed at Monticello.

Late on the eighteenth of April Jefferson started on his way back to Paris. The long drive across the plains of the Rhine and then the Vosges, with his servant Espagnol as his only companion, gave him ample time for observation of what was passing before him and for rumination on what he had seen. Now, like many a traveler, he found that the boundary of the Rhine did not make any essential difference in the customs of the inhabitants on either side. "The houses, as in Germany," he wrote, "are of scantling, filled in with wicker and mortar, and covered either with thatch or tiles." [57]

Then he philosophized on a favorite topic. "The women here, as in Germany, do all sorts of work. While one considers them as useful and rational companions, one cannot forget that they are also objects of our pleasures, nor can they ever forget it. While employed in dirt and drudgery, some tag of ribbon, some ring or bit of bracelet, earbob or necklace, or some thing of that kind, will show that the desire of pleasing is never suspended in them. It is an honourable circumstance for man, that the first moment he is at his ease, he allots the internal employments to his female partner, and takes the external on himself. ... Here, then, is so heavy a military establishment, that the civil part of the nation is reduced to women only. But this is a barbarous perversion of the natural destination of the two sexes. Women are formed by nature for attentions, not for hard labor. A woman never forgets one of the numerous train of little offices which belong to her. A man forgets often." [58]

Now his thoughts turned back to Frankfurt, in a flood of reminiscence, and he thought of the words he had written William Short from there, "The neighborhood of this place is that which has been to us a second mother country. It is from the Palatinate on this part of the Rhine that those swarms of Germans have gone who, next to the descendants of the English, form the greatest body of our people. I have been continually amused by seeing here the origin of whatever is not English among us. I have fancied myself often," he had concluded, "in the upper parts of Maryland or Pennsylvania." [59]

In speaking of Jefferson's Rhine journey one's mind inevitably turns to a similar journey made by Goethe in the summer of 1774. Although not a so-called picturesque journey, it may well be called the first of the romantic Rhine journeys which reached its apotheosis in Wagner's immortal *Siegfried's Rheinfahrt*. Indeed, Goethe's has been called "*die Rheinfahrt im Genierausch.*" Goethe was in the first flush of the Storm and Stress. He was described by one of his companions on this occasion as "a youth of twenty-five, who from the crown of his head to the soles of his feet radiates genius, power, and strength, who has a feeling heart, and a spirit of fire that soars with the wings of an eagle, *qui ruit immensus ore profundo.*" *Werther* had been finished in the spring of the year and was shortly to be published. His friends had already read the manuscript of this extraordinary work, and there was no doubt in their minds, or in that of the literary public, as to the genius of the author.

In July of that year Goethe had been sojourning at Ems with Lavater, the enlightened Swiss divine, and Basedow, the distinguished pedagogue. As has been remarked, it was the most curious group of congenial souls that can be imagined. In company with the two men Goethe started on the morning of the eighteenth for a trip to the lower Rhine. As in Jefferson's case, Goethe's objective was the gallery at Düsseldorf as well as the one at Bensberg. Fortunately for us, Lavater has left a fragmentary account of the trip in his journal. It was what the Germans call a *Bummelfahrt.* The three men set off in a bateau and proceeded down the lovely river Lahn. Wooded hills, picturesque towns, the ruins of castles floated by them. Basedow, uncouth and unattractive in appearance, sat smoking a pipe. Goethe sat with pencil and paper in hand, writing rhyme endings for the party. Coffee was passed and Basedow seized the occasion to make a witty speech about Goethe. At that moment, high above them on a rocky hill, the noble ruins of the castle of Lahneck came into view, looking peacefully down at the river. Goethe contemplated it for some minutes, then, like someone breaking into song, he began reciting the celebrated *Geistesgruss,* which the sight of the castle had inspired.

At three o'clock the bateau was to leave on the continuation of this leisurely voyage, but a sharp storm came up, and the party walked to Benndorf to take tea with friends. The obliging bateau stopped there for them, and they continued into Neuwied in the glow of a golden sunset. Once more Goethe was inspired to put his thoughts into verse in *Des Künstlers Vergötterung.* At Neuwied the party was received by the court chaplain, who entertained them at dinner in honor of

Lavater. Later they were received at court where there was a "brilliant assemblage of counts and countesses."

Two days later, Goethe and Lavater set out again at six o'clock of a rainy morning—"Goethe," his friend tells us, "a romantic figure in a gray hat and a treasured, half-withered boutonniere." He did not allow the weather to dampen his spirits, indeed he was effervescent. Until they reached Bonn, at noon, he versified or declaimed and read aloud passages from his operetta *Erwin und Elmira.* At Cologne the two friends parted, and Goethe, mounting his horse, rode on to Düsseldorf to enjoy the treasures of the art gallery.

The contrast between the Rhine journey undertaken by these two men, Goethe and Jefferson, whose life spanned almost exactly the same years, yet who never knew of each other, is the contrast of two worlds and two cultures. Although Goethe embarked on his tour fourteen years before Jefferson did, his outlook on it and the spirit he brought to it was already a harbinger of what was to come. He was a child of the future, not of the past. He had enthroned "the joyous heart" and deposed the pure reason of the eighteenth century. The same was true of his journeys to Switzerland in 1775 and 1777. "My first journey to Switzerland disclosed to me a wider view of the world," he writes. And again, standing on the Brocken in the Harz mountains in November, 1777, he exclaims, "Here standing upon the most ancient and eternal altar, built directly upon the profundity of creation, I bring an offering to the Being of Beings."

For Goethe a guide book setting down "a description of the principal cities and towns, the seats and palaces of the nobility, the produce of the country, the customs and manners of the people, their commerce, manufacture and bearing" was unthinkable. Such considerations did not too much concern him. Had he not prefaced his first journey to Switzerland by the remark, "*Ist mir toll und wunderlich über all wo ich bin?*"

Jefferson, however, clung to this staff of the traveler. He still needed to know about people and their commerce and their industry. He had not yet clearly heard the distant notes of the clarion call heralding a new manner of thought, which regarded nature as a never ending source of wonder and delight.

XII. Americans in Europe

JEFFERSON'S HOUSE in Paris early became the center of life for all Americans passing through Paris or living there, in a sense that had not been true of his predecessor's. Franklin, already an old man when he arrived, had settled down in Passy surrounded by a few old cronies and enjoyed life in quite a different sense from what Jefferson did. The latter undertook, as part of his mission, to assist and look out for any American who came to Europe and sought his counsel and assistance, as well as those who merely came with letters of introduction. No one with any intellectual pretensions could arrive in Paris without engaging Jefferson's interest and help, if needed. Almost always the relationship proved more than casual and lasted for years. It formed a happy chapter in his life.

There may be said to be three categories of Americans with whom he came in contact, those with whom it was of a purely social nature, those who sought him out, for one reason or another, in his official capacity, and the group of young men who wanted his advice and direction in their studies and travels.

By far the most agreeable social connection that Jefferson formed with an American in Paris was the one with that exceptional woman, Abigail Adams. She was a person of extraordinary gifts, not the least of which was an abundance of common sense. It was a friendship that was to survive all vicissitudes and subsequently to bloom anew toward the close of their lives. Mrs. Adams arrived in Paris on her first European visit about the middle of August, 1784, shortly after Jefferson. Her husband had already taken a large and handsome house at Auteuil, a village some four miles from Paris and one from Passy. Mrs. Adams was immediately taken into the same circle in which Jefferson moved, and there are frequent references in her letters, as also in those of her daughter, to the gentlemen of the American legation, Jefferson, Short, and Humphreys, as well as to the learned and jolly Abbés, of whom we have already spoken, the Marquis and Marquise de Lafayette, and other French people who were friendly with the Americans. They dined together weekly, went to the opera, the theater, to see the *fêtes* and other festivities that Paris afforded.

Thus on August 15, 1784, within a few days of their arrival, young Abigail is writing, "This day, by invitation, we dined with Mr. Barclay [the American account commissioner]. . . . Mr. Jefferson and daughter dined with us. . . . The dinner was in the French style. There is no such thing here as preserving our taste in anything," she remarks rebelliously. "We must all sacrifice to custom and fashion. I will not believe it possible to do otherwise for my pappa, with his firmness and resolution, is a perfect convert to the mode in everything, at least of dress and appearance." [1] Her "pappa" was equally firm about not introducing his wife and daughter to the most fashionable ladies in Paris society, whose morals and manners he considered questionable, making an exception only of the Duchesse d'Anville and the Marquise de Lafayette, "who seldom went out except into her family connections." [2]

The dinner in the French style at Mr. Jefferson's, to which young Abigail took exception, is described by her mother as one of the "very curious" customs of the country. "When company are invited to dine, if twenty gentlemen meet, they seldom or never sit down, but are standing or walking from one part of the room to the other, with their swords on, and their *chapeau de bras*, which is a very small silk hat, always worn under the arm. These they lay aside while they dine, but resume them immediately after. . . . At dinner the ladies and gentlemen are mixed, and you converse with him who sits next you, rarely speaking to persons across the table, unless to ask if they will be served with anything from your side. Conversation is never general as with us," Mrs. Adams continues, "for when the company quit the table, they fall into *tête-a-tête* of two, when the conversation is in a low voice, and a stranger, unacquainted with the customs of the country, would think that everybody had private business to transact." [3]

French or not, the dining back and forth continued, and Jefferson was otherwise equally indefatigable in his attentions. On the fourth of October he introduced the Adams' to the *concerts spirituels*, which were held in the Tuileries, and which he was so fond of attending. These concerts, established in 1725, were held in the Hall of the French Comedians, a theater illumed by nine great crystal chandeliers, in the big northern pavilion of the Tuileries. They took place on various religious holidays. In Jefferson's day M. le Gros was the musical director. He presented the finest music, both French and of other nations, performed by the most celebrated virtuosos.[4]

Ten days later Jefferson invited the Adams family to join him and Martha in witnessing the "ceremony of taking the veil in the convent where his daughter is to receive her education. We rose at seven, dressed, went into Paris and breakfasted with Madame Barclay," young Abigail writes. "We went to the church where we found a number of persons of our acquaintance. Upon this occasion we were admitted to the altar where the priest performs, which at other times is not allowed. It was separated from the place of the nuns and those of the convent, by iron grates. The place in which they were was a large apartment, with seats around. The floor was covered with an elegant carpet—here were the nuns only. When we first went they were repeating their prayers. Presently the curtains were drawn aside, the lady abbess and other nuns, with all the pensioners, came. The candles were lighted—each nun held a lighted candle in her hand. The two nuns who were to take the veil came forward, attended by two English ladies who were pensioners. Each held a large, lighted torch in her hand—they were elegantly dressed, and in all the vanities of the world.

"The two nuns were in fine, white woolen dresses, made like a parson's robes, loose and flowing, their veils were white.... They came and kneeled before the altar, there was much singing and chanting of prayers. It is impossible to describe the many different manners and forms, alternately kneeling and rising. The priest came to the altar and made many different signs that I did not understand." After commenting on the sermon, which began by "expatiating on the goodness of the King, then on the excellence of every particular class of people, from the throne to the footstool," she describes the further ceremonies in which the nuns "laid down upon their faces and there was brought in, by eight pensioners, a pall of black, crossed with white, which was held over them" for half an hour. "When they rise it is called the resurrection, after having been dead to the world." Miss Adams allows, "It was an affecting sight. I could not refrain from tears." She observed, however, that "the English girl who held the candle for all of them looked very sharp upon the other English girl, whose countenance expressed that she knew better than all this... quite right she." Miss Jefferson viewed the scene more sympathetically. She told Miss Adams that "they were very cheerful and agreeable. They seemed to take pleasure in contributing to the happiness of the pensioners." [5] It is not surprising to find that, after being exposed to scenes such as this for four years and more, Jefferson was to find that his child had decided that she was intended for this way of life.

On the seventh of February Jefferson asked the Adams' to dine and "see all Paris, which was to be seen on the streets today, it being the last day but one of the Carnival." His house, bordering as it did on the Champs-Elysées, afforded ample opportunity to observe the festivities there. He likewise asked his guests to go to the masked ball that evening, which began at one o'clock and continued until six in the morning. We know he attended such a one in 1786, on the very eve of setting out for England, but Miss Adams observes that she "had but little curiosity to go, the description of those who have seen it has not given me spirit enough to spend all the night to be perhaps not gratified." [6] Indeed, these austere New Englanders, to whom Sunday was synonymous with sermons, found difficulty in understanding the French *joie de vivre*, whether on the occasion of a *fête*, a carnival, or a Sunday. There is never a remark to indicate that Jefferson thought of such occasions as anything but part of the picture. Mrs. Adams, as well as her daughter, considered that for the French pleasure was the business of life. "We have no days with us," she writes, "by which I can give you an idea of the Sabbath here, except commencement and election." The Fourth of July had not yet entered this category. "Paris upon that day pours forth all her citizens into the environs for the purposes of recreation. We have a beautiful wood cut into walks within a few rods of our dwelling which, upon this day, resounds with music, jollity. In this woods booths are erected where cake, fruit and wine are sold. . . . I believe this nation is the only one in the world which could make pleasure the business of life and yet retain such a relish for it as never to complain of its being tasteless or insipid." [7]

A most impressive occasion presented itself on the thirtieth of March, 1785, when the King made one of his rare trips to Paris "to the church of Notre Dame to assist in the Te Deum which would be sung in that church to return thanks for the birth of a prince," the Duke of Normandy. He had been born three days before. The Marquise de Lafayette invited Jefferson and the Adams' to accompany her and sit "in her father's tribune at the church." This is described by young John Quincy Adams as "a gallery that commanded the choir." [8] He and his sister both picture the enormous crowds that filled the streets and bridges, which made it almost impossible for a carriage to pass. "Mr. Jefferson, who rode from the Marquis' with us, supposed there were as many people in the streets as there were in the State of Massachusetts, or any of the other states," young Abigail observes.

This solemn ceremony performed in the ancient cathedral, aglow with tapers and with the deep, jeweled light sifting in through tall windows, made an unforgettable impression upon the youthful Adams', to whom it was like a scene from fairyland. Each went home and silently recorded his impressions in the leather-bound volumes he thought no other eyes were destined to see. "In the middle of the choir below us," writes John Quincy, "were several rows of benches, upon which the King's train sat when he came, while he and his two brothers were before all the benches, and directly opposite the altar. When we arrived, we found the Parliament sitting in the choir on the right side, in scarlet and black robes; the Chambre des Comptes were seated in the same manner on the left side, in black and white robes. The foreign Ambassadors were in an enclosure at the right of the altar, and between them and the Parliament was a small throne, upon which the Archbishop of Paris officiated. Soon after we got there, the bishops arrived, two by two. There were about twenty-five of them.

They had black robes on with a white muslin skirt which descended from the waist down two thirds of the way to the ground, and a purple kind of a mantle over their shoulders. The Archbishop of Paris had a mitre upon his head. When the King came, he went out to the door of the church to receive him, and as soon as his Majesty had got to his place, and fallen upon his knees, they began to sing the Te Deum, which lasted about half an hour, and in which we heard some exceedingly fine music. The voices were admirable. The Archbishop of Paris sang for a couple of minutes near the end, that it might be said he had sung the Te Deum—his voice seems to be much broken. As soon as the singing was over the King and the court immediately went away. The King and all the court were dressed in clothes vastly rich, but in no peculiar form. After the ceremony was finished, we had to wait a long time for our carriages, and could not at last get them all, so that we were obliged to go away five in one chariot. We returned to the Hotel de Lafayette, and drank tea with Madame."

The observations of Miss Adams, rather more contemplative than her brother, were doubtless shared, as we shall see, by the gentleman for whom she had gradually acquired such a high regard. "It is impossible not to make many reflections upon this august and superb ceremony," she writes, with much of the good sense that distinguished her mother, "and upon the sentiments the people discovered for their King. But in this government I should judge it was right and necessary. If the man who has the whole kingdom at his disposal is not respected, and thought of next to their God, he will not long sustain his power. And however wrong it may be, it is unavoidable." [9]

In the purely social aspect of Jefferson's relations with Americans in Europe, American women very naturally play a rather more conspicuous rôle than do American men. It was the day when women were still regarded as the ornaments of society and a little gallantry was well in order. With one or two notable exceptions, Jefferson's connection with men was more likely to be a professional or business one. The question that has so often been asked is inevitably raised: Was Jefferson attractive to women? And was he attracted by them? From the number of friendships he formed with women at this period of his life, the conclusion is an inescapable affirmative to both. These friendships were not trifling love affairs but long-lasting attachments based on mutual interests and respect. The fact that two of these, and a third of a more passing character, were with three of the most beautiful women of their time would indicate that Jefferson was not oblivious to the physical charms of the opposite sex. As for their being attracted to him, what woman has ever found a tall, distinguished, chivalrous man of forty-odd actually distasteful?

On Jefferson's part we know that he had one lifelong love from which he never deviated and which he carried with him to his grave—that for Martha Wayles, whom he had married that snowy New Year's Day in 1772. It was in all truth that he had had inscribed on her tombstone, ten years later, the words from the Iliad proclaiming that her love would remain sacred to him and burn on through death. Even young Abigail sensed this one January evening when Jefferson came to dine. Lafayette had just brought him the news of the death of his youngest child. "Mr. Jefferson is a man of great sensibility and parental affection," she writes. "His wife died when this child was born, and he was almost in a confirmed state of melancholy, confined himself from the world and even from his friends for a long time, and this news has greatly affected him and his daughter." [10]

The women, both French and American, with whom he was thrown were, of course, married. It was a time when girls took their vows at an early age, and those who failed to do so usually remained in seclusion. The only widow that crossed Jefferson's path, he married. His French friends, such as Madame de Corny, wife of Ethis de Corny, the close associate of Rochambeau and Lafayette, and Madame de Tessé, to both of whom he was devoted, as well as Madame de Bréhan and Madame de Tott, painters of some distinction, and Madame de Staël, all had husbands in the background. They were old enough and sophisticated enough not to consider extraordinary a mild flirtation, intellectual or otherwise. In the numerous letters that passed between Jefferson and these women, which have been preserved, his attitude may be said to have been that of a whimsical gallantry and an almost youthful eagerness to please. The same is true of his relation with his American friends, such as Abigail Adams, Anne Bingham, and Angelica Church. Only once, in the course of these friendships, as we have seen, was Jefferson sorely tempted, and even this resolved itself into a true and lasting friendship.

Jefferson's tolerant persiflage toward the ladies is illuminated in his lively interchange of letters with Mrs. William Bingham after her return to America. It shows him to have been on what might be called teasing terms with this celebrated beauty, obviously enjoying the presence of this ornamental creature in a circle somewhat overburdened by age and distinction, yet fully conscious of her frailty and foibles. Mrs. Adams describes her as "a fine figure and a beautiful person, her manners are easy and affable, but she is too young to come abroad without a pilot, gives too much into the follies of this country, and has money enough and knows how to lavish it with an unsparing hand." [11] In 1784, four years after her marriage at the age of sixteen, she had come to Europe with her husband and they had established themselves in Paris with considerable display in the Hôtel Muscovy. Mr. Bingham was nominally on a business trip, but if we may judge from Abby's observations, he was actually more interested in climbing the social ladder, and his wife was not averse to it. " 'Tis said he wishes for an appointment here as foreign minister," Mrs. Adams says of him; "he lives at a much greater expense than any American minister can afford to do." [12] On the fourteenth of October, 1784, young Abigail notes in her diary, "Mr. Bingham came flourishing out in the morning to accompany Papa to Versailles to be presented to his most Christian Majesty, the King of France, with his four horses and three servants, in all the pomp of an American merchant." [13] Abigail, however, quickly succumbed to the charms of Mrs. Bingham. She "gains my love and admiration more and more every time I see her," she writes. "She is possessed of more ease and politeness in her behavior than any person I have seen." And again she confesses that "she has excellencies that overbalance every want of judgement, or that love for gay life, which is very conspicuous in her, but which I do not wonder at, at all." [14]

The Binghams dined regularly with the Adams' and with Jefferson, and on one of these occasions, it would appear, Jefferson made a wager with Mrs. Bingham that at the end of a stay of twelve months at home this social butterfly, whose good qualities he believed he discerned, would tell him "truly and honestly, whether you do not find the tranquil pleasures of America preferable to the empty bustle of Paris? For to what does that bustle tend? At eleven o'clock it is day, *chez Madame*," he begins and in the next pages paints an inimitable portrait of the life of a fashionable *Parisienne* in all its idleness and futility. "Thus the days of life are consumed, one by one, without an object but the present moment," he writes, "ever flying from the *ennui* of that, yet carrying it with us; eternally in pursuit of happiness, which keeps eternally before us.... In America, on the other hand, the children, the arrangements of the house, the improvements of the grounds, fill every moment with a useful and happy activity. The intervals of leisure are filled by the society of real friends, whose affections are not thinned to cobweb, by being spread over a thousand objects.... If we do not concur this year," he remarks, persuasively, "we shall the next, or if not then, in a year or two more. You see, I am determined not to suppose myself mistaken." [15]

Mrs. Bingham was too spirited and too fond of the way of life she had discovered to accept this moral lesson without a pert retort. "I agree with you that many of the fashionable pursuits of the Parisian ladies are rather frivolous," she replies, "and become uninteresting to a reflective mind." Whether this is a compliment or a sly reproof is left to the reader. "But the picture you have exhibited is rather overcharged. You have thrown a strong light upon all that is ridiculous in their characters, and you have buried their good qualities in the shade. ... The state of society in different countries requires corresponding manners and qualifications. Those of the French women are by no means calculated for the meridian of America, neither are they adapted to render the sex so amiable or agreeable in the English acceptation of those words. But you must confess they are more accomplished, and understand the intercourse of society better than in any other country. We are irresistibly pleased with them because they possess the happy art of making us pleased with ourselves.... The arts of elegance are there [in Paris] considered as essential, and are carried to a state of perfection, and there the friend of art is continually gratified by the admiration for works of taste. I have the pleasure of knowing you too well to doubt of your subscribing to this opinion."[16]

It cannot be said that Jefferson had not met a worthy adversary.

In Angelica Church he encountered a temperament of quite a different order from that of Anne Bingham. Less challenging, perhaps, but of a quiet serenity and understanding that leads a man to avow his trials and his triumphs and, before he knows it, to lay his heart at her feet. Miss Adams describes Mrs. Church as "a delicate little woman" and speaks of her "softness, sweetness and affability. Everything is delicate and agreeable, except her husband."[17] She was born Angelica Schuyler, the sister of Mrs. Alexander Hamilton, and is said to have been a great beauty. She had early eloped with John Church, an Englishman who passed in America under the *nom de guerre* of Carter, but who was now a member of Parliament. According to Trumbull, they were living in London at this time in great elegance.[18] Their child, Kitty, was in school at the Abbaye de Panthemont and was the inseparable companion of Jefferson's daughters.

Although, according to Mrs. Adams, Mrs. Church had been in Paris in December, 1784, Jefferson did not make her acquaintance until three years later, when she appears to have been staying with Madame de Corny. On Christmas Day, 1787, Maria Cosway wrote Jefferson, "Have you seen yet the lovely Mrs. Church? . . . If I did not love her so much I would fear her rivalship. But no, I give you free permission to love her with all your heart."[19] Early in January, 1788, Jefferson replied, "I never saw her before, but I find in her all the good the world has given her credit for. I do not wonder at your fondness for each other. I have seen too little of her as I did of you."[20]

Further acquaintance merely confirmed Jefferson's opinion of his new friend. When she had returned to London he could not resist writing to her. The half-serious, half-playful entreaties his letters embody must be taken in the spirit in which they were written. He begins his correspondence with the simple confession, "Many motives, my dear Madame, authorize me to write you, but none more than this, that I esteem you infinitely."[21] To be sure, he adds, "I have thought it safe to get Kitty to write also, that her letter may seem as a passport to mine, and shed on it the same *suave odeur* of those warm emotions it will excite in your breast. . . . I present myself, then, under the wing of Kitty, though she thinks of herself under mine." [22] It was July, a full six months after their meeting, and he begs her for another visit to her daughter and her friend. "Come then, Madame, to the call of friendship," he urges, "which does not issue from the chausée d'Antin alone [the residence of the de Cornys]. Your slender health requires exercise, requires amusement, and to be comforted by seeing how much you are beloved everywhere. . . . If you will install me as your physician, I will prescribe to you a journey a month to Paris." [23]

Meanwhile Mrs. Church, in sending Jefferson a gift of a silver urn, was writing with her natural affability of her tranquil life in London. "Mrs. Cosway and I are enjoying the quiet of the country, the plays and songs, and very often wish that Mr. Jefferson was here, supposing that he would be indulgent to the exertions of two little women to please him, who are extremely vain of the pleasure of being permitted to write him, and very happy to have some share of his favorable opinion. Adieu, my dear sir, accept the good wishes of Marie and Angelica. Mr. Trumbull has given us each a picture of you. Mrs. Cosway's is a better likeness than mine, but then I have a better elsewhere, and so I console myself." [24]

Jefferson was not slow in answering this letter and in taking up the challenge of the better likeness by which she, of course, meant the one in her heart. "The memorial of me which you have from Trumbull," he writes, "is the most worthless part of me. Could he paint my friendship to you, it would be something out of the common line. . . . I never blame heaven so much as for having clogged the ethereal spirit of friendship with a body which ties it to time and place. I am always with you in spirit; be you with me sometimes." He concludes his letter by pleading with her to make a proposed trip to her family in America coincide with his. "Think of it then, my friend, and let us begin a negotiation on the subject. You shall find in me all the spirit of accommodation with which Yoric began his with the fair Piedmontese. We have a thousand inducements to wish it on our part. On yours perhaps you may find one in the dispositions we shall carry with us to serve and amuse you on the dreary voyage." [25]

It was a scheme that failed of realization. Mrs. Church sailed for New York in the spring of 1789 and returned to England the very October Jefferson was leaving it. Although she corresponded with Jefferson until the time of her death, and her daughter Kitty did for many years after, a final message sent through Trumbull, then in dismal London, closes this period of the episode. "Say everything soft and affectionate for me to Mrs. Cosway and Mrs. Church," Jefferson writes. "They are a countervail to you for the want of a sun." [26] And the same thing could have been said of the writer. There was no sun in his heart.

From his early days, Jefferson, who was unquestionably a precocious and serious youth, had taken a great interest in the education and development of young men, often not much his junior. Among the earliest of his letters preserved is one written from Shadwell in February, 1769, to his uncle, Thomas Turpin, regretting that it was not in his "power to take the superintendence of your son in his studies," [27] owing to expected protracted absences from home. It was an unusual request for a man to make of a nephew not yet twenty-six years old, but he was doubtless already viewed as the flower of a family consisting largely of agriculturalists. Although obliged to decline the request, Jefferson felt free to give advice, replete with judgment beyond his years. "I always was of the opinion," he writes, "that the placing a youth to study with an attorney was rather a prejudice than a help. We are all too apt by shifting on them our business, to encroach on that time which should be devoted to their studies. The only help a youth wants is to be directed what books to read, and in what order to read them." He had therefore "laid down a plan of study" for his cousin, the first of many he was to make, "which will afford him all the assistance a tutor could." [28]

Not many years later the direction of the education of the children of his brother-in-law Dabney Carr fell to his lot and continued for some years. Peter, the most brilliant of the brood, was his particular charge. Throughout his stay in Europe Jefferson was buying and sending the boy books and guiding his education in a series of letters that are unequaled for the wisdom, the common-sense philosophy, and the high ideals they expound.[29] Now, in Paris, there was a new group of young men who sought his advice or whose fathers wrote to Jefferson soliciting his counsel on behalf of the sons whom they wished to give the benefit of European study and travel. Always Jefferson replied, as he did to Ralph Izard of South Carolina, once a fellow member of Congress, "Whenever you choose to send him, if I am here, and you think proper to accept my services towards him, they shall be bestowed with the same zeal as if he were my own son."[30] These young men passed through his friendly doors in what seems like a never ending stream, and none left without a sheet or two of notes written in the fine hand of the American Minister, or without a glimpse of new horizons.

However generous he was of his time and efforts, Jefferson's interest in these young men was not solely altruistic. Along with an innate kindness ran a powerful sense of duty toward his country, and he was ever conscious that he was training these youths for the service of the state. This is nowhere more strongly expressed than in a letter to Thomas Mann Randolph, Jr., after he had been in Edinburgh for two years and was asking for guidance as to his future course. "I am glad to find," Jefferson writes, "you have fixed on . . . politics as your principal pursuit. Your country will derive from this a more immediate and sensible benefit. She has much for you to do. For, though we may say with confidence, that the worst of the American constitutions is better than the best which ever existed before, in any other country, and that they are wonderfully perfect for a first essay, yet every human essay must have its defects. It will remain, therefore, to those now coming on the stage of public affairs, to perfect what has been so well begun by those going off it."[31]

The youths who particularly benefited from Jefferson's guidance were in some instances the sons of men he had known when he was at the Continental Congress, such as Ralph Izard, John Rutledge, and Thomas Shippen, or of fellow Virginians and relatives, as was the case with William Short, John Banister, John Wayles Eppes, who was to marry his Polly, and Thomas Mann Randolph, the future husband of Martha. The Mr. Fitzhughs, as Jefferson called them, were seemingly above or beyond needing advice on their European tour. Two notable non-Virginians who came under Jefferson's wing were Charles Bulfinch, the young Bostonian who speaks in his diary of Jefferson's attentions, and John Trumbull, the painter, whose relationship with Jefferson has already been discussed.

Jefferson's most celebrated utterance on education, more particularly on the relative advantages of a European and an American education, is contained in a letter to his old friend John Banister, Jr., of Petersburg, Virginia, a man of about his own age, who acted for a brief period as American consul at Nantes. After discussing the advantages of Rome over Geneva, which he thought were considerable, as there a man could acquire "a local knowledge of a spot so classical and so celebrated" along with "a true pronunciation of the Latin language and a first taste in the fine arts, more particularly those of painting, sculpture, architecture and music," he poses the question: "But why send an American youth to Europe for an education?" And he goes on to ask, "What are the objects of a useful American education?" His answer is, in many ways, as practical as it was more than a century and a half ago, despite the thousand theories that have had their ups and downs in that period. His terms may be outmoded but his common sense is immortal. "Classical knowledge," he replies, "modern languages, chiefly French, Spanish and Italian; mathematics, natural philosophy, natural history, civil history and ethics. In natural philosophy I mean to include chemistry and agriculture, and in natural history to include botany, as well as the other branches of those departments. It is true that the habit of speaking the modern languages cannot be so well acquired in America, but every other article can be as well acquired ... [there] as at any place in Europe."

Jefferson then proceeds to expatiate on the disadvantages of sending a youth to Europe. "To enumerate them all would require a volume," he tartly observes, and although he does not devote that much space to it, he does spend a good two pages picturing the unhappy fate of the American coming to Europe for an education who ends by losing "in his knowledge, in his morals, in his health, in his habits and in his happiness." Jefferson realizes, as he says, that he has delivered a sermon to his friend but justifies himself by saying that "the consequences of a foreign education are alarming to me, as an American."[32] Indeed, on another occasion he went so far as to say, "Of all errors which can possibly be committed in the education of youth, that of sending them to Europe is the most fatal. . . . I see [now] that no American should come to Europe under 30 years of age."[33] Nevertheless, once the youth had arrived in Europe, for whatever reason, there was little Jefferson would not do to render him assistance. There was only one point at which he drew the line, as he told Mazzei. That was asking them to live with him. This he felt would destroy the solitude without which he could not exist.

That his protégés found his company stimulating and were appreciative of his efforts is well indicated by John Quincy Adams, who came to Paris with his parents as a youth of seventeen, in August, 1784. As he and Jefferson saw each other nearly every day, there are not many written evidences of this relationship. There are various references in John Quincy's diary to dining with Jefferson or going to various spectacles, and on one occasion he observes, "Mr. Jefferson is a man of universal learning. Spent the evening with Mr. Jefferson, whom I love to be with."[34] Many years later John Adams was to write his old friend *à propos* of his son, "I call him our John because, when you were at the cul-de-sac at Paris, he appeared to me to be almost as much your boy as mine. I have often speculated upon the consequences that would have ensued from my taking your advice to send him to William and Mary College in Virginia for an education."[35]

By far the most beloved and, in Jefferson's eyes, the most important of his protégés was William Short, that most amiable of gentlemen from Jefferson's own Virginia. Jefferson had already known him well in Williamsburg where, despite his youth—he was twenty-four years old at the time—he had been chosen a member of the Executive Council of Virginia in June, 1783, as we have seen. Unwilling to follow in the footsteps of his father and become a planter, uncertain what occupation to pursue, he regarded Jefferson's invitation to accompany him to Europe as a godsend.[36] Jefferson, on his part, considered him a young man of unusual abilities and promise. He had in mind to appoint Short his secretary, but neither he nor Short could discover in the journals of Congress whether the commissioners were to be allowed such a functionary. Short replied that this did not matter to him, he would "be perfectly happy to be with you, and, although some employment under you would be agreeable, yet it will be enough for me to enjoy the advantages of your friendly instruction." [37] Never was there a more ideal relationship between master and disciple.

Short made a favorable impression upon the American circle in Paris. Mrs. Adams could pay him no higher compliment than to compare him to Mr. Tudor of Boston, "A better figure but much like him in looks and manners, consequently a favorite of mine.... Though one of Mr. Jefferson's family... he took a resolution that he would go into a French family at St. Germain and acquire the language; and this is the only way for a foreigner to obtain it." [38] Miss Adams found him equally attractive—"Very sociable and pleasant. He appears a well-bred man, without the least formality or affectation of any kind. He converses with ease and says many good things." [39] Young John Quincy also had his say by observing that Short "passed for a pretty good aristocrat." [40]

It was not only the Americans who found this soft-spoken Virginian attractive. His rapid mastery of the French language enabled him to consort with the leading French liberals and their ladies on a footing that was not possible for those who haltingly sought to present their ideas, or who stumbled through a compliment. It is significant that Jefferson once wrote him, "The difficulty of presenting my ideas justly in a foreign language often prevented my indulging myself in conversation with persons whose acquaintance I wished to cultivate, and with none more so than with Madame de la Rochefoucauld. But it did not prevent my being entirely sensible of her merit, and entertaining for her the highest esteem." [41] It was this very Madame de la Rochefoucauld, the young wife of Jefferson's friend, the Duke, who succumbed to Short's attractions and with whom he formed an attachment that lasted to the end of their lives.[42]

In Short's case there was, of course, no question of Jefferson's directing his formal education. This had been completed by his graduation from the College of William and Mary, where he had been one of the founders of the Phi Beta Kappa Society. It was rather a matter of perfecting his cultural background under Jefferson's aegis. This included a trip of some months to the Italy Jefferson had not been able to reach.[43] From Paris, Lyon, and then Geneva, Jefferson sent his alter ego across the Alps to Turin, Milan, and Venice, then through the ancient cities of Verona, Padua, Bologna, and on to Rome, where he remained for more than three months. From all these places Short delighted the heart of his patron by sending long accounts of everything that would interest him, from the making of wine and macaroni, to the glories of Rome, of which he had so long dreamed but which he was never to see. Now he viewed it all through the eyes of this young man, whom he had taught to see and think as he did, and who was more satisfactory than a son.

Two other youths who enjoyed the benefits of Jefferson's advice in regard to travel were young Thomas Lee Shippen of Philadelphia and John Rutledge, Jr., of Charleston. They arrived in London late in 1787, prepared to make the grand tour beloved of all well-to-do young men of the period. As is usual in such cases, the two gentlemen were presently short of money, and Jefferson was appealed to for help, a call to which he several times responded. After a protracted stay in London and a visit to Holland, the youths came to Paris in June, 1788. Although Jefferson had sent his young nephew Peter Carr a forceful indictment of the disadvantages of travel, declaring it "makes men wiser, but less happy,"[44] he presently gave young Shippen and Rutledge good advice on the opposite side of the subject in the form of some traveling notes for their tour. These are full of sense and practical wisdom, as good for the beginning traveler today as when they were written. This was on the third of June, 1788, not long after Jefferson's return from Germany. Unharassed by bad roads, worse weather, and the minor irritations of travel, he had had time to reflect on his trip, as well as on the one of the preceding year to France and Italy. In the sixteen pages of these notes he summarizes what he considers important for the young men to see in these various countries. At the same time he gives a glimpse of his own reactions on a similar trip and absolves himself of the charge of paying attention to things only of a practical nature. He advises them of the best wines to be had en route, the best inns, and even mentions certain very superior *valets de place*. He calls the attention of young Mr. Rutledge of rice-growing South Carolina to that raised around Milan, which he considers "the best of the Piedmont rice." In the next breath he tells them to make the trip from Nice to Tenda through the Alpes Maritimes, which caused him to fall on his knees and worship.

The notes begin with some "General Observations" in which Jefferson advises the young travelers that "on arriving at a town, the first thing is to buy the plan of the town and the book noting its curiosities. Walk round the ramparts when there are any, go to the top of a steeple to have a view of the town and its environs. When you are doubting whether a thing is worth the trouble of going to see, recollect that you will never again be so near.... But there is an opposite extreme, too, that is seeing too much. A judicious selection is to be aimed at.... Take care particularly," he adds—and every American who has ever visited a European palace or cathedral and listened to the discourses of this race of creatures, with its emphasis on the obvious and *fait à la main* will heartily and prayerfully agree—"not to let the porters of churches, cabinets, etc. lead you through all the little details of their profession which will load the memory with trifles, fatigue the attention, and waste that and your time." After advising the young men on what wines to select and where to stay, he observes, "The people you will naturally see the most of will be tavern keepers, *valets de place*, and postillions. These are the hackneyed rascals of every country. Of course they must never be considered when we calculate the national character."

Jefferson next takes up the "objects of attention for an American." Agriculture and "everything belonging to this art" he considers of the first importance, with particular reference to animals and plants which may be transported to the United States. Mechanical arts, such as boats and bridges merit scarcely less notice. Gardens are "peculiarly worth the attention of an American, because it is the country of all others where the noblest gardens may be made without expense." Architecture is "worth great attention... [and] among the most important arts." Furthermore "it is desirable to introduce taste into an art which shows so much"—a lesson America has not always learned.

Painting and sculpture he considers "worth seeing but not studying" for the average person as they are "too expensive for the state of wealth among us." Courts of Europe, and Jefferson cannot help giving a little sermon, are "to be seen as you would see the Tower of London or the menagerie of Versailles with their lions, tigers, hyenas and other beasts of prey. A slight acquaintance with them will suffice to show that, under the most imposing exterior, they are the weakest and worst part of mankind." Politics were of course of primary importance and "worth studying as far as respects internal affairs. Examine their influence on the happiness of the people," he writes and then makes a suggestion that must indeed have seemed formidable if not ludicrous to these young eighteenth-century plutocrats, who did not and could not have regarded the working man with the coddling eye of the present. "Take every possible occasion of entering into the houses of the laborers, and especially at the moments of their repast. See what they eat, how they are clothed, whether they are obliged to work too hard, whether their government takes from them an unjust proportion of their labor, on what footing stands the property they call their own, their personal liberty, etc." [45]

There is no record that the young gentlemen carried out their instructions to the fullest degree in this respect, but they had the grace to reward their mentor with a series of letters regarding their travels and what they had seen that must have compensated him for all the trouble he had taken and the hopes he had placed in the future of these young men as good citizens.[46]

No record of Jefferson's relation with Americans in Europe would be complete without mention of those two extraordinary and distinguished characters who crossed his path—John Ledyard and John Paul Jones. "While I resided in Paris," Jefferson writes, "John Ledyard of Connecticut arrived there, well known in the United States for energy of body and mind. He had accompanied Captain Cook on his voyage to the Pacific Ocean and distinguished himself on that voyage by his intrepidity. Being of a roaming disposition, he was now panting for some new enterprise." [47] Like "every American who comes into Paris, no matter from what state," as Abigail Adams writes, "makes his visit and pays his respects to the American Ministers, all of whom in return you must dine,"[48] Ledyard followed the pattern. Jefferson found in him "a person of ingenuity and information. Unfortunately, he has too much imagination."[49]

Nevertheless, Jefferson was intrigued by this unusual personality. Ledyard had in mind to satisfy his craving for adventure by forming a connection with "a mercantile company in the fur trade on the Western coast of America" but he failed in this and was now at loose ends. In long talks over the madeira at the Grille de Chaillot, Jefferson suggested the idea that he "go by land to Kamchatka, cross in some of the vessels to Nootka Sound, fall down to the latitude of the Missouri, and penetrate to and through that to the United States."[50] It was a bold and brilliant suggestion. Ledyard's imagination was aflame with it. He could not start too soon. There was, however, in those days quite as impenetrable an iron curtain about Russia as there is today. The permission of the Empress was necessary for any such expedition. Jefferson set about obtaining it through the Russian Ambassador, Monsieur de Sémoulin, and through Baron de Grimm, her special representative in Paris. On August 16, 1786, he wrote Ledyard, "I saw Baron de Grimm yesterday at Versailles and he told me he had received an answer from the Empress, who declines the proposition made in your account. She thinks it chimerical. I am in hopes your execution of it from our side of the continent will prove the contrary. I thought it necessary to give you this information that you might suffer no remorse from expectation of that quarter. I wish you success in whatever enterprise you adopt."[51]

Ledyard, however, declined to relinquish the proposition, "persuading himself that by proceeding to St. Petersburg he could satisfy the Empress of its practicability, and obtain her permission."[52] Some months later Jefferson received a letter from him. He was still full of confidence and, luckily, had a sense of humor to sustain him. He had reached St. Petersburg but had not been able to see the Empress, who was sojourning in the Crimea. In the letter he states that "he had but two shirts, and yet more shirts than shillings. Still he was determined to obtain the palm of being the first circumambulator of the earth. He says that, having no money, they kick him from place to place, and thus he expects to be kicked round the globe."[53]

Stout of heart, Ledyard continued on his way to within two hundred miles of Kamchatka, "where he was overtaken by an arrest from the Empress." [54] The police "put him in a closed carriage and conveyed [him] day and night, without ever stopping, till he reached Poland, where he was set down and left to himself. The fatigue of this journey broke down his constitution, and when he returned to Paris, his bodily strength was much impaired." [55] Thus Jefferson's dream and Ledyard's hopes were dashed at one blow.

Jefferson's relations with John Paul Jones had no such dramatic quality. The latter had been in Paris as early as 1780, where he became fantastically popular, despite his inability to speak French with any fluency, and where he was greatly admired, particularly by the ladies "who are all wild for love of him." [56] Like many men who enjoy this distinction, he lacked in stature and physical presence what he possessed in ardor. Now, in 1784, after further exploits, he was back and, of course, one of the American circle. Mrs. Adams has left none too flattering a picture of this man of such singular abilities. "He is a most uncommon character," she writes. "I dare say you would be as much disappointed in him as I was. From the intrepid character he justly supported in the American Navy, I expected to have seen a rough, stout, warlike Roman—instead of that I should sooner think of wrapping him up in cotton wool, and putting him into my pocket, than sending him to contend with cannon-balls. He is small of stature, well proportioned, soft in his speech, easy in his address, polite in his manners, vastly civil, understands all the etiquette of a lady's toilette as perfectly as he does the masts, sails and rigging of his ship. Under all this appearance of softness he is bold, enterprising, ambitious and active. He has been here often, and dined with us several times. He is said to be a man of gallantry and a favorite amongst the French ladies. . . . He knows how often the ladies use the baths, what color best suits a lady's complexion, what cosmetics are most favorable to the skin. We do not often see the Warrior and the *Abigail* thus united." [57]

Jones's business in Paris at this time was largely in connection with collecting the prize money due him and the officers and men who served under him. Numerous letters passed between him and Jefferson and the Commissioners of the Treasury on the subject at this time, and Jefferson's chief effort was to have this fairly adjusted. There seems to have been little personal intercourse between the two men, beyond Jefferson's undertaking to dispatch the countless plaster busts by Houdon with which Jones showered his friends. That he overlooked the man's inordinate appreciation of himself and valued his great gifts, we cannot doubt from the letters he wrote Washington and other of his friends.

Thus when a war between the Russians and Turks broke out, in 1788, Jones "was invited into the service of the Empress, with the rank of rear admiral, and to have a separate command," he writes. "I wish it corresponded with the views of Congress to give him that rank for the taking of the *Serapis*. I look to this officer as our great future dependence on the sea, where alone we should think of ever having a force. He is young enough to see the day when we shall be more populous than the whole British dominions, and able to fight them ship to ship. We should procure him, then, every possible opportunity of acquiring experience." [58]

Few men have filled the rôle of ambassador in its varied functions more faithfully or with greater imagination than Jefferson. The legation became a center of hospitality in a sense that had never been true before. As time went on, the Hôtel de Langeac saw a steadily increasing number of visitors, many of whom were glad to stay, in the hospitable Southern manner, for a few days to a few weeks. The even more hospitable table was always crowded. "You apologize for your letters of introduction to Americans coming here," Jefferson wrote William Stevens Smith. "It is so far from needing apology on your part that it calls for thanks on mine. I endeavor to show civilities to all the Americans who come here and who will give me opportunity of doing it, and it is a matter of comfort to know from a good quarter who they are and how far I may go in my attentions to them." [59] Even Gouverneur Morris had a good word to say for this man, whose abilities he secretly envied and begrudged. "Mr. Jefferson lives well," he writes, not long after his arrival in Paris. "Keeps a good table and excellent wine, which he distributes freely, and by his hospitality to his countrymen possesses very much their good will." [60]

XIII. The French Revolution through Jefferson's Eyes

AMONG THE MANY opportunities that his sojourn in Europe offered Jefferson, none was more unusual or more to his taste than that of being an observer of the revolution then developing in the country to which he was minister. "I considered a successful reformation of government in France as insuring a general reformation through Europe," he writes, "and the resurrection to a new life, of their people, now ground to dust by the abuses of the governing powers." [1] His close relationship with various leaders of the movement, such as La Rochefoucauld, more particularly with Lafayette and Malsherbes, with whom, he says, he had established "the most unreserved intimacy," [2] placed him in an unrivaled position. As he himself remarks in his autobiography, "I was in circumstances peculiarly favorable for a knowledge of the truth. Possessing the confidence and intimacy of the leading patriots, and more than all, of the Marquis Fayette, their head and Atlas, who had no secrets from me, I learned with correctness the views and proceedings of that party; while my intercourse with the diplomatic missionaries of Europe at Paris, all of them with the court, and eager in prying into its councils and proceedings, gave me a knowledge of these also." [3] Thus he followed the development of the upheaval with a passionate interest from its first murmurings until the very day of his departure. No father could more fondly have followed the uncertain footsteps of his firstborn then did Jefferson the early gropings of the French people toward freedom. Much as he felt the pull of private affairs drawing him home, he found difficulty in tearing himself away from scenes so absorbing.

Jefferson had the good fortune or, rather, he made the most of his opportunities, to be present on various occasions destined to become historic landmarks in this gigantic struggle. From the time of the first meeting of the States-General, he tells us, he drove "daily from Paris to Versailles and attended their debates, generally till the hour of adjournment. Those of the Noblesse were impassioned and tempestuous. They had some able men on both sides, actuated by equal zeal. The debates of the Commons were temperate, rational, and inflexibly firm." [4] The letters he subsequently wrote to Jay, to Madison, to Adams and certain other friends give a picture of the revolution that for vividness and immediacy has never been rivaled by any historian.

It is significant that the adoption of the Constitution of the United States should have coincided with the first violent onslaught of the French Revolution. In the first place, Jefferson felt it might well serve as a model for France. Indeed, he was shortly to write, "Ours has been professedly their model, in which such changes are made as a difference of circumstances rendered necessary." [5] Secondly, whether consciously or not, the circumstance caused in Jefferson's mind a resurgence of his theories of government and a sustained reflection on them. This by no means meant a revision, but rather a confirmation of his beliefs and theories and a more certain sense of their rightness, not only for his own country but for the oppressed of all nations. "Convinced," as he says, "that the republican is the only form of government which is not eternally at open or secret war with the rights of mankind," [6] we find him, at this period, expounding over and over again what he calls "the catholic principle of republicanism, to wit that every people may establish what form of government they please, and change it as they please, the will of the nation being the only thing essential." [7] Nowhere did he express his views on government and the fundamental rights of the people more firmly than in a letter to Humphreys in March, 1789. "There are rights which it is useless to surrender to the government, and which governments have yet always been found to invade. These are the rights of thinking, and publishing our thoughts by speaking or writing, the right of free commerce, [and] the right of personal freedom. There are instruments for administering the government, so peculiarly trustworthy, that we should never leave the legislature at liberty to change them. . . . There are instruments so dangerous to the rights of the nation, and which place them so totally at the mercy of their governors, that those governors whether legislative or executive, should be restrained by keeping such instruments on foot, but in well-defined cases. Such an instrument is a standing army" [8]—and he proceeds to discuss these principles in relation to the new constitution of the United States.

Jefferson was prepared to like the new constitution of the United States. He considered it "the wisest ever yet presented to men." [9] "A more able Assembly never sat in America," he wrote and added that "we may be assured their propositions will be wise. Happily for us," he continues, "that when we find our constitution defective and insufficient to secure the happiness of the people, we can assemble with all the coolness of philosophers and set it to rights, while every other nation on earth must have recourse to arms to amend or to restore their constitutions." [10] Nevertheless, only two months later, after learning what had been determined, we find him saying that "as to the new constitution, I find myself nearly a neutral. There is a great mass of good in it, in a very desirable form, but there is also, to me, a bitter pill or two." [11]

In a letter to Madison, written at the same time, he states in detail what he considers the good and the bad features of this document, which, as he says, "has been formed after hearing and weighing everything which the wisdom of man could offer on these subjects." [12] He writes, "I like much the general idea of framing a government, which should go on of itself, peaceably, without needing continual recurrence to the State legislatures. I like the organization of the government into legislative, judiciary and executive. I like the power given the legislature to levy taxes, and for that reason solely, I approve the greater House being chosen by the people directly. For, though I think a House so chosen, will be very far inferior to the present Congress, will be very illy qualified to legislate for the union, for foreign nations, etc., yet this evil does not weigh against the good of preserving inviolate the fundamental principle that the people are not to be taxed but by representatives chosen immediately by themselves.

"I am captivated by the compromise of the opposite claims of the great and little states," he continues, "of the latter to equal, and the former to proportional influence. I am much pleased, too, with the substitution of the method of voting by person, instead of that of voting by states; and I like the negative given to the Executive, conjointly with a third of either House. . . . There are other good things of less moment.

"I will now tell you what I do not like," he goes on, emphasizing what he considered the fundamental principles of government. "First, the omission of a bill of rights, providing clearly, and without the aid of sophism, for freedom of religion, freedom of the press, protection against standing armies, restriction of monopolies, the eternal and unremitting force of the habeas corpus laws and trials by jury in all matters of fact triable by the laws of the land, and not by the laws of nations. . . . Let me add, that a bill of rights is what the people are entitled to against every government on earth, general and particular, and what no first government should refuse, or rest on inference." [13]

Jefferson's second objection to the proposed constitution and one on which he expressed himself often and strongly was "the abandonment, in every instance, of the principle of rotation in office, and most particularly in the case of the President." Indeed, he goes so far as to say he is "a bad edition of a Polish King." [14] "Reason and experience tell us," he continues, "that the first magistrate will always be re-elected if he may be re-elected. He is then an officer for life." [15] Jefferson then goes on, as he did in every other letter to his friends in which he discussed the subject, to enlarge extensively on this evil, drawing examples from ancient as well as more recent history, to emphasize his point. With the election of Washington to the presidency, he was to modify his opinion to some extent. "I would not wish it to be altered during the life of our great leader," he writes Francis Hopkinson, "whose executive talents are superior to those, I believe, of any man in the world, and who alone, by the authority of his name and the confidence reposed in his perfect integrity, is fully qualified to put the new government so under way, as to secure it against opposition." [16]

"I do not pretend to decide," he concludes, "what would be the best method of procuring the establishment of the manifold good things in this constitution, and of getting rid of the bad.... At all events, I hope you will not be discouraged from making other trials, if the present one should fail."[17] "We are never permitted to despair of the commonwealth" he adds, as he once more gives utterance to his fundamental political faith. "I own I am not a friend to a very energetic government. It is always oppressive. It places the government indeed more at their ease, at the expense of the people," and he illustrates this by citing the examples of England, France, and Turkey, "where the sole nod of the despot is death," and "insurrections are the events of every day... And say, finally," he demands, as he launches upon a favorite theme, "whether peace is best preserved by giving energy to government, or information to the people. This last is most certain, and the most legitimate engine of government. Educate and inform the whole mass of the people. Enable them to see that it is their interest to preserve peace and order, and they will preserve them. And it requires no very high degree of education to convince them of this. They are the only sure reliance for the preservation of our liberty," he proclaims and adds, "After all, it is my principle that the will of the majority should prevail."[18]

Though, as he said, "forbidden by my character [*i.e.*, position] to meddle in the internal affairs of an allied state," it was "the wish of his heart" to see these principles inculcated in the new government that was evolving or, as he put it, "that their troubles may have such an issue as will secure the greatest degree of happiness." At the time he wrote these words, in December, 1787, Jefferson still regarded France very much as a clean slate upon which might be inscribed his dream of a free people. And he still hoped and believed it possible, as he stated at various times, that this might be accomplished without shedding a drop of blood or costing a human life. As late as August, 1788, he was to write, "I am in hopes her internal affairs will be arranged without blood. None has been shed yet. The nation presses on sufficiently upon the government to force reformations, without forcing them to draw the sword. If they can keep the opposition always exactly at this point, all will end well."[19] A year later his optimism was still not dulled. "I think it probable this country will, within two or three years, be in the enjoyment of a tolerably free constitution," he confided to Monroe, "and that without its having cost them a drop of blood; for none has yet been spilt, though the English papers have set the whole nation cutting throats."[20] Jefferson was, alas, not to prove a good prophet on this point.

The beginning of the year 1787 had marked a definite shift in Jefferson's interests. Hitherto his reflections, as revealed in his letters to his friends as well as in his official letters to Jay, had dealt primarily with general European politics and the usual imminence of war—this aside from what might be termed purely business letters regarding his mission to France. With the calling of the Assembly of Notables for the first time in 160 years, an event that, as he says, "occupies all conversation," the revolutionist in Jefferson was reborn. We find him enlarging with enthusiasm on a favorite theme, that "a little rebellion now and then is a good thing, and as necessary to the political world as storms in the physical.... It is a medicine necessary for the sound health of government."[21] To Colonel William S. Smith he expressed himself even more strongly *à propos* of the insurrection in Massachusetts. "God forbid that we should ever be twenty years without such a rebellion. The people cannot be all and always well informed.... We have had thirteen states independent for eleven years. There has been one rebellion.... What country can preserve its liberties if its rulers are not warned from time to time, that this people preserve the spirit of resistance? Let them take arms... what signify a few lives lost in a century or two? The tree of liberty must be refreshed from time to time, with the blood of patriots and tyrants. It is its natural manure."[22]

Henceforth Jefferson was to follow the internal politics of France with an avidness that could not have been greater had the country been his own. He was, of course, not so inexperienced politically, so unphilosophical, or so naïve as to believe the existing system could be swept out of existence by the stroke of a pen. He did not, through his friends among the patriots, advocate a declaration of independence, as had been made in America. France had far too old a history and institutions far too deeply rooted to consider such a step. She had, after all, legislative bodies of sorts, although they had not been convened for many years, in the Assemblée des Notables, which had last met in 1626, and in the all but forgotten Etats-Généraux, or States-General, composed of representatives of the nobility, clergy, and commons, the most recent session of which had occurred in 1614. Jefferson, as well as the liberal group with which he was connected, hoped that these might ultimately function so as truly to represent the people.

Although aware that the meeting of the Notables was "an event which will hardly excite any attention in America," Jefferson agreed with the French who "deemed [it] the most important one which has taken place in their civil line during the present century. Some promise their country great things from it, some nothing." [23] Even though not too hopeful, Jefferson took it as a good omen and a step in the right direction. The Assembly consisted "of various elements of the nobility: fourteen prelates, thirty-six great lords, thirty-three members of *parlements*, thirteen *intendants* and councillors of state, thirty-seven members of provincial estates and urban municipalities." [24] Lafayette, after first having had his name removed from the list, ultimately became a member of the Assembly. "This shows that his character is not considered an indifferent one," Jefferson writes, "and that it excites agitation. His education in our school has drawn on him a very jealous eye from a court whose principles are the most absolute despotism, but I hope he has nearly passed his crisis. The King, who is a good man, is favorably disposed toward him, and he is supported by powerful family connections and by the public good will." [25]

After a postponement due to the death of the Comte de Vergennes, the meeting finally took place on the twenty-second of February, 1787. The next day Jefferson sent a description of this historic occasion to his old friend Adams, as well as to John Jay. "The Assembly met yesterday," he writes. "The King, in a short but affectionate speech, informed them of his wish to consult them on the plans he had digested, and on the general good of the people.... The Garde des Sceaux [Keeper of the Seals] then spoke about twenty minutes, chiefly in compliment to the orders present. The Comptroller General [Calonne] in a speech of about an hour, opened the budget, and enlarged on the several subjects which will be under deliberation....

The Assembly was then divided into committees, with a prince of the blood at the head of each," which were to discuss separately "the subjects that will be submitted to them" and report to the Minister. He was ultimately to "submit them to the vote but I believe not to the debate of the General Assembly, which will be convened for this purpose one day in every week, and will vote individually." [26]

The effect was tremendous. "We talk and think of nothing here but the Assemblée des Notables," Jefferson writes. "Were all the puns collected to which this Assembly has given rise, I think they would make a larger volume than the *Encyclopédie*. The government is said to want eighty millions of livres revenue more than they have. They propose to give to the people provincial administrations, and to make other improvements." [27] To Lafayette, he sent some words of advice. "Keeping the good model of your neighboring country before your eyes, you may get on step by step, towards a good constitution. Though that model is not yet perfect, yet, as it would unite more suffrages than any new one which could be proposed, it is better to make that the object. If every advance is to be purchased by filling the royal coffers with gold," he adds philosophically, "it will be gold well employed. The King should be encouraged to repeat these Assemblies." [28]

Jefferson started on a tour of southern France and Italy shortly after this. From Nîmes, late in March, he wrote Madame de Tessé that his journey had given him leisure to reflect on the Assembly of Notables and he had concluded that "under a good and young King as the present... good may come of it." He then proceeds to lay before her his scheme for the reorganization of the government, well knowing that through her it would reach influential quarters. "Their first step should be to get themselves divided into two chambers instead of seven," he writes, "the Noblesse and the Commons, separately. The second, to persuade the King, instead of choosing the deputies of the Commons himself, to summon those chosen by the people for the provincial administrations. The third, as the Noblesse is too numerous to be all of the Assembly, to obtain permission for that body to choose its own deputies. Two Houses, so elected, would contain a mass of wisdom which would make the people happy, and the King great, would place him in history where no other act can possibly place him.... Should they attempt more than the established habits of the people are ripe for, they may lose all, and retard indefinitely the ultimate object of their aim." [29]

Shortly after Jefferson's return to Paris, in June, 1787, a change occurred in the ministry, which brought his old friend Malsherbes once more into power as a member of the King's Council. Jefferson's hopes rose with this appointment and he sent Madison a cheerful account of the political scene at that moment. "His [Malsherbes's] knowledge and integrity render his value inappreciable," he writes. "So far, too, I am pleased with Montmorin. His honesty proceeds from the heart as well as the head." Even the King came in for a good word. He "loves business, economy, order and justice, and wishes sincerely the good of his people, but he is irascible, rude, very limited in his understanding and religious bordering on bigotry. He has no mistress, loves his queen, and is too much governed by her." He pauses to add a phrase about the unfortunate Marie Antoinette, to the effect that she is "capricious like her brother [the Emperor Joseph II] and governed by him; devoted to pleasure and expense, and not remarkable for any other vices or virtues." [30]

Other changes in the ministry were made at the time Malsherbes was recalled. Chief among them was the appointment of Loménie de Brienne, archbishop of Toulouse, as Chef du Conseil de Finance. This remarkable man had been responsible for sending a certain Abbé to Vienna, before the marriage of Marie Antoinette, to perfect her in French. The Abbé, according to Jefferson, "either tutored by his patron, or prompted by gratitude, impressed on the Queen's mind the exalted talents and merit of the Archbishop, and continually represented him as the only man fit to be placed at the helm of affairs.... The Archbishop was named to the Assembly of Notables, had occasion enough there to prove his talents, and the Count de Vergennes, his great enemy, dying opportunely, the Queen got him the place. That he has imposing talents and patriotic dispositions, I think is certain. Good judges," he concludes, "think of him as a theorist only, little acquainted with the details of business," [31] but Jefferson continued to think of him as "a virtuous, able and patriotic character." [32]

Within a short time, the scene shifted again. Writing Jay on August 6, Jefferson rehearses the situation as it had developed. "You remember that the nation was in a delirium of joy on the convocation of the Notables," he writes, "and on the various reformations agreed on between them and the government. The picture of the distress of their finances was indeed frightful, but the intentions to reduce them to order seemed serious. The constitutional reformations have gone on well, but those of expenses make little progress. Some of the most obviously useless have indeed been lopped off, but the remainder is a heavy mass, difficult to be reduced. Despair has seized every mind, and they have passed from an extreme of joy to one of discontent. The Parliament, therefore, oppose the registering of any new tax, and insist on an assembly of the States-General. The object of this is to limit expenses and dictate a constitution.... It is evident, I think, that the spirit of this country is advancing towards a revolution in their constitution. There are not wanting persons at the helm, friends to the progress of this spirit." [33] In a postscript Jefferson adds that "the Parliament was received yesterday very harshly by the King. ... It may serve to show the spirit which exists between them." His answer to a deputation which waited on him at Versailles, "was in these words, and these words only: '*Je vous ferai savoir mes intentions. Allez-vous-en. Qu'on ferme la porte.*'" [34]

The day when a few haughty words might force an assemblage of men into submission had long since passed. In detailing the events of this moment, which he calls "perhaps the most interesting ever known in this country," Jefferson describes how "the King had been obliged to hold a bed of justice, to enforce the registering of the new taxes; the parliament on their side propose to issue a prohibition against their execution. Very possibly this may bring on their exile. The mild and patriotic character of the new ministry is the principal dependence against this extremity." [35] No ministry was able to prevent the exile to Troyes, however. It occurred on the fifteenth of August.

"In the meantime," Jefferson writes Adams, "all tongues in Paris (and in France it is said) have been let loose, and never was a license of speaking against the government exercised in London more freely or more universally. Caricatures, placards, bons mots have been indulged in by all ranks of people, and I know of no well-attested instance of a single punishment. For some time mobs of ten, twenty and thirty thousand people collected daily, surrounded the parliament house, huzzaed the members, and even entered the doors and examined into their conduct, took the horses out of the carriages of those who did well, and drew them home. The government . . . drew some regiments into the neighborhood, multiplied the guards, had the streets constantly patrolled by strong parties, suspended privileged places, forbade all clubs, etc. The mobs have ceased, perhaps this may be partly owing to the absence of parliament. The Count d'Artois [brother of the King] sent to hold a bed of justice in the *Cour des Aides*, was hissed and hooted without reserve by the populace. . . . The Queen, going to the theatre at Versailles with Madame de Polignac, was received with a general hiss. The King, long in the habit of drowning his cares in wine, plunges deeper and deeper. The Queen cries, but sins on."[36] It was not a pretty picture. It was far removed from the peaceful scene that had greeted Jefferson on his arrival three years before.

Less than a month later Jefferson was writing Jay, "It is confidently believed . . . that the Parliament will be immediately recalled, the stamp tax and the land tax repealed, and other means devised of accommodating their receipts and expenditures. Those supposed to be in contemplation are a rigorous levy of the old tax of the *deux vingtièmes* on the rich, who had in a great measure withdrawn their property from it, as well as on the poor, on whom it had principally fallen. This will greatly increase the receipts, while they are proceeding on the other hand to reform their expenses far beyond what they had promised . . . circumstances render these measures more and more pressing."[37]

Jefferson's prognostication was, indeed, fulfilled but, as he says, seeing "this was proposed by the King in lieu of the impost territorial, there is no doubt now that the latter, with the stamp tax, will be immediately repealed. There can be no better proof of the revolution in the public opinion, as to the powers of the monarch, and the force, too, of that opinion. Six weeks ago we saw the King displaying the plenitude of his omnipotence, as hitherto conceived, to enforce these two acts. At this day he is forced to retract them by public voice." [38]

A period of relative quiet followed, an interlude which enabled Jefferson to engage the attention of the Foreign Minister, Montmorin, for discussion of problems of immediate concern to America. Meanwhile he was hopeful for the future of France. "This nation is rising from the dust," we find him writing early in August, 1788. "They have obtained, as you know, provincial assemblies, in which there will be a more perfect representation of the people than in our state assemblies; they have obtained from the King a declaration that he cannot impose a new tax without the consent of the States-General, and a promise to call the States-General. When these meet, they will endeavor to establish a declaration of rights, a periodical national assembly, and a civil list." [39] No program could have sounded more reasonable or less difficult of achievement.

The very next day, however, Jefferson was recounting the insurrection of the nobles of Bretagne and sending Jay news of Lafayette's apparent disgrace by being relieved of his command in the South of France—although both Jefferson and the patriots considered that he was thus "honorably marked in the eyes of the nation. The ministers are so sensible of this that they have had, separately, private conferences with him, to endeavour, through him, to keep things quiet." [40]

A week later came the announcement of the momentous decision to call a meeting of the States-General for the first day of May of the following year. "This *arrêt* ought to have a great effect towards tranquilizing the nation," Jefferson observes. "There are, however, two circumstances which must continue to perplex the administration. The first is the want of money, occasioned not only by the difficulty of filling up the loan of the next year, but by the withholding of the ordinary supplies of taxes, which is said to have taken place in some instances. This gives apprehension of a bankruptcy under some form or other, and has occasioned the stocks to fall in a most alarming manner. The second circumstance is that justice, both civil and criminal, continues suspended. The parliament will not resume their functions, but with their whole body, and the greater part of the *baillages* decline acting. The present *arrêt* announces a perseverance in this plan." [41]

On the twentieth of August, 1788, Jefferson was informing his government of "the act of public bankruptcy which had taken place here" when an *arrêt* was published "suspending all reimbursements of capital, and reducing the payments of the principal mass of demands for interest to twelve sous in the livre, the remaining eight sous to be paid with certificates." The treasury "became literally moneyless." This, of course, caused a change of government, and Jefferson proceeds to describe the scene that followed when the first blood of the revolution was spilled by the excited mob. "The Archbishop [of Toulouse] was hereupon removed," he writes, "with Monsieur Lambert, the Comptroller General, and Mr. Necker was called in as Director General of the Finance.... The public joy on this change of administration was very great indeed. The people of Paris were amusing themselves with tying and burning the Archbishop in effigy. The commanding officer of the city guards undertook to forbid this, and not being obeyed, he charged the mob with fixed bayonets, killed two or three, and wounded many. This stopped their rejoicing for that day. But enraged at being obstructed in amusements wherein they had committed no disorder whatever, they collected in great numbers next day, attacked the guards in various places, burnt ten or twelve guard houses, killed two or three guards, and had about six or eight of their own number killed. The city was hereupon put under martial law and, after a while, the tumult subsided, and peace was restored. The public stocks rose ten percent on the day of Mr. Necker's appointment.... The whole kingdom seems tranquil at this moment." [42]

Jefferson's optimism persisted through the fall of 1788. In November he wrote Madison, "Here things internally are going well. The Notables now in session, have, indeed, passed one vote which augurs ill to the rights of the people; but if they do not obtain now so much as they have a right to, they will in the long run. The misfortune is that they are not yet ripe for receiving the blessings to which they are entitled. I doubt, for instance, whether the body of the nation, if they could be consulted, would accept a habeas corpus law, if offered them by the King. If the Etats-Généraux, when they assemble, do not aim at too much, they may begin a good constitution. There are three articles which they may easily obtain: their own meeting, periodically; the exclusive right of taxation; the right of registering laws and proposing amendments to them, as exercised now by the parliaments. . . . If they push at much more, all may fail." [43]

Attention was somewhat distracted from politics during the hard, cold winter of 1788–89, the coldest in nearly half a century when, as Jefferson says, "all communications, almost, were cut off. Dinners and suppers were suppressed, and the money laid out in feeding and warming the poor, whose labors were suspended by the rigors of the season. Loaded carriages passed the Seine on the ice, and it was covered with thousands of people from morning to night skating and sliding. Such sights had never been seen before, and they continued for two months." [44] Meanwhile the Notables remained in session, "their treasonable vote against the people [not] yet consolidated; but it will be. The Parliament have taken up the subject, and passed a very laudable vote in opposition. They have made it the occasion of giving sketches of what should be a bill of rights. Perhaps this opposition of authority may give the court an option between the two." [45]

All in all, Jefferson considered "the opposition to the revolution which is working . . . miraculously small, and he who would predict of its failure from the little obstacles which have happened, would be about as good a prophet as he who, from the loss of two or three skirmishes on our part, would have foretold our final failure in the American revolution. . . . The difficulties which now appear threatening to my mind," he observes, as an experienced politician, "are those which can result from the size of the Assembly. Twelve hundred persons of any rank and of any nation assembled together, would with difficulty be prevented from tumult and confusion. But when they are to compose an assembly for which no rules of debate or proceeding have yet been formed, in whom no habits of order have yet been established, and to consist, moreover, of Frenchmen, among whom there are always more speakers than listeners, I confess to you that I apprehend some danger." [46]

With breathless interest Jefferson watched the juggling and maneuvering of the various factions during these weeks, too numerous and too complicated to repeat here, and duly reported each detail to his correspondents in America. "The moment of crisis," he writes Jay, in January, 1789, discussing the question that was dividing the nation, "will be the meeting of the States [General], because their first act will be to decide whether they shall vote by persons or orders. The clergy will leave nothing unattempted to obtain the latter, for they see that the spirit of reformation will not confine itself to the political, but will extend to the ecclesiastical establishment also. With respect to the nobles, the younger members are generally for the people, and the middle aged are daily coming over to the same side; so that by the time the States meet, we may hope there will be a majority of that body also in favor of the people, and consequently for voting by persons and not by orders.... This country," he concludes, "advances with a steady pace towards the establishment of a constitution, whereby the people will resume the greatness of those powers so fatally lodged in the hands of the King." [47]

On March 14 we find him writing his friend Madame de Bréhan, who had gone to the United States with her brother the Comte de Moustier, the newly appointed French minister, "[Paris] is deserted, everybody being gone into the country to choose or be chosen deputies to the States-General. I hope to see that great meeting before my departure. A great political revolution will take place in your country, and that without bloodshed. A King, with two hundred thousand men at his orders, is disarmed by the force of public opinion and the want of money." [48]

Against this inflammable background the meeting of the States-General finally took place on the fifth of May, 1789. The significance of the occasion struck every heart. Jefferson has left no picture of the pageant, he merely observes that "had it been enlightened with lamps and chandeliers, it would have been almost as brilliant as the opera." [49] Gouverneur Morris, however, who was in Paris at the time and to whom Jefferson had given the ticket reserved by Mme. de Tessé for Short, gives a description of this historic occasion that brings the scene to actual life for us. The King and Queen had proceeded from the palace of Versailles to the Salle des Menus Plaisirs, which had been transformed from little more than a warehouse to a setting of great splendor, worthy of the King. The procession is described as being "very magnificent, through a double row of tapestry. Neither the King nor Queen appear too well pleased. The former is repeatedly saluted as he passes along with '*Vive le Roi,*' but the latter meets not a single acclamation. She looks, however, with contempt on the scene in which she acts a part and seems to say: 'For the present I submit, but I shall have my turn.'"

In a letter to Mrs. Robert Morris, Gouverneur Morris, who was much more vocal concerning his experiences in Paris than were his American contemporaries, has left an impressive picture of a ceremony. "A spectacle more solomn to the mind than gaudy to the eye," he writes, "and yet there was displayed everything of noble and of royal in this titled country. A great number of fine women and a very great number of fine dresses ranged round the hall. On a kind of stage the throne. On the left of the King and a little below him, the Queen. A little behind them to the right and on chairs, the princes of the blood. On the right and left, at some distance from the throne, the various princesses with the gentlemen and ladies of their retinue. Advanced on the stage to the left of the throne, the Keeper of the Seals. Several officers of the household, richly caparisoned, strewed about in different places. Behind the throne a cluster of guards of the largest size, dressed in ancient costume taken from the times of chivalry. In front of the throne on the right, below the stage, the Ministers of State with a large table before them. On the opposite side of the hall some benches on which sat the maréchals of France and other great officers. In front of the ministers, on benches facing to the opposite side of the hall, sat the representatives of the clergy, being priests of all colors, scarlet, crimson, black, white and grey to the number of three hundred. In front of the maréchals of France on benches facing the clergy, sat an equal number of representatives of the nobility dressed in a robe of black, waistcoats of cloth of gold, and over their shoulders so as to hang forward to their waist, a kind of lappet about a quarter of a yard wide at the top and wider at bottom, made of cloth of gold. On benches which reached quite across the hall and facing the stage, sat the representatives of the people, clothed in black. In the space between the clergy and nobles, directly in front of the representatives of the people and facing the throne, stood the heralds at arms with their staves, and in very rich dresses.

"When the King . . . had taken his seat he put on his hat, a round beaver ornamented with plumes, the part in front turned up with a large diamond button in the center. . . . The King rises to depart. The hall resounds with a long, loud, '*Vive le Roi!*' He passes the Queen, who rises to follow him. At this moment someone imbued with the milk of human kindness originates a faint '*Vive la Reine.*' She makes a humble curtsey." [50]

Jefferson writes of this occasion, "The King's speech was exactly what it should have been, and very well delivered. Not a word of the Chancellor's was heard by anybody so that, as yet, I have not heard a single guess as to what it was about. Mr. Necker's was as good as such a number of details would permit it to be. The picture of their resources was consoling, and generally plausible. . . . The Noblesse, on coming together, show that they are not as much reformed in their principles as we had hoped they would be. In fact, there is a real danger of their totally refusing to vote by persons. Some found hopes on the lower clergy, which constitute four-fifths of the deputies of that order. If they do not turn the balance in favor of the Tiers Etat, there is real danger of a scission. But I shall not consider even that event as rendering things desperate. If the King will do business with the Tiers Etat, which constitutes the nation, it may be well done without priests or nobles." [51]

The period immediately following this meeting was one of desperate confusion. Two weeks later Jefferson was writing that affairs were "at a dead stand." The three orders were still sitting in different chambers. "The great preliminary question, whether they shall vote by orders or persons, seems to threaten a scission. They have not yet ventured to present the question in form, but the votes which have been given by the separate chambers on the outworks of that question, enables us to see pretty clearly the strength of the two parties. For voting by persons are 1, the Tiers Etat, unanimous; 2, a good majority of the clergy, consisting of the *curés;* 3, fifty-four members of the Noblesse. For voting by orders are 1, the residue of the nobles, being about 190; 2, a minority of the clergy, consisting of the bishops, and archbishops, etc. All the world is conjecturing how they are to get over the difficulty. Abundance are affrighted, and think all is lost, and the nation, in despair at this unsuccessful effort, will consign itself to tenfold despotism. This is rank cowardice."[52]

It was impossible for the man who had successfully steered his country through the perils and intricacies of a revolution, to keep entirely aloof from the one then transpiring in a country toward which he felt as strongly as Jefferson did toward France, or to regard it from a purely intellectual point of view. For years, now, he had been pondering over the question of a declaration of rights, which he felt was sorely missing from the new constitution of his own country and which he likewise hoped would ultimately be embodied in that of France. The preceding January he had written Madison, "Everybody here is trying his hand at forming a declaration of rights. As something of that kind is going on with you also, I send you two specimens from hence." One had been written by Lafayette and contained "the essential principles of ours [*i.e.*, Virginia's], accommodated as much as could be to the state of things here."[53]

On the second of June Jefferson had gone to Versailles, as was his custom, to attend the meeting of the States-General. He was in the company of Short, Lafayette, and Rabaud de St. Etienne, a prominent liberal. The "difficulties which environed the country" were, as usual, the subject of conversation. "The idea was started," and a strong suspicion is inevitable that it originated with Jefferson, "of the King's coming forward in a *séance royale*," and offering "a charter containing all the good in which the parties agree." As he reflected, Jefferson confesses that he liked "the idea more and more." On his return to Paris that evening he put it "into form" and sent copies to Lafayette and St. Etienne. This declaration of rights, or charter, as he called it in this case, was to be signed by the King "and every member of the three orders," Jefferson writes St. Etienne. It was "to contain the five great points which the *Resultat* of December offered, on the part of the King, the abolition of pecuniary privileges offered by the privileged orders, and the adoption of the national debt, and a grant of the sum of money asked from the nation. This last will be a cheap price for the preceding articles. And let the same act declare your immediate separation till the next anniversary meeting. You will carry back to your constituents more good than was ever effected before without violence, and you will stop exactly at the point where violence would otherwise begin....

"I have ventured to send to yourself and Monsieur de Lafayette a sketch of my ideas of what this act might contain," Jefferson concludes, "without endangering any dispute. But it is offered merely as a canvas for you to work on, if it be fit to work on at all.... But after all, what excuse can I make, Sir, for this presumption? I have none but an immeasurable love for your nation, and a painful anxiety lest despotism, after an unaccepted offer to bind its own hands, should seize you again with tenfold fury." To Lafayette Jefferson remarks that he has thought best "to possess him [St. Etienne] immediately of the paper, because he may at the conference today sound the minds of the conferees." [54]

Jefferson's charter contains ten clauses. They provide for the annual meeting of the States-General, which "alone shall levy money on the nation and appropriate it." Laws were to be "made by the States-General only," with the consent of the King, and "no person was to be restrained of his liberty but by regular process from a court." The military was to be "subordinate to the civil authority." To make these and the further proposals palatable, "all debts already contracted by the King, are hereby made the debts of the nation," and eighty million livres, to be raised by a loan, "are now granted to the King." It was a simple document, with no elaborate preamble, no idealistic discussion of the rights of man.[55] However felicitous Jefferson's ideas may have been, they were not put into effect. Reared in the traditions of the proudest kings on earth, it was as yet impossible for Louis XVI to accept or carry out so democratic a procedure, much less for his advisers to suggest it.

Jefferson followed the deliberations of the States-General during the early part of June with the deepest interest and promptly relayed an account of the discussions to Madison and Jay. On the eighteenth he wrote that this body had "moved to declare themselves the National Assembly. The debates were finished yesterday, when the proposition was agreed to by four hundred and odd, against eighty odd. ... They then immediately made the proposition relative to taxes, which I enclose you.... We shall know, I think, within a day or two, whether the government will risk a bankruptcy and civil war, rather than see all distinctions of orders done away, which is what the Commons will push for.... The Commons have in their chamber almost all the talents of the nation; they are firm and bold, yet moderate.... Every step of this House has been marked with caution and wisdom. The Noblesse, on the contrary, are absolutely out of their senses. They are so furious, they can seldom debate at all. They have few men of moderate talents, and not one of great, in the majority. Their proceedings have been very injudicious. The Clergy are waiting to profit by every incident to secure themselves, and have no other object in view.... I give you these miscellaneous observations, that knowing somewhat the dispositions of the parties, you may be able to judge of the future for yourself, as I shall not be here to continue its communication to you." [56]

It is obvious that Jefferson had as yet no inkling how swiftly events were to move. Less than a week after the preceding letter he was writing Jay the startling developments of the past few days. It was a picture of intrigue without parallel: the continuing struggle of the various factions over the vote, the meeting of the King's Council at Marly when it was decided that "the King should interpose by a declaration of his sentiments at a *séance royale* on the 22nd," the closing of the Salle des Menus Plaisirs to further meetings of the Assembly until after the *séance*, and the famous oath of the tennis court, on June 20, where "they bound themselves to each other by an oath never to separate of their own accord till they had settled a constitution for the nation on a solid basis, and if separated by force, that they would reassemble in some other place.... The next day they met in a church, and were joined by a majority of the clergy. The heads of the aristocracy, viz: the Queen, Count d'Artois, and Prince de Condé saw that all was lost without some violent exertion. The King was still at Marly. Nobody was permitted to approach him but their friends. He was assailed by lies in all shapes. He was made to believe that the Commons were going to absolve the army from their oath of fidelity to him, and then raise their pay. The Queen abandoned herself to rage and despair."

Jefferson then recounts the intrigue against Necker, the minister of finance, who still retained the loyalty and confidence of the people and "whose plans were [now] totally dislocated, and that of the Count d'Artois inserted into it." When Montmorin and Necker offered their resignations, the Comte d'Artois savagely declared, "No, Sir, you must be kept as a hostage. We hold you responsible for all the ill which may happen." This change of plan, Jefferson continues, "was immediately whispered without doors. The nobility were in triumph, the people in consternation. When the King passed the next day through the lane they formed from the château to the Hôtel des Etats (about half a mile) there was a dead silence. He was about an hour in the house delivering his speech and declaration, copies of which I enclose you. On his coming out, a feeble cry of '*Vive le Roi*' was raised by some children, but the people remained sullen and silent. . . .

"He had ordered in the close of his speech that the members should follow him, and resume their deliberations the next day. The Noblesse followed him, and so did the Clergy, except about thirty who, with the Tiers, remained in the room and entered into deliberation. They protested against what the King had done, adhered to their former proceedings, and resolved the inviolability of their own persons. An officer came twice to order them out of the room, in the King's name, but they refused to obey.

"In the afternoon, the people, uneasy, began to assemble in great numbers in the courts and vicinities of the palace," Jefferson continues. It was obvious how completely the discipline of the guards and those responsible for the persons of the royal family had broken down. "The Queen was alarmed and sent for M. Necker. He was conducted amid the shouts and acclamations of the multitude, who filled the apartments of the palace. He was a few minutes only with the Queen, and about three quarters of an hour with the King. . . . The King was just going out to ride. He passed through the crowd to his carriage and into it without being in the least noticed. As M. Necker followed him, universal acclamations were raised of '*Vive Monsieur Necker!*

Vive le sauveur de la France opprimée.'... These circumstances must wound the heart of the King, desirous as he is to possess the affection of his subjects." [57]

The next day, the twenty-fifth, on his return from Versailles, Jefferson added a postscript, to the effect that the mob of Versailles had attacked the Archbishop of Paris, "who had been one of the instigators of the Court to the proceedings of the *séance royale.* They threw mud and stones at his carriage, broke the windows of it, and he in a fright promised to join the Tiers. This day (the 25th) forty-eight of the nobles have joined the Tiers. Among them is the Duke of Orleans. The Marquis de Lafayette could not be of the number, being restrained by his instructions. He is writing to his constituents to change his instructions or to accept his resignation. There are with the Tiers now one hundred and sixty-four members of the Clergy, so that the common chamber consists of upwards of eight hundred members....

"I found the streets of Versailles much embarrassed with soldiers," Jefferson adds. "There was a body of about one hundred horse drawn up in front of the hotel of the states, and all the avenues and doors guarded by soldiers. Nobody was permitted to enter but the members, and this was by order of the King, for till now the doors of the common room have been open, and at least two thousand spectators attending their debates constantly.... During the continuance of this crisis and my own stay," he concludes, "I shall avail myself of every private conveyance to keep you informed of what passes." [58]

An opportunity offered itself within a few days. It was very grave news Jefferson had to send. "I have before mentioned to you the ferment into which the proceedings at the *séance royale* of the 23rd had thrown the people. The soldiery also were affected by it. It began in the French guards, extended to those of every other denomination (except the Swiss) and even to the bodyguards of the King. They began to quit their barracks, to assemble in squads, to declare they would defend the life of the King, but would not cut the throats of their fellow citizens. They were treated and caressed by the people, carried in triumph through the streets, called themselves the soldiers of the nation, and left no doubt on which side they would be in case of rupture. Similar reports came in from the troops in other parts of the

Kingdom. . . . The operation of this medicine at Versailles was as sudden as it was powerful. The alarm there was so complete that in the afternoon of the 27th the King wrote a letter to the President of the Clergy, the Cardinal de la Rochefoucauld" and "the Duke de Luxemburgh, President of the Noblesse" in which he took the unprecedented step of recommending that they join the Tiers. "There was considerable opposition, when notes, written by the Count d'Artois to sundry members, and handed about among the rest, decided the matter, and they went in a body and took their seats with the Tiers, and thus rendered the union of the orders in one chamber complete.

"As soon as this was known to the people of Versailles, they assembled about the palace, demanded the King and Queen, who came and showed themselves on a balcony. They rent the skies with cries of '*Vive le Roi!*' '*Vive la Reine!*' They called for the Dauphin, who was also produced, and was the subject of new acclamations. . . . Similar emotions of joy took place in Paris, and at this moment the triumph of the Tiers is complete. . . . It remains to see whether they will leave to the Nobility anything but their titular appellations. I suppose they will not. . . . This great crisis being now over, I shall not have matter interesting enough to trouble you with as often as I have done lately." [59]

The great crisis was, alas, not over. Indeed, it had little more than begun. Meanwhile, however, during the first days of July, Jefferson had become involved in an incident that caused him considerable chagrin. The scarcity of bread at this time was so great that, as he says, "there has not been three days' provision beforehand in Paris for two or three weeks past." [60] Mirabeau, who was bitterly hostile to Necker, took occasion to announce to the Assembly that Jefferson had "made an offer to Mr. Necker to obtain from America a quantity of corn or flour which had been refused." [61] Jefferson was incensed. The possibilities of diplomatic complications were enormous. He immediately wrote Lafayette, who had informed him of what had happened, begging him "to satisfy Mr. Necker of the truth. It would be disagreeable, and perhaps mischievous," he adds, "were he to have an idea that I encouraged censures on him. . . . I do not know how Monsieur Mirabeau has been led into this error. I never in my life made any proposition to Mr. Necker on the subject; I never said I had made such a proposition." [62] Lafayette replied at once. "Before your letter came," he writes, "M. de Mirabeau had engaged to disown what he had advanced. On the receipt of yours, he did more. He undertook to read it to the Assembly and, telling everything that was in it, he laid it on the table. Somebody undertook to translate it, and the house called for the reading of the translation. I... said that... I took a second reading to be useless. Necker and Montmorin were very angry with me for it." [63] Jefferson immediately sent Necker a copy of his letter to Lafayette with a statement that Mirabeau had "acknowledged that he had been in error... and undertook to declare his error when the subject should be resumed by the Assembly, to whom my letter to the Marquis de Lafayette will also be read. I have thought it a duty, Sir, thus to correct in the first moment, an error by which your name had been compromitted by an unfounded use of mine." [64]

Although Jefferson admitted that in making these amends Mirabeau had performed "all that was requisite for any just purpose," he demanded one more safeguard. "As I was unwilling my name should be used to injure the Minister," he writes in a final letter to Lafayette on the subject, "I am also unwilling it should be used to injure Monsieur de Mirabeau. I learn that his enemies in Paris are framing scandalous versions of my letter. I think, therefore... it may be better to print it." [65] Thus Jefferson's letter, with an explanatory note by the editor, appeared in the *Journal de Paris* on the morning of July 11, and an international incident was averted.

On this same morning Lafayette, as he wrote Jefferson, proposed to introduce his bill of rights in the Assembly.[66] As early as January, 1789, as we have seen, Jefferson had sent Madison a copy of such a bill of rights by Lafayette. He appears to have had a copy in his own hands at this time, for on July 4 Lafayette had asked Jefferson to send him "my Bill of Rights with your notes." On the tenth of July Lafayette repeated the request with an urgent "be pleased to consider it again and make your observations." [67] There are, indeed, among Jefferson's papers two versions of this document, one of which bears two annotations in Jefferson's hand, as well as brackets about two phrases which he seems to have questioned. This is not the place to enter into a detailed discussion of Lafayette's ideas as expressed in his *Déclaration des Droits de l'Homme et du Citoyen*, but it may be said that he had drunk deep of the American cup. He owed much not only to his friend Jefferson, for his Declaration and his proposed constitution for Virginia,[68] but to George Mason for his Bill of Rights.

The discussion of Lafayette's *Déclaration* in the Assembly had scarcely ended and been referred to a committee, than Jefferson sat down to inform his fellow revolutionary Tom Paine of the success that seemed to be attending the efforts of the French toward a new life and government. "The National Assembly," he writes with rare enthusiasm, "having shown through every stage of these transactions a coolness, wisdom, and resolution to set fire to the four corners of the Kingdom and to perish with it themselves, rather than to relinquish an iota from their plan of a total change of government, are now in complete and undisputed sovereignty. The executive and aristocracy are at their feet; the mass of the nation, the mass of the clergy, and the army are with them. They have prostrated the old government, and are now beginning to build one from the foundation." After discussing at length what he calls "the order of proceedings," he recapitulates briefly what has been defined and what is being accomplished, "Declaration of the rights of man. Principles of the monarchy. Rights of the nation. Rights of the King. Rights of the citizen. Organization and functions of the Provincial and Municipal Assemblies. Duties and limits of the judiciary power. Functions and duties of the military power.

"You see," he concludes, "that these are the materials of a superb edifice, and the hands which have prepared them, are perfectly capable of putting them together, and of filling up the work of which these are only the outlines. While there are some men among them of very superior abilities, the mass possess such a degree of good sense, as enables them to decide well." [69]

In a struggle of the character and proportions such as this, it was difficult, if not impossible for a man of Jefferson's prestige, to say nothing of his obvious sympathy, to remain incognito. All the world was aware that the man who had led the American colonies to freedom was in

Paris, and it was inevitable that his advice should be sought. He had, as we have already seen, frequently been in informal conference with the various leaders among the patriots. Indeed, in his autobiography, Jefferson goes so far as to say, "I was much acquainted with the leading patriots of the Assembly. Being from a country which had successfully passed through a similar reformation, they were disposed to my acquaintance, and had some confidence in me." [70]

On July 20, 1789, this confidence was most fully expressed by the receipt of a letter from the Archbishop of Bordeaux, "chairman of a committee for the reduction of a *projet* of the constitution," as Jefferson puts it, "requesting me to attend and assist at their deliberations." The letter reads, "The Committee charged by the Assembly to draw up a project of a constitution, being eager to neglect nothing that may contribute to the perfection of so important an undertaking, is desirous of having a talk with you, and thus procuring the light of your reason and your experience for the benefit of France. We hope for this kindness from you, Monsieur. When the happiness of man is at stake, we no longer recognize the existence of foreigners. In this hope we have the honor to beg you to grant us an interview next Wednesday, in one of the offices adjoining the hall of the National Assembly, between five and six o'clock in the afternoon." [71]

It was, of course, an honor, and it must have been a temptation of the first order. Jefferson, however, very properly felt that his "mission was to the King as chief magistrate of the nation," and that his "duties were limited to the concerns of my own country and forbade me to intermeddle with the internal transactions of that, in which I had been received under a specific character only." [72] He seems to have given the matter some thought, however, for it was not until two days later that he replied to the Archbishop in a letter as full of grace as any Frenchman could have written, and thus closed the affair. It reads, in translation, "I am desolated, Monseigneur, to have received the request of the Committee named for drawing up the constitution at the very moment when dispatches for America are completely occupying my time, and when the vessel which is to carry them is about to sail. I beg you to express to them my deep regret. For me the loss is all the more grievous as I shall miss the most interesting possible discussions by the distinguished members of the most enlightened Assembly that exists. My feeble lights would have been of no value to them. They would have been too slight a compensation for the suspicion and perhaps for the calumnies which might have been aroused against the proceedings when it had been forgotten that a zealous republican had assisted in them, that a stranger especially accredited to the head of a nation had permitted himself to take part in discussions concerning the limitation of the powers of this head, and essentially changing the form of government. The situation which prevents me from accepting the invitation with which the Committee has honored me will protect their deliberations from that reproach, and permits me only to express my most sincere and heartfelt hopes for the success of your work." [73]

Although the Assembly was obliged to accept Jefferson's declination, the individual members did not feel bound to do so. Thus it happened that he became involved with certain of them in an incident that, as he says, had the most far-reaching consequences. Shortly after having written the Archbishop of Bordeaux at a time when "schism strongly marked, broke the Patriots into fragments of very discordant principles," Jefferson received an importunate letter from Lafayette. "I beg for liberty's sake," he writes, "you will break every engagement to give us a dinner tomorrow, Wednesday. We shall be some members of the National Assembly—eight of us, whom I want to coalize as being the only means to prevent a total dissolution and a civil war. . . . Those gentlemen wish to consult you and me. They will dine tomorrow at your house, as mine is always full. I depend on you to receive us—perhaps they will be late, but I shall be precisely at the house with you, and I think this dinner of an immediate and great importance." [74]

Fond as he was of Lafayette, and deeply immersed in the problem before him and his coadjutors, Jefferson could not say no to this request. "I assured him of their welcome," he writes, and when they arrived he found his guests to be "leading Patriots of honest but differing opinions, sensible of the necessity of effecting a coalition of mutual sacrifice, knowing each other, and not afraid, therefore, to unbosom themselves mutually." Aside from Lafayette his guests proved to be Barnave, a young lawyer from the Dauphiné, very active in the revolution, Alexandre la Meth, from Péronne, Duport, Dagout, Blacon, Maubourg, and Mounier, the man who proposed the oath of the tennis court.[75]

"The cloth being removed," Jefferson writes, "and wine set on the table, after the American manner, the Marquis introduced the objects of the conference by summarily reminding them of the state of things in the Assembly, the course which the principles of the constitution were taking, and the inevitable result, unless checked by more concord among the Patriots themselves. He observed . . . that a common opinion must now be formed, or the aristocracy would carry everything, and that, whatever they should now agree on, he, at the head of the national force would maintain.

"The discussions began at the hour of four, and were continued till ten o'clock in the evening, during which time I was a silent witness to a coolness and candor of argument, unusual in the conflicts of public opinion. . . . The result was, that the King should have a suspensive veto on the laws, that the legislature should be composed of a single body only, and that to be chosen by the people. This concordate decided the fate of the constitution. The Patriots all rallied to the principles thus settled, carried every question agreeably to them, and reduced the aristocracy to insignificance and impotence." [76]

Whatever sense of triumph Jefferson may have had that such a vindication of his dearest principles was established under his own roof, was tempered by what is apt to be known as a guilty conscience. The next morning, he writes, he waited on the Comte de Montmorin "and explained to him, with truth and candor, how it happened that my house had been made the scene of conferences of such a character. He told me he already knew everything which had passed, that so far from taking umbrage at the use made of my house on that occasion, he earnestly wished I would habitually assist at such conferences, being sure that I should be useful in moderating the warmer spirits, and promoting a wholesome and practical reformation only. I told him I knew too well the duties I owed to the King, to the nation, and to my own country, to take any part in its councils concerning their internal government, and that I should persevere, with care, in the character of a neutral and passive spectator.... I have no doubts, indeed, that their conference was previously known and approved by this honest minister, who was in conference and communication with the Patriots, and wished for a reasonable reform of the constitution." [77]

Although unable to participate in the discussions of the Assembly, Jefferson continued as an auditor and faithfully followed each development. He was deeply satisfied with the proceedings of the Assembly and reported to Jay that "matters went on well." To Madison, late in August, he sent an outline of the provisions expected to be embodied in the proposed constitution and concludes happily, "In short, ours has been professedly their model, in which such changes are made as a difference of circumstances rendered necessary, and some others, neither necessary nor advantageous, but into which men will ever run when versed in theory and new in the practice of government." And again, in the same letter, and with the same exultation, "It is impossible to desire better dispositions towards us than prevail in this Assembly. Our proceedings have been viewed as a model for them on every occasion; and though, in the heat of debate, men are generally supposed to contradict every authority urged by their opponents, ours has been treated like that of the Bible, open to explanation, but not to question." [78]

While Jefferson had thus been following each move of the National Assembly and reporting on them, events of the greatest moment, in which he was just as absorbed, had been taking place outside that august body. The few letters he was yet to write to America before forsaking the scene he found "too interesting to be left at present," give a vivid picture as seen by himself or some other eyewitness (for he and Short roamed the city for confirmation of what they heard), of the frightful crescendo of the revolution—the increasing lawlessness and terror, the storming of the Invalides and the Bastille, the murder of the defenders and the triumph of Lafayette. Writing Jay in the middle of July, Jefferson says it was observed that "troops, and particularly the foreign troops, were on their march towards Paris from various quarters.... The King was probably advised to this, under pretext of preserving peace in Paris and Versailles, and saw nothing else in the measure." The Marshal de Broglio, "a high flying aristocrat, cool and capable of anything," was placed in charge of all the troops. The States-General addressed the King to forbid their approach, which he declined to do. "In the meantime, troops to the number of about twenty-five or thirty thousand had arrived and were posted in and between Paris and Versailles. The bridges and passes were guarded. At three o'clock in the afternoon, the Count de la Luzerne was sent to notify Mr. Necker of his dismission and to enjoin him to retire instantly, without saying a word of it to anybody. . . . The next day . . . the whole ministry was changed, except Villedeuil, of the domestic department, and Barentin, Garde des Sceaux . . .

"This change," Jefferson continues, "however sudden it may have been in the mind of the King, was, in that of his advisers, only one chapter of a great plan, of which the bringing together of the foreign troops had been the first. He was now completely in the hands of men, the principal among whom had been noted through their lives for the Turkish despotism of their character . . .

"The news of this change began to be known in Paris about one or two o'clock. In the afternoon a body of about one hundred German cavalry were advanced and drawn up on the Place Louis XV and about two hundred Swiss posted at a little distance in their rear. This drew the people to the spot, who, naturally, formed themselves in front of the troops, at first merely to look at them. But as their numbers increased, their indignation rose. They retired a few steps, posted themselves on and behind large piles of loose stone, collected in that place for a bridge adjacent to it, and attacked the horse with stones. The horse charged, but the advantageous position of the people, and the shower of stones, obliged them to retire, and even to quit the field altogether, leaving one of their number on the ground. The Swiss in the rear were observed never to stir.

"This was the signal for universal insurrection," Jefferson goes on, "and this body of cavalry, to avoid being massacred, retired to Versailles. The people now armed themselves with such weapons as they could find in armorers' shops and private houses, and with bludgeons, and were roaming all night through all parts of the city, without any decided practicable object. The next day the States pressed on the King to send away the troops, to permit the *Bourgeoisie* of Paris to arm for the preservation of order in the city. . . . He refused all their propositions."

A defiant and desperate step was now taken. "A committee of magistrates and electors of the city were appointed by their bodies, to take upon them its government. The mob, now openly joined by the French guards, forced the prison of St. Lazare, released all the prisoners, and took a great store of corn, which they carried to the corn market. Here they got some arms, and the French guards began to form and train them." [79] Jefferson goes on to tell how it was determined to raise a city militia or Garde Bourgeoise of forty-eight thousand men. How the husband of his great friend, Mme. de Corny, was sent to the Hôtel des Invalides to demand arms and was refused, after which he returned home, to find Jefferson there and give him an account of what had happened.[80] The people then took possession of the arms. "It was remarkable," he adds, "that not only the Invalides themselves made no opposition, but that a body of five thousand foreign troops, encamped within four hundred yards, never stirred."

De Corny, a gentle soul, with five other men was now sent to the Bastille, the ancient prison and emblem of despotism, to demand arms. "They found a great collection of people already about the place," Jefferson continues, launching into an electrifying description of the scene, "and they immediately planted a flag of truce, which was answered by a like flag hoisted on the parapet. The deputation prevailed on the people to fall back a little, advanced themselves to make their demand on the Governor, and in that instant a discharge from the Bastille killed four people of those nearest to the deputies. The deputies retired, the people rushed against the place, and almost in an instant were in possession of a fortification, defended by one hundred men, of infinite strength, which in other times had stood several regular sieges, and had never been taken.

"How they got in has, as yet, been impossible to discover. Those who pretend to have been of the party tell so many different stories, as to destroy the credit of them all. They took all the arms, discharged the prisoners and such of the garrison as were not killed in the first moment of fury. [They] carried the Governor and the Lieutenant Governor to the Grève (the place of public execution) cut off their

THE OPENING OF THE STATES-GENERAL, MAY 5, 1789. From the engraving by Moreau le jeune. (*Courtesy of the New York Public Library*)

MARTHA JEFFERSON. Miniature by Joseph Boze. (*Courtesy of the American Embassy, Paris*)

heads and sent them through the city in triumph to the Palais Royal. About the same instant, a treacherous correspondence having been discovered in Monsieur de Flesselles, *Prévôt des Marchands*, they seized him in the Hotel de Ville, where he was in the exercise of his office, and cut off his head."

The effect of these terrifying events was twofold on the court. At first the King's Council urged that the principal members of the States-General be seized, that the army be marched upon Paris "to suppress its tumults with the sword. But at night," Jefferson continues, describing an unprecedented event, "the Duke de Liancourt forced his way into the King's bedchamber, and obliged him to hear a full and animated detail of the disasters of the day." It was probably the first time the King had ever heard such realistic words. "He went to bed deeply impressed," we are told. "The decapitation of M. de Launai," the Governor of the Bastille, Jefferson continues, "worked powerfully through the night on the whole aristocratical party." The candles at Versailles were not snuffed until the coming of dawn.

At eleven o'clock the next morning the King, accompanied only by his brothers, went "to the States-General and there read to them a speech, in which he asked their interposition to re-establish order. Though this be couched in terms of some caution, yet the manner in which it was delivered made it evident that it was meant as a surrender at discretion." He returned to the château on foot, accompanied by the entire assembly and all the inhabitants at Versailles.

Meanwhile "the alarm at Versailles increased instead of abating. They believed the aristocrats of Paris were under pillage and carnage, that one hundred and fifty thousand men were coming to Versailles to massacre the royal family, the court, the ministers and all connected with them, their practices and principles. . . . The foreign troops were ordered off instantly. Every minister resigned. The King confirmed Bailly as *Prévôt des Marchands*, wrote to Mr. Necker to recall him, sent his letter open to the States-General, to be forwarded by them, and invited them to go with him to Paris the next day to satisfy the city of his dispositions." [81]

Such a turn of fortune, and so sudden a one, had never before been known. Small wonder that such scandalous characters as the Comte d'Artois, the Prince de Condé, the Duc de Bourbon, the Queen's favorites, the scandalous Madame de Polignac and her confessor, the Abbé de Vermont, fled during the night and early morning, "we know not whither."

The seventeenth of July was to mark the real surrender of the royal power. It was likewise to mark the triumph of the man who had been doing lip service to his king although a patriot at heart—the Marquis de Lafayette. Leaving the Queen at Versailles "in consternation for his return," the King proceeded to Paris in a magnificent procession surrounded by his Horse Guards, his Garde de Corps, the uniformed militia, and the ragtag of the citizenry. The militia of Versailles escorted him as far as the Point-du-Jour on the road to Paris, where he was received by a double file of Parisian militia, which extended the long way to the Hôtel de Ville. "Omitting the less important figures in the procession," Jefferson says, "I will only observe that the King's carriage was in the centre, on each side of it the States-General, in two ranks, afoot and at their head the Marquis de Lafayette, as Commander-in-Chief [of the Milice Bourgeoise] on horseback, and Bourgeoise guards before and behind. About sixty-thousand citizens of all forms and colors, armed with the muskets of the Bastille and Invalides, as far as they would go, the rest with pistols, swords, pikes, pruning hooks, scythes, etc. lined all the streets through which the procession passed, and, with the crowds of people in the streets, doors, and windows, saluted them everywhere with cries of *"Vive la nation!"*; but not a single cry of *"Vive le Roi!"* was heard.

"The King stopped at the Hôtel de Ville." There this proudest of monarchs, who by this time was no more than a complaisant puppet in the hands of circumstance, was received by Bailly, the astronomer and popular representative of the Third Estate, who "presented and put into his hat the popular cockade, and addressed him. The King, being unable and unprepared to answer, Bailly went to him, gathered from him some scraps of sentences and made out an answer, which he delivered to the audience as from the King. On their return the popular cries were *'Vive le roi et la nation!'* " As a finale to this stupendous last act of the drama, the Garde Bourgeoise conducted the King back to the palace at Versailles, a distance of some twelve miles. "And thus,"

Jefferson observes, "concluded such an *amende honorable* as no sovereign ever made and no people ever received." [82]

Jefferson's activities during these exciting and terrible days can be followed to a great extent through his own notations and through those of Morris. On the twelfth Morris remarks for the first time, "Much alarm here. Paris begins to be in commotion." He speaks of a certain abbé who, "after sallying out in a fiacre, returns frightened because of a large mob in the rue St. Honoré... and who is confoundedly frightened at the commotions." Despite these disturbances Morris decided to call upon Jefferson after dinner, which was around four o'clock. "In riding along the Boulevards, all at once the carriages, horses, and foot passengers turn about and pass rapidly. Presently after we meet a body of cavalry with their sabres drawn and coming at half speed.... When we come to the Place Louis XV, observe the people, to the number of perhaps a hundred, picking up stones, and on looking back, find that the cavalry are returning." He then proceeds to describe the encounter that has already been related. Meanwhile, Jefferson was also abroad and driving through the Place Louis XV at the same moment. "Happening to be in my carriage on a visit," he writes in his autobiography, "I passed through the lane they had formed, without interruption, but the moment after I had passed, the people attacked the cavalry with stones." [83] The two men ultimately met at the Grille de Chaillot, where they exchanged experiences and where Jefferson gave Morris the latest news from Versailles, the dismissal of Necker "by the hands of Monsieur de la Luzerne, in which he orders him to leave the Kingdom.... In returning from Mr. Jefferson's," Morris concludes, "I am turned off to the left by the vidette posted on the road to the Place Louis Quinze."

On the fifteenth Morris again started for Jefferson's but was "stopped near the Pont Royale and obliged to turn into the rue St. Honoré. Stopped again at the Church St. Roch and a number of foolish questions asked... a few paces from the church I am again stopped and a vast deal of self sufficiency in the officer brings on an altercation with my coachmen. As everything is turned into this street and interruptions of the kind I experience are so frequent, the *embarras* is very great." It was after dinner before he finally reached the

Hôtel Jefferson, without further difficulties, and the two men were able to discuss the taking of the Bastille and the gruesome events that followed. "The carrying of this citadel is among the most extraordinary things that I have met with," Morris concludes.[84]

On the nineteenth of July Jefferson writes John Jay, "I went yesterday to Versailles, to satisfy myself what had passed there, for nothing can be believed but what one sees, or has from an eye witness. They believe there still, that three thousand people have fallen victims to the tumults of Paris. Mr. Short and myself have been every day among them, in order to be sure what was passing. We cannot find, with certainty, that anybody has been killed but the three before mentioned, and those who fell in the assault or defense of the Bastille."[85] It was fortunate for Jefferson that he spent his evenings in the cool of the Champs Elysées. The ink with which he had written these last words was scarcely dry when Gouverneur Morris, who was walking after dinner in the fashionable arcade of the Palais Royal, saw the head and body of Foulon, one of the ministers, "introduced in triumph. The head on a pike, the body dragged naked on the earth. ... This mutilated form of an old man of seventy-five is shewn to Bertier, his son-in-law ... and afterwards he is put to death and cut to pieces, the populace carrying about the mangled fragments in a savage joy. Gracious God, what a people!"[86] After this Morris paid a call.

From Jefferson's account book we gain the knowledge that on the seventeenth, the day of the King's appearance at the Hôtel de Ville in Paris, he visited the Bastille, paying two livres for the privilege. He went again on the twentieth after the destruction of the building had been ordered. According to Morris, it was necessary to secure a passport for this privilege. In his case and Jefferson's Lafayette provided one. "Some difficulty in getting thru the guards notwithstanding my passport," Morris writes. "We meet with the architect employed in the demolition ... who is glad to be useful. He shows us everything. More than I wish to see, as it stinks horribly."[87]

Jefferson was not to remain in France long enough to see the final outcome of the revolution or to see his dream of an ideal constitution come to realization. By the middle of August he was writing Jay, "The city is as yet, not entirely quieted. Every now and then summary execution is done on individuals by individuals, and nobody is in condition to ask for what, and by whom. . . . The details from the country are as distressing as I had apprehended they would be. . . . Abundance of châteaux are certainly burnt and burning, and not a few lives sacrificed. The worst is probably over in this city, but I do not know whether it is so in the country." [88]

His last letter from Paris to Jay, September 19, 1789, ended on a note of gloom. "The Assembly proceeds slowly in forming their constitution," he writes. "The original vice of their numbers causes this, as well as a tumultuous manner of doing business. . . . The sloth of the Assembly (unavoidable from their number) has done the most sensible injury to the public cause. The patience of the people, who have less of that quality than any other nation in the world, is worn threadbare. Time has been given to the aristocrats to recover from their panic, to cabal, to sow dissensions in the Assembly, and distrust out of it. It has been a misfortune that the King and aristocracy together have not been a sufficient resistance to hoop the Patriots in a compact body. The Assembly now consists of four distinct parties," which Jefferson proceeds to analyze at length. "This being the face of things, troubled as you will perceive," he concludes, "civil war is much talked of and expected." [89]

Many years later, in looking back over the momentous events that took place in July, 1789, and that culminated in the appearance of the King at the Hôtel de Ville, Jefferson was led to philosophize on them and their outcome. "The King," he writes, "was now become a passive machine in the hands of the National Assembly, and had he been left to himself, he would willingly have acquiesed in whatever they should devise as best for the nation. A wise constitution would have been formed, hereditary in his line, himself placed at its head, with powers so large as to enable him to do all the good of his station, and so limited, as to restrain him from its abuse. This he would have faithfully administered, and more than this I do not believe he ever wished.

"But he had a Queen," Jefferson adds, "of absolute sway over his weak mind and timid virtue, and of a character the reverse of his in all points. This angel . . . was proud, disdainful of restraint, indignant at all obstacles to her will, eager in the pursuit of pleasure, and firm enough to hold to her desires, or perish in their wreck. . . . Her inordinate gambling and dissipations . . . her inflexible perverseness and dauntless spirit, led herself to the guillotine, drew the King with her, and plunged the world into crimes and calamities which will forever stain the pages of modern history. I have ever believed, that had there been no Queen, there would have been no revolution. . . .

"The deed which closed the mortal course of these sovereigns," he concludes, "I shall neither approve nor condemn. I am not prepared to say that the first magistrate of a nation cannot commit treason against his country, or is unamenable to its punishment; nor yet, that where there is no written law, no regulated tribunal, there is not a law in our hearts, and a power in our hands, given for righteous employment in maintaining right, and redressing wrong." [90]

XIV. Farewell to France

On the nineteenth of November, 1788, after he had been in Europe well over four years and away from Virginia and his affairs a good five, Jefferson wrote the Secretary of Foreign Affairs, "I must now trouble Congress with a petition in my own behalf. When I left my own house in October, 1783, it was to attend Congress as a member, and in expectation of returning in five or six months. In the month of May, following, however, I was desired to come to Europe as a member of a commission which was to continue two years only. I came off immediately, without going home to make any other arrangements in my affairs, thinking they would not suffer greatly before I should return to them. Before the close of the two years, Dr. Franklin returning from his charge here, Congress was pleased to name me to it, so that I have been led on by events to an absence of five years, instead of five months. In the meantime matters of great moment to others as well as myself, and which can be arranged by nobody but myself, will await no longer. Another matter of still more powerful cogency on my mind is the necessity of carrying my family back to their friends and country. I must, therefore, ask of Congress a short leave of absence, allowing three months on the sea going and coming, and two months at my own house, which will suffice for my affairs. I need not be from Paris but between five and six months. I do not foresee anything which can suffer during my absence. ... Leave for me being obtained, I will ask it, Sir, of your friendship ... to convey me immediate notice of it, and relieve me, as soon as possible, from the anxiety of expectation, and the uncertainty in which I shall be."[1]

Jefferson had various reasons for wishing to return home after this long absence. For one thing, he felt he was getting out of touch with his country, and nothing could have been more distasteful to him. As he wrote Humphreys in the summer of 1789, "I hope to receive soon permission to visit America this summer, and to possess myself anew, by conversation with my countrymen, of their spirit and their ideas. I know only the Americans of the year 1784. They tell me this is to be much a stranger to those of 1789." Furthermore, no man had a more enduring love of his country than Jefferson. It is expressed over and over again in his letters during these years. "We all pant for America, as does every American who comes to Europe," [2] he wrote his brother-in-law within a year of his arrival, and all the honors, the pleasures, the distractions that he was to experience in Europe were never to change this feeling. As he remarked to Alexander Donald of Richmond, a friend of his earliest days, "Your letter had kindled all the fond recollections of ancient times, recollections much dearer to me than anything I have known since. There are minds which can be pleased by honors and preferments, but I see nothing in them but envy and enmity. It is only necessary to possess them to know how little they contribute to happiness. No attachments soothe the mind so much as those contracted early in life. I had rather be shut up in a very modest cottage with my books, my family and a few old friends, dining on simple bacon, and letting the world roll on as it liked, than to occupy the most splendid post which any human power can give." [3]

These remarks were no exaggeration. His attachment to his old friends was as deep as that to his country, and every letter he received from one of them brought a new wave of longing and remembrance. "The distance to which I am removed has given new value to all I valued before, in my own country," he writes his sister Mary Bolling, "and the day of my return will be the happiest in my life." [4] To his old friend George Gilmer, who lived at nearby Pen Park, he expressed himself no less nostalgically, "I am as happy nowhere else, and in no other society, and all my wishes end, where I hope my days will end, at Monticello. Too many scenes of happiness mingle themselves with all the recollections of my native woods and fields, to suffer them to be supplanted in my affection by any other. I consider myself here as a traveller only, and not a resident. My commission expires next spring, and if not renewed, I shall of course return then. If renewed, I shall remain here some time longer. How much, I cannot say; yet my wishes shorten the period. . . . If you knew how agreeable to me are the details of the small news of my neighbors, your charity would induce you to write frequently." [5]

Stronger than the call of his country, his friends, or his personal affairs was the duty he felt to take his daughters home. Martha or Patsy, the eldest, had, as we have seen, come with him to France as a young girl of twelve. She had been placed in a convent where she had remained nearly five years, except for visits twice a week to her father. It was, as Jefferson reassured his sister Mary, "a house of education altogether, the best in France, and at which the best masters attend. There are in it as many Protestants as Catholics, and not a word is ever spoken to them, on the subject of religion." [6] Now Martha was reaching the age where matrimony was the next step. A foreign alliance was unthinkable. It was necessary to get her back to her own country and her own people. Her cousin Thomas Mann Randolph, Jr., whom she was to marry within two months of her return to Virginia, had been in Paris during the summer of 1788 after studying for three years at Edinburgh, and it is more than possible that the romance with this promising and estimable young man had begun at that time.

Meanwhile, in the summer of 1787 Jefferson was writing Mrs. Eppes, his wife's sister, to whom his daughters "had been bequeathed" as he says and who had taken the place of their mother, "Patsy enjoys good health, and will write to you. She has grown much the last year or two, and will be very tall. She retains all her anxiety to get back to her country and her friends, particularly yourself. Her dispositions give me perfect satisfaction, and her progress is well. She will need, however, your instruction to render her useful in her own country. Of domestic economy she can learn nothing here, yet she must learn it somewhere, as being of more solid value than anything else." [7]

In July, 1787, Jefferson's youngest living daughter, Mary, or Polly as she was called, arrived in Paris to join her father and sister. After the death of her mother, when she was but four, the child had been left with Mrs. Eppes. Her father had been planning to send for her ever since he was settled in Paris, but she could not be prevailed upon to leave her aunt and cousins. A series of touching little notes, in the awkward hand of a very young child, were sent to "dear Papa" in Paris. "I long to see you, and hope you and sister Patsy are well . . . and hope you and she will come very soon to see us. I hope that you will send me a doll. I am very sorry that you have sent for me. I don't want to go to France. I had rather stay with Aunt Eppes." The next was more determined: "I should be very happy to see you, but I cannot go to France." And finally, "I want to see you and Sister Patsy, but you must come to Uncle Eppes's house." [8] Even her future husband, Jacky Eppes, scarcely older than Polly, was called on to assure his uncle that Polly could not come.[9]

How these letters wrung Jefferson's heart we see in a letter to Mrs. Eppes, dated September 22, 1785. "No event of your life has put into your power to conceive how I feel when I reflect that such a child, and so dear to me, is to cross the ocean, is to be exposed to all the sufferings and risks, great and small, to which a situation on board a ship exposes everyone. I drop my pen at the thought—but she must come. . . . My reason tells me the dangers are not great, and the advantages to her are considerable." [10] He had already written Mr. Eppes on August 30 details as to how to send the child, under the wing of "some good lady passing from America to France . . . or a careful gentleman who would be so kind as to superintend her, would do." In any case, "some woman who has had the smallpox must attend her—a careful negro woman, as Isabel, for instance, if she has had the smallpox would suffice." [11]

Meanwhile, he directed all his arts of persuasion on Polly. "I wish so much to see you," he writes, "that I have desired your uncle and aunt to send you to me. I know, my dear Polly, how sorry you will be, and ought to be, to leave them and your cousins, but your sister and myself cannot live without you, and after a while we will carry you back again to see your friends in Virginia. In the meantime you shall be taught here to play on the harpsichord, to draw, to dance, to read and talk French, and such other things as will make you more worthy of the love of your friends. . . . When you come here you shall have as many dolls and playthings as you want for yourself, or to send to your cousins whenever you shall have opportunities." [12]

The next summer came and the following one before Jefferson had the happiness of having his little daughter with him again. "I was never more anxious to hear from you than at present," Mrs. Eppes writes in March, 1787, "in hopes of your countermanding your orders with regard to my dear Polly. We have used every stratagem to prevail on her to consent to visit you, without effect. She is more averse to it than I could have supposed. Either of my children would with pleasure take her place for the number of things she is promised." [13] Finally, by sending the Eppes children on board ship with Polly for a few days, "which I hope will reconcile her to it," the little girl was induced to go, accompanied by her Negro maid. "I shall be truly wretched till I hear of her being safely landed with you," writes the distracted aunt. "For God's sake, give us the earliest intelligence of her arrival." [14]

Mrs. Adams took charge of the child on her arrival in London and kept her a fortnight until her father could send for her. "A finer child of her age I never saw," she writes. "So mature and understanding, so womanly a behavior, and so much sensibility united, are rarely met with.... She is a beautiful girl, too." [15] Jefferson was overjoyed to have his child and as pleased with her accomplishments as Mrs. Adams had been. "A parent may be permitted to speak of his own child when it involves an act of justice to another," he writes Mrs. Eppes. "The attentions which your goodness has induced you to pay her prove themselves by the fruits of them. Her reading, her writing, her manners in general, show what everlasting obligation we are all under to you. As far as her affections can be a requital, she renders you the debt, for it is impossible for a child to prove a more sincere affection to an absent person than she does to you. She will surely not be the least happy among us when the day shall come on which we may be all reunited. She is now established in the convent," he concludes, "perfectly happy. Her sister [who was fifteen at this time] came and staid a week with her, leading her from time to time to the convent, until she became familiarized to it. This soon took place, as she became a universal favorite with the young ladies and the mistresses." [16] Within a year Jefferson was reporting that his Polly "begins to speak [French] easily enough, and to read as well as English. She will begin Spanish in a few days, and has lately begun the harpsichord and drawing."[17] The advantages of a European education, which he had hoped for her, were being realized.

Jefferson had, indeed, somewhat expected and more than halfway hoped to return to the United States in 1788, on the expiration of his first appointment as minister. In June, 1787, he had written Madison, "Having been a witness, heretofore, to the divisions of Congress on the subject of their foreign ministers, it would be a weakness in me to suppose none with respect to myself, or to count with any confidence of the renewal of my commission which expires on the 10th of March next... Whenever I leave this place, it will be necessary to begin my arrangements six months before my departure, and these once fairly begun and under way, and my mind set homewards, a change of purpose could hardly take place. If it should be the desire of Congress that I should continue longer, I could wish to know it at farthest, by the packet which will sail from New York in September. Because were I to put off longer the quitting my house, selling my furniture, etc., I should not have time left to wind up my affairs.... I have never fixed in my mind the epoch of my return, so far as shall depend on myself, but I never supposed it very distant. Probably I shall not risk a second vote on the subject. Such trifling things may draw on me the displeasure of one or two states, and thus submit me to the disgrace of a recall."[18]

Jefferson's fears in this regard proved ungrounded. He was, of course, reappointed at the end of his three-year term, but his heart had become fixed on going home. It was thus that he asked for a leave of absence in November, 1788. Shortly after this he wrote Mrs. Eppes of his hope and expectations. "In my last of July 12th," he says, "I told you that in my next I would enter into explanations about the time my daughters would have the happiness to see you. Their future welfare requires that this should be no longer postponed. It would have taken place a year sooner, but that I wished Polly to perfect herself in her French. I have asked leave of absence of Congress for five or six months of the next year, and if I obtain it in time, I shall endeavor to sail about the middle of April. As my time must be passed principally at Monticello, during the two months I destine for

Virginia, I shall hope that you will come and encamp there with us a while." [19]

When no word had arrived from Congress by May, 1788, Jefferson decided to appeal to Washington. After expressing his "felicitations not to you, but to my country," on Washington's election to the presidency and observing that he is sensible of the sacrifice Washington is making in accepting the post, he mentions his own problem. The government under which he had been appointed and to which he had applied for leave was no longer in existence. It had been superseded by the new federal government. Jefferson writes that he had expected his letter to Jay "would have been received in time to be decided on by the government then existing. I know now that it would arrive when there was no Congress and, consequently, that it must have awaited your arrival in New York. I hope you found the request not an unreasonable one. I am excessively anxious to receive permission without delay, that I may be able to get back before the winter sets in. . . . Besides there has never been a moment at which the presence of a minister here could so well be dispensed with, from certainty of no war this summer, and that the government will be so totally absorbed in domestic arrangements, as to attend to nothing exterior." [20]

Shortly before writing this letter an incident had occurred that made Jefferson more determined than ever to take his daughters home. One April morning he found in his mail a letter from Martha asking his permission to become a *religieuse*, as the French call a nun. Jefferson was too much of a philosopher and too well acquainted with human nature to be entirely taken aback. He had grown up with six sisters, and from them he had doubtless learned something of the emotional topsy-turvy that plagues the breast of the adolescent female. Far better to place his daughter where she would be assailed by the importunities of suitable young men than by religious qualms. He did not permit himself to show surprise or disturbance. According to the Jefferson family, he drove by the abbey, explained the situation to the Abbess, a thoroughly worldly and understanding woman, and took his daughter home with him to the lovely house at the Grille de Chaillot.

The leave of absence was finally granted in the middle of June, 1789, but word of it did not reach Jefferson until the end of August. As he wished to avoid the storms that often attend the equinox, he fixed his sailing for October. There was little packing to be done, no furniture and household goods, for he expected to return in the spring. The last weeks were spent in settling affairs and saying good-by to friends and to Paris. Even in the short time Jefferson had been there many important changes had taken place. In writing Humphreys he observed that "wonderful improvements are making here in various lines. In architecture, the wall of circumvallation round Paris, and the palaces by which we are to be let out and in, are nearly completed; four hospitals are to be built instead of the old Hôtel-Dieu; one of the old bridges has all its houses demolished, and a second nearly so; a new bridge is begun at the Place Louis XV; the Palais Royal is gutted, a considerable part of the centre of the garden being dug out, and a subterranean circus begun." [21] To Madame de Bréhan, the sister of the French Minister to Washington, he wrote after she had gone to America, "A new theatre is established since your departure, that of the Opera Buffons, where Italian operas are given, and good music"—indeed, Jefferson often frequented it. "Paris is every day enlarging and beautifying. I do not count among its beauties, however, the wall with which they have enclosed us. They have made some amends for this by making fine boulevards within and without the walls. These are in considerable forwardness and will afford beautiful rides around the city between fifteen and twenty miles in circuit." [22]

The question of a suitable ship for the return voyage naturally arose, and on September 1 Jefferson wrote William Ast, who was acting as American consul at Lorient, to inquire what French ships would be sailing from France about the first of October, bound for "either Chesapeake or Delaware." At the same time he wrote Trumbull for similar information in regard to a British vessel. On September 11 Trumbull replied that "the Clermont, Captain Colley, will sail so as to be at the Isle of Wight by the 11th of next month. Should you be disappointed at Havre, you have only to inform me as early as possible and I shall direct him to put into Cowes for you. He will give you his whole cabin . . . and furnish you stores for 100 guineas. Beds you of course furnish yourself. His port is Norfolk." [23]

On the twenty-fifth of September Jefferson "pd. servant's wages, 343 livres," and the following morning, after putting "into Petit's hands for travelling expenses 402 livres," for Petit was to accompany him to Havre, he "left Paris," as he notes in his account book.[24] The travelers followed the well- known road to Havre along the Seine, familiar to all of them. This time there was no sight-seeing. They spent the first night at Vernon, the second at Bolbec, almost within sight of Havre, which they reached the following morning. Here the party put up at L'Aigle d'Or, although Jefferson notes that "la Bienvenu chez Durand is the best hotel." In this barren port, Jefferson was detained by contrary winds until the eighth of October, when he left at "half before one o'clock in the morning on board the packet *Anna,* Captain Wright." This first stage of his journey took him only to Cowes, on the Isle of Wight, where he arrived on the ninth "at half after two in the morning," and lodged at the Fountain Inn. In the best eighteenth-century tradition of traveling, there was another delay of ten days, which, according to Martha, "were spent in visiting different parts of the island when the weather permitted, among others Carisbrook Castle, remarkable for the confinement of Charles the First, and also for a well of uncommon depth." [25]

A good deal of time was filled up by shopping, buying books, "shoes for Polly, half galoshes for Patsy," "trifles," and the all-important provisions for the trip. A "*chienne bergère* big with pup" was added to the party and doubtless consigned, as still today in the good English fashion, to the care of the butcher's boy.

On the third of October Trumbull informed Jefferson at Cowes that he had ordered the *Clermont* to stop there. The ship had sailed "on Tuesday the 27th, but the wind since has been such that he is still in the Downs and must remain there." [26]

On the seventeenth Jefferson hopefully wrote Short, "Our ship has arrived here this morning and if wind permits we shall sail tomorrow. We have now lost exactly three weeks by contrary winds, so that in spite of my efforts to be in readiness for a passage between the equinox and winter we shall surely be thrown into December and perhaps into January, for our captain tells us we cannot expect less than a nine weeks' passage. The ship is of 300 tons, on her 4th voyage, a good sailor, and we shall go the southern route, so that we may hope for good weather till we approach the coast of America.... Having nothing to communicate and pressed with preparations for departure," he concludes, "I shall only beg you to remember me to all my American friends at Passy, to those at Chaville, of the Hôtel de la Rochefoucauld, Mr. Mazzei, the abbés and their house." [27]

Finally, at noon on the twenty-second of October, Jefferson and his family embarked on the *Clermont,* and at daybreak "in company with upwards of thirty vessels which had collected there and been detained, as we were, by contrary winds," weighed anchor from Yarmouth. Jefferson was on deck, as we have remarked, to hand a last letter to the pilot and to cast a last, long look at the retreating shores of the Old World. His thoughts were turned toward France and in his mind were forming the words he was to pen many years later, "I cannot leave this great and good country, without expressing my sense of its preeminence of character among the nations of the earth. A more benevolent people I have never known, nor greater warmth and devotedness in their select friendships. Their kindness and accommodation to strangers is unparalleled, and the hospitality of Paris is beyond anything I had conceived to be practicable in a large city. Their eminence, too, in science, the communicative dispositions of their scientific men, the politeness of the general manners, the ease and vivacity of their conversation, give a charm to their society, to be found nowhere else." [28]

Never was a more noble tribute paid to a noble people.

Notes

The spelling and punctuation of all quotations have been modernized. Quotations from the French and German have been translated.

CHAPTER I

1 See Marie Kimball, *Thomas Jefferson's Cook Book*, p. 105. James is mentioned as the cook at Monticello in the manuscript cook book.

2 Martha Jefferson to Elizabeth Trist. Ms. copy, Edgehill Randolph Collection, Alderman Library, University of Virginia.

3 Paul Leicester Ford, *The Writings of Thomas Jefferson* (cited henceforth as Ford), Vol. IV, p. 5.

4 Jefferson account book, for 1784. Massachusetts Historical Society.

5 Sarah Nicholas Randolph, *The Domestic Life of Thomas Jefferson* (cited henceforth as *Domestic Life*), (1939), p. 47.

6 *Memoirs of John Quincy Adams*, Vol. I, p. 317. However, John Adams quotes Duane as saying Jefferson knew Spanish in 1775. *Works*, Vol. II, p. 430.

7 James T. Austin, *Life of Elbridge Gerry*, p. 453.

8 A. E. Lipscomb and A. E. Bergh, *The Writings of Thomas Jefferson* (cited henceforth as Lipscomb), Vol. XIX, pp. 14-15.

9 Ford, Vol. IV, p. 5.

10 Worthington Chauncy Ford, *Thomas Jefferson Correspondence, Printed from the Originals in the Collection of William K. Bixby* (cited henceforth as Bixby), p. 19.

11 Martha Jefferson to Elizabeth Trist.

12 *Ibid.* Martha's observations on her father's lack of ability to speak French are sometimes surprising, as Jefferson has usually been considered a good linguist. Like many since, he was doubtless able to read the language but not speak it. On arrival he said: "I understand the French so imperfectly as to be uncertain whether those with whom I speak and myself mean the same thing." Albert H. Smyth, *The Writing of Benjamin Franklin* (cited henceforth as Smyth), Vol. I, p. 216. After he had been

in France two years, he wrote Crèvecoeur: "Being unable to write in French so as to be sure of conveying my true meaning, or perhaps any meaning at all, I will beg of you to interpret what I have now the honor to write." Ford, Vol. IV, p. 253.

13 Ford, Vol. IV, p. 5.

14 Jefferson was traveling in the phaeton he had brought from America.

15 Martha Jefferson to Elizabeth Trist.

16 John Adams, *Works* (cited henceforth as Adams, *Works*), Vol. III, p. 298.

17 *The Letters of Mrs. Adams*, p. 193.

18 *Ibid.*

19 Martha Jefferson to Mrs. Trist.

20 For the location of other buildings on the street see de Gèze, *Etat ou tableau de la ville de Paris* (1760), p. 68, also Jaillot, *Plan de la ville et des faubourgs de Paris* (1727), and Lefeuve, *Histoire de Paris, rue par rue, maison par maison* (1875), *tome* I, p. 494.

21 Pocket account book, 1784, August 7 and 20.

22 In his account book for this year Jefferson gives the name of his landlord. *The Atlas de la Censive de l'archevêché dans Paris, par* A. Brette, *tome* I, *planche* VII, likewise mentions M. Guereau as the owner of the house at that number.

23 *Letters of Mrs. Adams*, p. 191.

24 *Ibid.*, p. 207.

25 Frank Landon Humphreys, *Life and Times of David Humphreys* (cited henceforth as Humphreys), Vol. I, p. 317.

26 *Letters of Mrs. Adams*, p. 238.

27 *Ibid.*, p. 207.

28 *Ibid.*, p. 192.

29 *Ibid.*, p. 207.

30 Ford, Vol. IV, pp. 11-12.

31 Jefferson Papers, Library of Congress.

32 Ford, Vol. IV, p. 54.

33 Tronchin à Puérari, Archives d'état de Genève. Reference through courtesy of Howard C. Rice.

34 Martha Jefferson to Elizabeth Trist.

35 Jefferson Papers, Library of Congress.

36 Gijsbert Karel van Hogendorp, *Brieven en Gedenkschiften*, Eerste Deel, p. 365.

37 *Letters of Mrs. Adams*, p. 216.

38 Ford, Vol. IV, pp. 41-42.

39 *Ibid.*, p. 46.

40 *Domestic Life* (1939), p. 54.

41 Lipscomb, Vol. XIX, pp. 11-12.
42 *Ibid.*, Vol. V, pp. 152-53.
43 *Domestic Life* (1939), p. 53.
44 Lipscomb, Vol. V, p. 154.

CHAPTER II

1 Smyth, Vol. VII, p. 223.
2 Adams, *Works*, Vol. III, p. 123.
3 Edmund C. Burnett, *Letters of Members of the Continental Congress* (cited henceforth as *Letters Members Continental Congress*), Vol. VII, p. 530.
4 *Ibid.*, p. 529.
5 *Ibid.*, p. 527.
6 Ford, Vol. IV, p. 25.
7 Lipscomb, Vol. I, p. 96.
8 *Ibid.*, Vol. V, p. 169.
9 *Ibid.*, Vol. I, p. 93.
10 *Ibid.*, Vol. V, p. 108.
11 Ford, Vol. IV, p. 104.
12 *Ibid.*, pp. 54-58.
13 *The Diplomatic Correspondence of the United States*, from September 10, 1783, to March 4, 1789 (cited henceforth as *Diplomatic Correspondence*), Vol. I, p. 503.
14 *Ibid.*, p. 503-4.
15 Humphreys, Vol. I, p. 328.
16 Lipscomb, Vol. I, p. 42.
17 *Diplomatic Correspondence*, Vol. I, p. 518.
18 Ford, Vol. IV, p. 7.
19 Oscar Browning, *Despatches from Paris*, 1784-1790.
20 *Diplomatic Correspondence*, Vol. I, pp. 542-43.
21 Ford, Vol. IV, p. 21.
22 Lipscomb, Vol. I, p. 93.
23 Humphreys, Vol. I, p. 322.
24 Ford, Vol. IV, p. 31. A treaty had already been concluded with Sweden in April, 1783, and with the Netherlands, by John Adams, in 1782.
25 *Diplomatic Correspondence*, Vol. I, p. 513.
26 Ford, Vol. IV, p. 7.
27 *Diplomatic Correspondence*, Vol. I, p. 575.
28 Adams, *Works*, Vol. VIII, p. 189.
29 *Ibid.*, Vol. IX, p. 274.
30 *Ibid.*, Vol. VIII, p. 183.

31 *Ibid.*, pp. 195-96. This letter, along with a translation of the projected treaty, appears in *Diplomatic Correspondence*, Vol. I, pp. 442-53.
32 *Diplomatic Correspondence*, Vol. I, p. 505.
33 *Ibid.*, pp. 518-19.
34 *Ibid.*, p. 531.
35 *Ibid.*, pp. 532-33.
36 Marie Joseph Paul de Lafayette, *Memoirs, Correspondence and Manuscripts*, Vol. II, p. 121.
37 *Diplomatic Correspondence*, Vol. I, pp. 553-60.
38 *Ibid.*, p. 546.
39 Adams, *Works*, Vol. VIII, p. 225.
40 Franklin signed the treaty before leaving France in July. Jefferson signed it July 28. His secretary, William Short, carried it to London for Adams' signature August 5. He then proceeded to the Hague, where it was signed by Thulemeier, before Short and C. W. F. Dumas, the American agent, on September 10.
41 Adams, *Works*, Vol. VIII, p. 201.
42 *Report to the Mediterranean Trade*, Lipscomb, Vol. III, p. 94.
43 Ford, Vol. III, p. 493.
44 Smyth, Vol. X, p. 352.
45 *Ibid.*, Vol. VII, p. 328.
46 Ford, Vol. III, p. 493.
47 *Diplomatic Correspondence*, Vol. I, p. 537.
48 Humphreys, Vol. I, p. 333.
49 Ford, Vol. IV, p. 25.
50 Humphreys, Vol. I, p. 340.
51 *Diplomatic Correspondence*, Vol. I, pp. 632, 635-37. In the Jefferson Papers, Library of Congress, is an undated memorandum in Jefferson's hand of the sums paid by France, England, Denmark, Sweden, Portugal, and Venice to the Barbary powers during the years 1773-83.
52 Ford, Vol. IV, pp. 10-11.
53 *Diplomatic Correspondence*, Vol. I, p. 638.
54 Adams, *Works*, Vol. VIII, pp. 400-1.
55 Lipscomb, Vol. V, pp. 365-66.
56 *Ibid.*, Vol. XVII, pp. 145ff. Also Vol. I, pp. 97ff.
57 *Ibid.*, Vol. XVII, p. 146.
58 *Ibid.*, Vol. I, p. 100.
59 Gilbert Chinard, *The Letters of Lafayette and Jefferson*, p. 101.
60 Lipscomb, Vol. I, pp. 100-1.
61 See *Diplomatic Correspondence*, Vol. I, p. 655.
62 *Ibid.*, p. 581.
63 *Ibid.*, p. 751.

64 *Ibid.*, Vol. II, p. 28.
65 *Ibid.*, Vol. I, p. 798.
66 Lipscomb, Vol. V, p. 20. See also letter to Adams, *Ibid.*, pp. 31-33.
67 *Letters Members Continental Congress*, Vol. VIII, pp. 580-82.

CHAPTER III

1 *Letters Members Continental Congress*, Vol. VIII, p. 25.
2 *Idem.*
3 *Ibid.*, p. 26.
4 *Diplomatic Correspondence*, Vol. I, p. 612. The original is in the Jefferson Papers, Coolidge Collection, Massachusetts Historical Society.
5 *Ibid.*, pp. 613-14.
6 Adams, *Works*, Vol. VIII, p. 38.
7 *Diplomatic Correspondence*, Vol. I, p. 164.
8 Humphreys, Vol. I, p. 317.
9 *Mémoires du Comte de Cheverny*, Vol. I, pp. 82-84.
10 Humphreys, Vol. I, p. 328.
11 Jefferson Papers, Library of Congress.
12 Lipscomb, Vol. I, p. 96.
13 Jefferson Papers, Library of Congress.
14 The documents mentioned are in the Jefferson Papers, Library of Congress.
15 Lipscomb, Vol. I, p. 96.
16 Ford, Vol. IV, p. 50.
17 Lipscomb, Vol. VI, p. 70.
18 Pocket account book.
19 Lipscomb, Vol. VI, p. 70.
20 *Ibid.*, pp. 71-72.
21 *Ibid.*, pp. 342-43.
22 *Diplomatic Correspondence*, Vol. I, p. 693.
23 *Ibid.*, p. 686.
24 *Ibid.*, p. 693.
25 *Ibid.*, p. 695.
26 *Idem.*
27 *Ibid.*, pp. 696-97.
28 *Ibid.*, pp. 698-703.
29 *Ibid.*, pp. 703-4.
30 Morris' contract is printed in *Diplomatic Correspondence*, Vol. I, pp. 760-63.
31 Lipscomb, Vol. V, p. 254.
32 *Ibid.*, p. 354.

33 *Diplomatic Correspondence*, Vol. I, p. 311.
34 Lipscomb, Vol. V, p. 530. See also, *Diplomatic Correspondence*, pp. 757-65.
35 *Diplomatic Correspondence*, Vol. I, p. 282.
36 *Ibid.*, p. 824.
37 *Ibid.*, p. 758.
38 *Idem.*
39 *Ibid.*, p. 759.
40 *Ibid.*, p. 764.
41 Gouverneur Morris wrote Robert Morris, July 21, 1789, "I have never yet mentioned to you that Mr. Jefferson, shortly after my arrival, in speaking of the affair of Berni, told me that he had constantly insisted on a compliance with your treaty, though from a letter written to him and published in America the reverse would appear, I doubt not the truth of this assertion." *A Diary of the French Revolution*, Vol. I, p. 159, note. See also Jefferson to Monroe, Lipscomb, Vol. VI, p. 15.
42 *Diplomatic Correspondence*, Vol. I, pp. 822-23.
43 Lipscomb, Vol. VI, pp. 69-70.
44 *Ibid.*, Vol. V, pp. 401-2.
45 *Ibid.*, pp. 371-76. See also *Diplomatic Correspondence*, Vol. I, pp. 823-26.
46 *Diplomatic Correspondence*, Vol. I, pp. 821-22.
47 *Ibid.*, pp. 827-29.
48 *Ibid.*, p. 822.
49 *Idem.*
50 Lipscomb, Vol. I, p. 96.
51 *Ibid.*, Vol. VII, p. 94.
52 *Ibid.*, Vol. VI, pp. 180-87.
53 *Ibid.*, pp. 160-65.
54 *Ibid.*, p. 101.
55 *Ibid.*, Vol. XVII, pp. 377-78.
56 *Ibid.*, Vol. VII, p. 60.
57 *Diplomatic Correspondence*, Vol. I, p. 766.
58 *Ibid.*, p. 767.
59 *Ibid.*, Vol. II, p. 20.
60 *Ibid.*, pp. 22, 23.
61 *Ibid.*, Vol. II, p. 193.
62 Lipscomb, Vol. VII, pp. 59-60.
63 *Ibid.*, pp. 142-43.
64 *Diplomatic Correspondence*, Vol. II, pp. 224-31.
65 Lipscomb, Vol. XVII, pp. 378-79.
66 *Diplomatic Correspondence*, Vol. II, p. 259.

67 *Ibid.*, p. 260.
68 Jefferson's letters to Adams at this period, particularly those of July 1, 1787 (*Diplomatic Correspondence*, Vol. II, pp. 63-64), and of December 5, 1788 (*Ibid.*, pp. 259-60), give a detailed account of his efforts.
69 Gouverneur Morris, *A Diary of the French Revolution*, Vol. I, p. 5.
70 *Idem.*
71 *Ibid.*, p. 476.
72 *Ibid.*, p. 159, note.

CHAPTER IV

1 W. W. Hening, *Statutes at Large*, Vol. XI, p. 552.
2 Charles Henry Hart and Edward Biddle, *Jean Antoine Houdon* (cited henceforth as Hart and Biddle). Not in the printed *Official Letters of Governors of Virginia.*
3 Information on Peale letters kindly furnished by Charles Coleman Sellars.
4 *Calendar of Virginia State Papers*, Vol. IV, p. 24.
5 See Marie Kimball, *Jefferson: War and Peace*, p. 359.
6 Hart and Biddle, pp. 184-85. This letter is likewise not in the published *Official Letters of the Governors of Virginia*, Vol. III.
7 Ford, Vol. IV, pp. 26-28.
8 Jared Sparks, *Correspondence of the American Revolution*, Vol. IV, p. 83.
9 J. C. Ballagh, *The Letters of Richard Henry Lee*, Vol. II, p. 405.
10 Hart and Biddle, p. 197.
11 Lipscomb, Vol. V, p. 33.
12 *Ibid.*, p. 142.
13 *Ibid.*, p. 214.
14 Ford, Vol. IV, pp. 72-75.
15 *Diplomatic Correspondence*, Vol. I, pp. 777-79.
16 *Idem.*
17 Hart and Biddle, p. 197.
18 J. C. Fitzpatrick, *The Diaries of George Washington*, Vol. II, p. 419.
19 *Ibid.*, p. 426.
20 *Ibid.*, p. 420.
21 Charles Seymour, "Houdon's Washington at Mount Vernon Re-examined," *Gazette des Beaux Arts*, Series 6, Vol. XXXV (March, 1948), pp. 137-58.
22 Hart and Biddle, pp. 204-5.
23 *Ibid.*, p. 205.

24 Lipscomb, Vol. XIX, p. 23.
25 Lafayette, *Memoirs,* Vol. II, p. 125.
26 Lipscomb, Vol. V, p. 314.
27 *Ibid.,* Vol. XIX, p. 23.
28 Hart and Biddle, pp. 208-9.
29 Lipscomb, Vol. VI, pp. 274-75.
30 Hart and Biddle, pp. 209-10.
31 W. W. Hening, Vol. XI, p. 552.
32 Lipscomb, Vol. V, pp. 280-81.
33 *Idem.*
34 W. W. Hening, Vol. X, p. 569.
35 John C. Fitzpatrick, *Writings of Washington,* Vol. XXVII, p. 319.
36 Hart and Biddle, pp. 228-29.
37 W. W. Hening, Vol. XI, p. 553.
38 Hart and Biddle, p. 231.
39 Lafayette, *Memoirs,* Vol. II, p. 148.
40 *Calendar of Virginia State Papers,* Vol. IV, p. 49.
41 Hart and Biddle, p. 232.
42 *Idem.*
43 Bachaumont, *Mémoires Secrètes,* August 25, 1787, Vol. XXXVI, p. 396.
44 Lipscomb, Vol. V, p. 84.
45 Hart and Biddle, p. 233.
46 Lipscomb, Vol. V, pp. 428-29.
47 *Idem.*
48 *Idem.* See also M. Thiéry, *Guide des amateurs et des étrangers voyageurs,* Vol. II, pp. 685-86.
49 Owing to a mistake in reading the ancient script, the name Jefferson has heretofore wrongly been printed *Sesseron.*
50 Friedrich Melchior von Grimm, *Correspondence Litteraire,* Vol. XV, p. 572.
51 Humphreys, Vol. I, p. 324.
52 *Diplomatic Correspondence,* Vol. II, p. 40.
53 Lipscomb, Vol. V, pp. 228-29.
54 Jefferson Papers, Library of Congress.
55 Lipscomb, Vol. VIII, p. 28. For Gateau see Lipscomb, Vol. VII, p. 10.
56 *Diplomatic Correspondence,* Vol. II, pp. 40, 41.
57 Lipscomb, Vol. XIX, p. 55.
58 Ford, Vol. II, pp. 106-7.
59 W. W. Hening, Vol. X, pp. 85-86.
60 *Ibid.,* Vol. XI, p. 496.
61 Lipscomb, Vol. V, p. 136.

62 For a full discussion of these early designs see Fiske Kimball, "Jefferson and the Public Buildings of Virginia, I. Williamsburg 1770-1776," *The Huntington Library Quarterly*, Vol. XII, No. 2, pp. 115-20.

63 For an authoritative and comprehensive discussion of these drawings and the next one to be mentioned, see Fiske Kimball, "Jefferson and the Public Buildings of Virginia, II. Richmond, 1779-1780." *The Huntington Library Quarterly*, Vol. XII, No. 3, pp. 303-10.

64 Lipscomb, Vol. I, p. 68.

65 Fiske Kimball, *The First Monument of the Classical Revival in America*, p. 11.

66 *Ibid.*, pp. 11-12. Jefferson writes in his autobiography that while in France he heard of a society that had successfully introduced solitary confinement, and saw the drawings of a prison at Lyons in France formed on this idea. In June, 1786, he sent the governor of Virginia "the Lyons plan, accompanying it with a drawing on a smaller scale better adapting it to our use." (Lipscomb, Vol. I, pp. 257-58.) The design for such a prison was made by Pierre Gabriel Bugnet or Bugniet, and appeared in the *Mercure de France*. Clérisseau worked on the design for Virginia, as his bill contains the item "less plans de prisons coupe et elevation 2 louis." This plan appears to have been lost. The name of the architect and the reference to the *Mercure de France* were kindly supplied by Mlle. Leonie Villard, through Howard C. Rice.

67 *Ibid.*, p. 12.

68 *Idem.*

69 Manuscript in Henry E. Huntington Library.

70 Fiske Kimball, *The First Monument of the Classical Revival in America*, p. 15.

71 Ford, Vol. IV, p. 133.

72 Fiske Kimball, *The First Monument of the Classical Revival in America*, p. 13.

73 *Ibid.*, p. 14.

74 *Ibid.*, p. 13.

75 Lipscomb, Vol. XVII, p. 354.

76 Duc de la Rochefoucauld-Liancourt, *Voyage dans les Etats Unis d'Amérique*, Vol. IV, p. 299.

CHAPTER V

1 Nelson to William Short, March 12, 1790. Short Papers, Library of Congress, Vol. V.

2 Lafayette, *Memoirs*, Vol. II, p. 192.

3 *Ibid.*, p. 133.

4 Jefferson Papers, Library of Congress.
5 Lipscomb, Vol. I, p. 103.
6 Lafayette, *Memoirs*, Vol. I, pp. 94-95.
7 Lipscomb, Vol. I, p. 103.
8 Lafayette, *Memoirs*, Vol. I, pp. 129-30.
9 George W. Corner, *Autobiography of Benjamin Rush*.
10 Adams, *Works*, Vol. I, p. 660.
11 Ford, Vol. V, p. 293.
12 *Private Correspondence of Daniel Webster*, Vol. I, p. 373.
13 Jefferson Papers, Library of Congress.
14 Smyth, Vol. VII, p. 16.
15 *Ibid.*, p. 10.
16 *Ibid.*, Vol. IX, p. 71.
17 *Ibid.*, pp. 131-32.
18 Adams, *Works*, Vol. III, pp. 137-38.
19 *Ibid.*, p. 352.
20 *Ibid.*, Vol. IX, p. 623.
21 *Ibid.*, p. 624.
22 See Marie Kimball, "William Short, Thomas Jefferson's Only 'Son'," *North American Review*, Vol. CCXXIII, No. 3 (November, 1926), pp. 471-86.
23 Howard R. Marraro, *Memoirs of the Life of Philip Mazzei*, p. 296.
24 For a discussion of the *Notes on Virginia*, see Marie Kimball, *Jefferson: War and Peace*, pp. 259-305.
25 Lipscomb, Vol. XIX, pp. 18-19. The writer was in correspondence with the Duc de la Rochefoucauld some years ago, and has talked to the present Duke and Duchess. Their papers of this period were destroyed in the Revolution.
26 *Ibid.*, Vol. VIII, pp. 18-19.
27 The name is variously spelled d'Anville and d'Enville, even by the Duchess herself.
28 Smyth, Vol. X, p. 467.
29 *Biographie Universelle*, Vol. II, pp. 295-96.
30 Adams, *Works*, Vol. IX, p. 591.
31 *Ibid.*, Vol. III, p. 122.
32 Mrs. Adams was mistaken in the age of the Duchess. It has been impossible to ascertain the exact date of her birth, but in the article just referred to, "William Short, Jefferson's Only 'Son'," p. 482, this writer states that in 1793 the Duchesse d'Anville was nearly seventy-eight years old. Information as to the relationships and ages of the members of his family at that time was supplied to the writer by the Duc de la Rochefoucauld in 1926.

33 *Letters of Mrs. Adams,* pp. 250-51.
34 Lipscomb, Vol. VIII, pp. 17-18.
35 Short Papers, in private possession.
36 Jefferson Papers, Library of Congress.
37 Adams, *Works,* Vol. III, p. 137.
38 Gouverneur Morris, *A Diary of the French Revolution,* Vol. I, pp. 220-21.
39 Ford, Vol. V, p. 379.
40 Lafayette, *Memoirs,* Vol. I, p. 6.
41 Adams, *Works,* Vol. III, p. 149.
42 *Official Letters of the Governors of Virginia,* Vol. II, p. 383.
43 Lipscomb, Vol. I, p. 96.
44 Adams, *Works,* Vol. III, p. 148.
45 *Ibid.,* p. 149.
46 *Letters of Mrs. Adams,* p. 215.
47 *Ibid.,* p. 236.
48 *Ibid.,* p. 215.
49 *Biographie Universelle,* Vol. XXX, pp. 118-24.
50 Franklin Papers, University of Pennsylvania.
51 Smyth, Vol. X, p. 426.
52 *Letters of Mrs. Adams,* pp. 241-42.
53 La Duchesse d'Abrantès, *Histoire des salons de Paris,* Vol. I, pp. 361-406.
54 *Idem.*
55 *Mémoires de l'Abbé Morellet,* Vol. I, p. 286.
56 The translation of the *Notes on Virginia* and Morellet's part, has been discussed in Marie Kimball, *Jefferson: War and Peace,* pp. 297-99.
57 *Mémoires de l'Abbé Morellet,* Vol. II, p. 437.
58 Smyth, Vol. IX, p. 546.
59 *Letters of Mrs. Adams,* p. 90.
60 Adams, *Works,* Vol. III, p. 135.
61 Ford, Vol. IV, p. 68.
62 Lipscomb, Vol. VII, pp. 73-79.
63 *Memoirs of John Quincy Adams,* Vol. I, p. 15.
64 Lipscomb, Vol. XIX, p. 34.
65 Jefferson Papers, Library of Congress.
66 H. A. Marraro, *Memoirs of the Life of Philip Mazzei,* pp. 291-93.
67 Gouverneur Morris, *A Diary of the French Revolution,* Vol. I, p. 335.
68 Ford, Vol. IV, p. 63.
69 *Private Correspondence of Daniel Webster,* Vol. I, pp. 371-73.
70 See Hippolyte Buffenoir, *La comtesse d'Houdetot, une amie de Jean Jacques Rousseau,* pp. 75ff, pp. 327-30.

71 Pocket account book, October 23, 1785.
72 Gilbert Chinard, *Les amitiés américaines de Madame d'Houdetot*, p. 45.
73 Lipscomb, Vol. VIII, p. 15.
74 Max von Boehn, *Rokoko Frankreich im 18. Jahrhundert*, p. 396.
75 *Private Correspondence of Daniel Webster*, Vol. I, p. 373.
76 The *salon* of Madame Necker is described in the *Histoire des salons de Paris*, by the Duchesse d'Abrantès, Vol. I, pp. 83-213.
77 Lipscomb, Vol. XIX, p. 243.
78 *Ibid.*, Vol. XIV, p. 468.
79 Bixby, p. 7.
80 Gouverneur Morris, *A Diary of the French Revolution*, Vol. I, p. 6.
81 *Ibid.*, p. 161.
82 Gilbert Chinard, *Trois amitiés françaises de Jefferson*, pp. 74-75.

CHAPTER VI

1 Fiske Kimball, *Thomas Jefferson, Architect*, p. 149, fig. 118a.
2 Humphreys, Vol. I, p. 317.
3 Jefferson Papers, Library of Congress.
4 M. Thiéry, *Guide des amateurs et des étrangers voyageurs*, Vol. I, p. 42.
5 *Idem.*
6 *Ibid.*, p. 53.
7 Fiske Kimball, *Thomas Jefferson, Architect*, p. 148, fig. 118.
8 Howard C. Rice, *L'Hôtel de Langeac*, plates 4-10.
9 Henry E. Huntington Library.
10 Jefferson Papers, Library of Congress. See also Marie Kimball, "Thomas Jefferson's French Furniture," *Antiques*, Vol. XV, No. 2, pp. 123-28.
11 Ford, Vol. IV, pp. 99-100.
12 Marie Kimball, "Thomas Jefferson's French Furniture," *Antiques*, Vol. XV, No. 2, pp. 123-28.
13 Pocket account book, March 8, 1785.
14 Roger de Felice, *Les meubles français sous Louis XVI et sous l'Empire*, pp. 67-74.
15 Marie Kimball, *Jefferson: The Road to Glory*, p. 154. Also, Fiske Kimball, "Jefferson and the Arts," *Proceedings of the American Philosophical Society*, Vol. LXXXVII, No. 3, pp. 238-45.
16 A *Catalogue Raisonée* of the Cosway sale is in the Doucet Library in Paris.
17 F. Lugt, *Répertoire des catalogues des ventes publiques*, pp. 66-67.

18 The writer is indebted to Monsieur Michel Benisovitch of Paris for information about the contemporary catalogues.
19 Marie Kimball, *Jefferson: War and Peace,* pp. 356-67. See also Fiske Kimball, "Joseph Wright and his Portraits of Washington," *Antiques,* Vol. XV, pp. 377-82.
20 Jefferson's manuscript catalogue.
21 William Kirby, *Notes on American Artists,* New York Historical Society, 1922.
22 Jefferson Papers, Library of Congress.
23 *Ibid.*
24 Ford, Vol. V, p. 2.
25 Fiske Kimball, "The Life Portraits of Jefferson," *Proceedings of the American Philosophical Society,* Vol. LXXXVIII, p. 501.
26 Ford, Vol. IV, p. 299.
27 John Trumbull, *Autobiography* (cited henceforth as Trumbull), p. 93.
28 *Ibid.,* p. 95.
29 Trumbull to Jefferson, December 26, 1816, Jefferson Papers, Library of Congress.
30 Trumbull, p. 147.
31 *Ibid.,* pp. 150-51.
32 Jefferson's head from this painting forms the frontispiece of Marie Kimball's *Jefferson: The Road to Glory.*
33 See Fiske Kimball, "The Life Portraits of Jefferson," *Proceedings of the American Philosophical Society,* Vol. LXXXVIII, p. 503.
34 Short Papers, Library of Congress, No. 1514, August 15, 1790.
35 *Ibid.,* November 22, 1790.
36 Lipscomb, Vol. XIV, p. 132.
37 Jefferson Papers, Library of Congress.
38 Lipscomb, Vol. XIV, p. 178.
39 Jefferson Papers, Library of Congress.
40 The list of paintings belongs to a descendant of Jefferson, who has kindly given the writer permission to print it.

A Washington half length of full size or larger, an original taken by Wright (son of Mrs. Wright, famous for her works in wax). When General Washington attended the meeting of the Cincinnati in Philadelphia, May, 1784, when passing through that city on my way from Annapolis to Boston to embark for Europe, I could only allow Wright time to finish the head and face and sketch the outlines of the body. These and the drapery were afterwards finished at Paris by Trumbull.

James Madison by Pine. Taken about the year 1790.

Mons. de Lafayette, taken at Paris in 1789.

An Ecce Homo, a ¾ length of full size on canvas. The subject is taken from John 19 (?) or 10. Jesus is represented as clothed in a purple robe, a wreath of thorns on his head, his wrists bound together with a cord and a reed in his hand. This last circumstance is taken from Matt. 27.29. Drops of beads are trickling from the wounds made by the thorns and his countenance, a little thrown up, expresses the anguish of his trial. Given to Petit

A St. Joseph, the husband of Mary, the mother of Jesus, a ¾ length of full size on canvas. A book is lying open by him, his hands interlocked with energy and his head and eyes cast up to heaven and his mouth open as in the act of fervent prayer.

A bust of full size on canvas (Supposed of St. Joseph).

A bust of a nun of full size on canvas.

Another bust, companion to the former.

A head of St. Peter weeping, of full size on canvas. The cock in the background shows it was in the moment of Matt. 26.75 "and Peter remembered the words of Jesus which said unto him 'before the cock crow, thou shalt deny me thrice' and he went out and wept bitterly."

[This is crossed out beginning with "the cock in the background, etc.]

A head of an apostle in meditation, of full size on canvas.

A head with finger on the lips, indicating silence. Of full size on canvas.

A bust of a St. Jerome in meditation, his head reclined on his right hand and a book in his left. Of full size on canvas.

A Virgin Mary weeping on the death of Jesus. Her hands are clutched together and her eyes uplifted as in ejaculation to Heaven. She is clothed with a blue drapery and her head covered with a veil. A half length of full size on canvas. See the catalogue De Billy No. 21.

[This next item is crossed out.]

A naked figure of a man, at whole length, 2 ft. 3 inches high, his head bound round with a fillet, a leaf in his left hand, while in his right he grasps a staff. The muscles are strong and contracted and the whole figure braced. (etc.)

An academical figure of a man naked and showing all the muscles in front with precision and energy, etc.

Two busts, larger than the life, one of them holding a sword in his hand, the point downwards, the other a musical instrument. Canvas.

An Ecce Homo, a bust of about ⅔ the natural scale on canvas. He is clothed in a simple robe, with a crown of thorns on his head and a cord round his neck.

A head of an old man, of full size on canvas. He had spectacles on his nose as if reading.

A St. John, a whole figure of about 16 inches on wood. He is sitting, the garment of camel's hair loosely round his waist, has a cross in his right hand, while his left is pressing to him the lamb, his usual attribute, which is reared with its forefeet on his lap.

A Magdalen composed and placid, her right hand pointing to Heaven, etc. [This crossed out.]

Jesus disputing with the doctors, Luke 3.46, his right hand pointing to Heaven, the left pressing his breast, the drapery blue and purple, the hair flowing loose, a half length figure of full size seen in profile. Canvas.

A Magdalen in a state of pity and faith, smiling and pointing to Heaven with her right hand, while the left, shaded and almost hid by that, is scarcely seen, etc. [This item crossed out.] On canvas.

An Infant Jesus at prayer. He is kneeling, his hands pressed together, his look amiss, a glory round his head, his robes white and blue. Near him are the instruments of his fatal execution. A whole length of about 7 inches on copper. [This item crossed out. Written opposite "Given to Petit."]

The flight of Aeneas on copper.

A landscape on canvas.

An Adoration of the Kings and Magi. A group of 17 figures. Those in the foreground are about 9 inches. They are whole length in wood. Matt. 2.11.

The Sacrifice of Isaac. He is placed on the pile on his knees, his wrists bound. Abraham, with his left hand grasping the back of his neck, a naked sword in his right uplifted and ready to sever the head.... An angel is hovering about him.... The figures are full length, that of Abraham on a scale of not quite half the natural size. On canvas. Gen. XXII.

Democrites, called the laughing and crying philosopher, and Heraclites, the former smiling, the latter railing the father of mankind. The figures are ¾ length, larger than life, on canvas. They are of the collection of St. Severin, catalogue 215.

Daphne transformed into a laurel. Apollo is seizing her round the waist to bear her off, but her father, the river god Peneus, in that instant transforms her into a laurel. On the left are two female figures struck with dismay, and above a cupid flying off.... The figures are whole length, that of Daphne 12 inches on canvas. Original. Taken from Ovid's Metamorphoses. (Latin quotations written opposite.)

A Descent from the Cross, a group of five figures. The corpse of Jesus is reclined on the background, the head and shoulders supported in the lap of his mother, who with four others are weeping over him. The figures are full length, the principals are 13 inches on wood.

A St. John, a whole figure of 22 inches. The garment of camel's hair is round his waist, a cross in his left hand, etc. On canvas.

A group of figures, half-length of full size, on canvas. [Crossed off.]

Diogenes with a lantern in midday, looking for a man.... Group of 6 figures, half-lengths of full size on canvas.

A Flagellation of Christ, a group of 10 figures, the principal of which is 21 inches. He is bound to a post, two soldiers whipping him. On wood. Matt. 27.26.

The Translation of Enoch. He is just risen from the ground, borne by 3 angels, one of which is pointing his way to Heaven. The principal figure is 22 inches. On canvas. Gen. V, 24.

Opposite this is written "St. Paul carried up into the third Heaven." Poussin. The original is in the collection of the King of France. The principal figure is 22 inches on canvas.

Jephtha leading his daughter Leila to be sacrificed. On one side is the altar and the High Priest with the implements of sacrifice, etc. There are 12 figures, the principal of which is 16½ inches. Canvas.

Herodiade bearing the head of St. John on a platter, a ¾ length of full size on canvas by Simon Vouët, purchased from St. Severin's Collection, catalogue 248.

A Magdalen penitent, sitting, her hair dishevelled, her eyes looking up to Heaven, a book in her right hand and the left resting on a skull, a ¾ length of full size on canvas by Joseph de Ribera, called Espagnolet, purchased from St. Severin Collection, catalogue No. 59.

The Prodigal Son. He is in rags kneeling at the feet of his father who extends his hands to raise him. The mother and sister appear. The figures are full size on canvas, purchased from St. Severin Collection, catalogue No. 306.

A Crucifixion. The instant seized is that of the expiration....

A Presentation, three figures with the Virgin, an Infant Jesus and the prophetess Anna. ¾ length of four inches on copper.

St. Peter weeping for his offence. His hands are pressed together.... Near him is the cock. A half length of full size on canvas by Guido, purchased from St. Severin Collection, catalogue No. 36.

The Cyclops forging thunder bolts, a group of 9 figures of about 8 inches on wood.

Christ bearing his cross. A half length on wood. Scale about 3/5 of the life.

A group of 7 figures. Spanish of full length and about half the natural height.

Jesus driving the money changers out of the Temple. 7 figures of full length and about half the natural module.

A group of 9 figures of about 1/3 the natural height, the subject unknown. It is believed to be a trial before a bishop for a rape by a young man on a young woman who is present.

Susanna and the Elders. Three figures of about an eighth of the natural module. On canvas, from Coypel.

Jesus on the praetorium stripped of the purple, as yet naked and with the crown of thorns on his head. He is sitting. A whole length of about 4 feet....

A Jesus on the Cross, but not yet expired.

A descent. The Christ is of about ten inches. Behind him is the Virgin weeping. On each side angels. On copper.

The baptism of Jesus by John. The figures are whole length of ten inches on wood.

A Transfiguration.... Whole length figures of 6 inches on canvas.

Danaë visited by Jupiter. She is reclined, naked, the gold showering about her and a cupid at her feet looking with affright to the cloud from whence it issues. A whole length of full size on canvas.

The Roman daughter suckling her father.

David with the head of Goliath. A whole length of 2 feet, 6 inches on canvas.

Aeneas bearing off Anchises on his shoulders. Whole length of 3 feet, 6 inches on canvas.

The priest of Jupiter at Lystra going to sacrifice to Paul and Barnabas from Le Sueur.

The testament of (Damias).

Game, vegetables, etc.

Dr. Franklin, an original, drawn for the Abbé Very, by Greuze.

In January, 1950, the University of Virginia acquired from one of Jefferson's descendants a list showing the disposition of his collection of paintings and sculpture at Monticello. It is written on paper bearing the date 1801. This document will be discussed by the writer in a forthcoming article in *Antiques*.

41 Jacques Herrisay, *Le Mont Valérien*.

42 Kindly communicated by Mr. Howard C. Rice.

43 *Letters of Mrs. Adams*, pp. 249-50.

44 *Diplomatic Correspondence*, Vol. II, p. 162.

45 *Letters of Mrs. Adams*, p. 222.
46 Pocket account book, December 16, 1785.
47 Marie Kimball, *Thomas Jefferson's Cook Book*, pp. 27-38.
48 *Diplomatic Correspondence*, Vol. I, p. 331.
49 *Ibid.*, Vol. II, p. 160.
50 In the Jefferson Papers, Library of Congress, Vol. XII, Nos. 2042-67, is a memorandum of 25 pages entitled "My Account with the United States, Chronologically Stated." In this Jefferson lists in detail his expenses as minister from August, 1784, to September, 1789—his house rent, the salary of his secretary, his traveling expenses on business for the United States, stationery, postage, and couriers, court fees, translators, and charity to various stranded American sailors. It is the basis of his letters to Jay and Madison.
51 *Diplomatic Correspondence*, Vol. II, pp. 160-63.
52 Ford, Vol. V, p. 15.
53 *Diplomatic Correspondence*, Vol. I, pp. 166-67.
54 *Letters Members Continental Congress*, Vol. II, pp. 799-800.
55 *Ibid.*, p. 806.
56 Ford, Vol. V, p. 15.

CHAPTER VII

1 Adams, *Works*, Vol. III, p. 374.
2 *Ibid.*, p. 374.
3 *Ibid.*, p. 375.
4 Katherine Metcalf Roof, *Colonel William Smith and Lady*, p. 129.
5 *Idem.*
6 Adams, *Works*, Vol. VIII, p. 368.
7 Jefferson Papers, Library of Congress.
8 *Letters of Mrs. Adams*, p. 274.
9 Lipscomb, Vol. V, pp. 286-87.
10 *Diplomatic Correspondence*, Vol. I, p. 720.
11 Katherine Metcalf Roof, *Colonel William Smith and Lady*, p. 57.
12 *Ibid.*, p. 56.
13 Thomas Blaikie, *A Diary of a Scotch Gardener at the French Court*, p. 189.
14 The trip is described in a letter to Short, *William and Mary Quarterly*, Series 2, Vol. XI, p. 336.
15 *London and Its Environs* (1761), Vol. III, p. 47.
16 *Diplomatic Correspondence*, Vol. I, pp. 728-29.
17 Lipscomb, Vol. I, p. 95.
18 *Ibid.*, Vol. V, p. 295. Pinto was authorized only to negotiate, not to sign.

19 *Ibid.*, Vol. I, p. 95.
20 Jefferson Papers, Library of Congress.
21 *Idem.*
22 *Diplomatic Correspondence*, Vol. I, p. 729.
23 *Ibid.*, Vol. I, p. 601.
24 *Idem.*
25 *Ibid.*, p. 726.
26 Lipscomb, Vol. V, pp. 322-23.
27 *Diplomatic Correspondence*, Vol. I, p. 726.
28 Lipscomb, Vol. I, pp. 94-95.
29 *Ibid.*, Vol. VI, p. 324.
30 *Gazetteer and New Daily Advertizer* for March 17, 18, and 21, 1786.
31 Adams, *Works*, Vol. VIII, pp. 255-59.
32 Pocket account book for 1786, Massachusetts Historical Society.
33 Lipscomb, Vol. I, p. 94.
34 Adams, *Works*, Vol. VIII, p. 258.
35 *Gazetteer and New Daily Advertizer* records the performance given on the dates Jefferson attended.
36 *Ibid.*, March 20, 1786.
37 *Ibid.*, March 23, 1786.
38 *Ibid.*, April 22, 1786.
39 *Letters of Mrs. Adams*, pp. 297-98.
40 *Ibid.*, p. 297.
41 *Gazetteer and New Daily Advertizer*, March 22, 1786.
42 Lipscomb, Vol. V, p. 305.
43 *Ibid.*, p. 294-95.
44 Jefferson Papers, Library of Congress. See so-called Epistolary Record under that date.
45 Pocket account book, August 16, 1784.
46 Lipscomb, Vol. V, p. 110.
47 *Ibid.*, Vol. VI, pp. 72-73.
48 A. B. Shepperson, *John Paradise and Lucy Ludwell*, pp. 210-11.
49 *Letters of Mrs. Adams*, p. 268.
50 Lipscomb, Vol. V, p. 293.
51 *Letters of Mrs. Adams*, pp. 280-81.
52 Adams, *Works*, Vol. III, p. 393.
53 To R. H. Lee, Lipscomb, Vol. V, p. 292.
54 Marie Kimball, *Jefferson: The Road to Glory, 1743-1776*, pp. 160-65.
55 *Letters of Mrs. Adams*, p. 287.
56 Adams, *Works*, Vol. III, pp. 394-95.
57 Lipscomb, Vol. IV, p. 304.

58 *London and Its Environs*, Vol. II, p. 112.
59 Lipscomb, Vol. XVII, p. 237.
60 *London and Its Environs*, Vol. II, p. 115.
61 Lipscomb, Vol. XVII, p. 237.
62 *London and Its Environs*, Vol. VI, p. 211.
63 For description see Lipscomb, Vol. XVII, p. 237.
64 *London and Its Environs*, Vol. III, p. 162.
65 *Idem.*
66 Lipscomb, Vol. XVII, p. 237.
67 Thomas Whately, *Observations on Modern Gardening* (cited henceforth as Whately), p. 50.
68 Lipscomb, Vol. XVII, pp. 237-38.
69 *London and Its Environs*, Vol. II, pp. 277-78.
70 Lipscomb, Vol. XVII, p. 238.
71 *London and Its Environs*, Vol. II, pp. 139-40.
72 Whately, p. 186.
73 *London and Its Environs*, Vol. V, pp. 101-2.
74 Lipscomb, Vol. XVII, p. 238.
75 *London and Its Environs*, Vol. V, pp. 60-61.
76 *Ibid.*, Vol. III, p. 132.
77 *Ibid.*, Vol. VI, p. 361.
78 Whately, p. 176.
79 *Ibid.*, p. 177.
80 *Ibid.*, pp. 177-78.
81 *Ibid.*, pp. 178-79.
82 *Ibid.*, p. 179.
83 *Ibid.*, pp. 179-80.
84 Lipscomb, Vol. XVII, p. 238.
85 *Ibid.*, p. 239.
86 Whately, p. 84.
87 *Ibid.*, p. 88.
88 Lipscomb, Vol. XVII, p. 239.
89 J. Seeley, *Description of House and Gardens at Stowe*, pp. 9-10.
90 Lipscomb, Vol. XVII, p. 240.
91 J. Seeley, *Description of House and Gardens at Stowe*, pp. 10, 25, 32.
92 Adams, *Works*, Vol. III, p. 394.
93 Marie Kimball, *Jefferson: The Road to Glory, 1743-1776*, pp. 148-49.
94 Whately, pp. 169-70.
95 Lipscomb, Vol. XVII, pp. 240-41.
96 *Ibid.*, p. 242.
97 *Idem.*
98 *Letters of Mrs. Adams*, pp. 336-40.
99 *London and Its Environs*, Vol. III, p. 275.

100 *Letters of Horace Walpole* (Toynbee), Vol. VIII, pp. 291-92.
101 Adams, *Works*, Vol. III, p. 397.
102 Jefferson Papers, Library of Congress.
103 *London and Its Environs*, Vol. III, p. 69.
104 Adams, *Works*, Vol. III, p. 386.
105 Lipscomb, Vol. VI, p. 380.
106 *Ibid.*, p. 339.
107 *Ibid.*, Vol. V, pp. 304-5.
108 *Ibid.*, Vol. VI, p. 145.

CHAPTER VIII

1 Trumbull, p. 95.
2 Jefferson Papers, Library of Congress.
3 Lipscomb, Vol. V, pp. 400-1.
4 Trumbull, p. 96.
5 Lipscomb, Vol. VII, p. 308.
6 Trumbull, p. 96.
7 George C. Williamson, *Richard Cosway*, p. 12.
8 *Ibid.*, p. 13.
9 Trumbull, p. 118.
10 Lipscomb, Vol. V, p. 435.
11 George C. Williamson, *Richard Cosway*, p. 27.
12 Trumbull, p. 101.
13 *Ibid.*, pp. 101-2.
14 *Ibid.*, pp. 101-2.
15 Lipscomb, Vol. V, p. 433.
16 *Ibid.*, pp. 433-34.
17 *Ibid.*, p. 434.
18 Trumbull, p. 147.
19 Jefferson to Mrs. Cosway, January 14, 1788, Coolidge Collection, Massachusetts Historical Society.
20 Lipscomb, Vol. V, p. 434.
21 *Ibid.*, p. 435.
22 Thomas Blaikie, *Diary of a Scotch Gardener at the French Court*, p. 187.
23 M. Piganiol de la Force, *Description de Paris*, Vol. IX, p. 276.
24 Thomas Blaikie, *Diary of a Scotch Gardener at the French Court*, p. 163.
25 *Memoirs of Vigée Lebrun*, p. 17.
26 Lipscomb, Vol. V, p. 434.
27 *Correspondence Secrète*, Vol. XII, p. 80.

28 Franklin Papers, American Philosophical Society, Vol. CVII, p. 15. Martha Jefferson says her father fractured his wrist (Randall, Vol. I, p. 456). On November 13, 1786, he writes M. le Roy that he has dislocated it (Lipscomb, Vol. V, p. 463), and on December 25 he makes the same statement to Dumas (*Ibid.*, Vol. VI, p. 26). Veillard uses the verb *se desunir*, which means the same thing.

29 Jefferson Papers, Library of Congress, October 22, 1786.

30 *Domestic Life* (1939), p. 59.

31 Gouverneur Morris, *A Diary of the French Revolution*, Vol. I, p. 491.

32 M. Thiéry, *Almanach du Voyageur* (1786), p. xix.

33 See L. H. Butterfield and H. C. Rice, "Jefferson's Earliest Note to Maria Cosway," *William and Mary Quarterly*, Series 3, Vol. V, pp. 26-33. This writer cannot agree that the note was written on Thursday, October 5, the day the Cosways left Paris, as Jefferson was able to accompany his friends on that occasion. She believes it was written on September 21, the Thursday after the accident.

34 *Domestic Life* (1939), pp. 59-60.

35 Lipscomb, Vol. V, pp. 430-31.

36 The quotations in this section from the *Dialogue of the Head and Heart* are in Lipscomb, Vol. V, pp. 430-47.

37 *Ibid.*, pp. 448-49.

38 Manuscript in Massachusetts Historical Society. A portion of the letter, along with others quoted henceforth, was published by the writer in "Jefferson's Farewell to Romance," *Virginia Quarterly Review*, Vol. IV, No. 3, pp. 402-19.

39 November 29, 1786. Manuscript Division, Alderman Library, University of Virginia (cited henceforth as University of Virginia). Large parts of the letters there were published by Helen D. Bullock, *My Head and My Heart* (1945).

40 Coolidge Collection, Massachusetts Historical Society.

41 *Idem.*

42 November 19, 1786, University of Virginia.

43 November 29, 1786, *idem.*

44 March 6, 1787, Coolidge Collection, Massachusetts Historical Society.

45 University of Virginia.

46 Coolidge Collection, Massachusetts Historical Society.

47 Jefferson Papers, Library of Congress.

48 July 1, 1787, University of Virginia.

49 July 9, 1787, *idem.*

50 Jefferson Papers, Library of Congress.

51 *Ibid.*, August 30, 1787.

52 *Idem.*

53 In his *Memoirs,* Mazzei mentions two ladies of this name who belonged to the circle Jefferson and Mrs. Cosway frequented, Princess Lubomirski, sister of Prince Adam Czartoriski and cousin of the King of Poland, another the wife of Prince Alexander Lubomirski. See pp. 299, 311.
54 April 24, 1788, University of Virginia.
55 Quoted by H. D. Bullock, *My Head and My Heart,* p. 78.
56 January 14, 1788, Coolidge Collection, Massachusetts Historical Society.
57 Undated, Jefferson Papers, Library of Congress.
58 Coolidge Collection, Massachusetts Historical Society. Published in *Virginia Quarterly Review,* Vol. IV, No. 3, p. 410.
59 Christmas Day, 1787, Coolidge Collection, Massachusetts Historical Society.
60 *Ibid.,* January, 1788.
61 April 29, 1786, University of Virginia.
62 *Ibid.,* July 27, 1788.
63 *Ibid.,* September 26, 1788.
64 March 6, 1788, Coolidge Collection, Massachusetts Historical Society.
65 Jefferson Papers, Library of Congress. On August 19, 1788, Mrs. Cosway wrote Jefferson that Trumbull had finally presented her with his portrait. He gave one at the same time to Angelica Church.
66 July 30, 1788, University of Virginia.
67 *Ibid.,* January 14, 1789.
68 *Ibid.,* February 6, 1789.
69 *Ibid.,* October 14, 1789.

CHAPTER IX

1 Ford, Vol. IV, p. 18.
2 Lipscomb, Vol. VI, pp. 108-9.
3 Ford, Vol. IV, p. 367.
4 Lipscomb, Vol. VI, pp. 106-9.
5 *William and Mary Quarterly,* Series 2, Vol. XI, p. 244.
6 *Ibid.,* p. 246.
7 Lipscomb, Vol. XVII, pp. 153-54.
8 *Ibid.,* p. 154.
9 Jefferson does not mean maize or Indian corn, but uses the word for the predominant cereal crop of the region, wheat, rye, barley, or oats, as the case might be.
10 Letter to William Short, *William and Mary Quarterly,* Series 2, Vol. XI, pp. 244ff.

11 *Idem.*
12 *Ibid.*, p. 247.
13 Lipscomb, Vol. XVII, pp. 162-63.
14 *William and Mary Quarterly*, Series 2, Vol. XI, pp. 246ff.
15 Lipscomb, Vol. XVII, p. 164.
16 *Ibid.*, p. 163.
17 *Ibid.*, pp. 164-65.
18 "Traveling Notes for Mr. Rutledge and Mr. Shippen," Coolidge Collection, Massachusetts Historical Society. A small fragment of these notes is printed in Lipscomb, Vol. XVII, pp. 290-93.
19 Lipscomb, Vol. VI, pp. 102-6.
20 *Diplomatic Correspondence*, Vol. II, pp. 47-52.
21 The amphitheater was cleared of the dwellings of the numerous poor who inhabited it in 1825-30.
22 Lipscomb, Vol. XVII, pp. 171-72.
23 *William and Mary Quarterly*, Series 2, Vol. XI, pp. 245-46.
24 *Ibid.*, p. 248.
25 *Ibid.*, p. 247.
26 *Diplomatic Correspondence*, Vol. II, p. 46.
27 Lipscomb, Vol. XVII, pp. 177-78.
28 *Ibid.*, Vol. XIX, pp. 32-33.
29 *Diplomatic Correspondence*, Vol. II, p. 46.
30 Ford, Vol. IV, pp. 442, 443.
31 Lipscomb, Vol. XVII, p. 182.
32 "Traveling Notes for Mr. Rutledge and Mr. Shippen," Coolidge Collection, Massachusetts Historical Society.
33 Lipscomb, Vol. VI, p. 110.
34 This quotation and the one preceding are in the "Traveling Notes for Mr. Rutledge and Mr. Shippen."
35 Lipscomb, Vol. VI, p. 170. See also pp. 147, 193-204, 209-10.
36 *Ibid.*, Vol. XVII, p. 194.
37 "Traveling Notes for Mr. Rutledge and Mr. Shippen."
38 Ford, Vol. IV, p. 387.
39 Lipscomb, Vol. XVII, p. 202.
40 *William and Mary Quarterly*, Series 2, Vol. XI, p. 339.
41 Lipscomb, Vol. XVII, pp. 228-29.
42 *Ibid.*, pp. 234-35.
43 *Ibid.*, Vol. IV, p. 59.

CHAPTER X

1 Lipscomb, Vol. VI, p. 434.
2 *Ibid.*, Vol. V, pp. 192-93.
3 *Ibid.*, pp. 45-46.
4 *Ibid.*, p. 65.
5 *Diplomatic Correspondence*, Vol. I, pp. 813-14.
6 Lipscomb, Vol. VI, p. 28.
7 *Diplomatic Correspondence*, Vol. II, pp. 31-33.
8 *Ibid.*, Vol. I, pp. 173-74.
9 *Ibid.*, pp. 214-15.
10 *Ibid.*, Vol. II, p. 30.
11 Lipscomb, Vol. VI, p. 394.
12 *Ibid.*, pp. 62-63.
13 *Ibid.*, pp. 248-49.
14 *Ibid.*, Vol. VII, pp. 10-11.
15 *Ibid.*, Vol. VI, p. 394.
16 *Ibid.*, pp. 429-30.
17 *Ibid.*, pp. 402-3.
18 *Ibid.*, pp. 419-20.
19 *Ibid.*, p. 437.
20 *Ibid.*, pp. 443-45.
21 *Ibid.*, p. 135.
22 *Diplomatic Correspondence*, Vol. II, p. 135.
23 Lipscomb, Vol. I, p. 123.
24 *Ibid.*, Vol. VI, pp. 419-20.
25 *Ibid.*, pp. 421-23.
26 *Ibid.*, p. 434.
27 Jefferson Papers, Library of Congress.
28 Lipscomb, Vol. VI, pp. 451-53.
29 *Ibid.*, Vol. VII, p. 1.
30 *Ibid.*, Vol. XVII, p. 250.
31 *Ibid.*, pp. 244-49.
32 *Ibid.*, Vol. VII, pp. 9, 22.
33 *Ibid.*, pp. 136-37.
34 *Diplomatic Correspondence*, Vol. II, p. 275. The letter to the bankers is on pp. 278-79.
35 *Ibid.*, p. 288.
36 *Ibid.*, p. 186.
37 *Ibid.*, p. 326.

CHAPTER XI

1 Lipscomb, Vol. VI, p. 441.
2 *Ibid.*, Vol. I, p. 126.
3 See Marie Kimball, *Jefferson: The Road to Glory*, p. 68.
4 *Ibid.*, pp. 108-9.
5 Ford, Vol. IV, p. 259.
6 Lipscomb, Vol. I, p. 259.
7 The book was first published in 1749; second edition, 1756; third edition, 1778.
8 Trumbull, p. 94.
9 *Idem.*
10 *Ibid.*, p. 131. By the North River he means the Hudson.
11 Jefferson Papers, Library of Congress.
12 Johann Wolfgang von Goethe, *Von deutscher Art und Kunst* (1773), pp. 127-28.
13 Pocket account book for 1788.
14 "Traveling Notes for Mr. Rutledge and Mr. Shippen," Coolidge Collection, Massachusetts Historical Society.
15 *Idem.*
16 Lipscomb, Vol. XVII, pp. 252-53.
17 "Traveling Notes for Mr. Rutledge and Mr. Shippen."
18 *Goethe's Briefe* (Weimar edition, 1887), Vol. II, p. 179.
19 The pictures of the Düsseldorf Gallery were removed to Munich in 1805, and were subsequently placed in the Alte Pinakothek.
20 Lipscomb, Vol. VII, p. 307.
21 *Ibid.*, Vol. XVII, p. 254.
22 Trumbull, p. 137.
23 *Schriften der Goethe-Gesellschaft*, Vol. XVI, Goethe und Lavater, p. 426.
24 Victor Hugo, *Le Rhin* (1858), p. 119.
25 Nugent, *The Grand Tour* (1778), Vol. II, pp. 318-19.
26 "Traveling Notes for Mr. Rutledge and Mr. Shippen."
27 Lipscomb, Vol. XVII, pp. 254-55.
28 *Ibid.*, pp. 255-56.
29 *Ibid.*, pp. 256-57.
30 Marie Kimball, *Jefferson: The Road to Glory*, p. 171.
31 Lipscomb, Vol. IX, p. 14.
32 *Ibid.*, Vol. VI, p. 198.
33 *Ibid.*, Vol. XII, p. 91.
34 *Ibid.*, Vol. XIV, p. 263.
35 Nugent, *The Grand Tour*, Vol. II, p. 405.

36 Lipscomb, Vol. XVII, p. 259.
37 *Ibid.*, Vol. XVII, pp. 259-60.
38 *William and Mary Quarterly*, Series 2, Vol. XI, p. 341.
39 *Idem.*
40 "Traveling Notes for Mr. Rutledge and Mr. Shippen."
41 Lipscomb, Vol. XVII, p. 264.
42 *Ibid.*, p. 266.
43 Jefferson's pocket account book for 1788, Coolidge Collection, Massachusetts Historical Society.
44 Lipscomb, Vol. XIX, p. 72.
45 *Ibid.*, Vol. XVII, p. 263.
46 *Idem.*
47 "Traveling Notes for Mr. Rutledge and Mr. Shippen."
48 Nugent, *The Grand Tour*, Vol. II, p. 394.
49 "Traveling Notes for Mr. Rutledge and Mr. Shippen."
50 Lipscomb, Vol. XVII, p. 272.
51 *Ibid.*, p. 273.
52 *Ibid.*, p. 275.
53 *Idem.*
54 *Ibid.*, pp. 276-77.
55 "Traveling Notes for Mr. Rutledge and Mr. Shippen."
56 Nugent, *The Grand Tour*, Vol. IV, p. 207.
57 Lipscomb, Vol. XVII, p. 278.
58 *Ibid.*, pp. 279-80.
59 *William and Mary Quarterly*, Series 2, Vol. XI, p. 341.

CHAPTER XII

1 *Journal of Miss Adams*, p. 14.
2 *Ibid.*, p. 59.
3 *Letters of Mrs. Adams*, pp. 240-1.
4 Thiéry, *Guide des amateurs et des étrangers*, Vol. I, pp. 393-94.
5 *Journal of Miss Adams*, pp. 23-27.
6 *Ibid.*, pp. 46-47.
7 *Letters of Mrs. Adams*, p. 201.
8 *Diary of John Quincy Adams*, p. 17.
9 *Journal of Miss Adams*, p. 68.
10 *Ibid.*, p. 45.
11 *Letters of Mrs. Adams*, p. 208.
12 *Idem.*
13 *Journal of Miss Adams*, pp. 27-28.
14 *Ibid.*, pp. 29, 44.

15 *Domestic Life* (1939), pp. 68-69.
16 *Ibid.*, pp. 70-71.
17 *The Journal of Miss Adams*, p. 36.
18 Trumbull, p. 97.
19 Marie Kimball, "Jefferson's Farewell to Romance," *Virginia Quarterly Review*, Vol. IV, p. 411.
20 H. D. Bullock, *My Head and My Heart*, pp. 84-85.
21 Bixby, p. 32.
22 *Ibid.*, p. 31.
23 *Ibid.*, p. 32.
24 Jefferson Papers, Library of Congress.
25 Bixby, pp. 32-33.
26 Jefferson Papers, Library of Congress.
27 *Two Letters from Thomas Jefferson*, edited by Marie Dickoré. The Oxford Press, Oxford, Ohio.
28 *Idem.*
29 See Lipscomb, Vol. V, pp. 82-87, and Vol. VI, pp. 256-62.
30 *Ibid.*, Vol. VII, p. 72.
31 *Ibid.*, Vol. VI, p. 165.
32 *Ibid.*, Vol. V, pp. 185-88.
33 *Virginia Magazine*, Vol. XLII, p. 317.
34 Quoted from the diary by Samuel Flagg Bemis, *John Quincy Adams*, p. 141.
35 Adams, *Works*, Vol. X, p. 414.
36 See letters of May 8, 1784, May 14, 1784, and July 28, 1784, Short to Jefferson. Jefferson Papers, Library of Congress.
37 *Idem.*
38 *Letters of Mrs. Adams*, p. 240.
39 *Journal of Miss Adams*, p. 45.
40 *Memoirs of John Quincy Adams*, Vol. I, p. 80.
41 Short Papers, Library of Congress.
42 See Marie Kimball, "William Short, Jefferson's Only 'Son'," *North American Review*, Vol. CCXXIII, No. 3, pp. 471-86.
43 Short made the trip partly in company with Mr. and Mrs. Paradise and John Rutledge, Jr. For this as well as Jefferson's relation to the Paradises, see A. B. Shepperson, *John and Lucy Paradise of London and Williamsburg*.
44 Lipscomb, Vol. VI, p. 261.
45 "Traveling Notes for Mr. Rutledge and Mr. Shippen."
46 See Jefferson Papers, Library of Congress, for series of fourteen letters from Rutledge, beginning January 2, 1788. Also eight from Shippen.
47 Lipscomb, Vol. XVIII, p. 143.

48 *Letters of Mrs. Adams*, p. 214.
49 Lipscomb, Vol. VI, p. 312.
50 *Ibid.*, Vol. XVIII, p. 143.
51 Jefferson Papers, Library of Congress.
52 Lipscomb, Vol. I, p. 102.
53 *Ibid.*, Vol. VI, p. 130.
54 *Ibid.*, Vol. I, p. 102.
55 *Ibid.*, Vol. XVIII, p. 144.
56 Mrs. Reginald de Koven, *The Life and Letters of John Paul Jones*, Vol. II, p. 76.
57 *Letters of Mrs. Adams*, p. 208.
58 Lipscomb, Vol. VII, pp. 38-39.
59 November 13, 1787, Jefferson Papers, Library of Congress.
60 Gouverneur Morris, *Diary of the French Revolution*, Vol. I, p. 476.

CHAPTER XIII

1 Lipscomb, Vol. I, p. 139.
2 *Ibid.*, Vol. VI, p. 131.
3 *Ibid.*, Vol. I, pp. 158-59.
4 *Ibid.*, p. 136.
5 *Ibid.*, Vol. VII, p. 447.
6 *Ibid.*, Vol. VIII, pp. 6-7.
7 *Ibid.*, Vol. I, p. 330.
8 *Ibid.*, Vol. VII, p. 323.
9 *Ibid.*, p. 322.
10 *Ibid.*, Vol. VI, p. 295.
11 *Ibid.*, pp. 394-95.
12 *Ibid.*, p. 391.
13 *Ibid.*, pp. 386-89.
14 *Ibid.*, p. 370.
15 *Ibid.*, pp. 389-90.
16 *Ibid.*, Vol. VII, pp. 301-2.
17 *Ibid.*, Vol. VI, p. 391.
18 *Ibid.*, pp. 391-92.
19 *Ibid.*, Vol. VII, p. 103.
20 *Ibid.*, p. 113.
21 *Ibid.*, Vol. VI, p. 65.
22 *Ibid.*, pp. 372-73.
23 *Ibid.*, p. 56.
24 Georges Lefebvre, *The Coming of the French Revolution*, pp. 25-26.
25 Lipscomb, Vol. VI, p. 56.

26 *Diplomatic Correspondence,* Vol. II, pp. 42-43.
27 Lipscomb, Vol. VI, pp. 100-1.
28 *Ibid.,* pp. 101-2.
29 *Ibid.,* p. 105.
30 *Ibid.,* p. 134.
31 *Diplomatic Correspondence,* Vol. II, pp. 109-10.
32 Lipscomb, Vol. VI, p. 287.
33 *Diplomatic Correspondence,* Vol. II, p. 70.
34 *Ibid.,* p. 72.
35 Lipscomb, Vol. VI, pp. 276-77.
36 *Ibid.,* pp. 286-87.
37 *Diplomatic Correspondence,* Vol. II, pp. 87-88.
38 *Ibid.,* pp. 90-91.
39 Lipscomb, Vol. VII, p. 100.
40 *Diplomatic Correspondence,* Vol. II, p. 174.
41 *Ibid.,* p. 182.
42 *Ibid.,* pp. 188-89.
43 Lipscomb, Vol. VII, pp. 184-85.
44 *Ibid.,* p. 308.
45 *Ibid.,* p. 235.
46 *Ibid.,* pp. 291-92.
47 *Diplomatic Correspondence,* Vol. II, pp. 263-64.
48 *The Domestic Life* (1939), p. 111.
49 Lipscomb, Vol. VII, p. 367.
50 Gouverneur Morris, *A Diary of the French Revolution,* Vol. I, p. 68, note. Baron Grimm likewise gives a vivid description of the magnificence of the colonnaded hall, adorned with baldequin and regal hangings of gold-fringed violet velvet embroidered with fleur-de-lis of gold. Quoted in L. Dussieux, *Le château de Versailles,* pp. 437-38.
51 Lipscomb, Vol. VII, pp. 337-38.
52 *Ibid.,* pp. 367-68.
53 *Ibid.,* p. 268.
54 *Ibid.,* pp. 370-72.
55 *Ibid.,* pp. 372-74.
56 *Ibid.,* pp. 387-90.
57 *Diplomatic Correspondence,* Vol. II, pp. 297-99.
58 *Ibid.,* pp. 299-300.
59 *Ibid.,* pp. 301-2.
60 *Diplomatic Correspondence,* Vol. II, p. 303.
61 Lipscomb, Vol. VII, pp. 400-1.
62 *Idem.*
63 Gilbert Chinard, *Letters of Lafayette and Jefferson,* pp. 132-33.

64 Lipscomb, Vol. VII, pp. 401-2.
65 *Ibid.*, p. 404.
66 Chinard, *The Letters of Lafayette and Jefferson*, p. 130.
67 *Ibid.*, p. 135. The two versions of this document are printed in French and in translation, the one with Jefferson's annotations in facsimile, on pp. 136-42.
68 Ford, Vol. II, pp. 7ff.
69 Lipscomb, Vol. VII, pp. 405-8.
70 *Ibid.*, Vol. I, p. 139.
71 The letters of the Archbishop and of Jefferson are printed in French in Chinard, *The Letters of Lafayette and Jefferson*, pp. 143-45. There is a translation of the former.
72 Lipscomb, Vol. I, p. 154.
73 The fact that the copy of this letter, preserved among his papers, is in Jefferson's hand is no proof that he wrote it unaided, as has been claimed. It is doubtful that his French, even at this time, was sufficiently fluent for him to do so.
74 Chinard, *The Letters of Lafayette and Jefferson*, p. 145.
75 Lipscomb, Vol. I, p. 155. See also Georges Lefebvre, *The Coming of the French Revolution*, p. 68.
76 *Ibid.*, p. 156.
77 *Ibid.*, p. 157.
78 The letter to Madison is in Lipscomb, Vol. VII, pp. 444-53.
79 *Diplomatic Correspondence*, Vol. II, pp. 304-6.
80 Lipscomb, Vol. I, p. 147.
81 *Diplomatic Correspondence*, Vol. II, pp. 306-7.
82 *Ibid.*, pp. 303-9.
83 Lipscomb, Vol. I, p. 145.
84 The quotations from Morris are from *A Diary of the French Revolution*, Vol. I, p. 143.
85 *Diplomatic Correspondence*, Vol. II, p. 309.
86 The various quotations from Morris are from *A Diary of the French Revolution*, Vol. I, pp. 144, 150, 156, 158-59.
87 *Diplomatic Correspondence*, Vol. II, p. 317.
88 *Idem.*
89 *Ibid.*, p. 327.
90 Lipscomb, Vol. I, pp. 150-51.

CHAPTER XIV

1 *Diplomatic Correspondence*, Vol. II, pp. 234-35.
2 Lipscomb, Vol. XIX, p. 22.

3 *Ibid.*, Vol. IV, p. 427.
4 *Domestic Life* (1939), p. 39.
5 Lipscomb, Vol. IV, p. 265.
6 *Domestic Life* (1939), pp. 99-100.
7 *Ibid.*, p. 97.
8 *Ibid.*, p. 76.
9 Jefferson Papers, Library of Congress.
10 *Domestic Life* (1939), p. 76.
11 *Ibid.*, pp. 77-79.
12 *Ibid.*, p. 75.
13 *Ibid.*, p. 94.
14 *Idem.*
15 *Letters of Mrs. Adams*, p. 328.
16 *Domestic Life* (1939), pp. 96-97.
17 *Ibid.*, p. 106.
18 Lipscomb, Vol. VI, pp. 136-37.
19 *Domestic Life* (1939), p. 116.
20 Lipscomb, Vol. VII, pp. 349-50.
21 *Ibid.*, Vol. VI, p. 278.
22 *Ibid.*, Vol. VII, 307-8.
23 Jefferson Papers, Library of Congress.
24 The passport for Jefferson, his family, and servants is preserved in the Jefferson Papers, Library of Congress.
25 *Domestic Life* (1939), p. 118.
26 Jefferson Papers, Library of Congress.
27 *Ibid.*
28 Lipscomb, Vol. I, p. 159.

Index

Abbeville, 130
Abdrahaman, 127-128, 131-132
Abrantès, Duchesse d', 97, 104
Acacia, 101
Académie des Inscriptions et Belles-Lettres, 67-68
Académie des Sciences, 84
Académie Française, 95
Adam, Robert, 154
Adams, Abigail (Abby), 127-130, 140, 243, 247, 257
——, Abigail (Mrs. John), 9, 10-11, 14, 87, 95, 96, 98, 112-113, 122, 123, 137, 138, 139-140, 152, 154, 242-246, 248, 249, 251, 257, 260, 262, 305
——, John, 5, 9, 11, 17, 18, 22, 24-25, 27, 30, 33, 36, 58, 83-84, 86-87, 94, 98, 109, 116, 117, 124, 127-129, 131-135, 139-142, 145, 147, 148, 151, 154, 156, 159, 202, 204, 207, 210, 211, 213, 215, 242-247, 256, 264, 270, 273
——, John Quincy, 4, 99, 246-247, 256, 257
Africa, 22
Agriculture, 7-8, 146, 147, 185, 186, 187, 188, 191-192, 193-199, 212, 217-218, 221-222, 223, 225-226, 228, 229, 231, 232-234, 255, 259
Aix-en-Provence, 184, 189, 192
Aix-la-Chapelle, 223
Albenga, 197
Alembert, 84, 91, 95, 102, 104, 105
Alexis, 192
Algiers, 22, 28-34, 128, 131, 215
"Alhambra," Kew, 153
Alps, 195, 219, 258
Alsace, 239
Amboise, 200
Americus Vespucius, 119
Ampuys, 188
Amsterdam, 202, 207, 211, 213, 214, 215, 217, 220
Animal magnetism, 99
Antibes, 194
Antiquities, 187, 188, 189, 191, 192, 195, 222
Antwerp, 212
Anville, Duc d', 86
——, Duchesse d', 82, 84, 85, 86-91, 163, 243, 320
Apennines, 197
Appiani, 196
Aranda, Count de, 23
Archimedes screw, 153
Architecture, 16, 105, 187, 218, 255, 259, 308
Aristotle, 238
Arles, 191
Arminius, 226
Arnault, Abbé, 82, 98-100, 187, 243, 310
Arpajon, 201

Arrowsmith, 136
Art, 16, 55-77, *see also* Architecture, Painting, Sculpture, Music
Artois, Comte d', 164, 274, 283, 284, 286, 296
Assemblée des Notables, 206, 269-272, 273, 276, 277
Assembly, National, 282-290, 292, 299
Ast, William, 308
Astorg, Madame d', 88-90
Auteuil, 17, 109, 242
Auxerre, 186
Avignon, 189
Ayen, Duc d', 94

Baalbec, 74
Bacharach, 220
Bacon, 120
Baden, 237
Baden, Markgraf of, 237
Barbary States, 28-33, 127-128
Bailly, 295, 296
Bancroft, Dr., 140
Banister, John, 254, 299
Barclay, Mrs., 244
——, Thomas, 32, 33, 35, 64-65, 123-124, 243
Barentin, 293
Barnave, 291
Barthalemen, Mrs., 136
Barthélemy, Abbé, 82
Bartolozzi, 160
Basedow, 240
Baskerville types, 238
Bazin, 113
Beaujolais, 186
Beaumarchais, 206
Beavers, 237
Beccafias, 197
Beggars, 8, 237
Belisard, 160
Bellini, Carlo, 15, 16
Benndorf, 240
Bensberg, 227, 240
Bergen, 232
Bergstrasse, 237
Berthelemy, 110
Bertier, 298
Billy, de, collection, 114-115
Bingen, 220, 235
Bingham, Anne (Mrs. William), 248, 249-251
——, William, 249
Birmingham, 151
Blacon, 291
Blaikie, Thomas, 131, 165, 166
Blair, Mrs. Elizabeth, 6
Blenheim, 151-152
Bolbec, 309
Bolling, Mary (Jefferson), 302
Bologna, 258
Bonn, 220, 223, 228, 241
Books, 7, 16, 139, 189, 214, 231, 238
Bordeaux, 199
Bordeaux, Archbishop of, 289
Borelli, château, 193
Boston, 3
Botany, 106
Botetourt, Lord, statue, 63
Bouchardon, 58
Bourbon, Duc de, 296
Bourget, 156
Boze, Joseph, 119
Braine le Comte, 211
Brazil, 190
Bréhan, Madame de, 248, 278, 308
Breteuil, 130

Bridges, 142, 146, 148, 152, 187, 189, 259, 308
Brienne, Loménie de, 272
Brillon, Madame, 96
Brittany, 199
Broglio, Marshall, 292
Brown, Launcelot, 152
——, Mather, 61, 116-117
Brussels, 211
Btorki, Count, 179
Buchanan, James, 72
Buckingham, Duke of, 153
——, Marquis of, 148
Buckles, 9
Buffon, 104
Bulfinch, Charles, 255
Burgundy, 186
Burlington, Earl of, 142, 152

Cabanis, 98
Cabot, Mr., 4
Cabriolet, 123, 129
Cadiz, 29
Cadogan, Lord, 147
Calais, 130, 131, 156
Calonne, 41-42, 48, 49, 50, 53, 54, 204, 270
Canals, 184, 191, 224-225
Cannes, 194
Canterbury, 156
Cape of Good Hope, 228
Capel, Lord, 153
Capers, 194
Carmathen, Marquis of, 21, 132-134, 155, 156
Carmichael, William, 24, 29, 139
Carnival, 245
Carr, Dabney, 254
Carriages, 8, 10, 12, 123, 129, 163, 198, 225
Cary, Archibald, 5
Cassel, 228
Catherine II, 58, 69, 73, 105, 212, 261, 263
Cavallo, 139
Caversham, 147
Ceres, 3, 5
Cette, 198
Chabot, Comte de, 90, 91
Chalgrin, 109
Chalut, Abbé, 82, 98-100, 187, 243, 310
Chambers, Sir William, 153
Champagne, 221
Chantilly, 129-130
Chariot, 123, 225
Charlemagne, 234
Charpentier, 139
Chastellux, Marquis de, 95, 104, 139, 199
Chatham, Earl of, 133, 152; statue, 63
Chaumont, Le Ray de, 17
Chaville, 106-107, 310
Cheverny, Comte de, 37
Child, Sir Francis, 154
——, Lady, 154, 155
China, 10
Chiswick, 142
Choiseul, Comte de, 77
——, Duc de, 200
Church, Angelica Schuyler (Mrs. John), 248, 251-253
——, Catharine, 251-252, 253
Cincinnati, Order of the, 66
Cipriani, 160
Claremont, 144
Clemens Wenceslaus, 231

Clérisseau, Charles-Louis, 73-77
Clermont, 221
Clermont, 308, 309-310
Cleves, *see* Kleve
Clive, Lord, 144
Clocks, 238
Coachmen, 10, 11, 12
Coblentz, 220, 230-231, 235
Col de Tenda, 177, 195, 259
Colle, 231
Colley, Captain, 308
Cologne, 220, 222, 223, 226-227, 229, 241
Columbus, 119, 120
Commerce, 4-5, 17-34, 38-39, 42-48, 192, 199, 228
Commissioners to negotiate treaties of commerce, 17-34
Condé, Prince de, 283, 296
Condorcet, Marquis de, 78, 82, 84, 85, 91-93, 95, 101
Congress, Continental, 11, 12, 17, 18, 19-20, 21, 24, 25, 29, 30, 31, 32, 33, 34, 47, 51, 53, 58, 60, 67, 68, 124-126, 128, 189, 202, 203, 204, 205, 206, 207, 212, 215, 216, 263-266, 301, 306, 307
Coni, 195
Connecticut, 84
Constitutions, American, state, 83, 84; federal, 216, 265, 266-268; French, 268-299
Consuls, 50-53
Convention, National, 92
Cook, Captain, 260
Copley, John Singleton, 61, 116
Copying press, 138-139, 214
Cornwallis, Lord, 27
Corny, Ethis de, 66, 248, 294
——, Madame de, 157, 248, 294
Correspondence littéraire, 105
Cortez, 119
Cosway, Maria (Mrs. Richard), 114, 160-183, 248, 251, 252
——, Richard, 114, 160-161, 164, 169, 170
Côte d'Azur, 185, 194-195
Côte Rôtie, 188
Coudrieux, 188
Cowes, 5, 183, 308, 309
Crèvecoeur, 82, 95
Crimea, 261
Currie, James, 5, 13, 14, 74
Curtains, 108, 113-114

Dagout, 291
Dauphiné, 187
David, Jacques-Louis, 159, 178, 227
Debts, war, 202-217
De Dominis, 99
Deer, 237
Deffand, Madame de, 78
Denmark, 22, 23
Descartes, 99
Désert de Retz, 167-168, 177
Dessein, 130, 156
Deux-Ponts, 221
Devonshire, Duchess of, 160
Dialogue of Head and Heart, 162-172
Diderot, 81, 95, 102, 104
Dijon, 185, 186
Directors of Public Buildings, 69-76
Donald, Alexander, 302
Dorset, Duke of, 21, 156
Dover, 156
Drayton, William, 230
Drusus, 222, 229
Dubarry, Madame de, 166

Dubourg, Dr., 81
Dugazon, Madame, 192
Dugnani, Count, 82, 139
Duisburg, 225, 226
Dumas, C. W. T., 204, 208
Dumbwaiters, 113
Dunmore, Lord, 70
Duport, 291
Dupré, 68
Dürckheim, 220
Düsseldorf, 220, 223, 226, 240, 241
Duvivier, 68

Eaux Forges, 89-90
Education, 3, 253-260, 268
Egypt, 218
Empire, 23
Ems, 240
"Encyclopédie," 78
Enfield Chase, 152-153
England, 20-22, 23, 127-158, 309
"English garden," *see Jardin anglais*
Epernay, 221
Eppes, John W., 13, 254, 304
——, John W., Jr. (Jacky), 304, 305
——, Mrs. John W., 13, 303, 304, 305, 306
Erbach, 233
Erechtheum, 74
Esher Place, 143-144
Espagnol, 224, 238
Estaing, Comte d', 68
Etampes, 201

Falconet, 58
Fareham, 5
Farmers-General, 38, 44-45, 50, 98
Ferme ornée, 145, 150
Figs, 197, 199
Fille, 194
Fiseaux and Co., 208-209
Fish, 4, 38, 39, 43
Fitzhugh, Mr., 27, 254
Flesselles, 295
Florida, 23
Fontainebleau, 185
Forges, 89-90
Foulon, 298
Fouquet, 77
Frankfurt, 219, 220, 222, 231-233, 237, 239
Franklin, Benjamin, 17, 18, 25, 27, 28, 33, 35, 50, 52, 56, 59, 60, 67, 80-81, 82, 83, 84, 87, 96, 98, 102, 116, 118-119, 124, 126, 301
——, William Temple, 61, 139
Franks, David, 12
Frederick the Great, 22, 24-27, 79, 105
—— V, 59
French language, 7, 44, 221, 305, 311, 312
Friseur, 9
Frotteur, 11, 123
Furnishings, 108, 111-114, 122, 130, 214
Fürstemberg, Cardinal, 238
Fuschias, 200

Gaillon, 7
Gardens, 105-107, 130, 141-152, 164, 166, 167-168, 200, 232, 236, 237, 259
Gaspard, 10
Gates, Horatio, 68
Gatteaux, 68
Geismar, Baron de, 231-232, 233

Geneva, 258
Genoa, 195, 196-197
Gentil, 199
Geoffrin, Madame, 78, 95, 101, 104
George III, 132, 133, 134-135, 137-138, 153, 157; statue, 63
Georgia, 44
Gérard, Conrad Alexandre, 41, 54
German language, 218, 221
Germany, 163, 218-241
Gerry, Elbridge, 4
Gilmer, George, 302
Girardon, 162
Gisors, 90
Glass, 10
Gluck, 97
Goats, Angora, 237
Goethe, 218, 223-224, 226, 239-241
Goldsmith, 139
Gosport, 6
Gothic, 8, 130, 143, 146, 148, 149, 167, 196, 211, 220, 223, 224
Goujon, 123
Gournay, 89
Gouvion, Colonel, 207
Grand, Ferdinand, 206, 215, 216
Grand Tour, 219, 258
Grasse, Comte de, 69
Grayson, William, 33
Greene, Nathanael, 67, 68
Greenwich, 156
Greuze, 119
Grey, Captain, 6
Grillement, château de, 199
Grimm, Melchior de, 38, 82, 104-105, 261
Grouchy, Sophie de, 92
Guireau, 10
Haarlem, 214
Habrecht, 238
Hadfield, Mrs., 160
Hagley Park, 151
Hague, The, 210, 211, 212
Haltenheim, 233
Ham Farm, 145
Hameau, 130
Hamilton, Charles, 145
——, Mrs. Alexander, 251
Hampton Court, 143
Hancarville, Monsieur d', 160, 170, 178
Hansa towns, 31, 49
Harcourt, Earl of, 140
Hardy, Samuel, 5
Hares, 5
Harrison, Benjamin, 5, 17, 55-56, 57, 63-64
Hartley, David, 20, 21
Hats, 9
Havre, 6-7, 8, 59, 77, 308, 309
Hay, William, 72
Heidelberg, 235-236
Heliotropes, 200
Helvétius, 78, 104
——, Madame, 98, 101, 104
Hennin, Pierre-Michel, 41
Henry, Patrick, 59, 64, 65, 79
Hewson, Mary, 83
Hochheim, 231, 232
Hock, 233, 234
Hogendorp, Count van, 5, 14, 19
Hogs, 228
Holbach, 104, 105
Holland, 23, 128, 202, 204, 212, 213, 217, 218, 224-225, 258
Hope, 214
Hopkinson, Francis, 267

Houdetot, Comtesse d', 101-103
Houdon, Jean-Antoine, 56-63, 65, 66-67, 114, 116, 159, 162, 263
——, Madame, 159, 162
Hudson, 220, 222
Hugo, Victor, 227
Humphreys, David, 11, 21, 29, 36, 38, 47, 67, 95, 108, 128, 159, 264, 302, 308
Hyères, 184, 194

Indigo, 43
Inns, 130-131, 226, 230, 259, 309
Instruments, 138, 157
Ironwork, 108
Italy, 176-177, 184, 195-196, 218, 219, 258
Izard, Ralph, 39, 254

Jacob, 111, 112
James, 3
Jansen, 109
Jardin anglais, 106, 111, 130, 165, 167, 232, 236
Jay, John, 10, 11, 23, 25, 26, 30, 32, 35, 39, 42, 47, 48, 51, 58, 68, 79, 124-126, 127, 129, 133, 134, 135, 189, 192, 203, 209, 213, 214, 216, 217, 264, 269, 270, 273, 274, 275, 278, 282, 283, 292, 299, 300, 301, 307
Jefferson, Lucy Elizabeth, 13
——, Maria (Polly), 13, 200, 254, 303-306, 309
——, Martha (Patsy), 3, 5, 6-7, 9, 12-13, 94-95, 200, 254, 303, 304, 305, 306, 307, 309
——, Martha Wayles (Mrs. Thomas), 248
——, Thomas, voyage to Europe, 4-9; establishment in Paris, 9-16; treaties, 17-34; ministry to France, 35-54; and the art world, 55-77; and the circle of literati, 78-107; house and possessions, 108-126; trip to England, 127-158; romance with Maria Cosway, 159-183; trip to South of France and North Italy, 184-201; negotiates war debts, 202-216; Rhine journey, 218-241; and Americans in Europe, 242-263; and the French Revolution, 264-299; leaves France, 301-310
Health, 13-14, 168-170, 184, 192, 332; paintings, collection, 114-120, 323-327; portraits of, 66-67, 116, 118, 182; "Notes on Virginia," 85, 93, 97
Johann Wilhelm, 227
Johannisberg, 232, 233, 234
John, 129, 142
Joigny, 186
Jones, Inigo, 156
——, John Paul, 30, 67, 69, 116, 260, 261, 262-263
Joseph II, 213, 272
Journal de Paris, 287
Justine, 192

Kamchatka, 261, 262
Karl Theodore, 236
Karlsruhe, 236-237
Kauffmann, Angelica, 131, 160
Kent, William, 144, 148
Kew, 153, 167
Kingston, Duchess of, 168
Kleve, 225, 237
Kress, 225
Krumpfholz, Julie, 163

Lafayette, Marquise de, 12, 80, 94-95, 243, 247
——, Marquis de, 27, 31, 45-49, 60, 63-66, 68, 78, 80, 82, 93-95, 107, 116, 119, 139, 157, 185, 206, 246, 248, 263, 270, 271, 275, 281, 282, 286-288, 290-291, 296
La Harpe, 104
Lahn, 231
Lahneck, 240
Lamb, John, 32
Lambert, 53, 276
La Meth, Alexandre, 291
Lamps, 10
Langeac, Comte de, 109-110
Lansdowne, Marquis of, 133, 140
La Roche, Abbé, 96, 98
La Rochefoucauld, Cardinal de, 286
——, Duc de, 78, 81, 82-87, 92, 93, 95, 257, 264, 310
——, Duchesse de, 82-84, 86, 87-90, 257, 310
La Rochefoucauld-Liancourt, Duc de, 77, 295
LaRoche-Guyon, château de, 82, 85, 88
Launay, de, 295, 296
Lavater, 240-241
L'Aye Epinay, château de, 186-187
Leasowes, 147, 150-151
Le Brun, Mme. Vigée, 160, 178
Ledyard, John, 260-262
Lee, Arthur, 126
——, Richard Henry, 57, 139
Legrand, 162-163
Le Gros, 244
Leonardo, 114, 196
Leoni, Giacomo, 152
Lespinasse, Mlle. de, 78
Letter press, 138-139, 214
Lewis, Nicholas, 5
Liancourt, Duc de La Rochefoucauld-), 77, 295
Lincoln, Earl of, 145
Linen, 10, 24
Lisbon, 128
Livingston, Robert R., 83
Locke, 120
Loire, 200
London, 131-145, 147, 153-156, 258; Tower of, 153, 260; Buckingham House, 154
Lorient, 46, 199, 308
Lorraine, 221, 239
Louano, 197
Louis XIV, 198
—— XV, 58
—— XVI, 36-37, 41, 47, 50, 57, 92, 246-247, 249, 270, 271, 273, 274, 278-280, 282, 283, 284, 285, 292, 293, 296
Louisburg, 86
Louveciennes, 166
Lubomirski, Princess, 179, 333
Luxembourg, Duc de, 286
Luzerne, Chevalier de la, 54
——, Comte de la, 53, 293, 297
Lyon, 187, 258

Mably, Abbé de, 82, 85
Macaroni, 258
Madison, James, 40, 47, 62, 70, 120, 126, 139, 184, 204, 217, 264, 266, 276, 279, 282, 287, 292, 306
——, Reverend James, 99
Madrid, 23-24
Magellan, 119
Main, 231, 233
Mainz, 220, 222, 233, 234, 235

Malsherbes, 272
Malta, 31
Manners, 15-16, 54, 87, 95, 101-105, 140, 192, 243, 245, 250, 262
Mannheim, 219, 235-236
Mantes, 8
Mantua maker, 9
Manuel, 84
Maratti, Carlo, 115
Marc, 10, 77, 123
Marco-Brunnen, 233, 234
Marie-Antoinette, 164, 166, 272, 274, 278-280, 283, 284, 296, 299-300
Marigny, Marquis de, 200
Marlborough, Duchess of, 152
Marly, 8, 163, 165-166, 177, 179, 283
Marmontel, 82, 96, 100, 104
Marseille, 192-193
Martin, 196
Maryland, 45, 239
Massachusetts, 4, 84
Mathurins, 32
Maubourg, 291
Mayan, Madame, 10
Mazet, 192
Mazzei, Philip, 85-86, 100, 119, 193, 199, 229, 256, 310
Mechanical arts, 138, 157, 259
Medals, 67-69, 215
Meeks, Dr., 5
Melun, 185
Menageries, 237, 260
Menander, 238
Menars, château de, 200-201
Metz, 219, 220, 221
Metza, 95
Meudon, 106
Mignard, 163
Milan, 196, 258
Milliner, 9
Mirabeau, 81, 286-287
Mississippi, 23
Mockingbirds, 198
Moerdyke, 212
Mole, river, 143, 144
Molinos, 162-163
Molyneux, Mr., 153
Monaco, Princesse de, 104
Monroe, James, 11-12, 14, 17, 19, 21, 23, 29, 201, 269
Mons, 211
Mont Calvaire, 121
Mont Valérien, 120, 121, 165, 179
Montagnes Noires, 198
Montesquieu, 84
Monticello, 3, 71, 107, 108, 111, 112, 114, 120, 123, 141, 142, 146-147, 150, 151, 153, 154, 214, 224, 231, 237, 238, 302, 307
Montmorin, Comte de, 18, 49-50, 52, 54, 272, 275, 291
Montreuil, 130
Monville, Monsieur de, 167
Moor Park, 152
Morellet, Abbé, 82, 95-98, 100, 101, 104
Morocco, 22, 28-34, 124, 131
Morris, Gouverneur, 53-54, 93, 101, 106, 164, 169, 263, 278, 297-298
——, Robert, 45-47, 67, 138
——, Mrs. Robert, 279
Moselle, 221, 223
Mosque, 153
Mounier, 291
Mount Vernon, 60-61
Moustier, Comte de, 157, 278
Mules, 193, 197
Music, 16, 163, 244, 308

Nantes, 199
Naples, 30, 31
Nassau, 231
Natural Bridge, 175
Navy, 30, 262
Necker, 41, 50, 53, 54, 101, 103, 122, 276, 280, 284, 286-287, 293, 295, 297
——, Madame, 101, 103-105
Neuilly, 109; Pont de, 120, 162, 165
Neuwied, 220, 240
Newcastle, Duke of, 144
New Haven, 102
Newton, 99, 120
New York, 307
Nice, 194-195, 197, 259
Niederwald, 234
Niemsewicz, 179
Nightingales, 197, 198-199
Nijmegen, 225
Nîmes, 99, 189-191; Maison Carrée, 76, 148, 189
Noailles, Duc de, 94
——, Maréchal de, 165
Noli, 197
Nootka Sound, 261
Normandy, Duke of, 246
"Notes on Virginia," 85, 93, 97
Novara, 196
Nugent, "Grand Tour," 219, 223

Oatlands, 145
Obelisk, 142, 143, 151, 167
"Observations on Modern Gardening," 145
Odiot, 74
Olives, 184, 193, 194, 199
Opera, 97, 136, 308
Oppenheim, 220, 222, 235
Oranges, 184, 189, 194, 197
Orléans, 201
Orléans, Duc d', 160, 285
Ortolans, 197
Osterley Park, 154-155
Outfit, 11-12, 123-126

Padua, 258
Pagan, Père, 96
Page, John, 141, 157
Pagoda, 153, 200
Paine, Thomas, 117, 288
Painshill, 144-145
Painting, 16, 109, 114-120, 130, 154, 159, 163, 178, 187, 218, 220, 223, 226, 227, 235, 241, 255, 259; Jefferson's collection, 114-120, 323-327
Pajou, 162
Palatinate, 221, 239
Palladian bridge, 148
Palladio, 74, 142
Palms, 194, 199
Pantheon, London, 136
Panthemont, Abbaye de, 12, 13, 95, 305, 307
Paradise, John, 139, 156, 338
——, Lucy (Mrs. John), 139, 338
Paris, 9-14, 78, 123, 156, 159-183, 242-300, 303-308; Arc de l'Etoile, 109; Archbishop of, 285; Bagatelle, 164; Bastille, 292, 294, 298; Bibliothèque du Roi, 162; Bois de Boulogne, 120, 163, 164, 179; Boulevards, 297, 308; Champs-Elysées, 108, 109, 245, 298; Cul-de-sac Taitbout, *see* Hôtel de Landron; Faubourg St. Honoré, 109; Grille de Chaillot, *see* Hôtel de Langeac; Halle aux Blés, 162-

163; Hôtel de Lafayette, 247, de Landron, 10, 108, 109, 114, 123, de Langeac, 100, 108-114, 121-122, 263, 297, 298, 307, de La Rochefoucauld, 10, 82, 85, des Monnaies, 92, Muscovy, 249, d'Orléans, rue de Richelieu, 9, d'Orléans, rue des Petits-Augustins, 9-10, de Ville, 66, 295, 296, 298; Invalides, 292, 294; Louvre, 162; Luxembourg, 162; Madrid, château de, 164; Notre Dame, 246-247; Palais Royal, 162, 178, 181, 298, 308; Panthemont, Abbaye de, 12, 13, 95, 305, 307; Panthéon, 162; Place de la Grève, 294, Louis XV, 293, 297; Pont Royal, 279; Porte St. Denis, 170; rue de Berri, 110, des Petits-Augustins, 9, de Richelieu, 9, St. Honoré, 297; St. Lazare prison, 294; St. Philippe du Roule, 109; St. Roch, 297; St. Sulpice, 109; Ste. Geneviève, 162; Tuileries, 88, 96, 244
Parlément, 273, 274, 277
Parmesan cheese, 196
Partridges, 5, 197
Passy, 17, 98, 109, 310
Pavia, 195; Certosa, 196
Peaks of Otter, 175
Peale, Charles Willson, 55
Pelham, Henry, 144
Pelts, 43, 48
Pennsylvania, 239
Peronne, 211
Peter the Great, 58
Peters, Lord, 145
Péthion, 88
Petit, 129, 142, 156, 166
Petrarch, 198, 236
Phaeton, 8, 10, 123, 163
Pheasants, 5, 197, 237
Phi Beta Kappa, 258
Piccini, 97
Picturesque, the, 7, 130, 199, 219, 235
Piedmont, 193
Pierrelatte, 184
Pilat mountains, 188
Pinckney, Thomas, 24
Pine, Robert Edge, 120
Pinto, Chevalier de, 128, 132, 155
Pitt, William, 133, 152; statue, 63
Plateaux de dessert, 112-113
Plato, 238
Poggi, Alexander di, 219
Polignac, Duchesse de, 274, 296
Politics, 260, 264-299
Pompadour, Madame de, 200, 201
Pont du Gard, 189
Pope, Alexander, 142-143
Poplar Forest, 146
Portchester, 5
Portmore, Earl of, 145
Portsmouth, 5, 6
Portugal, 23, 30, 31, 128, 132, 141
Postillions, 232, 259
Prévôt des marchands, 66, 295, 296
Price, Richard, 133
"Progrès de l'esprit humain," 92
Prussia, 22, 24-27, 225, 237

Quail, 197
Quesnay, 78

Rabbits, 5
Rainbow, 99
Randall, Paul R., 35
Randolph, Roy, 72
——, Thomas Mann, 254, 303
Raphael, 114
Raynal, Abbé, 85, 104

Rayneval, Joseph-Mathias Gérard de, 41, 43, 44, 45, 52
Reading, 148
Reni, Guido, 115
Retz, Désert de, 167-168, 177
Revolution, French, 264-287
Reynolds, Sir Joshua, 160
Rheinberg, 225
Rheingau, 233
Rhine, 197, 218-241
Rhone, 187, 191
Ribera, 115
Rice, 38, 39, 43, 48, 193, 195-196, 259
Richmond, Va., 69-75; Capitol, 69-77; Governors' House, 71, 73; Halls of Justice, 69, 71; market, 162; prison, 73, 74, 319
Riedesel, General von, 229
Rights, Bill of, 267, 281-282, 287-288
Rivers, Lady, 160
Riviera, 185, 194-195, 196
Roads, 195, 197, 226, 231, 237
Robert, Hubert, 178
Rochambeau, 68, 248
Rochester, 156
Rohan, Cardinal de, 238
Roland, 178
Rolls, 230
Rome, 176, 258
Rose, Guelder, 193
Rotterdam, 212
Rouen, 7, 8
Rousseau, 78, 101
Roye, 156
Rozzano, 196
Rubens, 114, 223, 226
Rüdesheim, 232, 233, 234
Ruggieri, 163
Ruins, 146, 150, 153, 236
Rush, Benjamin, 81
Russia, 261-262, 263
Rutledge, Edward, 195
——, John, 189, 200, 224, 226, 227, 230, 234, 235, 238, 254, 258

Saarbrücken, 220
St. André, Monsieur de, 179
St. Barbe, Captain, 5
St. Cloud, 161, 163, 168, 179
St. Denis, 170
St. Etienne, Rabaud de, 281-282
St. Florentin, Comte de, 110
St. Foin, 201
St. Germain, 8, 165, 178, 179, 257
St. Lambert, 101-102, 104
St. Ouen, 156
St. Raphael, 194
St. Remy, 191
St. Petersburg, 261
St. Séverin, collection, 115
Saliari, 136
Salons, 78, 96-97, 101-104; of 1787, 175; of 1789, 67
Sannois, 101-102
Santerre, 90
Saorgio, château de, 177, 195
Saxe-Gotha, 104, 105
Saxony, 23
Say, Jean Baptiste, 230
Schwalbach, 231
Schwetzingen, 236
Science, 16
Sculpture, 109, 113, 116, 187, 218, 255, 259; in America, 63
Seine, 8, 77, 163, 165, 277, 309
Sémoulin, Monsieur de, 261

Senlis, 211
Sens, 185-186
Sentimental Journey, 130
Serapis, 263
Servants, 10-11, 12, 77, 123, 129, 142, 156, 166, 185, 187, 224, 309
Shakespeare, 120, 149, 150
Shay's Rebellion, 269
Shells, 199-200
Shenstone, William, 150-151
Shipbuilding, 43, 48
Shippen, Thomas Lee, 189, 200, 224, 226, 227, 230, 234, 235, 238, 254, 258
Shirts, 9
Shoemakers, 9, 131
Short, William, 11, 24, 66, 71-72, 84, 85, 119, 185, 187, 191, 195, 198, 212, 231, 234, 243, 254, 256-258, 278, 281, 292, 298, 309
Sicily, 23, 31
Siddons, Sarah, 135-136
Sigond, Chevalier de, 205
Silver, 10, 112, 122
Slavery, 92
Slaves, 3, 7, 305
Slodtz, Michel-Ange, 187
Smiths, 108
Smith, William Stephens, 116, 127, 128, 129, 139, 140, 145, 263, 269
Soderini, Count, 140
Somme, 211
Soufflot, 200
South Carolina, 39, 196, 259
Southgate, Philip, 145
Spain, 23-24, 30, 202, 218
Spanish language, 4, 306
Spithead, 5
Städel, 220
Staël, Baron de, 122
——, Madame de, 101, 104, 122
Stanitski, 209
States-General, 93, 264, 270, 273, 275, 277, 278-281, 282, 284-285, 293, 295, 296, 340
Stay maker, 9
Steam, 138
Sterne, 130, 156
Stiles, Ezra, 117
Stowe, 144, 148-149, 167
Strassburg, 218, 237
Stratford on Avon, 149-150
Strawberries, 193
Sully, 59
Suresnes, 121, 161
Surtouts de table, 112-113
Sweden, 23, 25
Switzerland, 210, 241
Swords, 9, 67
Syon House, 154

Tailors, 9, 131
Tain, 188
Tea, Hyson's, 214
Te Deum, 246-247
Temples, garden, 143, 145, 147, 148-149, 151, 152, 153, 167, 236
Tenda, Col de, 177, 195, 259
Terrier, Madame de, 101
Tessé, Comtesse de, 104, 105-107, 189, 248, 271, 278
Thames, 137, 143, 144, 145, 148, 153, 155
Theater, 130, 131, 135-136, 192, 195, 196, 231, 235
Thompson, Samuel, 6
Thomson, Charles, 60
Thulemeier, Baron de, 24-27
Titchfield, 5

Tobacco, 24, 38, 39, 42-43, 50
Toiles de Jouy, 108, 114
Tott, Madame de, 248
Toulon, 194
Toulouse, 198, 199
Toulouse, Archbishop of, 272, 276
Tours, 199, 200
Tracy, Nathaniel, 3, 4, 5, 89
Traiteur, 10, 123
Travel, 4-9, 129-157, 184-201, 211-212, 214, 218-241, 255-256, 258-260, 309-310
Treasury, Board of, 206, 207, 209, 210, 211, 212, 215, 216
Treaties, 17-34
Tripoli, 22, 28-34, 127-128, 131-132
Trist, Mrs. Elizabeth, 3, 8, 13, 14, 16
Tronchin, 109
Trotti, Marquis, 160
Troyes, 273
Trumbull, John, 61, 105, 113, 116, 117-118, 120, 123, 159-163, 164, 170, 176, 177, 178, 182, 183, 219-223, 226, 251, 252, 255, 308, 309
Tudor, Mr., 257
Tulips, 214
Tunis, 22, 28-34, 131
Turgot, 78, 84, 95, 116
Turin, 195-196, 258
Turkey, 263, 268
Turpin, Philip, 253
——, Thomas, 253
Tuscany, 22, 105
Twickenham, 143

University of Virginia, 8, 70, 166, 196
Unternach, 222
Upper Ossory, Countess of, 154
Utrecht, 214, 224, 225

Valadée, Marquis de, 79
Valenciennes, 211
Valets, 10, 11, 185, 259
Vanbrugh, Sir John, 144, 149
Van der Werff, Adrian, 227
Van Dyck, 114
Varus, 226
Vaucluse, 199, 236
Vaudreuil, Marquis de, 160
Venice, 30, 31, 177, 258
Vercelli, 195
Vergennes, Comte de, 18, 31, 36, 38, 39, 40-41, 42-47, 49, 50, 52, 54, 129, 203, 270, 272
Vermanton, 186
Vermont, Abbé de, 296
Vernon, 89, 309
Verona, 258
Versailles, 8, 36, 40, 42, 93, 129, 159, 162, 166, 178, 249, 260, 261, 273, 281-286, 292, 293, 295-296
Vetayard, 66
Vienna, 272
Vienne, 187-188, 189
Villedeuil, 293
Virginia, 45; Assembly, 55, 62, 63, 64, 69, 70; Council, 64, 72; Capitol, 69-77; Governors' House, 71, 73; Halls of Justice, 69, 71
Voltaire, 57, 78, 116, 199-200, 238
Vosges, 237, 238
Voss, Edward, 72
Vouët, 115

Waal, 225
Waffle iron, 214

Wales, Prince of, 132, 136, 161
Walpole, Horace, 151, 154
Warville, Brissot de, 95
Washington, Capitol, 162; White House, 113, 130
Washington, George, 29, 212-213, 267, 307; medal, 67; portraits, 55-63, 115-116, 122
"Werther," 240
Wescot, Lord, 151
West, Benjamin, 116, 159, 219
West Indies, 22, 23, 48
Westphalia, 228
Weybridge, 145
Whale oil, 38, 43, 48
Whately, Thomas, 141, 142, 144, 145, 146, 148, 150, 151
Wheelbarrow, 214
White House, 113, 130
Wiesbaden, 231
Wight, Isle of, 5, 183, 308
Wigs, 9
Wilhelmsbad, 232
William III, 143, 156
William and Mary College, 70, 256, 257
Williamos, Mr., 11
Williamsburg, 256; Capitol, 72; chapel, 70-71
Willincks and Van Staphorsts, 202, 208-209, 215, 216
Windsor, 137-138
Wine, 4, 48, 186, 187, 188-189, 193, 197, 198, 199, 221, 223, 228, 229, 232-233, 235, 258, 263
Woburn Farm, 146-147
Wolsey, Cardinal, 143-144
Women, labor of, 186, 199, 233-234, 239
Worms, 220, 221, 235
Woronzow, Count, 140
Wotton, 148
Wren, Sir Christopher, 143
Wright, Joseph, 56, 115
Wythe, George, 218

Xanten, 225

Yarmouth, 183, 310
Yonne, 186
York, Duke of, 27
Young, Sir George, 140

to Paris 1784 · Returned to America 1789
to London & Some of the Gardens of England · 1786
into Southern parts of France and Northern Italy 1787
to Amsterdam, Strassburg, back to Paris 1788
Rennes
Lorient
LaRochelle
Rochefort
Bordeaux
ENGLAND
LONDON
Amsterdam
GERMANY
Antwerp
Cologne
Rennes
PARIS
Nancy
Lorient
Strassburg
Tours
Nantes
Dijon
FRANCE
Bordeaux
Lyon
Milan
Turin
ITALY
Toulouse
Nîmes
Genoa
Aix
Marseille
HARTM'N